Caste and kinship in Kangra

International Library of Anthropology

Editor: Adam Kuper, University of Leiden

Arbor Scientiae
Arbor Vitae

Caste and kinship in Kangra

Jonathan P. Parry

Routledge & Kegan Paul
London, Henley and Boston

First published in 1979
by Routledge & Kegan Paul Ltd
39 Store Street,
London WC1E 7DD,
Broadway House,
Newtown Road,
Henley-on-Thames,
Oxon RG9 1EN and
9 Park Street,
Boston, Mass. 02108, USA
Set by Hope Services, Wantage
and printed in Great Britain by
Redwood Burn Ltd,
Trowbridge and Esher

British Library Cataloguing in Publication Data

Parry, Jonathan P

Caste and kinship in Kangra. – (International library of anthropology).
1. Caste – India – Kangra
I. Title II. Series
301.44'0954'52 HT720 78-40549

ISBN 0 7100 0012 X

To E. R. L. as Gurudaksina

Contents

Illustrations

Tables

Preface

This report on fieldwork carried out between October 1966 and December 1968 is a revised version of a PhD thesis submitted to the University of Cambridge in 1971. Though my stay was very brief, I was fortunate to be able to revisit Kangra in 1974, and this provided me with an opportunity to check on various points of detailed ethnography.

My original plan when I went to the field was to study local-level politics. Though I did in fact devote a good deal of time to this interest throughout the fieldwork, I found myself becoming increasingly interested in the classic topics of caste and kinship, and it is on this aspect of my material that the present study is focussed.

Throughout the period of fieldwork my headquarters were located in *mauza* Chadhiar in Palampur sub-division, though I also stayed for some weeks in *mauza* Khera (also in Palampur) and in *mauza* Indaura in Nurpur sub-division. In addition I made a series of more cursory visits to various other parts of the district, and became quite familiar with much of Palampur sub-division. But I write primarily about the locality I know well, and cannot claim with confidence that all my data are equally valid for the whole district. When I speak of this or that as Kangra custom, I ask the reader to bear this qualification in mind.

I am also conscious that the view of Kangra society I present is one seen through the eyes of the higher castes. In Chadhiar I lived with a Brahman family; and this fact has undoubtedly had a good deal of influence on the nature of my material since it tended to restrict my contacts with people of the very lowest castes. Though a significant proportion of my closest friends and best informants were Kolis – an untouchable though not one of the most polluting castes – it was otherwise the case that my freest contacts were with people of 'clean' caste.

In the interests of the general reader I employ English equivalents of those caste names which denote a specific occupation; and I have taken the liberty of pluralizing Indian terms in English fashion by adding an 's'. I do so with apologies to the Indian reader who finds this as ludicrous as *chevals* would be to a Frenchman reading a monograph on the Provençal horse-trade; and on the plea that some of the most eminent Indian anthropologists adopt the same expedient. Throughout the text I use the real names of places but (generally) pseudonyms for people. At various points in the text I use the conventional shorthand for kinship relations:

B brother
C child
D daughter
e elder
F father
H husband
M mother
S son
W wife
y younger
Z sister

Thus eBWM denotes the elder brother's wife's mother; HyZS, the husband's younger sister's son, etc.

During the period of fieldwork an enormous number of Kangra people went out of their way to help me with my research, and received me with kindness and hospitality. Since it is impossible to list them all, and would be invidious to list a few, I must thank them collectively for their generosity and forbearance. I cannot, however, avoid a special mention of Pt Kesho Ram Vaid, Smt Beasan Devi and Prito Devi, who gave me a home in Chadhiar and who paid me the honour of treating me as a member of their family. Shri Om Prakash Vedwe, who worked as my assistant throughout the second year of fieldwork, also has a very special claim on my gratitude.

During the course of writing various drafts of this book I have made constant and quite unreasonable demands on my wife, Margaret, and on various of my long-suffering friends. I am under a special obligation to Roger Ballard, Maurice Bloch, Tony Carter, Adam Kuper, Chris May,

Mike Norris and Julia Stevens; and to Jock Stirrat, whose telephone bills bear irrefutable testimony to hours of patient advice and moral support. Professors Meyer Fortes and David Pocock examined the original thesis, and Professors Adrian Mayer and S. J. Tambiah generously gave of their time to comment on various aspects of my data. I gratefully acknowledge their many useful criticisms. Professor André Béteille acted as my supervisor during the period I was working in India, and Professor E. R. Leach supervised the rest of the research. My debt to both is immeasurable. I also record my thanks for the infinite care and patience shown by Janet Baker, who drew the maps and diagrams, and by Terry Clarke, who typed the final manuscript.

The fieldwork was generously supported by an Anthony Wilkin Studentship, and by grants from the Smuts Memorial Fund and the Emslie Horniman Scholarship Fund.

July 1976

'I mean to marry Mari Sancha off all right, wife, so high that no one'll get near her without calling her "*your ladyship*".'

'No, no, Sancho,' replied Teresa. 'Marry her to her equal. That's the best thing. . . .'

'Be quiet, silly,' said Sancho. 'All she needs is two or three years' practice. Then the grand manner will come to her as if she were born to it. And if not, what does it matter? Let her be "*her ladyship*", come what may.'

'Keep to your own station, Sancho,' replied Teresa. 'Don't try to raise yourself higher, and remember the proverb: "take your neighbour's son, wipe his nose, and ask him home". It would be a fine thing indeed to marry our Maria to a great count or a fine gentleman. He might take another look at her when the fancy took him, and then call her a peasant, the daughter of clodhoppers and flax-spinners. . . .'

'Come here, beast,' replied Sancho, 'wife of Barabbas. Why do you want to hinder me now, for no reason at all, from marrying my daughter to someone who will give me grandsons who'll be called "*your lordships*"?'

Cervantes, *Don Quixote*, Pt II, Ch. V.

Part one

Inter-caste relations

1 Introduction: the axiom and idiom of inequality

This study is intended as a descriptive analysis of caste and kinship in the Kangra hills of north-west India. The first part is primarily concerned with relations between the units conventionally described as 'castes'; the second part with the internal structure of these units. The thread which runs throughout is that there are certain common principles which operate at both levels.

Following Béteille (1964, 1965) and Dumont (1970) I show that Kangra people conceptualize their society in terms of a segmentary model and that neither in language nor in behaviour do they signal any radical or absolute distinction between the nature of groups of different orders of inclusiveness. The boundaries which mark divisions within the caste, divisions between castes, between 'clean' and 'untouchable' castes and even between men and gods are not of qualitatively different kinds, but are different only in the degree of emphasis and elaboration they receive.

Whether we focus on relationships between members of different castes or on relationships between members of the same household, inequality is almost axiomatic in all dyadic relations, and this inequality is expressed in the same idiom throughout. It is therefore impossible to draw the kind of clear-cut distinction between 'castes' and 'grades within a single caste' which Leach (1960) has insisted on; and it is by no means 'absurd' – as Pocock (1972:65) has recently asserted – to speak of 'status' within the caste and thus to imply that the relationship between different levels within the caste is homologous to the relationship between different castes. 'There is', as Dumont (1957) puts it, 'no absolute distinction between what happens inside and outside a caste group, and we may expect to find in its internal constitution something of the principles which govern its external relations.'

Each caste is associated in the popular imagination with a set of customs and a style of life of greater or lesser purity and prestige; while relations between castes are governed by a set of interactional rules restricting potentially polluting contacts with those of inferior status and requiring deference to those of superior status. People of a higher caste may not, for example, smoke from the same hookah stem as, or accept certain kinds of food cooked by, anybody of a lower caste. Men of inferior caste may remove the plates off which their superiors have eaten, but a superior cannot come into contact with the used utensils of an inferior without incurring pollution. In ideal terms at least, low-caste people should greet their superiors first, should touch their feet on certain symbolic occasions, should appear before them with their heads covered, address them by an honorific and adopt the respectful pronoun forms when talking to them, and should build their houses at lower elevations.

In Kangra each caste is divided into a number of named exogamous patriclans which may be dispersed over a wide area. The clans of each of the highest castes are ranked on a hierarchical scale. Marriage is patrilocal and status within this intra-caste hierarchy is expressed by hypergamy: clans of lower status giving daughters in marriage to those immediately above them. Clans of approximately equal status form a single *biradari*, and those girls who are not given to grooms of superior *biradari* are exchanged on a symmetrical basis within the *biradari*. I aim to show that the relationship between one *biradari* and another within the caste is in many respects analogous to the relationship between one caste and another. That is, each *biradari* is associated with a distinctive style of life and a distinctive set of customs, and interactions between *biradaris* are again ordered by a set of transactional rules governing the exchange of food, hookahs, greetings and – of course – women.

But whether they belong to different *biradaris* or not, the hypergamous marriage formula defines wife-givers as inferior to wife-takers, and this inequality is acted out in the most explicit manner. When two affines of the same generation meet, the man of the wife-giving group touches the feet of the man of the wife-receiving group. People of superior status are never addressed by their personal names but always by an honorific or by a kinship term. Wife-takers of the same generation are addressed by a kinship term, but wife-givers by their personal names.

The Brahman is worshipped as a deity, and the wife-taker – though a non-Brahman by caste – is worshipped as if he were a Brahman. Both are appropriate recipients of *dan*, a charitable and meritorious donation for which no return may be accepted without cancelling the merit to be acquired by the act of giving. As a consequence the patron may not accept any kind of hospitality from the Brahman priest who officiates at his domestic rituals and to whom he offers *dan*, any more than the wife-giver may accept from the wife-taker. When a number of Brahmans are summoned to receive gifts at the house of the deceased on the fourth anniversary of a death, various wife-taking affines are treated as if they were Brahmans and included in the invitation. In yet other contexts the wife-takers are directly equated with the gods. So, for example, a married daughter of the lineage is a 'goddess' to her brother's wife, who worships her as a divinity when she first returns to her natal home after marriage.

The general point here, then, is that even within the *biradari* the asymmetrical and inegalitarian relationship between wife-givers and wife-takers has something of the same quality as the relationship between one *biradari* and another, and between one caste and another.

Precisely the same can be said of relations between junior members of the lineage (and of the household) *vis-à-vis* their seniors. A younger brother, for example, may remove the used plate of his elder brother; but not vice versa. He should call his elder brother by the appropriate kinship term while the latter refers to him familiarly by name; he should build his house at a lower elevation, should touch his feet when they meet after a period of separation, should never appear before him without some form of head covering and must shave his head in mourning on the latter's death.

Again the same kind of deference is ideally due from a house-tenant to his landlord, from subjects to their raja and from men to gods. As Sharma (1969, 1970) has documented for a village in the extreme south of Kangra, the relationship between mortals and deities has a very similar character to the relationship between low and high castes. Just as a low-caste Leather-worker must remove his shoes before entering the courtyard of a high-caste household, so the worshipper must remove his shoes before entering a temple or approaching the gods. A Brahman is greeted by a non-Brahman in the same way as a god is greeted by the worshipper; and just as the polluted remnants (*jutha*) on the plate of a high-caste diner are regarded as pure enough for the consumption of the lowest castes, so the *jutha* of the gods – the sacramental *prasad* which is distributed and consumed after an act of worship – edifies the worshippers.

The whole of Kangra society can thus be seen in terms of a series of oppositions in which:

> junior agnates : senior agnates : : wife-givers : wife-takers : :
> low castes : high castes : : men : gods.

The 'encompassing' ideology of hierarchy permeates every sphere of social life, and even the subordination of the tenant to his landlord and of the subject to his ruler – which may appear to be of a qualitatively different kind – is expressed in the same symbolic language. But it is not only the principle of hierarchy which runs all the way through Kangra society, for we shall also find that the twin processes of inclusion and exclusion (Pocock 1957) recur at a number of different levels.

These continuities between what happens at different levels of the system form, as it were, the theoretical skeleton which is used to structure the ethnographic material. Within this general framework, a whole range of narrower and more specific issues are taken up in individual chapters of the book.

Chapter 3 attempts to assess the economic significance of caste; and to show that some reconciliation is possible between the apparently incompatible views of those who emphasize the harmonious interdependence brought about by the division of labour between castes and those who argue that integration is based purely on assymetrical power relations and the coercive sanctions of the dominant caste. Chapter 4 focuses on the hierarchical aspects of caste. Here I consider certain problems with a purely interactional model of caste ranking; emphasize the need to distinguish between different degrees of untouchability, and show that there is an indeterminacy in the line which separates 'clean' from 'untouchable' castes and that the traditional view which sees untouchability as absolutely immutable is too simple. In this context I also draw attention to the traditional role of the raja in manipulating the order of caste precedence; to the politics of social mobility, and to the way in which the strategies pursued by an upwardly mobile low caste have been complicated by the Government policy of 'protective discrimination'.

The second part of the study deals with the internal composition of the caste. Chapter 5 describes the structure of unilineal descent groups and bears directly on my central theme that the caste is ordered internally by the same principles which govern relations between castes.

Chapter 6 deals with relations within the household and explores the interrelationship between the developmental cycle of the domestic group and the remittance economy. The more general issue here concerns the way in which 'traditional' family structures respond to a diversification of the economy and to a situation in which a substantial proportion of men are employed away from home for long periods.

The four final chapters of the study are all in one way or another concerned with marriage and affinity, and focus attention on the hypergamy of the high castes. Chapter 7 has an historical perspective and offers a general account of the hypergamous hierarchy of the dominant caste; while the argument of the following chapter is that this hierarchy is subject to periodic upheavals which are the product of structural contradictions inherent within the system itself. The data here are of direct relevance to the wider debate about the 'instability' of regimes of generalized exchange. Chapter 9 looks at the empirical pattern of marriage alliances and the relationship which these bear to the status aspirations of those who contract them; and Chapter 10 at the actors' models of non-agnatic kinship and affinity. Much of this discussion relates to a set of problems arising out of Dumont's (1964, 1966) analysis of marriage in north India and to his proposition that an alliance pattern exists in north India in a 'disguised' form.

2 The setting

2:1 Geographical sketch

District Kangra lies in the hill country to the north of the Punjab plains (Map 1). It covers an area of 2,554 square miles and its predominantly Hindu population numbered just over one million at the 1961 census (Census of India, Paper No. 1, 1963).[1]

On the north a massive snow-covered wall of mountains known as the Dhaula Dhar, a range of the outer Himalayas with an average height of 15,000 feet and with some peaks rising to over 18,000 feet, forms a natural barrier between Kangra and district Chamba. The southern slopes of the Dhaula Dhar fall precipitously away to the lush fertile Kangra valley below, so that the mountains appear from a distance to rise almost perpendicularly out of the green valley. The area is one of such startling natural beauty that even the normally dead-pan authors of the nineteenth century Settlement literature could not resist an occasional lapse into purple prose:

> No scenery, in my opinion, presents such sublime and delightful contrasts. Below this lies the plain, a picture of rural loveliness and repose, the surface is covered with the richest cultivation, irrigated by streams which descend from the perennial snows, and interspersed with homesteads buried in the midst of groves and fruit trees. Turning from this scene of peaceful beauty, the stern and majestic hills confront us; their sides are furrowed with precipitous water-courses; forests of oak clothe their flanks, and higher up give place to gloomy and funereal pines; above all are wastes of snow on pyramidal masses of granite too perpendicular for snow to rest on (Quoted in Kangra District Gazetteer, 1926:4).

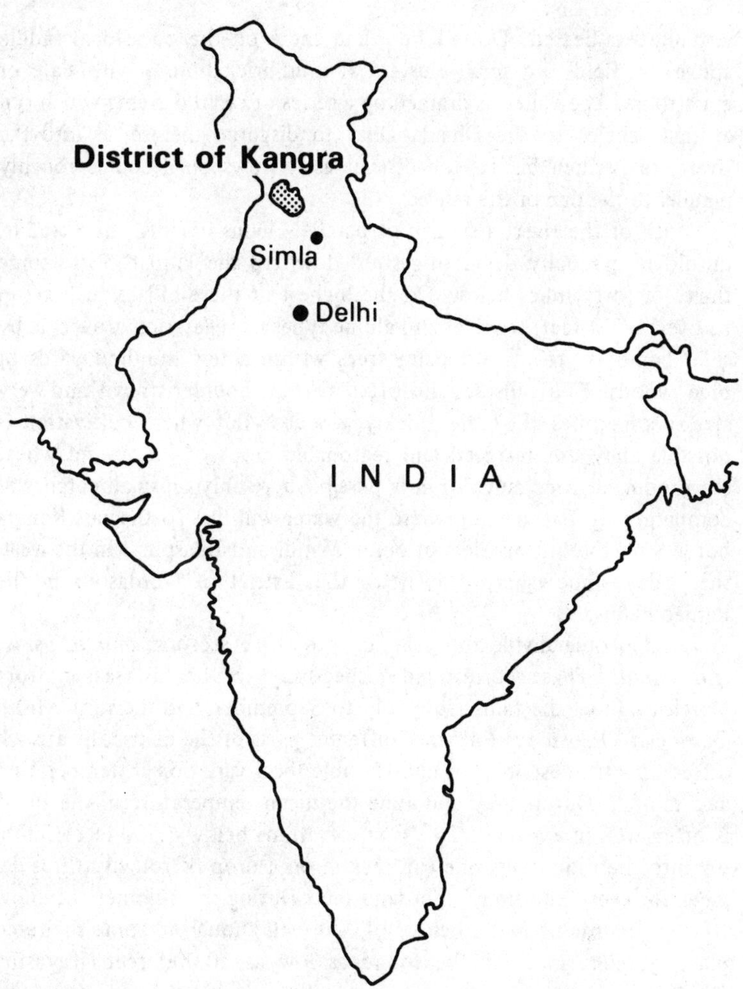

MAP 1 *Location of Kangra District*

On average some six miles broad, the gently sloping valley runs parallel to the mountain ridge for more than twenty miles at an elevation of between 2,300 and 4,000 feet. Most of this tract – the most fertile in the district – is covered with a patchwork of tiny terraced paddy-fields, which are waterlogged during the monsoons, and in which mosquitoes breed prodigiously. Malaria used to be common but has now been virtually eradicated. Dotted here and there on the occasional saddle above the fields are small clusters of mud-brick houses with slate or grass roofs. The valley is drained by a series of rapid torrents which run at right angles to the Dhaula Dhar to disgorge themselves into the river Beas, which bisects the district as it flows on a course roughly parallel to the line of the range.

South of the river, a system of parallel chains of hills, the Siwaliks, unfold in gradually decreasing steps down to the Punjab plains some thirty or forty miles below. On the highest of these hills, which go up to over 4,500 feet, tropical and alpine types of vegetation grow side by side; bamboo groves and palm trees within a few hundred yards of pine woods. The hillsides are often barren, boulder-strewn and very steep; sometimes they are thickly wooded. But where cultivation is possible they are terraced and reasonable crops of maize and wheat are produced. Rice cultivation is possible here only on small patches of comparatively flat ground where the water will lie. To the east Kangra borders on the hill districts of Kulu, Mandi and Bilaspur. On the west, the valley slopes sharply away to the district of Gurdaspur in the Punjab plains.

Local people divide the year up into three seasons: *taundi*, *barsat* and *yunhd.* These correspond respectively to the hot season from March to June; the rains from July to September, and the winter from October to February. But since different parts of the district lie at such different altitudes, there is considerable local variation in temperature and rainfall. During May and June the mean temperature in the shade is often well in excess of 100°F at elevations below 4,500 feet. Climbing into the mountains one can reckon on a drop of roughly three degrees for every additional thousand feet. During the summer the snow on the mountains melts below 14,000 feet, though in some sheltered places glaciers may still be found as low as 10,000 feet (Kayastha 1964:41).

Average winter temperatures in the valley are around 53°F (Kangra District Gazetteer, 1926:31) and the nights and early mornings are often bitterly cold. Heavy snow falls on the Dhaula Dhar though it seldom lies for long below 6,000 feet, and is unusual below 4,500 feet. In the valley the mornings are frosty. Light rains – on which the wheat crop in the unirrigated parts of the district is dependent – occur in December, January and February, though they are apt to be unreliable. Melt-water from the snows of the Dhaula Dhar ensures a minimal supply of water to the irrigation channels in the valley throughout the year.

The monsoon in Kangra is extremely heavy and more than three-quarters of the annual precipitation falls between July and September. Sometimes it rains continuously for several days and storms of dramatic ferocity are not infrequent. The heaviest rainfall is on the lower slopes of the Dhaula Dhar. Towards the south the altitude decreases and so does the rainfall. At 4,000 feet the average annual precipitation is 116 inches; at 1,500 feet it is only 50 inches (Kayastha 1964:42–4). In Palampur sub-division it can be taken as a rough guide that the annual rainfall decreases by about one inch for every quarter of a mile that you go away from the high mountains. The rains, however, are rather unpredictable and variable, a range of between 48·8 and 153·7 inches per year being recorded for Dharamsala, the district headquarters, which is located in the belt of highest rainfall (Kangra District Gazetteer, 1926:31–2).

2:2 Historical sketch

In pre-British days, Kangra and the surrounding hill districts were divided into numerous petty states. Although the figures never add up consistently, there are conventionally said to have been twenty-two states between the rivers Chenab and Sutlej, and these were divided by the river Ravi into two groups of eleven each. The most powerful of the western group was Jammu, and of the eastern group the Katoch kingdom of Kangra (Hutchinson and Vogel 1933).

Many of the smaller states are reputed to have been founded by a younger son of a raja of one of the larger ones, though it is impossible to say whether such traditions have any historical validity, or simply reflect contemporary political and status relations between the royal clans. Whichever the case, the tradition of a common origin is preserved, and is embodied in the sharing of a common *gotra* and, until recently, a ban on intermarriage. Those ruling families which did not claim to be related as distant agnates intermarried. But neither putative agnatic descent, nor repeated intermarriage, seem to have inhibited the rajas from frequent attacks on each others' territory (though kinship considerations may perhaps have moderated their excesses).

> The history of these hill States is one of almost continuous warfare. When a strong ruler rose to power the larger states made tributary their smaller neighbours, but these again asserted their independence as soon as a favourable opportunity offered. These wars did not lead

> to any great political changes, for on the whole the hill Chiefs were considerate of each others' rights. Being all of the same race and faith and also nearly related to one another by marriage and even closer family ties, they were content to make each other tributary, or to replace a deposed chief by one of his kinsmen (Kangra District Gazetteer, 1926:47).

The isolation of the hill states allowed them to retain their independence from the plains until they were brought under Moghul suzerainty early in the Emperor Akhbar's reign in the middle of the sixteenth century. The extent to which the Moghul emperors were able to exercise any real control over either the local rajas or the commanders of their own garrisons seems to have been closely related to the internal stability of their own regimes, and varied considerably. For much of the time, Moghul rule does not appear to have been particularly burdensome. Although the rajas had to pay tribute and a fee of investiture to the Emperor, and were sometimes required to send their sons as hostages to the imperial court, they continued to wage war on each other without restraint, and there was little direct interference in their internal affairs. But when the insubordination of the hill states got out of hand and when events at the centre allowed, an expeditionary force would be despatched to bring the recalcitrant rajas to heel. Jahangir, for example, captured the strategically crucial fort at Kangra in 1610, annexed the surrounding area, and reduced the once powerful Katoch rajas to the status of minor vassals.

With the decline of the Moghul empire the hill states reasserted their independence from Delhi. But for many of them this simply meant a change of old masters for new, since they immediately fell victim to the expansionist ambitions of a resurgent Katoch kingdom. Raja Ghamand Chand (1751-74) recovered most of the territory which had earlier been ceded to the Moghuls. But the Kangra kingdom reached its height under Sansar Chand (1775-1823), who imposed his overlordship throughout the neighbouring hill areas. During his reign the Kangra court became a major centre for the patronage of the arts. Several fine palaces were built, and the Kangra school of painting was at its most vigorous.

Sansar Chand's policy of predatory aggrandizement eventually provoked a coalition of the smaller states, who allied themselves with the Gurkha army which was occupying the hills to the east, and which invaded Kangra in 1805. The result was a period of total anarchy, during which the local peasantry fled *en masse* across the hills into Chamba or down to the plains. 'In the fertile valleys of Kangra, not a blade of cultivation was to be seen, grass grew up in the towns and tigresses whelped in the streets of Nadaun' (ibid., p. 72). Sansar Chand was forced to enlist the help of Ranjit Singh, the Sikh raja, who marched on Kangra in 1809. Ranjit Singh got rid of the Gurkhas, but Sansar Chand could never get rid of Ranjit Singh, who annexed the most fertile part of the valley. The neighbouring rulers were also reduced to the position of tributaries to the Sikhs, who proved less indulgent masters than the Moghuls and who encroached still further on their authority.

Sikh domination came to an abrupt end after the First Sikh War in 1846, when the whole area passed into British hands. The rajas were assigned only small areas of their former kingdoms as *jagirs*, in which they had rights to the revenue and the authority of a magistrate. Some of them attempted to resist this emasculation of their royal powers, and a series of minor insurrections broke out before the area was finally pacified. But even though the British reduced the rajas to the position of petty *jagirdars*, and severely curtailed their traditional rights in the soil, their subjects continued to pay them a certain amount of formal respect. At the *seri* festival, for example, they would offer the raja presents, the landholders giving baskets of fruit and vegetables, and the artisans tools that they had made. When he died, the whole kingdom was expected to observe mourning, and ideally a man of each house should shave his head (Lyall 1889:34). Long after their administrative and judicial authority had all but disappeared, the rajas continued to wield a certain authority in matters of caste precedence.

2:3 Administrative sub-divisions

Throughout the British period, and during the early years after Independence, Kangra remained an administrative district of the Punjab. But when the State was carved up into Hariana and the Punjabi Subah in November 1966, Kangra – along with the other Himalayan districts of the old Punjab – was merged with neighbouring Himachal Pradesh.

The division was made on what was euphemistically characterized as a 'linguistic basis', though most observers were agreed that this was just a polite fiction designed to gloss over the contradiction between the officially secular ideology of the Congress government and the concession of the new Sikh-dominated Punjabi Subah (cf. Nayar 1966,

1968; Pettigrew 1975). But this piece of political humbug did have the effect of forcing much of the public debate into a linguistic idiom and, as far as Kangra was concerned, the controversy ostensibly hinged on whether the local dialect has more affinities with Punjabi or Pahari. The evidence here is highly equivocal. In his still authoritative survey of 1916, Grierson describes *Kangri boli* as one of three sub-dialects of Dogra, which he classifies as a dialect 'intermediate between standard Punjabi and the Pahari of the lower Himalaya' (Grierson 1916:IX:608, 637). Those with an axe to grind dug up other 'competent authorities' and invoked the 'latest research' to support their case, though it was plain to all concerned that the real issues were rather less academic.

The political elite of the district was hopelessly divided on the question. On the one hand, there was a widespread feeling that in terms of development grants Kangra had always had a raw deal from the government of the old state and had been poorly represented in successive Congress ministries. Along with this went a strong feeling of cultural distinctness from the plains, and the shrewd calculation that the Kangra elite would be powerful enough to make their voices heard in the smaller and more backward state of Himachal Pradesh. On the other hand, there were those who felt that their best interests lay in being associated with the far richer Punjab, and who were disquieted by the much tougher land reform legislation in force in Himachal Pradesh.

Eventually Kangra was merged with Himachal, and Tehsil Una – a former sub-division of district Hoshiarpur – was merged with Kangra. At the time of my fieldwork, then, the district consisted of six sub-divisions, each under the overall administrative jurisdiction of a sub-divisional magistrate, who was responsible to the District Commissioner in Dharamsala. It was also divided into 21 Community Development Blocks, each under a Block Development Officer.

I shall continue to refer to the whole of this unit as Kangra, though in fact the district was split up in 1972 to form two new districts, Kangra and Hamirpur. This was a move which had been widely canvassed in the late 1960s by the political bosses from Hamirpur, and which seemed likely to find favour with the established state-level Congress leadership, for whom the possiblity of a unified Kangra lobby in state politics represented a major threat.

All-weather roads connect the sub-divisional headquarters with Dharamsala and there is an extensive network of dirt roads all over the district. A metre-gauge railway runs through the valley from Pathankot in district Gurdaspur to Jogindernagar in district Mandi.

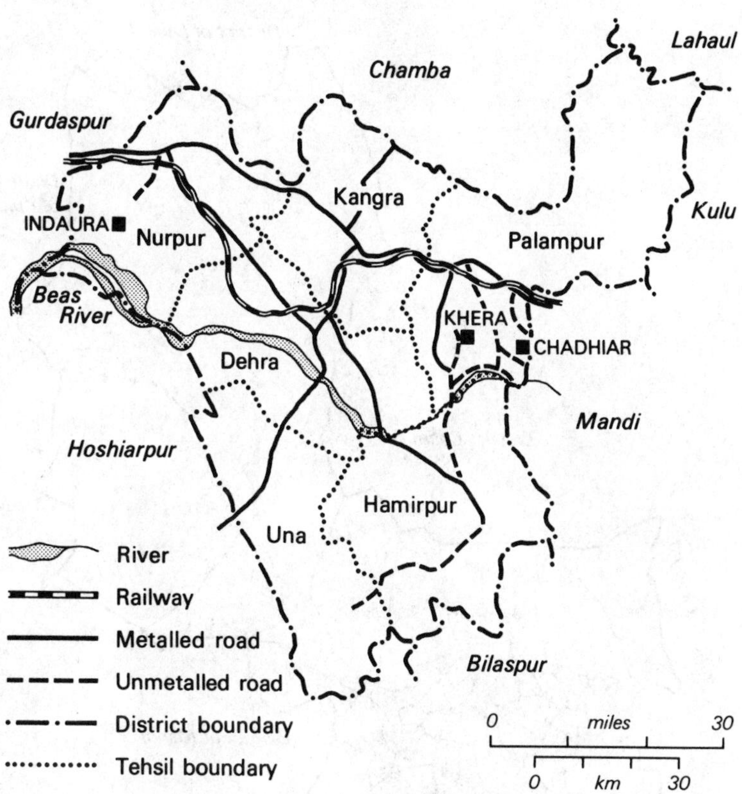

MAP 2 *Kangra District*

Map 2 shows the district and sub-division boundaries, the location of Chadhiar (my headquarters throughout the fieldwork) and of the other two revenue circles (*mauzas*) in which I spent any appreciable time. Most of my material relates to Palampur sub-division, which is located in the north-east corner of Kangra (Maps 2 and 3). The *tehsil* (sub-division) has an area of 724 square miles, is divided into four Community Development Blocks, and had a population of 199,494 at the 1961 census. The largest town was Palampur itself with a population of a little over 2,000.

The *tehsil* falls naturally into four geographical regions which local people distinguish as Palam, Changer, Dhar and Bir-Bangahal. Palam and

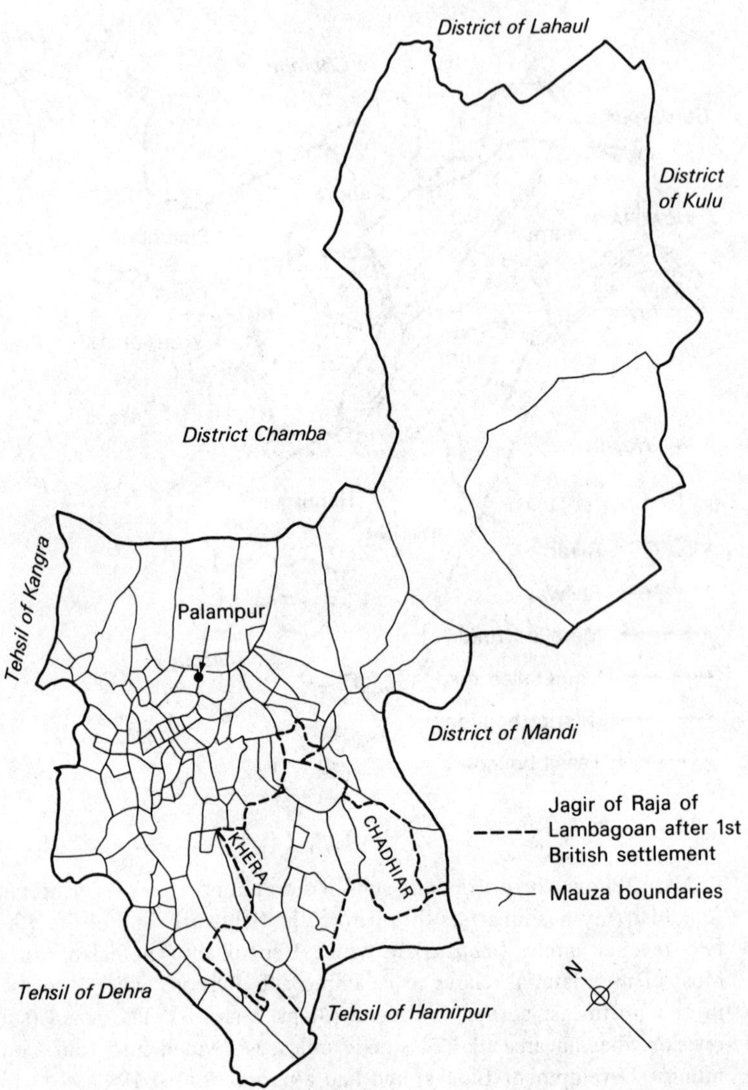

MAP 3 *Map of Palampur sub-division (district Kangra)*

Changer, where the land is comparatively flat and the soil very fertile, form part of the main Kangra valley; 49·4 per cent of the total cultivated area of the sub-division is irrigated, and a large proportion of this is located in Palam (Kayastha 1964:82). But while Palam is extensively irrigated, and regularly produces one of the best paddy harvests in the district, the Changer area relies largely on natural rainfall. On the southern side of the valley, running parallel to the high mountains, is a broken ridge roughly 14 miles long and reaching an altitude of 4,625 feet. This area is known as the Dhar. Here much of the land is either too steep for cultivation or the soil too poor. Of the land which is cultivated only a tiny fraction is irrigated, though there are patches of plateau where a fair rice crop can be produced. The main crops on the Dhar, however, are maize and wheat.

The Bir-Bangahal area is the largest of these natural divisions of Palampur. But since most of it lies in the high mountains it is also the most sparsely populated. The northern part of this area is known as Bara Bangahal and consists of a large valley lying on the far side of the Dhaula Dhar. Surrounded on all sides by high mountains – some of them over 20,000 feet – Bara Bangahal is snow-bound throughout the winter and supports only one village. The valley is separated from Chhota Bangahal to the south by a 10,000-foot range of mountains; and a further range separates this valley from the Bir tract which lies on the southern slopes of the Dhaula Dhar above the rice-fields of Palam.

Each of these divisions corresponds rather roughly to the *talukas* which were important units of local administration under the rajas, although today they have no administrative significance. But they do tend to be the object of a certain amount of local patriotism. Tiny differences of vocabulary and minor variations in custom and diet distinguish the people of the Dhar, for example, from those of Palam. Palam people tend to pride themselves on being more 'cultured' than the roughnecks of the Dhar; while Dhar people secretly think of Palam people as slightly soft and effeminate. But the inhabitants of Nurpur *tehsil*, which borders on the plains in the extreme west of the district, have a single stereotype for all Palampur people, who are seen as a bunch of hill-billies. Faced with outsiders, however, people from all parts of the district tend to close ranks and emphasize their common style of life and a common culture of great antiquity; while the more sophisticated take pride in the wide renown of the Kangra valley paintings.

2:4 The settlement pattern

There are no nucleated villages in Palampur. For administrative purposes the smallest unit of local organization is the *tika*, or hamlet, which consists of a residential site (*abadi*), and area of arable land (*masrua*), and an expanse of waste land (*shamlat*). The *patwari*, or village accountant, keeps a separate record of rights (*jamabandi*) and a separate field map for each *tika*. The houses of a hamlet spread out chain-wise along the crest of a ridge or are scattered haphazardly over steep slopes where agriculture is either difficult or impossible. The level areas of land are too valuable and too swampy to be used for building and form an open stretch of cultivation.

The boundary between one *tika* and another is seldom obvious and it is common to find people who are not sure whether a particular house belongs to their *tika* or to an adjacent one. As Map 5 illustrates, one hamlet often seems to merge rather indiscriminately into the next. In fact, formal boundaries were the creation of the British revenue Settlements and only in part did they follow locally established divisions (Kangra District Gazetteer, 1926:383-5). It is not surprising, then, that the *tika* as such receives no explicit social recognition and that there is no ritual at which its members unite. At one time the British tried to introduce *tika* headmen, but the experiment soon fizzled out (Lyall 1889:151). Nor is it *de jure* an exogamous unit though it tends to be so in practice, since the chances of finding an eligible spouse within your own hamlet are small, and since anyway people don't like to marry too close to home.[2]

Tikas vary enormously in population. Sometimes they may contain only one or two houses, and exceptionally none at all. The 1926 edition of the District Gazetteer (p. 122) gives an average population of 129; while the upper limit would be around 750. The hamlet is usually a multi-caste unit, though most specialist services are provided by outsiders. The fields which its inhabitants cultivate are likely to be scattered over a number of different hamlets.

When *tika* boundaries were first defined it was often found that a family or group of lineage members of one *tika* owned comparatively large patches of land some way from their home *tika*, in an area where most of the cultivation belonged to the members of another *tika*. These patches were sometimes detached from the *tika* into which they naturally fell and were declared to be the *chak karz* of that *tika* by which they were owned. For example, the cultivators of *tika* A may have owned a substantial area of land in the fields surrounding *tika* B some way away. This area may then have become *chak karz* A, an isolated pocket of land forming part of *tika* A but separated from it and surrounded on all sides by *tika* B (cf. Middleton 1919b:13).

Smaller than the hamlet, but more significant in terms of social relations, is the *narar* or house-cluster. Two or more *narar* may be distinguished within a single *tika*. Generally they are more or less nucleated knots of houses – anything from two to twenty – separated from other house-clusters by a patch of waste ground. But again there is sometimes no very apparent boundary between them. Typically, the houses will be built around a series of interlocking courtyards, or even a single courtyard if there are only three or four houses in the *narar*.

The house itself – which may occasionally contain more than one domestic group defined by reference to a common hearth – is almost invariably a two-storied mud-brick structure with a sloping roof of thatch or slate. Thatch roofs need to be renewed every four or five years. Not only are they less convenient than slate, and a greater fire risk, but also less prestigious, as thatch is taken to be an indication of poverty. At the other end of the scale, a concrete floor on the ground storey is *de rigueur* for the really affluent. Most houses have four or five rooms. The top storey, or *bohri*, consists of a kitchen and storeroom. On the ground floor is a living room, known as the *oan*, where guests are entertained and where most of the family sleeps at night. Leading off the *oan* is the *obari*, a smaller and more private room, where the family's more valuable movable assets are usually stored in large tin trunks. A certain amount of ribald innuendo focusses on the *obari*, for it is here that a newly-married couple traditionally spend their first nights together. In the less well-to-do households, the furniture is generally sparse and often consists of little more than a string-cot or two, a couple of tin trunks and a straw mattress. But the more prosperous run to tables, chairs and a cupboard; and perhaps also to a sofa, a radio and a sewing machine. The house fronts on to a courtyard (*angan*), around which other houses are built. In the middle of the courtyard is a small shrine. Behind the house lies the cattle-shed (*gharal*).

Although the inhabitants of a house-cluster may belong to more than one caste, there is a tendency for the members of a single agnatic lineage to predominate, and for the *narar* to take its name from this dominant lineage. For example, Buhli Waziron da *narar* – the lower *narar* of the Wazirs – is named after the Wazir lineage although it also includes representatives of three other castes. Such agnatic groups are the product of the repeated partition of joint families. Given patrilocal marriage, the scarcity of land suitable for building, and a general preference for constructing a new house on the nearest available site to the old one, lineages tend to take on a residentially compact character and a man's closest agnates are usually also his closest neighbours.

Typically these core lineages are of high caste, and their members claim to be the descendants of the original founders of the *narar* who imported the forebears of the low-caste households as their servants. Relative altitude of settlement has shadowy status connotations and the high-caste households tend to live higher up the hillsides than their low-caste neighbours. (Associated with the same general phenomenon is a propensity for the more mountainous tracts to be areas of Rajput domination; while the Girths – a relatively inferior caste of Cultivators – tend to predominate both numerically and economically in the low-lying valleys.)

Whatever their caste, the people of one house-cluster rate as neighbours (*parosi*) and are expected to behave in a neighbourly sort of way. Between them lots of small items may be borrowed or lent. If there is a death, or a marriage, or any other important ritual in the *narar*, then each household should take a share in the preparations for the guests. Those of one *narar* should have *bartan* ('transactions based on relations of amity') expressed in reciprocal prestations of cloth and money at marriages and funerals. If a *parosi* dies, other members of the house-cluster irrespective of caste are expected to observe certain minimal mourning restrictions. The women should put off all their ornaments until the purificatory ritual of *kapar-dhuai*, at which a man from each house should be shaved; though if the family priest belongs to the same *narar*, his household is exempted. That, at least, describes the ideal position. In practice, land disputes and accusations of witchcraft (*jadu*) often disrupt this ideal unity.

The *narar* has no administrative status and no corporate interests in land or office. It is a rather indistinct territorial group defined primarily by the interactions of its members; and as a result of this its boundaries tend to be rather fluid at the edges. Although there is a broad consensus about which houses belong to which *narar*, there are occasionally one or two houses on the fringe which some members of the *narar* will include and others exclude. For example, A may include X's house in his *narar* because it is close by and because he has *bartan* with X. But A's brother and near neighbour B may repudiate X's membership because he is on bad terms with X and has no *bartan* with him.

A series of hamlets are grouped into a *mauza*, which is a revenue circle or 'parish' (in the civil rather than the ecclesiastical sense). The *mauza* generally consists of between 10 and 20 hamlets, though exceptionally it may contain as many as 100. In *tehsil* Palampur there are a total of 113 *mauzas* made up of 1,151 hamlets. (The 'parish' boundaries are shown in Map 3.) These divisions were originally the old fiscal units of the rajas, have little importance for the organization of social relations, and many people are unable to say whether a particular *tika* belongs to their *mauza* or to an adjacent one. The District Gazetteer (pp. 368–9) describes their formation like this:

> each one . . . was so constituted in respect of size and physical characteristics as to represent just that amount of land which one man could efficiently supervise, with the assistance of a 'complete and numerous set of officials', all of whom were the raja's servants. In order to secure this result the circuits were of various dimensions, according to the nature of the country, extensive in hilly tracts, where population and arable land are scarce; contracted in the open and closely cultivated valleys.

In general, then, the settlement pattern in Palampur has a rather fuzzy character, in that for most purposes territorial boundaries have little social significance. This general impression of amorphousness is strengthened by the striking ignorance of nearby hamlets which some of my high-caste informants occasionally displayed. I had, for example, to point out the house of a very prominent Rajput leader to a middle-aged friend of mine, himself a Rajput, who lived less than a mile and a half away. This ignorance – whether real or pretended – stems partly from the number of men employed away from home for substantial periods, partly from the fact that high-caste women do not (or rather should not) visit strange houses; and partly from the notion that respectable people stay at home and do not call without a purpose, and that only anthropologists and loafers in search of mischief wander aimlessly about the place.

2:5 Land tenure: a historical note

The general vagueness which surrounds territorial boundaries and their lack of social significance has to be seen in the light of certain historical facts about land tenure in Kangra. Before the British annexed the area in 1846 land was held in severalty, and neither the *tika* nor the *mauza* had any corporate property in the waste, nor any joint responsibility for the raja's revenue.

> In former times each family holding, and in some tracts each plot or field, was assessed separately. If the rent of such holding or plot was not paid, the State proceeded against the individual holder only, . . . the other landlords of the circuit had nothing to do with the matter (Lyall 1889:28).

Of the period before the area came under British administration, Barnes records:

> Each member lives upon his own holding, and is quite independent of his neighbour. There is no identity of feeling, no idea of acting in concert. The headman, who is placed over them, is not of their own choice, but has been appointed by the Government. In short, the land enclosed by the circuit, instead of being a co-parcenary estate, reclaimed, divided and enjoyed by a united brotherhood, is an aggregation of isolated freeholds quite distinct from each other, and possessing nothing in common, except that, for fiscal convenience, they have been measured together under one jurisdiction (Barnes 1889:16).

The Kangra rajas claimed extensive rights in the land, though they would sometimes alienate a part of their prerogatives in favour of the descendants of cadets of the royal house (Lyall 1889:26). In fertile tracts the raja's share (*sath*), which was normally paid in kind where the crop was a subsistence one, amounted to half the gross produce; on less favourable land the demand was between a third and a quarter (Lyall 1889:31, 45; Bhai Mul Raj 1933:52). From the Chadhiar area he claimed one third (Moorcroft and Trebeck 1841:1:151). But the more avaricious, or perhaps simply the more powerful, rajas added to these basic rates a whole host of additional levies: an army tax and a war tax, for example, a weighman's tax, a money-tester's tax or a tax to cover the cost of transporting the grains to the royal granaries; and – what must have been most galling of all – a tax to cover the cost of writing receipts (Kangra District Gazetteer, 1926:406). The Sikhs seemed to have pushed their luck even further, for they generally demanded half the total output on all qualities of land, and made their collection before the harvest was in. The result was that the money-lenders did excellent business and that 'the burdens of the people were as heavy as they could bear' (Kangra District Gazetteer, 1926:411). In general, then:

> a holding in these hills was held very cheap, . . . a man who tilled his land with his own hands could earn a humble subsistence, but if he employed farm servants or sublet to a tenant, the profit, if any, was very small (Lyall 1889:35).

The ideological justification for these heavy revenue demands was provided by a theory of land tenure in which 'the people's rights approach nearer to those of occupancy tenants than of proprietors' (Suket State Gazetteer, 1904:40).

> The Raja was not, like a feudal king, lord paramount over inferior lords of manors, but rather, as it were, manorial lord for his whole country. . . . The waste lands, great or small, were the Raja's waste, the arable lands were made up of the separate holdings of his tenants. . . . Every several interest in land, whether the right to cultivate certain fields, to graze exclusively certain plots of waste, work a water-mill, set a net to catch game or hawks on a mountain, or to put a fish-weir in a stream, was held direct of the raja as a separate holding or tenancy. The incumbent or tenant at the most called his interest a *warisi* or inheritance, not a *maliki* or lordship (Lyall 1889:26).

The raja could resume the land of a cultivator who died without heirs (Kangra District Gazetteer, 1926:442); and usually claimed the right to debar an heir 'if the claimant be fractious or have given offence' (Suket State Gazetteer, 1904:40), for in theory the land 'escheated to the crown' on the death of the holder and 'not until the Raja had passed orders in person had the heirs the least right or title' (Howell 1917:79). From the statistical information provided by the early British settlement officers there are some indications that these powers were used quite extensively in practice. The figures indicate that only about one-third of the landholders in the 1870s could trace their title back beyond their grandfather (Lyall 1889:p. 71 para. 73; Kangra District Gazetteer, 1926:374); though it is likely that the unsettled political conditions in the valley during the Gurkha invasion were at least in part responsible for the turn-over.

The cultivator's rights were contingent on prompt payment of the revenue and proper use of the land. He had no right to sell his holding, though in Kangra – but not in neighbouring Mandi – he could under certain circumstances give it in mortgage. No new field could be carved out of the waste without a grant (*patta*) from the raja; and the local community, including both the landholders and the landless, had only certain customary rights of usage in the wasteland – the right, for example, to pasture cattle and to collect firewood (Lyall 1889:26).

In marked contrast, then, to the joint villages they had been used to dealing with elsewhere in the north-west provinces, in the Punjab hills the early British settlement officers were faced with a species of land tenure which Baden-Powell (1892:II:537) considered 'as nearly *raiyatwari* as possible' and which seemed to display all the characteristic hallmarks of the severalty village: influential headmen appointed by an external authority; separate holdings which were not regarded as shares of a unit estate; and an absence of any joint responsibility for the revenue or joint rights in wasteland available for partition (cf. Baden-Powell 1899:19).

The first regular British settlement in 1849, based on a model imported from the plains, undermined the fundamental principles of this severalty system and had the effect of creating incipient joint villages (cf. Baden-Powell 1892:I:142). Four major changes can be singled out. In the first place, the landholders of each *mauza* were made jointly responsible for the payment of the revenue, and were given 'the right to collect and divide among themselves certain items of fluctuating and miscellaneous rent' (Lyall 1889:28).

Second, the revenue was now generally commuted into cash, and the demand remained fixed for a minimum of 20 years and often for longer. At the first regular settlement the revenue burden was anyway somewhat lightened; but – combined with steadily rising prices throughout the post-annexation period – the results of these measures was that the state's share, seen as a proportion of the total value of the crop, diminished quite rapidly. While in some areas the rajas had levied up to, or even in excess of, half the total production, Bhai Mul Raj (1933:54) estimates for one part of the district that between 1920 and 1930 the demand represented not more than 8 per cent of the value of the total output.

The third really significant change was that the landholders now acquired firm rights to alienate their land, and in effect became 'owners' in a conventional European sense. These new rights, along with a constant demand for cash to keep up with the system of marriage prestations (see Chapter 7), an expansion of the market economy and wider opportunities for wage labour, soon led to a significant turn-over in the ownership of land. By 1890, 13·62 per cent of the total cultivated area of the district was under mortgage and a further 5 per cent had been sold (Anderson 1897:2). A large proportion of this alienation was a result of money-lenders foreclosing on debts. Most of the big money-lenders belonged to the trading castes (Mahajans, Suds and Kayasthas) concentrated in the commercial centres, and generally they would accept only the best land as surety. The Punjab Alienation of Land Act of 1900, which prohibited members of castes classified as 'agricultural' from alienating land in favour of 'non-agricultural' castes, curbed this trend towards a rapid accummulation of land by money-lending absentee landlords. The immediate effect of the Act was to reduce the average amount of land sold per year by about half, and the reduction of the area under mortgage was even more dramatic (Kangra District Gazetteer, 1926:262–4).

The fourth important change brought in by British Settlement was to make the body of landowners co-proprietors of the wasteland (Barnes 1889:19). Most of this *shamlat* was vested in the proprietory body of the *tika*. In some cases it was included within the boundary of one *tika* but declared to be the common property of two or more *tikas*. Other areas of waste, known as *chak shamlat deh*, became the property of the landholders of the *mauza* as a whole. The British, then, created corporate rights in the waste and these rights were vested in a body made up of those who paid the revenue. Each landowner held a share in the *shamlat* proportional to the amount of revenue he paid, and, with the consent of the Government and the joint body of proprietors, could bring an area of wasteland, up the amount of his share, under cultivation (Lyall 1889:114). One of the effects of all this was to exclude the rights of those who had no land of their own, and were not paying any revenue.

In the political *jagirs* which the British had assigned to the old rajas of the former Kangra states, the position was much the same, though here it was the raja's permission, rather than that of the British authorities, which was necessary before the waste could be broken up for cultivation. Except in certain forest lands, known as *nagban*, which were demarcated as his full property, the raja could no longer give grants in the waste without the consent of the local landholders

(Kangra District Gazetteer, 1926:442).

The present position is that the *shamlat* is under the management of the *gram panchayat*, an elected council with a constituency of several hamlets. Each *mauza* is likely to contain several such *panchayats.* The legislation (The Punjab Common Land (Regulation) Act of 1961) gives them the right to give grants of *shamlat* to landless tenants for house-sites, and to give short-term leases for cultivation to those who own less than 10 acres of land, which in Kangra means practically everybody.

2:6 'Village' officials

The *mauza* is not always congruent with the *patwar* circle of the village accountant. The more extensive *mauzas* are generally divided between two or even three *patwaris* and a larger number of *lambedars.* The *patwari*, who is the most junior official in the revenue administration, keeps a complete record of all landholdings, tenancies and transfers of land in his circle. But it is the *lambedar* as revenue headman who actually collects the tax from the landowners of the group of *tikas* under his jurisdiction. These two posts are not directly related in the hierarchy of bureaucratic authority. While the *lambedar* is an influential local man who acts as an intermediary between the villagers and bureaucracy, and as the representative of both, the *patwari* is an outsider, a government employee who is eligible for transfer and promotion.

Besides collecting the revenue, the *lambedar*'s other duties include reporting crimes to the police, assisting them and other officials who visit his area, and giving character references for men of his circle who want to join the army or take any sort of job in a government department. Two or three watchmen (*chowkidars*) are appointed to help him with his police duties and to run errands for him and the *patwari*. The *lambedar*'s post is hereditary, though succession is subject to the confirmation of the District Commissioner. One of the conditions of this confirmation is that he should be among the largest landowners of the *mauza*, a precaution by which the government seeks to insure itself against any possible embezzlement of the revenue, and to ensure the influence of its local representative.

The British grouped a number of adjacent *lambedari* circles into a *zail*, over which they appointed a *zaildar* in a supervisory capacity. The *zaildar* was again one of the largest landlords of his area, and his duties involved helping the authorities with the investigation of crime and with the recruitment to the army, and general liaison with the Government. At the last count before the office was finally abolished, there were 52 *zaildars* in the district and 11 in Palampur sub-division.

In the days of the British raj the *lambedar* was a minor potentate in his own area, for he had a virtual monopoly over contacts with the administration. But since Independence there has been a marked decline in his influence and authority. His post does not carry a salary, though he is entitled to a given percentage of the revenue he collects. This used to represent a rather substantial sum. But since the land revenue has remained constant for many years, while a general inflation of prices has led to a dramatic fall in the purchasing power of money, the *lambedar*'s legitimate rewards today amount to a pittance. These days, then, being a *lambedar* is not nearly such a remunerative business as it used to be, though there are still a large number of more or less illicit ways in which the post can be made to pay.

But the most important reason why the *lambedar*'s influence has declined is that, by the *panchayati raj* legislation of the post-Independence period, the government created a new structure of power within the local community. The *gram panchayats* now control very substantial patronage in the form of development grants and the right to allocate the *shamlat*. This patronage is far more extensive than anything that the *lambedar* has at his disposal. What's more, the latter is no longer the sole intermediary between the local farmers on the one hand, and the bureaucracy and the political elite of the sub-division on the other. His old authority has been largely usurped by the chairman (*sarpanch*) of the *gram panchayat*. The more astute among the *lambedars* were quick to realize what was happening and used the influence they derived from their old positions to gain control of these new institutions. Where they failed to do so, they have typically become the leaders of the dissident faction in the *panchayat*, implacably opposed to the *sarpanch*.

The *panchayat* structure has also provided a base from which those with political aspirations have been able to challenge the position of established leaders at higher levels in the political system. The *panchs* of every *gram panchayat* in the Block form a constituency which elects the *Panchayat Samiti* (Block council). In turn, each of the 24 *Panchayat Samitis* in Kangra elects representatives to the *Zila Parishad* at the district level. Due to their control of a very substantial amount of patronage the *Zila Parishad* and *Panchayat Samiti* Chairmen are considerable figures in local politics, and often find themselves in direct competition for influence with the local members of the State Assembly (MLAs). During the 1967 General Elections there were 23 Assembly seats for district Kangra. The Chairman and Vice-Chairman of the *Zila Parishad*, and at least 14 of the *Samiti* Chairmen, contested the election and all but two of them stood against the official Congress nominees. It came as no surprise, then, that shortly after the election a somewhat weakened Congress government introduced new legislation designed to draw the teeth of these institutions. It was similar motives which had earlier led to a brief revival of the office of *zaildar* – originally abolished at Independence – by a State cabinet anxious to create a malleable counter-weight to the growing influence and independence of those who had gained control of the *panchayats.*

2:7 'Mauza' Chadhiar

Mauza Chadhiar covers an area of 14·62 square miles of the Dhar area of *tehsil* Palampur and lies at an average height of around 4,000 feet. The *mauza*, which contains the circles of two *patwaris* and four *lambedars*, is divided into 9 *gram panchayat* areas (belonging to the Baijnath Development Block) and 37 *tikas*. An outline of the *mauza* and *tika* boundaries is shown in Map 4. (Each of the numbers in parenthesis alongside the *tika* name refers to one of the castes listed in Table I and indicates that this caste is represented in the *tika*). On a larger scale, Map 5 shows the three centrally located hamlets of Ruperh, Chhek and Matial Kalan; and provides some idea of the way in which the houses of different castes tend to be interspersed, and of the way in which they are scattered over the surface area of the land.

The total population of Chadhiar at the 1961 census was 9,040, a figure which excludes the very substantial number of men employed away from home. The dominant caste in the *mauza* and in the surrounding area are the Rajputs. They account for 764 of Chadhiar's total of 1,481 households. The remaining 717 households belong to the 16 other castes listed in Table 1.

There is no evidence as to how long Chadhiar has been settled. The English traveller Moorcroft passed through the *mauza* in the early nineteenth century and mentions the existence of a number of the present-day hamlets (Moorcroft and Trebeck 1841:I:149). The old foundations of substantial stone buildings in some *tikas* suggest resources on a scale which are no longer available to even the largest landlords in the area, and also perhaps that Chadhiar was not always the remote backwater

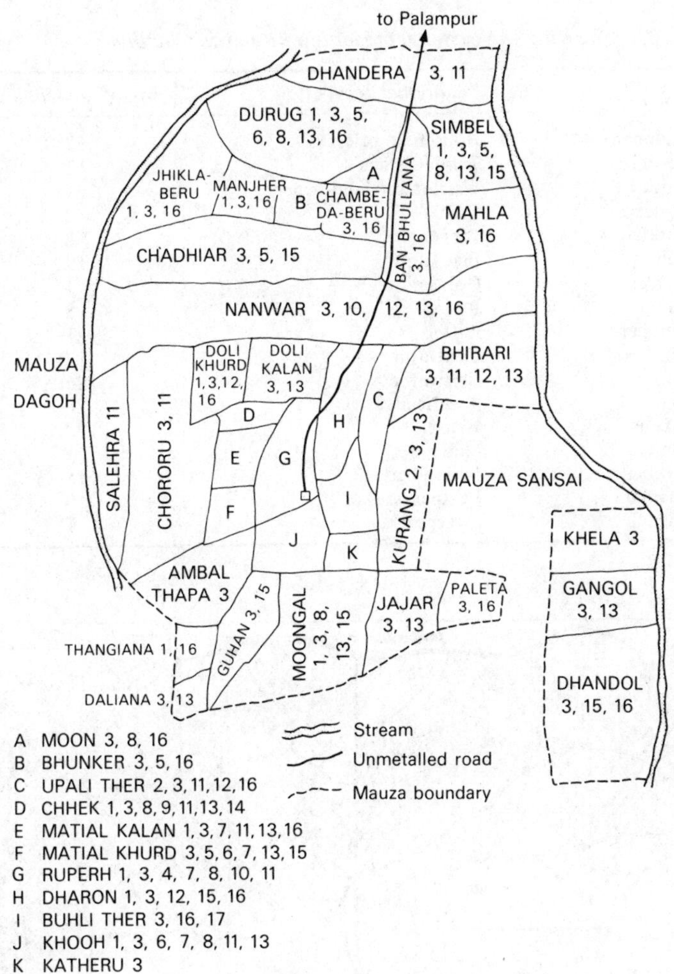

MAP 4 *Map of* mauza *Chadhiar*

it subsequently became. Local tradition has it that these buildings were destroyed by the Gurkha army as it rampaged through the district in 1806. Before the British took over the area, Chadhiar was part of the territory of the Raja of Kangra. After annexation the Raja was assigned a small *jagir* in the Lambagoan area and was given the title of Raja of Lambagoan. Chadhiar was one of the *mauzas* which made up this *jagir* (the extent of which is shown in Map 3). The first British

TABLE 1 *Showing the castes represented in* mauza *Chadhiar*

Caste	*Traditional occupation*	*No. of households*
1 Brahman	Household priest	52
2 Bhojki	Temple priest	11
3 Rajput	Warrior and landowner	764
4 Mahajan	Trader	2
5 Turkhan	Carpenter	18
6 Lohar	Blacksmith	19
7 Sonyar	Goldsmith	4
8 Nai	Barber	18
9 Kumhar	Potter	1
10 Girth	Cultivator	17
11 Koli	Cultivator	226
12 Jogi	Ascetic and beggar	20
13 Jullaha	Weaver	102
14 Sanhai	Musician	1
15 Dumna	Basket-maker	15
16 Chamar	Leather-worker	210
17 Bhangi	Sweeper	1

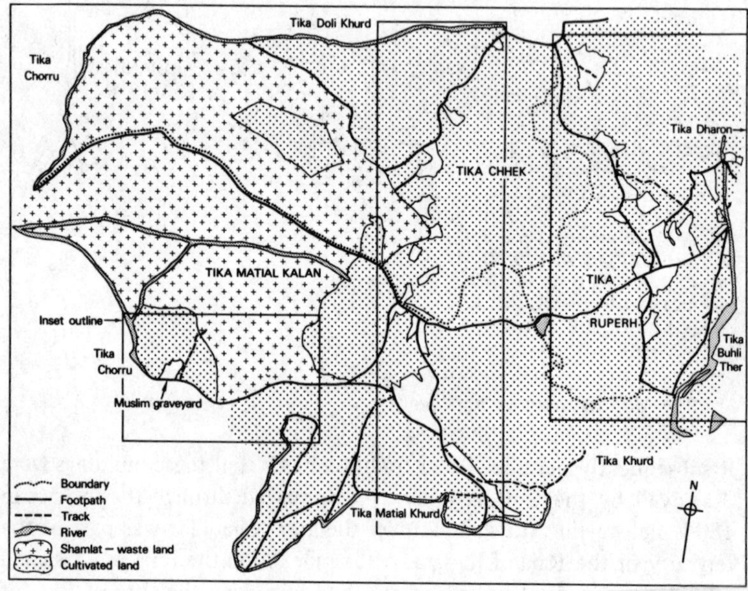

MAP 5 (a) *Map of three* tikas *of* mauza *Chadhiar*

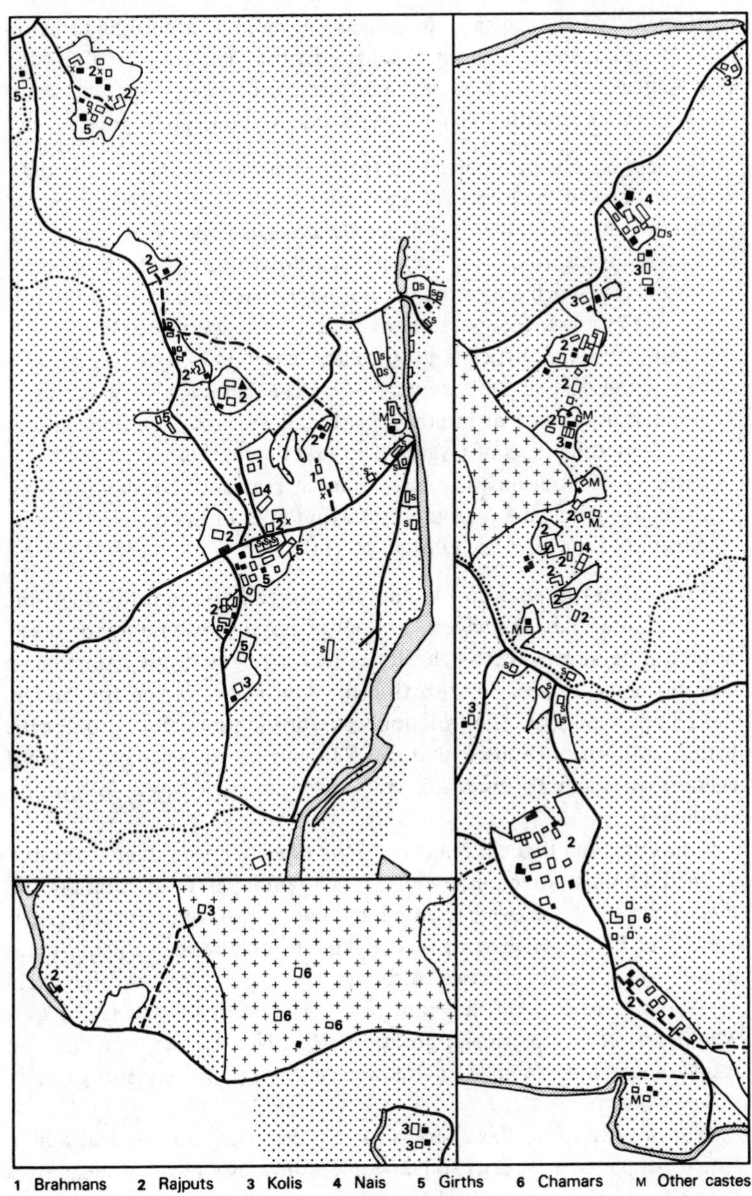

MAP 5 (b) *Inserts of residential sites*

Settlement left the *jagirdars* to collect the revenue 'according to native fashion and ancient custom' (Kangra District Gazetteer, 1926:440). But 'native fashion and ancient custom' soon turned out to be somewhat at variance with the new rulers' ideas about good government:

> the *jagirdar* does not collect his *rurhu* when the crops are harvested. He waits until the prices are high, often allowing three instalments to fall into arrears and when the people have consumed their grain, and then sends his officials to collect; their procedure is to fix a price for the grain high above the price at harvest and collect the amount in cash in a manner most disadvantageous to the *zamindars*. . . . Again, the Raja's officials go to collect in bodies of 8 or 10 men who live at the cost of the *zamindars*. . . . The *jagirdar* also levies his revenue by threats of imprisonment, and by actual confinement. . . . Many other acts of tyranny and exaction have been proved beyond all doubt against the *jagirdar* and his servants. On the other hand the *zamindars* retaliate by buying inferior grain to pay the demand of the *jagirdar* (O'Brien 1891).

Long after its abolition in the areas directly administered by the British, forced labour (*begar*), as well as certain irksome minor taxes, were still being exacted by the Raja. This, along with his extortionate revenue demands, led to an artificially low market value for land in the Lambagoan *jagir*. The situation was worrying enough to prompt the British authorities to insist that the Raja put his house in order, and it encouraged them to encroach still further on what was left of his autonomy.

I have stressed that the *mauza* and the *tika* are both rather arbitrarily defined administrative units whose inhabitants shared no corporate interests before these were created by the British administration. But even after British settlement neither kind of unit became a major focus of important social activities. Although there are three small fairs held in Chadhiar each year they are not the concern of the *mauza* as a whole, nor of any particular group of *tikas*. Nor are the four tiny and rather dilapidated temples in the *mauza* centres for any sort of communal worship.

Yet in spite of all this there is some rather vague and general way in which people – or at least some people– obviously identify themselves with Chadhiar as a unit. It is tempting to attribute such expressions of local loyalty largely to the development of a politics of patronage. Chadhiar has achieved a certain degree of notoriety all over Kangra for being one of the most politically-conscious *mauzas* in the district. Its leaders are important not only at the level of the *mauza*, but also in the wider political arenas of the constituency and district. One of them was for some time a Deputy Minister in the Congress government of the Punjab, and another was elected in 1967 as a Communist member of the Himachal Pradesh State Assembly. In the General Elections of that year there were four candidates from Chadhiar contesting in four different constituencies. Chadhiar people are proud of their favourite sons; and well they might be, for although the *mauza* lies in one of the remotest and least accessible parts of the district, it has received a quite disproportionate share of the development cake.

There is now a once daily bus service along the newly constructed dirt road which connects Chadhiar to the sub-divisional headquarters at Palampur twenty-two miles away. The only Primary Health Centre in Baijnath Development Block is located in Chadhiar – which means, incidentally, that it is totally inaccessible to the vast majority of the inhabitants of the Block. There are also two high schools, eight primary schools and a small veterinary centre in the *mauza*. The centrally located *tikas* – which are also the *tikas* of the henchmen of the ex-Minister – are served by a piped water-supply scheme which cost the Punjab government several hundred thousand rupees. Many of the more prosperous houses of these hamlets have electricity. Chadhiar people, then, are able to identify themselves with an area which has made rapid progress since Independence. Moreover, development funds are seen as a limited good, one area's gain being another's deprivation; and the effect of this is to strengthen parochial identities.

But, significantly, the people of those hamlets which lie around the periphery of *mauza* Chadhiar and which have benefited comparatively little from its material progress continue to regard it as an arbitrary collection of hamlets. In fact, they will sometimes talk of 'going to Chadhiar' – by which they mean the area surrounding the ex-Minister's house – as though their own *tika* were not part of the same *mauza*. The obvious conclusion, then, is that local loyalties have been greatly strengthened by the system of political patronage, and are more developed in some *tikas* than in others. They are strongest of all amongst those who have the greatest stake in Chadhiar's identity: the high-caste members of the Congress faction in the centrally located *tikas*.

But outsiders, too, have a vague idea of Chadhiar as a unit, and quite a vivid image of what sort of unit it is. Chadhiar is envied for its rapid development and notorious for its vicious political in-fighting. For a government employee who is posted there it is an exile, since it is far away from any urban centre, and since it has the reputation of being none too gentle with any outsider unwise enough to get embroiled in its factional politics. In the 12 years since the veterinary centre was opened, 9 compounders have been transferred as the result of complaints made by local people. In the same number of years 40 teachers were transferred from one of the primary schools which has a staff of only two. It is hardly surprising, then, that many of the Government employees in Chadhiar seem to spend their posting in a state of near paranoia. After an altercation about a minor impropriety of which some of the high school girls were guilty, the headmaster took three days off work to tail one of the local *sarpanchs* surreptitiously to Palampur and Dharamsala with the object of discovering whether an official complaint was to be made. When, in 1967, the sub-Post Master was due for a month's leave, a temporary replacement was to be appointed by the head office in Palampur. Five clerks were in turn detailed to take over the Chadhiar office, but one after the other they reported sick.

3 The economy

The present chapter is devoted to the broad theme of the Kangra economy, and is divided into four sections. In the first, I focus on the extent of Kangra's integration into the wider economy and the dependence of the majority of families on money remitted by men employed away from home. I then briefly sketch the structure of agrarian class relations in the subsistence sector. The third part of the chapter deals with the concentration of resources in the hands of the dominant caste; and the final section with what is conventionally known as the *jajmani* system.

3:1 The remittance economy

The rural population density of the Palampur sub-division is 235 per square mile (Kayastha 1964:205), but this figure gives a false impression of the real pressure on the land since large areas in the high mountains are very sparsely populated, and since only 22·1 per cent of the total area is cultivable (ibid., p. 77). The actual density per cultivated square mile is 1,513, which approaches the figure for the middle Ganges valley. The corresponding statistics for *tehsil* Kangra, which neighbours on Palampur to the west, is 1,718 (ibid., p. 209). The 1926 edition of the District Gazetteer (p. 121) records that Kangra had at that time the highest density per unit of cultivation in the whole of the Punjab.

Pressure on the land, then, is terrific, and nearly all the arable waste has long since been brought under the plough. The evidence would suggest that by the beginning of the 1890s practically all the available land was already being cultivated, and that between 1891 and 1914 there was no significant expansion of the cultivated area in either

Palampur or Kangra sub-divisions (Boughey 1914; Middleton 1915).

The 1897 Settlement report for Kangra observes that 'it is hard to see how the land could support a much larger population than it does at present' (Anderson 1897:2). Yet between 1891 and 1951 the population of Palampur increased by 34·2 per cent (Kayastha 1964: 196–8). The eradication of malaria and a general improvement in medical facilities contributed to a further sharp rise of 15·3 per cent in the district as a whole between 1951 and 1961. Chemical fertilizers and higher-yielding varieties of seed, which have been adopted by some of the richer and more progressive farmers, have resulted in some increase in production since Independence, but this has nothing like kept pace with the growth in population.

TABLE 2 *Average size of holdings in 1897 by sub-division*

Tehsil	*Acres per owner*	*Acres per house of 5 persons*
Kangra	1·3	2·6
Palampur	1·7	3·1
Hamirpur	2·9	6·0
Dehra	1·8	4·2
Nurpur	3·1	4·9
Average	2·6	3·9

Throughout the district individual holdings tend to be small and scattered. Table 2, adapted from Anderson (1897:10), provides a broad picture of the situation at the turn of the century, though his figures somewhat underestimate the size of holdings since they take no account of the fact that many owners hold land in more than one *tika*. In the area of Palampur sub-division which includes the Dhar and Lambagoan *jagir* 80 per cent of holdings were less than 4 acres in 1891 (O'Brien 1891). The growth in population and the repeated partition of joint estates mean that the size of the average holding has subsequently diminished further. At the time of my fieldwork there were only 58 holdings in the whole sub-division which were recorded in the official revenue papers as including more than 10 standard acres[1] of cultivable land.[2] But even this figure is something of an exaggeration since a number of these holdings are in the names of different members of the same joint family, or of closely related agnatic kin, but have been registered separately to circumvent the legal limit of 30 standard acres per owner imposed by the Punjab legislation.[3] In fact only 30 different small-scale lineages are represented on the list. Of those who own more than 5 (ordinary) acres in the *tehsil*, over half own less than 8.[4]

In Table 3, 472 households have been categorized according to the amount of land that they own. These households represent a total population of 3,061[5] living in 8 of the 37 hamlets of *mauza* Chadhiar. Table 4 shows the population of each of the 13 castes represented in these *tikas*; while Table 5 provides a detailed break-down of the ownership pattern by caste. These ownership figures obviously take no

TABLE 3 *472 households of* mauza *Chadhiar classified according to acreage owned*

Area owned (in ordinary acres)	Number of households	Percentage of households
1 Landless	109	23·1
2 Less than 1 acre	109	36·2 (rows 2–3)
3 1 to 2 acres	62	
4 2 to 3 acres	43	23·3 (rows 4–6)
5 3 to 4 acres	36	
6 4 to 5 acres	31	
7 5 to 7 acres	20	17·4 (rows 7–11)
8 7 to 10 acres	25	
9 10 to 15 acres	17	
10 15 to 20 acres	6	
11 More than 20 acres	14	

TABLE 4 *Population of eight hamlets of* mauza *Chadhiar*

Caste	Number of households	Population
1 Brahman	19	122
2 Temple priest	10	67
3 Rajput	198	1,280
4 Blacksmith	1	10
5 Goldsmith	3	15
6 Barber	4	37
7 Potter	1	7
8 Girth-cultivator	17	102
9 Koli	122	867
10 Jogi-ascetic	5	27
11 Weaver	28	162
12 Musician	1	1
13 Leather-worker	63	364
Total	472	3,061

TABLE 5 *Ownership pattern of 472 households classified according to caste*

Size of holding (acres)	*Brahman*	*Temple priest*	*Rajput Biradari 1*	*Rajput Biradari 2*	*Rajput Biradari 3*	*Rajput Biradari 4*	*Total Rajput*	*Blacksmith*	*Goldsmith*	*Barber*	*Potter*	*Girth-cultivator*	*Koli*	*Jogi-ascetic*	*Weaver*	*Musician*	*Leather-worker*	*Total*
Landless	2		1	1		5	7		3		1	5	28	5	18	1	39	109
0 to 0·5	6	1			1	2	3			4		9	24		4		18	69
0·5 to 1	2			1	8		9	1				2	19		3		4	40
1 to 1·5	1			1	8	6	15						12					28
1·5 to 2	3	2	3	2	7	5	17					1	8		1		2	34
2 to 3	3	4	3		9	11	23						13					43
3 to 4	2		1	3	14	3	21						11		2			36
4 to 5		1	8	4	13	4	29						1					31
5 to 6		2		3	3		6						1					9
6 to 7				7	3		10						1					11
7 to 8				4	3	3	10						2					12
8 to 9			2	3	3		8											8
9 to 10			2		1	1	4						1					5
10 to 12.5			1	4	3	1	9											9
12·5 to 15			2	6			8											8
15 to 17·5					4		4						1					5
17·5 to 20						1	1											1
20 to 25					4		4											4
25 to 30					3		3											3
More than 30			1	2	4		7											7
Total	19	10	24	41	91	42	198	1	3	4	1	17	122	5	28	1	63	472

account of tenancy contracts, and it should be noted that the majority of those who are shown as landless in fact cultivate a few fields as tenants. The figures also reflect the total area of land owned – up to a third of which is uncultivated grassland – and not the area of arable cultivation. In other words, they greatly exaggerate the extent of productive land.

The broad picture which emerges from these tables is of a majority of households having either very small holdings or no land at all. Only 17·4 per cent have more than 5 acres, while 50·3 per cent own less than 2 acres.

Nearly all the cultivated land in Palampur is devoted to the production of the three subsistence cereal crops – rice, maize and wheat – which form the staples of the local diet. A couple of varieties of millet, pulses, vegetables and tobacco are also grown but in a very subsidiary sort of way. The only cash crop produced in the sub-division is tea. In the Palam area there are the run-down remnants of what were once sizeable and fairly profitable gardens. But competition from the better quality produce of Assam and Sri Lanka proved too much for the Kangra tea industry, which has declined steadily over the last 50 years.

The subsistence crops produce two harvests in the year: *seri* and *niai*. The *seri* crops of rice and maize are sown towards the end of the hot season; the rice on the flatter land known as *jol*, and the maize on the *lahar*, or terraced hillsides. After the monsoon has broken, the young paddy seedlings are transplanted and pulses are sown. Then, in the middle of August, people start to cut hay from the grass preserves (*kharetr*) on the hillsides. The ripened paddy and maize are harvested after the rains in September. Ploughing then begins for the wheat crop (*niai*), which is sown on both types of land in late October or early November, and harvested in early May. Work in the fields goes on almost continuously throughout the nine months of the year from the middle of March to the middle of December. There is then a lull in agricultural operations, during which most of the local fairs fall due and most marriages are celebrated.

In the summer of 1968 I made a survey of the amounts of grain which had been bought and sold over the previous twelve months by 335 of the households of my census. The autumn's harvest of rice and maize had been fairly good but the last wheat crop was poor. The results of my survey are shown in Table 6: 280 (83·6 per cent) of the households had not been able to meet all their own basic requirements from their own land, from land held on a share-cropping basis, or from

TABLE 6 *Showing the number of households who bought and sold cereals in 1967–8*

	No. of households	*Per cent of total*
1 Bought rice, maize and wheat	199	59·5
2 Bought two cereals	47	14·0
3 Bought one cereal	34	10·1
4 Broke even (neither bought nor sold)	15	4·5
5 Both bought and sold	16	4·7
6 Sold one cereal	7	
7 Sold two cereals	9	7·2
8 Sold three cereals	8	
Total no. of households	335	100

grain payments received from labour or from the performance of traditional service duties; 199 households (59·5 per cent) of the total had purchased varying quantities of all three staple cereals, and only 24 (7·2 per cent) had shown a clear surplus for sale. The remaining 9·2 per cent of the sample had either broken even, or had bought one sort of grain (usually rice) and sold another (usually maize). In the poorest hamlet of my census, which has an exclusively low-caste population, only four out of 101 households had managed to meet all their own needs. It almost goes without saying that the amount of grain put on the market by those who had shown a clear surplus for sale was nothing like large enough to meet the demand of those who were forced to buy.

As far as the quality of land is concerned, Chadhiar is among the less well favoured *mauzas* in the sub-division, and its rice production is certainly considerably lower than that of the irrigated areas in the Palam valley. But the overall picture of small-holdings, with a majority of households failing to meet their own basic requirements, is not substantially different elsewhere. In fact, Kangra as a whole has long been a deficit area importing large quantities of grains from the plains of the Punjab.

There are no large-scale industries in the district, so in order to import grain Kangra has to export labour; and this it does in a big way. I estimate that around one-fifth of the total domiciled population of *mauza* Khera was employed outside in 1968. My figures for Chadhiar are more precise. From the 8 hamlets of my census there were 859 adult men between the ages of fifteen and fifty-five; 487 (56·7 per cent) of these were employed outside the *mauza* and most of them outside the district. A further 18 had some form of salaried employment which allowed them to live at home. Of the 373 men over the age of twenty who were not employed, and who were living in Chadhiar at the time of my census, 230 (61·7 per cent) had at some time or other been employed outside.

In one month of 1968, the Chadhiar sub-Post Office received a total of Rs. 43,290 in money orders sent back to their families by local men working outside. The sub-Post Office has a catchment area with a population of around 13,000. Through 1968, the average monthly remittances disbursed by one of the branch Post Offices, which serves the low-caste hamlet of 101 households included in my census, was Rs. 3,300. At a rough estimate these figures would account for only about half the cash being pumped into the economy, the balance being brought by the employees themselves when they come on holiday, or being sent with friends, relatives or neighbours returning from the cities. A substantial amount of money is also paid out by the local Post Office in the form of pensions to ex-soldiers.

The largest single employer of those who leave the district to find work is the military. In Kangra as a whole there are some 30,000 ex-soldiers, in addition to a further 30,000 men from the district who are currently serving in the armed forces.[6] This represents a significant percentage of the total number of able-bodied men born in the district. Out of the 487 men of my census who are employed outside, 179 (36·8 per cent) are in the army. That is, 20·4 per cent of all the males of the appropriate age-group are soldiers. Of the 230 men over the age of twenty who now live at home, but who were previously employed outside, 91 (39·6 per cent) were at one time or another in the military.

Throughout most of the district the dominant caste are the Rajputs, and the martial ethic with which they are associated permeates the whole ideology of Kangra society. The value that people attach to this ethic is, perhaps, the major reason why the military recruitment figures are so high, and why high army rank has such enormous prestige in the villages. But there is also another important incentive for those who want to get ahead to opt for the army rather than a civilian job. Few people in Kangra can afford a college education for their sons, and the standard of secondary education in the district is poor. This puts young men from Kangra at a serious disadvantage when they have to compete for jobs with city-bred boys from the plains. A high proportion of those who work in the cities are unskilled labourers or domestic servants and will never be anything else. Even the lucky ones who have passed the higher secondary examination and been taken on as clerks in a government department find promotion slow and unspectacular. By contrast, the army offers an avenue of mobility for even the barely literate. While it would be overstating the case to say that every Private carries a Field Marshal's baton in his knapsack, the ambitious young recruit can at least aspire to retiring as an Honorary Captain. As I shall argue when I come to talk about hypergamy, this new achieved status can, with advantage, be converted into prestigious marriage alliances on the traditional ladder of ascribed status.

For the more prosperous households it is social considerations of this sort, rather than the mere requirements of subsistence, which encourage the family to send its young men out to make their way in the world. A Captain, a teacher or a *babu* (clerk) in the family is a matter of pride in itself. But a dutiful and successful son will also contribute the financial means for a man to provide his daughter with the spectacular dowry which will enable her to marry well, to pursue a protracted piece of litigation, or to celebrate his household rituals with becoming dignity.

Employment outside the district is nothing new to Kangra people. By the turn of the last century they were leaving home by their thousands to work in the cities or enlist as soldiers (O'Brien 1891; Middleton 1915). Even in the pre-British period large numbers of Rajputs – perhaps encouraged by the necessity of meeting the extortionate revenue demands of the state – had been mercenaries in the Sikh and Moghul armies. When the Sikh army was disbanded after the annexation of the Punjab by the British, many Kangra families were left destitute (Barnes 1889:54); though this situation was soon remedied when the British themselves started to recruit from the area on an even larger scale. Before the First World War their policy was to enlist only Rajputs, but during the course of the war they were forced to modify this practice, though they never did abandon it completely (cf. MacMillan 1968; Mason 1974; Bristow 1974). A total of 17,113 Kangra men served during the war, well over half of whom were Rajputs (Kangra District Gazetteer, 1926:465). By 1921 there were an estimated 40,000 servicemen from the district (ibid., p. 125).

Although the Rajputs had a monopoly on army recruitment during the British period, members of different castes were finding other sorts of work outside the district. Large numbers of Leather-workers from Chadhiar, for instance, were coolies and rickshaw-pullers in Simla, and there was a seasonal migration of labour from the *mauza* to the tea-estates in the Palam valley. Set in the British era, Mulk Raj Anand's celebrated novel *Coolie* paints a moving if somewhat romanticized picture of the hardships which confront a young Rajput orphan from Kangra who becomes a domestic servant in the plains and eventually a rickshaw coolie in Simla.

But although Kangra people have long exploited the outside labour market, they now do so on a scale which was previously unknown. In 1915 there were just 37 men, including the soldiers, from the 8 *tikas* of my census who were employed by the Government in one capacity or another.[7] Now there are over 200.

Not only have more and more men left the district to find work, but the kinds of job that they do are increasingly varied. In the past, those who went to the cities went as menials and labourers, and those who enlisted in the army found that promotion beyond a certain point was contingent on caste and clan status (cf. Cunningham 1932:101), and on racial qualifications. But today, with a general rise in educational standards, and with an expansion of the absolute number of jobs – a larger proportion of which are, theoretically at least, open to competition irrespective of criteria ascribed by birth – Kangra people are becoming increasingly heterogeneous in terms of occupational status. Within the 8 *tikas* of my census are the homes of several teachers, a lawyer and a District Employment Officer. Table 7 provides a general idea of the way in which the 308 civilian employees from these hamlets divide up between different broad occupational categories. Despite the theory, in practice the more prestigious jobs tend to be monopolized by the Rajputs, as are the higher ranks in the army. While they now account for less than half the total numbers of

TABLE 7 *Occupations of 308 civilian employees*

1 Professional:	(a)	teachers	12
	(b)	other	3
2 White-collar (clerks, etc.)			22
3 Skilled labour:	(a)	mechanics and electricians	18
	(b)	drivers	24
	(c)	barbers and tailors	8
	(d)	other	5
4 Unskilled labour:	(a)	Industrial workers	20
	(b)	Police, guards and watchmen	21
	(c)	Orderlies and domestic servants	84
	(d)	Labourers	75
	(e)	Others	16

serving soldiers from these *tikas* (86 out of 179), the two Commissioned Officers and all but one of the 22 Junior Commissioned Officers[8] are Rajputs.

In this connection I am reminded of an interminable evening spent with two gawkish twelve-year-old boys, one an aristocratic Rajput and the other a Carpenter by caste. To fill one of many awkward silences I desperately asked the lads what they intended to do after they had left school. The Rajput's world, it appeared, was his proverbial oyster, for he couldn't decide whether to be an engineer or a doctor. His friend was less easy to draw out, and before he could answer the other had chipped in with great finality: 'He's a Turkhan. He'll be a carpenter – what else?'

Although large numbers of men go outside to work, and although they sometimes take their wives and children with them, very few families uproot themselves completely and abandon their village home forever. In spite of being forced to participate in the cash economy, very few people who have any option in the matter are prepared to commit themselves to it entirely. The main reason why this is so, is that even a small amount of land on tenancy is security against losing a job. Many know from bitter experience that jobs are hard to come by and that at any moment they might suddenly and arbitrarily find themselves out of work. They also know that sickness, or old age, may leave them destitute unless they retain an interest in the land. Wages are often so low that few can afford to support their families from their salaries alone. To make ends meet, a cash income must usually be backed up by participation, in some form or other, in the subsistence sector of the economy. Moreover, living conditions in the city are cramped, accommodation expensive and the cost of living high.

But in addition to all this, there are other, less tangible reasons why few people would care to settle permanently in the city. Partly this is the result of a strong emotional attachment to the valley, and partly because so few of them put down real roots in the urban environment. Even those who have been employed in the city for twenty years or so tend to remain villagers at heart, and most of their contacts outside working hours are with other Kangra people. This was forcefully brought home to me when I stayed with my adoptive sister and her fireman husband in Delhi. There was always a constant stream of visitors who dropped by, but never did I meet anyone whom I could not place in the village context.

Kangra, then, is a district with a high population density and insufficient land to meet even the barest subsistence requirements of its people. A large proportion of the adult men are forced to look for work outside, but because even the smallest holdings offer a degree of security and even the most factious kin groups will preserve their own from total destitution, few abandon their villages altogether. These social and demographic conditions allow the city access to a vast pool of cheap labour; while – to a significant degree – the urban economy supplies the material base for the perpetuation of the rural social structure (cf. Rowe 1973:242). Provided that it is understood that the local community only maintains itself as a community to the extent that it retains its peasant basis, we might characterize the Kangra economy as a remittance economy backed up by subsistence agriculture.

3:2 Landlords, labourers and tenants

The local dialect makes a consistent distinction between two varieties of tenant: *pahu* and *sajhi*. The essential difference between them is that while the *pahu* is a house-tenant, who may perhaps also cultivate some of his landlord's fields, the *sajhi* is simply a tenant of arable land. The landlord stands in the relationship of *bajhiya* to both *sajhi* and *pahu*.

If the *pahu* is a specialist craftsman the rent for his house-site is occasionally paid in the form of his specialist service or product. A barber, for example, may shave his *bajhiya* without payment; a weaver may give a length of cloth, a basket-maker a number of baskets. It was on this basis that, in the old days, a large number of craftsmen throughout Kangra used to hold their house-sites direct from the rajas (Anderson 1897:76; Kangra District Gazetteer, 1926:400). It is only very rarely that the *pahu* pays a cash rent. In the vast majority of cases he pays no fixed rent at all, but is expected to do chores and run errands for his landlord. On these occasions the *pahu* should be given food and tobacco, but he will not be paid. The extent of this labour-service is not defined, and tends to vary considerably with the power and influence of the *bajhiya*. Although the latter's right to his tenant's labour is entered in the official revenue records, he can no longer legally enforce his claims, since house-tenants now theoretically enjoy absolute security against eviction. But in practice landlords can – and occasionally do – use strong-arm methods to evict a recalcitrant *pahu*; and in many cases the mere threat of this allows them to continue to command their *pahu*'s services. But in general the amount of work that they are now able to extract is undoubtedly a good deal less than it used to be.

The status of a house-tenant is a very demeaning one, and the *pàhu* is expected to act out his subordination in a number of ways. He should never appear before his *bajhiya* without some form of head-covering, and when they meet he should touch his feet. At the *seri* festival, which marks the end of the rains, the *pahu* makes a gift of walnuts to his landlord. If the latter should die he must shave his head and observe a seven-day period of mourning. No child of his may be given the same name as any member of the *bajhiya*'s household, or of a closely related household of the same lineage. That, at least, describes what the landlords consider to be appropriate, though these days few tenants are prepared to be quite so punctilious in matters of deference.

Each one of these ritual acts of subordination is the conventional form toward a senior agnate (Chapter 5:5), and in ideal theory, the *pahu-bajhiya* relationship has a quasi-kinship content. The landlords like to conceptualize their role as that of a sort of benevolent patriarch to the *pahu*'s family. In a perfect world the *bajhiya* would lend his *pahu* money and grains, give him wood for his house and grass for thatching, and even perhaps arrange the marriages of his children. People recognize, however, that the world is manifestly imperfect.

The term *sajhi*, by contrast with *pahu*, has definite implications of equality or partnership. It can be used to describe a partner in a business enterprise, or an agnate with whom you have undivided joint property. Although labour service may occasionally be demanded of a *sajhi* as it is of a *pahu*, a landlord's legitimate claims on his *sajhi*'s time are considered to be very much more restricted. The words generally used to refer to such services neatly catch the difference in status between the two types of tenant. While the *sajhi* works on his *bajhiya*'s land as *jowari* ('mutual help between friends') the tasks required of a *pahu* would generally be described as *kar-begar*, or 'forced labour'.

Sajhi cultivate either for a fixed grain rent (*rurhu*), or for a share of the crop (*gala-batai*). Of these, the share-cropping system is by far the more common. In Chadhiar, the landlord traditionally takes half the produce after the revenue has been deducted, and after payment has been made out of the undivided heap to those specialist craftsmen like the carpenter and the blacksmith whose prompt service is essential to the success of the harvest. Other kinds of craftsmen (like the barber and shoemaker) who do not contribute directly to the harvest are paid separately by the landlord and tenant out of their individual shares, though it seems that in the past they too were customarily paid from the common heap (Boughey 1914). But the precise details of the division between the landlord and tenant vary from one part of the district to another. In many parts the craftsmen are paid by the tenants alone, and elsewhere the landlord has customarily received a small additional allowance in recognition of his responsibility for the revenue (cf. Connolly 1911).

Even within Chadhiar shares tend to vary slightly from case to case, depending on who provided the seed and who supplied the plough and oxen. A *sajhi* may hold land from more than one *bajhiya* and his arrangements with each of them may be different. These are often quite complicated and sometimes they involve a deal about labour service. A common pattern is for the tenant to cultivate his holding with the plough and oxen supplied by his landlord, and for the crop from this land to be split on a fifty-fifty basis. In addition, he also cultivates the rest of his *bajhiya*'s land without either taking a share of the crop or being paid wages, though while he is working on this land he gets his food, and at the end of the rains he can cut as much hay as he needs from his landlord's grass preserves. Sometimes such arrangements acquire a quasi-hereditary character.

Throughout the last century the landlord's bargaining position *vis-à-vis* his *sajhi* was greatly weakened by the fact that the demand for tenants generally exceeded the supply (Lyall 1889:47; Kangra District Gazetteer, 1926:395; Middleton 1915, 1919b). The major reason for this was simply that the tenants had a hard time making an adequate living. Their difficulties must have been most extreme during the pre-British period when the combined share of the state and the *bajhiya* amounted to between two-thirds and three-quarters of the crop, while the tenant often had to meet the entire costs of production including the seed and the fees of the specialist craftsmen. It is hardly surprising then, that:

> the proprietors used to have to coax their tenants to settle down and stick to their farms: the proprietor's interest was in those days a sufficient guarantee to the tenant that he would not be evicted except for some very grave cause; and if he was evicted, he could easily get another farm, or if enterprising enough, get land from the State and become a proprietor (Lyall 1889:47).

Evictions of tenants were still very rare at the turn of the century (Anderson 1897) while in the years immediately preceding the First

World War 'the high rates of rent which are imposed by custom probably leave the tenants less profit than they can obtain by equal labour in non-agricultural occupations outside the district' (Middleton 1915). During the same period the shortage of labour in Palampur was sufficiently acute to force the tea-planters to employ coolies for the whole year in order to meet their requirements at peak seasons (Boughey 1914).

Since that time, however, a number of factors have combined to reverse this situation and there are now many more would-be tenants than there is land to go round. The growth in population, and the almost total exhaustion of the supply of cultivable waste, have swelled the pool of aspirants for tenancy contracts. Inflation has also had a hand here, for tenancy on a share-cropping basis becomes increasingly profitable as escalating prices progressively erode the real value of the fixed cash revenue, which now represents a tiny fraction of the total value of the crop, leaving a correspondingly larger share for division between the landlord and tenant. Involvement in subsistence production also gains in attractiveness when, as in recent years, grain prices rise faster than the purchasing power of the wages commanded by many urban employees. This, combined with recent tenancy legislation, has at the same time created a new reluctance – often stridently expressed but hard to demonstrate statistically – to lease land out; and has helped many Rajput and Brahman landlords to overcome some of their aristocratic disdain for farm work, and even for ploughing.

The record shows that nearly 35 per cent of the total cultivable area of *tehsil* Palampur was held by tenants in the mid-1920s (Kangra District Gazetteer, 1926:282). It is difficult to provide precise figures for the current situation. The village accountant's revenue papers for the eight *tikas* of my census give a total of 27 per cent, but this somewhat underestimates the true position since many tenancies are not entered in the records. The reason for this is that the Punjab Security of Land Tenures Act of 1955 makes it very difficult to evict a *sajhi*, and limits the landlord's share of the produce to one-third. Forewarned of the provisions of the Act, a considerable number of landlords evicted their tenants before it became law. Some, however, were evicted on paper only. Land which was previously recorded as the holding of a tenant is now shown as being cultivated by the owner himself, although in fact it is the tenant who is still farming the land. This, of course, deprives the tenant of his legal rights and allows the landlord to continue to demand half the crop, and to evict whenever he feels like it. It almost goes without saying that virtually none of the land given to new tenants within the last 15 years is entered in the records. My estimate is that in Chadhiar these unofficial contracts account for between 10 and 15 per cent of the cultivation.

Even those who are entered in the records, and who are supposedly protected by the Act, often find themselves under heavy pressure either to give half the crop or to quit the land. An influential landlord can get away with this because there are still a large number of ways in which he can make life tough for his tenants. The most straightforward of these is the crude threat of violence or malicious damage to the standing crops. But it is often just as effective to exploit the tenant's reluctance to get involved in a legal action, for most people have little faith in the impartiality of the courts and the landlords have the best opportunities to influence their decisions. Furthermore, court actions are lengthy and very expensive, and even if the case initially goes in favour of the tenant, a rich landlord can wage a campaign of attrition by instituting a series of appeals which place an intolerable strain on his opponent's financial resources. Coercive measures are by no means equally effective against all tenants, however. Those who have some land of their own are much less vulnerable. Sometimes it is the tenant who is the more financially secure of the two, in which case it may be he who trades on the *bajhiya*'s incapacity to sustain a lengthy court case by withholding full payment of his share of the crop.

A very substantial proportion of all cases which do eventually come before the courts involve disputes between *bajhiya* and *sajhi*. I was able to trace records in the District Commissioner's court of 118 civil suits involving people from the 8 *tikas* of my census. Of these cases 53 were between landlord and tenant.

In general, it seems clear that the government legistlation has failed to provide the security of tenure which was its ostensible aim; and, by encouraging the immediate eviction of many tenants, has in fact swelled the ranks of the landless labourers. This may partly explain the discrepancy between the comparatively low proportion of landless labourers noted by some of the earlier sources (cf. Kangra District Gazetteer, 1926:234) and my own more recent (though admittedly more selective) observations.

Of the 373 adult men who were actually living at home at the time of my Chadhiar census, just under 100 had worked as labourers for some time during the past twelve months. The vast majority of these were of low caste, though the figure included a handful of impoverished

Brahmans. In many cases the total number of days that they were employed did not amount to more than two or three weeks, and the money that they earned as labourers was only a subsidiary source of income. For most of the year the supply of labour exceeds the demand, and even those whose livelihood depends almost exclusively on wage labour are often unemployed for long periods. But at harvest and ploughing times, when the pressure of work in the fields is heaviest, there are not enough labourers to go round and many women, predominantly of low caste, are also employed. In Chadhiar, the demand for hired labour is greatest among Rajputs of high standing whose women do not work in the fields.

By all accounts permanent farm servants were common in the past; but today the great majority of labourers work on a daily-wage basis. At peak periods of agricultural activity the daily rate tends to be slightly inflated, but throughout the rest of the year it remains pretty stable. In terms of real wages labourers are probably slightly worse off, and certainly no better off, than they were at the beginning of this century. In 1909 a casual labourer was paid 4 annas a day in addition to his food. With 4 annas he could buy 3 kilos of wheat (Kangra District Gazetteer, 1935, Tables, 25, 26). When I first arrived in Chadhiar in October 1966, the going rate was two meals a day plus Rs. 2 for a man, and Rs. 1 for a woman. Rs. 2 would buy 2·6 kilos of rice or wheat at rationed government fixed-price rates, or 1·7 kilos on the open market. Coarser grains, like maize, were slightly cheaper. A family of two adults and two adolescent children may be reckoned to consume about 50 kilos of grains per month.

During the period of my fieldwork there was an increase in daily wages, so that by the time I left Chadhiar in December 1968 the standard rate for men was Rs. 2·50 to Rs. 3. But even so, the arithmetic leads inexorably to the simple conclusion that a labourer is barely able to cover the cost of enough staple cereals to feed his family. Unless he has some other source of income – a few fields on tenancy, a craft speciality, or a son or brother sending regular remittances from outside – the chances are that he will be heavily in debt. I found it impossible to collect accurate and systematic information about the extent of indebtedness, but nearly all the landless families in my census admitted to owing money. The largest creditors are the shopkeepers.[9]

The problems of skilled labourers – like carpenters and masons – are much less acute, since the demand for their services is more constant, and since their daily wage rates are double those of unskilled labourers. Most masons are carpenters too, and for most carpenters work on a casual daily basis is not a major source of income. Their bread and butter comes from seasonal contracts with the farmers for a grain payment.

A ploughman, or *hali*, is sometimes engaged by one or more landowners for the whole period during which the crop is sown. The *hali* just does the ploughing and family members or hired labourers do the rest of the work. The demand for his services comes largely from households in which all the able-bodied men are employed outside, from households which do not keep a pair of oxen because their holding is too small to merit the investment, and from aristocratic Rajput and Brahman families whose high standing would be compromised by ploughing. The arrangement is a purely contractual one; there is absolutely no obligation to continue it from one harvest to the next, and in practice a *hali* is seldom engaged by the same landowner for more than two or three harvests in a row. Sometimes he will get an agreed quantity of grains for the whole job, but more usually payment is calculated by the number of days it takes to do the ploughing. If he uses his employer's plough and oxen he is paid Rs. 3 per day and given his food while he works. But those *halis* who provide their own plough animals get Rs. 5 per day plus food.

The employment of a *kama*, or general farm servant, is more long-term than that of a *hali*. Though these days it is becoming increasingly common to take one on for the harvest period only, a *kama* is generally engaged on a semi-permanent basis. I have no evidence, however, that his relationship with his master's household ever had the kind of hereditary character described for other parts of India (cf. Breman 1974). The *kama* is required to do pretty well every sort of work from ploughing to collecting firewood; but since he is likely to be of low caste and his employer of high caste, there are a number of tasks – like fetching drinking water from the often distant springs – which he cannot appropriately perform. Though excluded from the kitchen, he sometimes virtually lives in his master's house. In addition to his food and clothing, he is paid between Rs. 85 and Rs. 200 per year. The position of the *kama* is both unprofitable and highly unprestigious, and most labourers would sooner try their luck at finding a job in the cities. For their part few but the richest landowners can really afford to feed another mouth throughout the year. It is not surprising, then, that these days there are very few permanent farm servants in Chadhiar, though they are said to have been much more common in the past. Old men recall the time when even the moderately affluent Rajput households employed three or four. But if these reminiscences are strictly accurate, it would seem that their employment must – at least in part – have been dictated by considerations of prestige and political influence, for even though the women of such households would not have worked in the fields the marginal product of so much additional labour on such comparatively small holdings must have been very small (cf. Breman 1974:46).

Today, when the financial standing of many families is so heavily reliant on those who are employed outside, individual households tend to move up and down the economic ladder rather rapidly. A family with no wage-earners, with only a tiny holding and a number of children to raise, finds it extremely difficult to make ends meet. But one day the sons will be grown up; and with luck they will find themselves jobs and start to contribute to the family economy. When regular remittances are coming in from three or four employees in the city, there may well be a surplus left over after the subsistence requirements of those at home have been met, and in such circumstances a relatively rapid accumulation of capital becomes possible. This may be invested in land (preferably rice land in Palam), or in some small-scale enterprise like a shop or a flour-mill, or in a College education – and thus hopefully in eventual white-collar employment – for a son or a younger brother.[10]

At the time of his death, Bhuri Singh shared a joint household with his four brothers. But shortly afterwards, the brothers decided to partition, allegedly to shed the burden of supporting his widow and twelve children (cf. Chapter 6:7). At the time this left the fatherless family virtually destitute. But now that all the girls are married and all six boys are employed, they are decidedly prosperous. With help from his brothers one of the sons has purchased his own taxi in Delhi.

But this new prosperity is often rather short-lived, and any number of possible combinations of circumstance may lead to its even more rapid dissipation. The family may have several children to marry off; and marriages involve not only expensive rites but also substantial prestations. A land dispute may wind up as a protracted court case which frequently costs more than the value of the land itself, but which becomes a matter of family honour to be seen through to the bitter end. Alternatively a sudden death requiring a costly funeral, extensive house-repairs after the rains, or the need to replace bullocks or a water-buffalo, may combine to place an intolerable strain on the family resources. In addition to all this there is the continual threat that those outside may lose their jobs.

Even if the family manages to ride out all these difficulties without losing its footing on the economic ladder, its property will not survive indefinitely as part of a single estate. Unless there is only one heir, the joint estate will eventually be partitioned after the death of the members of the senior generation (if not before). It is significant that 8 of the 20 holdings of more than 5 acres in Tables 3 and 5 belong to men who were only sons. When there are several heirs none of them may be able to support themselves and their dependants from their share of the land alone. Partitions of even the larger estates may mean, then, that the whole cycle of rags to moderate riches will have to start all over again.

One fairly common pattern, represented by several of my Rajput case-histories, is for the barely literate eldest son of an impoverished family to enlist in the military in his late 'teens, or to take some rather unglamorous employment in the city. The remittances that he sends back, and the grains which are saved in his absence, then subsidize the education of his younger brothers, who are consequently in a position to get better jobs. As subsequent brothers leave home, the educational attainments of those that remain tend to rise, and as a result the individual's chances of carving out an eminent career for himself seem to relate quite closely to his position in the birth order of siblings. As the upward employment spiral of a Rajput or Brahman sibling group continues, the prestige of hypergamous marriage alliances contracted by the family begin to reflect its progress. Both the commissioned army officers in my census, for example, are amongst the youngest of several brothers and enlisted as graduates. Both have also made highly advantageous marriages. But ironically there are some indications that such families are subject to greater pressures to partition than more homogeneous ones. The danger is that the educated army officer, with whom many fathers of high ranking clans would welcome alliance, begins to regard an illiterate elder brother, on whose back he has probably ridden to glory but who is now a spent asset, as something of a liability (especially in the matter of marriage negotiations), and may even secretly come to despise him.

This whole process of accumulation and rapid dissipation of wealth has inhibited both the formation of very rigid class barriers within Chadhiar, and the association of particularly distinctive styles of life with social class. The opportunity to earn money outside, and to invest this money in land at home, allows for a degree of mobility between classes. These days even the largest landowners in Chadhiar will work in the fields alongside the labourers they employ, though if they are Brahmans or aristocratic Rajputs they probably do not plough. The land reforms have had a great effect here. Since the landlords are now reluctant to give their land to tenants, and since most of them cannot afford to employ labourers to do all the work, they simply have to participate in the cultivation themselves. But in the Palam area class differences are sharper, the rich are richer, and the big landlords never work in the fields themselves.

Nowhere in the sub-division, however, can social classes be visualized as a series of tidy pigeon-holes into which each individual can be unambiguously fitted. A landlord in the village may be a member of the industrial proletariat in the city. More importantly, many small landowners also cultivate as tenants, and a few of them work as labourers for part of the year, as do a substantial proportion of tenants. A single individual, then, may simultaneously occupy the roles of landlord, tenant and textile worker. *A priori*, it might be argued that such a situation is likely to inhibit the development of class-consciousness and class conflict. But – as my figures for the number of court cases between *sajhi* and *bajhiya* indicate – it is clear that empirically conflict is by no means absent from the agrarian scene in Palampur. There is, however, some evidence that the degree of antagonism is softened by the extent to which the classes overlap. At least, that is how I am inclined to interpret my general impression that class conflict is much more acute in the Palam area, where there are a number of large non-cultivating landlords and where fewer landlords are also tenants, than on the Dhar where a larger number of farmers occupy both roles.

It was the big landlords of Palam who provided the leadership for an eventually successful campaign to suppress the new tenancy bill which was introduced into the Himachal Pradesh State Assembly in 1968. Their opposition to the bill aroused strong feelings throughout the district, and had the effect of polarizing landlords and tenants into rival pressure groups which were formed to fight on specifically economic issues, and which recruited supporters from a number of different castes on the basis of their class interests.

Class interests as a focus for political action, however, are not a development of the last few years. The 1926 District Gazetteer (p. 390) records that:

> A fierce struggle is going on between the landlords, and the tenants over the *batais* [relative shares] and deductions to be made from the common heap. . . . In several places lands have been left uncultivated owing to the uncompromising attitude of the tenants.

But it should be emphasized that in many political situations it is impossible to make any clear distinction between class and caste conflict. Broadly speaking, the high castes control most of the land, and the majority of low-caste people are either tenants or landless labourers. Given this, caste conflict often implies conflict between members of different classes, and class conflict a clash between those at the top of the hierarchy and those at the bottom.

3:3 The dominant caste and the control of resources

The largest caste in the district as a whole are the Rajputs, who account for 30·8 per cent of the total population. Next in size are the Girth-cultivators and Brahmans with 15·1 per cent and 13·4 per cent respectively. Together these castes account for roughly three-fifths of the total population of the district. Table 8 shows the population of each of the castes represented in Chadhiar as a rough proportion of the population of the *mauza* and of the district.[11]

TABLE 8 *Relative proportions of the population of the 17 castes of Chadhiar*

Caste	*Percentage of district's population*	*Percentage of mauza's population*
1 Brahman	13·4	3·5
2 Bhojki	<1·0	<1·0
3 Rajput	30·8	51·6
4 Mahajan	1·3	<1·0
5 Turkhan	1·8	1·2
6 Lohar	1·8	1·3
7 Sonyar	<1·0	<1·0
8 Nai	1·0	1·2
9 Kumhar	1·0	<1·0
10 Girth	15·1	1·2
11 Koli	4·6	15·3
12 Jogi	1·2	1·3
13 Jullaha	3·8	6·9
14 Sanhai	<1·0	<1·0
15 Dumna	1·3	1·0
16 Chamar	7·3	14·1
17 Bhangi	<1·0	<1·0

British Settlement papers record that in the latter part of the nineteenth century the Rajputs, Brahmans and Girth-cultivators owned nearly 90 per cent of the total cultivated area of the district between them. Of this the lion's share (58 per cent) belonged to the Rajputs, 18 per cent to the Brahmans and around 13 per cent to the Girths (Lyall 1889:60). The proportion of land owned by each of these castes at the beginning of this century is shown for each sub-division in Table 9.[12] In all but one case the Rajputs owned the largest area. In the *jagir*

TABLE 9 *Proportion of land held in each sub-division by Brahmans, Rajputs and Girths at the beginning of the century*

Sub-division	*Brahman (%)*	*Rajput (%)*	*Girth (%)*
1 Palampur	21·0	38·1	9·1
2 Nurpur	12·6	75·1	2·5
3 Dehra	17·7	57·0	14·3
4 Hamirpur	23·6	65·0	12·7
5 Kangra	11·5	27·1	33·1

of the Raja of Lambagoan they owned 58·1 per cent of the cultivation, and the Brahmans a further 20·5 per cent (O'Brien 1891). If the Chadhiar figures are anything to go by, there is little reason to suppose that there has been any very substantial redistribution of land in favour of the lower castes since that time (see Chapter 7:4, Table 21).

But although it is the Rajputs who in absolute terms own the largest proportion of the land, there are – today at least – comparatively few Rajputs among the very biggest landlords in Palampur sub-division. Of the 58 holdings of over 10 standard acres, 18 belong to Brahman landlords from Palam, 25 to the trading-caste families who had profited so enormously as money-lenders in the period following the first British Settlement, and only 9 to the Rajputs.

Not only do the Rajputs, Brahmans and a few trading-caste families control a disproportionate share of the land, but until comparatively recently they have been in a position to corner an overwhelming majority of the most prestigious jobs on the outside labour market. Army recruitment, as I noted earlier, has traditionally been a monopoly of the Rajputs. But white-collar jobs, too, tended to be confined mainly to the high castes, for it was only they who had the wherewithal to send their sons to school. It was the Brahmans and trading castes, however, who did so the more conscientiously since the Rajputs knew that their sons could join the army without much schooling, and since anyway Rajput values tend to rate academic attainments rather less highly than skills of a more martial nature. In the 1920s the Mission School at Palampur was the only high school in the sub-division. Out of 590 pupils who were enrolled between 1923 and 1933, 203 were Brahmans, 177 were Rajputs and 125 members of the trading castes. In other words, 505 (85·6 per cent) of the students belonged to this group of castes. What all this meant in effect was that achieved status was kept broadly congruent with ascribed (caste) status. Although the high castes still retain a monopoly on College education, their stranglehold on secondary education has been largely broken, and it is becoming increasingly possible for low-caste individuals to get a high school education and take up white-collar jobs.

Between them the Rajputs and Brahmans occupy an overwhelming majority of the key positions in the formal structures of power. Out of 165 *lambedars* in Palampur sub-division, 88 are Rajputs and 50 are Brahmans; of the 151 *sarpanchs*, 60 are Rajputs and 44 Brahmans. The same pattern is repeated at the higher levels in district politics. Before the office was abolished 42 of the 53 *zaildars* in the district were Rajputs and a further 8 were Brahmans. All but 12 of the 52 elected representatives on the *Zila Parishad*,[13] all but 5 of the 19 members of the State Assembly from Kangra who were elected from general constituencies in 1967, and all but two of the directors of the District Co-operative Bank and District Wholesale Society – which stand at the apex of a whole pyramid of co-operative societies – belong to these castes.

Considered as a pair, then, the Rajputs and Brahmans display what Srinivas (1959) has characterized as 'decisive dominance'. Not only are they numerically the largest castes in the district and economically and politically the most powerful, but they also have the highest ritual status and the highest educational standards. Though it is perhaps questionable to describe these two castes as united in – rather than as competing for – dominance; and though I have somewhat over-simplified the picture by speaking as if each constituted a homogeneous unit, when in fact there are endless discriminations of rank and a great deal of economic graduality within them, the broad picture of a fantastic concentration of power and resources at the top of the hierarchy is nevertheless clear enough.

In any one *mauza* their influence is unlikely to be evenly matched. In Chadhiar it is the Rajputs who combine most of the elements of dominance though it is, of course, the Brahmans who stand unambiguously at the top of the hierarchy. The *sarpanchs* of all the nine *gram panchayats* in the *mauza* are Rajputs and so are nearly all the other important political leaders. While the Brahmans own only 3·5 per cent of the total cultivated area, the Rajputs own more than four-fifths of it. The extent of their control over the land has changed very little over the last 75 years or so. In 1891 they owned 86·9 per cent of the area, compared with 87·8 per cent in 1934 and 86·3 per cent today.[14] As a consequence it is they who are the main employers of labour and the principal patrons of those specialists who pursue their traditional caste calling.

3:4 Caste and the division of labour

The 17 castes represented in *mauza* Chadhiar are associated with a wide range of occupations, and most essential specialist services of a traditional kind are available within the *mauza*, though few of them are to be found within any one *tika*, and though people who live in one of the peripheral *tikas* are equally likely to patronize specialists from the neighbouring *mauza*. The only essential specialists who are missing from the Chadhiar hierarchy, and who invariably have to be called in from outside, are the Funeral priests. Also notable for their absence are representatives of the Washerman caste, but their services are dispensed with since they are not felt to be absolutely necessary. In *mauza* Khera there are a number of Washerman-caste households but they have long since abandoned their traditional calling in an attempt to launder their blemished status. The women-folk wash the clothes of their own family members. On profane occasions laundering clothes – other than those soiled by menstruation – is not felt to be particularly polluting. My own washing was often done by a Brahman girl with whose family I lived, and nobody seemed to think twice about it.

There is only one family of Sweepers in Chadhiar, and they are recent immigrants who work on a salaried basis cleaning the high school. They have no private patrons at all. People go out into the extensive wasteland to defecate and the night-soil is eventually washed away by the heavy rains.

In practice only a small proportion of the men who live at home, and an even smaller proportion of the total labour force, are actually pursuing their caste-specific occupation. The vast majority are either employed outside, or engaged in agriculture in some capacity or other; while others who have remained in the village work in one of the traditionally caste-free occupations as, for example, teachers, tailors, masons, village watchmen, forest guards or *vaids* (Ayurvedic doctors).[15] Table 10 shows the proportion of adult men from the 8 *tikas* of my census who were in any way engaged in their caste occupation. I have excluded the purely agricultural and mendicant castes from the table as they cannot be said to be specialized in quite the same way as the others.

Leaving aside the cultivating castes and ignoring the anomalies for the time being, the majority of caste occupations sort out into three broad categories: *purohits* ('priests') who receive *dan* (an unsolicited gift); *kamin* ('craftsmen') who receive *gadi-kalothi* (a payment); and a third category which is not normally named but which may sometimes be descriptively labelled *magne-wallahs* ('those who beg') who receive *bitsha* or 'alms'. Table 11 shows how these categories apply to the castes of the Chadhiar hierarchy. Each category of specialist seems to enjoy a qualitatively different kind of relationship with its patrons.

(1) *Purohit/jajman* relations: In Kangra the terms *jajman* and *jajmani* are used in accordance with their religious etymology:

> It can be seen that etymologically the *jajman* is the master of the house who employs a Brahman as a sacrificer. The religious connotation is important, and is still present today, although there is no longer any question of Vedic sacrifice. A Hindi dictionary gives for *jajman*: 'he who has religious (*dharmik*) rites performed by Brahmans giving them fees, etc.' . . . for *jajmani*: 'the privilege (*adhikar*) of performing the function of domestic priest (*purohit*), barber, *bari* (a helper) on the occasions of marriage, etc.' (Dumont 1970:97–8).

As far as Chadhiar people are concerned a *jajman* is a patron of either a Brahman or a Barber or of a Funeral Priest. When he is working as a ritual cook the Brahman is a *boti* to his *jajman*, but as a priest he is a *purohit*. The Barber, in his capacity as an essential functionary at life-cycle rituals, also stands in the relationship of *purohit* to his *jajman*. None of these terms could appropriately be used in the context of any other employer-employee relationship.

In theory, a clan of any caste which is entitled to the services of a Brahman has a fixed relationship with a particular clan of *kul-purohits*. The *kul-purohit* officiates at all household ceremonies and at all life-cycle rituals with the exception of mortuary rites. In addition to this, clans of the twice-born castes are allied to a second Brahman clan who

TABLE 10 *Showing the number of adult men engaged in their caste-specific occupation (Census of eight* tikas*)*

Caste	Traditional occupation	No. living at home	No. employed outside	Following caste occupation as: Main source of income	Following caste occupation as: Subsidiary source of income
1 Brahman	Priest	23	13	4	7
2 Bhojki	Temple priest	6	13		
3 Mahajan	Trader	1		1	
4 Lohar	Blacksmith	2		2	
5 Sonyar	Goldsmith	3	3	1	1
6 Nai	Barber	10	5	8	1
7 Kumhar	Potter	1		1	
8 Jullaha	Weaver	22	26		
9 Chamar	Leather-worker	53	63	2[1]	4[1]

[1] These figures relate to Chamars who actually work as cobblers and tanners (*mochis*) and not to those who simply remove dead cattle.

are their *guru-purohits*. It is the *guru-purohit* who whispers the *gyatri mantra* to initiates during the sacred thread ceremony (*janeo sanskar*). When a *jajman* meets any male member of his *purohit* clan he will touch his feet and address him as *purohit Ji*.

In the ideal model it is whole clan groups which are related in this way. In other words, people talk as if all the members of their clan, wherever they might happen to live, are *jajman* to the same two Brahman clans. But in reality the *jajman/kul-purohit* relationship is between sub-clans, defined as localized segments of the clan. The Awasti sub-clan of *mauza* Khera, for example, claim that the Vedwe are their *kul-purohits*; while at Paprola, some fifteen miles away, it is said that properly the Tugnaiths are *kul-purohits* of all Awastis.

Between *jajman* and *purohit* sub-clans there is a relationship which is thought of as permanent. Within this alliance an individual *jajman* household will have an hereditary relationship with an individual household of the *purohit* sub-clan, and in theory this relationship lasts from one generation to the next. In fact the ties between particular *jajman* and *purohit* households do not have quite this long-term immutability, since few of Chadhiar's Brahmans are actually priests (as Table 10 shows) and since a priest's sons frequently take to secular occupations. When a *purohit* dies his *jajmans* often redistribute themselves among the other *purohits* of the deceased's sub-clan. But during his lifetime switches are very rare. Despite extensive enquiries I encountered only two cases in Chadhiar where a practising *kul-purohit* had been deserted by former *jajmans*. Both of these involved rather exceptional circumstances and in both the switch was to another member of the *kul-purohit* sub-clan. In one other case the *jajmans* had started to patronize a household priest of a different clan on the death of their former *purohit*. But while the reality of the *jajman/kul-purohit* relationship corresponds fairly closely to the theory, the insistence on an enduring relationship with an entirely separate *guru-purohit* clan seems in practice to be an elaboration of the aristocratic Rajputs, and in general people are a good deal less fussy about recruiting their preceptor from the appropriate clan.

It was my own lack of discretion on an occasion when an elderly Rajput widow was to perform the marriage of Tulsi Mata that gave me my first real insight into the value which is attached to the permanence of the *kul-purohit/jajman* relationship. Tulsi Mata is a manifestation of the goddess Lachmi, and is represented in material form by the basil plant (*tulsi*) which occupies a shrine in the centre of most Brahman and

TABLE 11 *Showing categories of caste occupation in* mauza *Chadhiar*

Caste	Occupation	No. of Households	Customary reward for performance of caste occupation	Category of specialist	Notes
1 Brahman	Household priest	52	*Dan* (= *Nasran* + *Brasod* + *Dakshina* + *Dharmarth*)	*Purohit/Boti*	As ritual cooks sometimes receive seasonal grain payments (*brasod*); otherwise paid on piece-work basis.
2 Bhojki	Temple priest	11	*Dan* (= *Dharmarth* + offerings at temple)	*Purohit*	Perform no temple duties in Chadhiar. All secular.
3 Rajput	Warrior and land owner	764			
4 Mahajan	Trader	2			Recent immigrants
5 Turkhan	Carpenter	18	*Gadi-kalothi*	*Kamin*	Lohars and Turkhans intermarry and are considered equal in status. Many are both blacksmiths and carpenters by trade.
6 Lohar	Blacksmith	19	*Gadi-kalothi*	*Kamin*	
7 Sonyar	Goldsmith	4	Cash		Piece-work rates even in the past
8 Nai	Barber	18	*Gadi-kalothi* + separate remuneration at life-cycle rituals	*Purohit/Kamin*	

9 Kumhar	Potter	1	*Gadi-kalothi*	*Kamin*	Recent immigrants
10 Girth	Cultivator	17			
11 Koli	Cultivator	226			
12 Jogi	Ascetic and beggar	20	*Bitsha*	*Magne-wallah*	
13 Jullaha	Weaver	102	Cash?	*Kamin*	Long since ceased to weave
14 Sanhai	Musician	1	*Bitsha*	*Magne-wallah*	Recent immigrants
15 Dumna	Basket-maker	15	*Gadi-kalothi/Bitsha*	*Kamin/ Magne-wallah*	As funeral drummer receives shroud (*kaphan*) and classified as 'the eater of the shroud' (*Kaphan-kho*).
16 Chamar	Leather-worker	210	*Gadi-kalothi*/hide of animal	*Mochi* + *Kamin*	Receives *gadi-kalothi* as specialist leather-worker (*mochi*) and not as scavenger of dead animals.
17 Bhangi	Sweeper	1	?	?	Recent immigrants. Work as Government employees for school and not on private basis at all.

aristocratic Rajput courtyards.[16] At *Tulsi Mata da biah* the plant is symbolically married to a stone representing Salig Ram, an incarnation of Vishnu. The ritual takes exactly the same form as a real marriage and confers great merit and prestige on the *jajman*, largely on account of the substantial dowry which is given along with the bride. Salig Ram's marriage party sets off from the *purohit*'s house, to which it returns along with the bride and her dowry, after the rites have been performed at the *jajman*'s house. In this particular case what happened was that the *purohit*'s *chachi* (FyBW) died shortly after the marriage was due to take place, and by all the rules no marriages should have been celebrated in his house for at least three months after the death. This left the widow in something of a quandary since she had already made all the preparations, invited the guests and bought the dowry which was earmarked for the forthcoming marriage of the *purohit*'s daughter. Various compromise solutions were put forward; my own contribution being to suggest that the widow get herself a new *purohit* for the occasion. This suggestion, I was patiently given to understand, was not only quite irrelevant but also in distinctly bad taste, for it is the hereditary *purohit*'s right to perform the ceremony and to take the dowry. Calling in another Brahman was simply not an option.

If for any reason it is impossible for a *purohit* to attend to his obligations in a *jajman*'s house, it is his duty to provide a substitute, and it would be out of place for the *jajman* to make separate arrangements without consulting him. Some *purohits* are much more sophisticated than others in their knowledge of the often elaborate and complicated rituals. If an hereditary *purohit* does not know how to conduct a particular ceremony a second *purohit* will be invited to perform it. But it is the hereditary *purohit* who will collect the payment, and he will divide it with his colleague by a private arrangement, which is no concern of the *jajman*.

The word *jaddi* means 'ancestral property' and normally it refers to land. But a Brahman's *purohitchari* is also *jaddi*. Like land it is heritable and divisible among male heirs, or at least among those who are practising priests. These rights are not marketable, however, and people I asked about this made a show of being shocked at the very idea. The *jajmani* rights of the funeral Brahmans, on the other hand, can be bought and sold or even mortgaged, transfers usually being accompanied by a written document.

On death the soul becomes a *pret*, a marginal state dangerous both to itself and to the survivors. On the thirteenth day after death, or thereabouts,[17] the *sapindi* rite is performed at which the deceased re-joins his ancestors and himself becomes an ancestor (*pitr*). At the rite he is represented by a ball of flour (*pind*) which is cut into three by the chief mourner, and is merged with three other *pind*s which represent his father, father's father and *his* father. In many parts of orthodox Hindu India this *pret/pitr* distinction corresponds to a division of labour between the specialists who handle the marginal *pret* and those who will preside only after the *pret* has been assimilated to the category of *pitr* (between, for example, the Mahabrahman and the Panda).

In Kangra there are three kinds of funeral priest: the Sanyasi, the Charaj and the Parcharaj. It is only with the first two, however, that Chadhiar people have any dealings. The inferior Charaj presides over the ceremonies directed towards the *pret*: that is, the rites immediately following the death up until the *sapindi* ritual which transforms the deceased into a *pitr*, and which marks – for the chief mourner – the end of the period of the most intense pollution. After *sapindi* the Sanyasi takes over the monthly rituals which are performed for the first year after death (*masik saradh*), and for the first three of the four annual rituals. It is only on the fourth anniversary (*chabarakh*) of the death that a pure Brahman will officiate. The Parcharaj, who are not represented in the immediate vicinity of Chadhiar, perform the duties of Charaj to the Charaj. In ritual contexts the Sanyasi to the Sanyasi, like the Barber to the Barber, is a member of a wife-taking clan – a fact which is clearly closely related to the hypergamous marriage formula prevalent in the area.

When a funeral priest dies his *purohitchari* is divided amongst his heirs in a way significantly different from that of pure Brahmans. It is not particular households of *jajmans* which are allocated between the heirs, but rather days in the month. For example, if there are two heirs, then one will be responsible for all deaths which occur in the first half of the month in the *jajman*'s houses, and the other for the second half of the month.

By way of remuneration the *purohit* receives a series of prestations which fall into the general category of *dan*. *Dan* also occurs in contexts outside the system of customary rewards. A pre-pubescent bride, for example, is offered along with a dowry as *dan* to the groom's family. But whatever the context, the morality of *dan* is fundamentally distinct from the morality of a commercial payment. It has rather the character of a charitable donation humbly offered to somebody of superior status, whose condescension in accepting the gift allows the donor to acquire merit. Under no circumstances may any material return be accepted, for a counter-prestation would cancel out the merit acquired by the original gift. It is for this reason that an orthodox and conservative Rajput will not eat at a Brahman's house, any more than he will eat in his married daughter's house. When several Rajput households of the Wazir lineage of *tika* Ruperh clubbed together to finance the marriages of two Brahman sisters, they all came to attend the rites, though none of them would stay for the wedding feast which they themselves had provided. A respectable man gives as much as he can afford in *dan*, and the bigger the gift, the more the merit. The *purohit*'s takings, then, are neither rigidly fixed nor subject to bargaining.

The Brahman receives several different kinds of *dan*. On the occasions when he officiates as a *purohit* he takes away a quantity of grains (*brasod*), some money and various articles of clothing.[18] He does not receive a fraction of the crop at harvest time. But on certain festival days and at *sagrand*, the first day of the Hindu month, he has the right to go from house to house and collect from each a handful of grains, known as *nasran*. If a Brahman eats in a non-Brahman house, the honour should be acknowledged by *dakshina*, which usually consists of just a small coin. But far more substantial than either *nasran* or *dakshina* is *dharmarth*, by which a landlord will make over the produce of a certain field on a permanent basis to a particular Brahman household. The land usually remains under the cultivation of the donor, or his tenant, and the crop (or the landlord's share of it) is sent to the Brahmans. Alternatively, the land itself, as distinct from its produce, is given over to the Brahman who will then arrange for the cultivation himself. Another variety of *dharmarth* is when a well-to-do landowner finances all the wedding expenses of a Brahman girl.

It should not be imagined, however, that patrons distribute their largesse indiscriminately to an undifferentiated collectivity of importunate Brahmans. Most are far too canny to squander their resources on those whose standards of orthodoxy fall below par, for it seems as if the merit and prestige which are the indeterminable fruits of *dan* are best guaranteed by the impeccable status of the recipient. As a result, some impoverished Brahmans seem to be caught in a kind of poverty trap: since they cannot afford to renounce certain degrading practices (like ploughing) they disqualify themselves from all but the crumbs of the munificence of wealthy patrons.

By way of summary we can characterize the Brahman's relationship with his *jajman* as an ideally hereditary tie between two households which is part of a permanent alliance between two sub-clans. The *purohit* has an obligation to serve his *jajman*, or to provide a substitute; and the *jajman* has an obligation to utilize his services and to reward him to the limit of his capacity. Even if he is incompetent to perform a particular ritual, and a better qualified Brahman has to be invited, the prestations are his. A *purohit*'s rights are his *jaddi*, or ancestral property, and in the case of funeral priests they can be bought and sold.

(2) *Kamins*: In marked contrast to all this is the more contractual nature of the relationship between a *kamin* and his patron.

It is essentially those who pursue an artisan-type occupation who are labelled *kamin*, and this craft aspect of their specialization is emphasized by their adoption of Viswakarma – the artisan god and architect of the universe – as a patron deity. At the time of the *Diwali* festival, all those who rate as *kamins* (including the anomalous cases of the Barber and the Basket-maker) worship the tools of their trade and make a thank-offering to Viswakarma. The Tailor and the Goldsmith (who are not strictly speaking *kamin*) also make such an offering but none of the 'non-technical' specialists do so.

The patron of a *kamin* is probably a *zamindar*, or landowner, but this pair of terms are not reciprocals in the strict way that *purohit-jajman* are. While the word *purohit* is an honorific and implies superiority of status, *kamin* has distinctly derogatory connotations and always applies to inferiors. For this reason it is impolite to refer to somebody as a *kamin* in his presence, though the term will be used freely of those who are out of earshot. A *kamin* is ideally supposed to act out his subordination in much the same way as a house-tenant (see above), and makes identical offerings to his patron at the *seri* festival. Like the *pahu*, he is called to weddings and other major rituals in his patron's house, though these days he is likely to ignore the summons since he knows that he will be letting himself in for a whole series of menial chores; and instead of being fed with the guests he will be given a pile of cooked rice to take home to consume with his family.

The relationship which links the *zamindar* and his *kamin* is *kalothi-badh*, and the traditional payment is *gadi-kalothi. Gadi* refers to a sheaf of paddy; *kalothi* to a basket used for storing maize. But due to the great shortage of rice-land in Chadhiar, very few landholders in the *mauza* are these days prepared to give paddy to their *kamins*. At the *seri* crop they give maize; at *niai* a quantity of wheat, most of it as grains but perhaps one or two unthreshed sheaves (*puliyan*) as well.

In return for this payment the artisan is expected to provide prompt and efficient service throughout the months from the first ploughing until the crop is in. At sowing time and harvest time the pressure of work on the Carpenter and Blacksmith is extremely heavy as impatient farmers with an eye on the weather make urgent demands that a plough be mended, a new ploughshare forged, or a sickle sharpened. The Potter and the Basket-maker, who provide enough pots and baskets to cover the basic needs of their patron's households, work at a more sedate pace since the demand for their services is not so pressing.

On jobs like house-building, Carpenters are remunerated on a daily-wage basis. These days, too, many other artisans do much of their work for piece-work rates. But even where there is a *kalothi-badh* relationship not all services are included in the grain payment. Broadly speaking anything not normally needed in the day-to-day running of the house or farm is paid for in cash. On certain ritual occasions some special article of the artisan's manufacture may be required, and for this he should get separate remuneration, though in practice he may waive payment from his landlord or from a powerful patron. When a man dies, for example, the Carpenter makes the bier (*sihar*) for his corpse. When he gets married he makes the *ved*, or marriage booth. For the *panjap* ceremony, celebrated 13 days after birth, the Potter is asked to provide special pots and the Basket-maker a cradle.

In contrast to *dan*, *gadi-kalothi* is explicitly a payment. Although the old papers of the village accountant list fixed rates for each variety of *kamin*, nobody in Chadhiar takes a blind bit of notice of them, and even 50 years ago they do not seem to have been observed. The District Gazetteer (1926:235) notes that 'none of (the *kamins*) has fixed perquisites, and their duties and remuneration vary in different parts'. In my own experience the details of *gadi-kalothi* payments are subject to a good deal of bargaining, and disputes between artisan and patron are common. The general complaint amongst the *kamin* is that the size of the *gadi-kalothi* payment has diminished steadily over recent years. The amount paid corresponds roughly to the amount of work done during the season, but it also depends on how large the crop has been. An artisan, then, may find that his income varies a good deal from harvest to harvest.

Amongst themselves *kamin* may sometimes exchange services, but on the whole this is rather rare, as it is distinctly unusual for any two of them to require an equivalent amount of each other's product or service. The Barbers, for example, have virtually no land, so for them the question of a reciprocal exchange of services with the Blacksmiths does not arise. When this sort of arrangement does occur it is an entirely private affair between individuals and in no way involves whole groups of specialists. None of the cases I recorded involves a Brahman *purohit* as one of the partners. This, I was assured, could never be the case, for it would be directly contradictory to the ideology of *dan*. A *purohit*'s services are simply not commensurate with the services of a *kamin*.

A *kamin* does not have the right to serve his *zamindar* in the same way as a *purohit* has a right to serve his *jajman*. There is no question of *jaddi* ('ancestral property') here; the term would be quite inappropriate. Although a *kamin* may take over his father's clientele he will soon find that they go elsewhere if he is not a competent craftsman. Either party can terminate the contract at will though it is considered only right and proper to wait until the crop is in. But it sometimes happens that at busy times in the year an irate cultivator will switch to a new carpenter or blacksmith if he thinks that he is not being served quickly enough. As the Kangra adage has it, 'at the time of sowing and reaping the *zamindar* is nobody's friend'. During my stay in Chadhiar one of the blacksmiths was ill for most of one season. By the time the next season came around he found that he had lost 28 of the households he had formerly served.

Most people who have any land at all have *kalothi-badh* with a carpenter and a blacksmith. Cultivators say that in this case they prefer to have seasonal contracts than to pay piece-work rates because it ensures that they are served promptly when they are in a hurry. If the artisan were employed on the basis of once-off cash transactions he could afford to turn a customer away when he was busy. But with a *gadi-kalothi* arrangement, where the rates are variable and the payment delayed until the harvest, he is rather unwise to refuse a patron. In view of the general shortage and high price of grains, the artisans are for their part happy to continue the arrangement.

Carpentry and iron-work are the most competitive trades in the *mauza*, partly because they are particularly open to interlopers from other castes. Among the inhabitants of the 8 *tikas* of my census, for example, there were 3 Kolis, 5 Leather-workers and a Jogi-ascetic who were pursuing these occupations as full-time specialists. For the most part it is low-caste people who have infiltrated these trades, though in another *mauza* of the sub-division I knew two Brahman brothers, one of whom was a carpenter and the other a blacksmith.

The only potter in Chadhiar is a recent immigrant from a

neighbouring *mauza* where his brother still supplies their old clientele. About two-thirds of his business is for cash and the rest is by *gadi-kalothi* arrangement. Population pressure on the land, enormously inflated grain prices, and competition from manufactured products have combined to eliminate almost completely the Shoe-maker (*mochi*) and the Basket-maker from the *gadi-kalothi* system. Sometimes they are paid in grains on a piece-work basis, but for the most part they are now paid in cash. The Weavers have long since ceased to pursue their traditional caste calling, and most of those who have remained at home are landless labourers.

In general, there has been little positive action that the *kamins* have been able to take in order to preserve their caste occupation as a monopoly free from outside interlopers and secure against competition from the wider market. Everywhere in Kangra almost all the caste *panchayats* are now either defunct or largely impotent. For the most part they seem to have been concerned with matters of status and I have no evidence that they ever functioned as trade guilds. In fact, the caste *panchayats* which have been most effective over the last fifty years have been those of the Kolis, Girth-cultivators and Rajputs, and these are agricultural castes with no such monopoly to protect. I never came across a case in which a specialist caste had itself successfully initiated the boycott of a patron, and nobody I asked seemed to think that this would be possible. On the other hand, I recorded several instances in which the dominant Rajputs had successfully denied an offender access to the services of the specialist castes.

(3) *'Those who beg'*: The *purohits* who condescend to accept *dan*, and the *kamin* who are paid *gadi-kalothi* are distinguished from 'those who beg' for *bitsha* or alms. Such are the Jogis, who rate as Ascetics to their face and Beggars behind their backs, and who have the privilege to go from courtyard to courtyard at certain times of the year singing ballads about the exploits of various deities and quasi-divine folk heroes, and to receive from each household a small quantity of grains. Again it is the Musicians' privilege after the harvest to make music at the houses in the area around which they live. Before Partition, when those who were not slaughtered fled to Pakistan, a caste of Muslim Drummers were also entitled to collect *bitsha* in the *mauza*.

It is obviously difficult to compare the security enjoyed by the recipient of *bitsha* with that of the other two categories since they are not tied to individual employers in quite the same way. Theirs is the right to beg from all the houses in their local area (though the obligation to give is a good deal less marked than with *gadi-kalothi* or *nasran*) and they continue to enjoy this right as they have always done. But today a number of the younger men refuse to exercise their traditional privilege, which they see as degrading. Others complain that the high price of grains has made the *zamindars* less liberal than formerly. But even so they don't do too badly, and I noted one case where a Jogi-ascetic collected fifteen kilos of maize in a single day.

Reference to Table 10 will show that in reality the individual castes of the Chadhiar hierarchy cannot all be unambiguously assigned to one of these three categories. On the face of it at least, the boundaries are blurred by the Basket-makers who receive both *gadi-kalothi* and *bitsha*, and by the Barbers who rate both as *purohits* and as *kamin*. In fact, however, the tripartite schema I have outlined is nevertheless preserved by the people themselves, who in these cases appear to distinguish either different aspects of their caste occupation, or entirely different occupational roles performed by caste members, and to classify these in different ways.

This is perhaps clearest in the case of the Dumnas who, as Basket-makers and workers in bamboo, rate as *kamin* and traditionally receive *gadi-kalothi*, though these days they are steadily being forced out of business altogether by products sold in the local markets.[19] But during the month of *Chet*, the Dumna also performs what might loosely be described as a 'ceremonial' role as a singer of ballads known as *dolru*, for which his customary reward is *bitsha*. By contrast with his superannuated function as basket-maker, only the most tight-fisted of householders would begrudge him the handful of grains he customarily receives as ballad-singer.

The Dumnas perform *dolru* at every clean-caste house, and before their visit there is a taboo on the name of the month. The names of other months should not be used until they have been heard from an auspicious individual, preferably a Brahman. But *Chet* is an inauspicious month, and the Dumnas ('the thirteenth caste') are a proverbially inauspicious bunch of people. A much quoted ditty sums up the general sentiment:

Gujar se ujar bhali,	Barren ground is better than a Gujar,
Us se bura Labana;	Worse is a Labana;
Basi khili pani hoye	But if the village site is to be empty
Tan Dumna basana	Then settle a Dumna on it

The reason why the Dumnas are held to be so inauspicious is that they perform a third function as drummers at mortuary rituals. In this capacity their customary reward is the shroud of the corpse (*kaphan*) and for this reason they are known as *kaphan-kho*, 'the eaters of the shroud'. This perquisite is quite distinct from either *gadi-kalothi* or *bitsha*.

In the same general way it seems possible, in the case of the Barbers, to discriminate one aspect of their traditional occupation in which they are *purohits*, and another in which they are merely *kamin*. It is *par excellence* at life cycle ceremonies, when he has certain essential ritual duties to perform, that the Barber rates as a *purohit* to his *jajman*. On such occasions it is as if he in some way shares in the qualities of the Brahman, for in most of these rituals they are strikingly paired. Where, for example, the Brahman receives gifts at the beginning of the ceremony, the Barber receives identical gifts at the end.[20] Though the individual prestations bear the same names, I do not think that the word *dan* would be used as a generic term for the Barber's perquisites here. But nor are they part of the *gadi-kalothi* payment which is his reward as a *kamin* who shaves and cuts the hair of his patrons on ordinary profane occasions. Paradoxically, the Barber may at such times be jocularly addressed as '*raja sahib*' (cf. Tandon 1972:125), a title which is popularly held to derive from the fact that aside from the raja only he may lay his hands on the head of a Rajput aristocrat without causing grave offence.[21]

The right to wear the sacred thread is, of course, theoretically confined to the twice-born castes, which in much of Kangra traditionally meant only the Brahmans and the aristocratic – though not the plebeian – Rajputs (cf. Cunningham 1932:72; and also Chapter 7). But the Barbers, who rate as Shudras, were even in the past an exception here, though they had to content themselves with a thread of only three *aggars* (or strands) as opposed to the six-stranded *janeo* worn by the Rajputs and Brahmans and the nine-stranded *janeo* of the Bhojkis.[22] On the face of it, it is rather puzzling that the Barbers alone, out of all the castes in the middle ranges of the hierarchy, should have had this privilege. The reason, I suggest, is that in certain contexts they belong to the category *purohit*, which marks them off as essential ritual specialists, and identifies them with the Brahmans.

In the next chapter I aim to show that there are various degrees of untouchability. In the present context it is enough to note that all those below Koli are 'untouchable' or *baharke*; that the Kolis themselves are in an anomalous position; and that people discriminate between those who are literally untouchable, and those who are untouchable only in the limited sense that they pollute the food, water and utensils of the clean castes. I introduce this here since it is relevant to the distinction between the Barber's everyday trade and his role as a ritual specialist essential to the performance of a marriage.

Both a Barber and a Brahman *purohit* will officiate at the rituals of all castes down to and including the Kolis. But on profane occasions the Barber's range is rather wider and he serves the Jogi-ascetics, Weavers and (theoretically) the Musicians, though some Barbers will insist on shaving the men of the last two castes in the open and will not go to their houses, while one or two claim that they will only lend them scissors and won't actually do the work themselves. To simplify the pattern slightly, what all this seems to amount to is that the Barber uses the distinction between 'clean' (*andarke*) and 'untouchable' (*baharke*) castes to discriminate between those he will serve as a *purohit*, and those he will serve only in contexts less highly charged with religious significance. The distinction between those who are 'untouchable' in the limited sense of polluting food, water and utensils of clean castes, and those who pollute by physical contact alone, corresponds to the distinction between those whom the Barber will serve only on profane occasions and those he will not serve at all.

In these two capacities – as a kind of 'tradesman' and as a kind of 'priest' – the Barber experiences a qualitatively different kind of relationship with his patrons. Though most landowning households of any substance do in fact continue to pay *gadi-kalothi* to the Barber, others have attempted to economize by eliminating him from the system of customary rewards. The men of such families now shave themselves and have their hair cut on a cash basis, either locally or on a trip to town. Even when the household does maintain the *gadi-kalothi* relationship, some young dandies from Chadhiar refuse to patronize their family Barber because, they complain, he is only fit for rustic fashions.

But as an essential functionary at life-cycle rituals, the Barber's relationship to his patron is of a much more durable nature. In the course of the year the latter may be shaved and have his hair cut by a series of different Barbers to whom he pays cash. But when it comes to a wedding, then there will generally be one special Barber household on whom he will call. While the Barber's rights here are by no means as strong as those of the Brahman *purohit*, have no market value, and are not part of a permanent alliance between sub-clans, there would nevertheless have to be a very good reason for ignoring his claims on ritual occasions. Each year the Barber issues, as it were, a reminder of these obligations when on the night before the *seri* festival he visits each of the *jajman* households (including those from whom he receives no *gadi-kalothi*) and collects from each a small quantity of grains and at least Rs. 1 in cash.

The participants' categories, then, divide the majority of caste-ascribed occupational roles into three groups, each of which is associated with a different customary reward and governed by a different transactional morality. At first sight it is tempting to gloss these three categories as 'religious', 'secular' and 'ceremonial' occupations respectively. But while the term 'religious' retains the habitual sense it has acquired in the sociology of India as an adjective for anything positively charged with status-purity implications, it is grossly misleading to characterize the Kangra distinction between *purohit* and *kamin* as a distinction between religious and secular specialists. The inappropriateness of such a translation is clear from the fact that the Barbers and Leather-workers rate as *kamin*, although both are (in this sense) religious specialists who restore purity to their patrons by removing pollution, the Chamars by disposing of the carcasses of dead cattle and the Barbers by barbering. That even on profane occasions the barber refuses to serve the lowest castes, while the patron suffers mild impurity from his ministrations and sprinkles his head with water in token of a bath, should warn us against viewing barbering as a purely technical act devoid of status implications for either party. It would seem, then, that a more satisfactory gloss on the participants' categories is that they reveal a systematic distinction between 'those who beg' for *bitsha*; the *purohits* who are essential to the performance of life-cycle rituals, and the *kamins* who pursue a craft speciality which may either be religiously neutral (e.g., carpentry) or religiously significant (e.g., barbering and leather-work).

All this would seem to have some bearing on the striking disparity between those authorities who conceptualize the division of labour between castes in terms of a harmonious interdependence in which the 'special privileges' of the low castes are guaranteed (e.g., Wiser 1936; Leach 1960) and those who emphasize the asymmetrical power relations between patrons and specialists and insist that 'any integration possible is of a coercive nature' (e.g., Beidelman 1959:68).

In a postscript to this debate, Epstein (1967) has attempted to reconcile these two extreme positions. Her argument starts from the premise that the service castes are rewarded in terms of fixed quantities of produce sufficient to guarantee their minimum subsistence needs. In order to be able to make such payments, the peasant landlords of the two south Indian villages she studied have to accept a relatively small proportion of the crop in poor seasons, when the total product of the village is distributed in a relatively egalitarian way. But when there is a bumper harvest it is the peasants who rake in the surplus, while the service castes continue to receive the same subsistence allowance. In good years the system offers the patron windfall profits and an assured supply of labour at periods of peak demand; in bad years it offers security to the specialist, and to both parties it consistently offers a whole series of diffuse benefits of a non-economic kind. The net effect is that the economic differentiation emphasized by Beidelman's 'exploitative' model is marked in good years, but is minimal in bad years when the guaranteed security of employment and subsistence which is stressed by Leach and Wiser is the most conspicuous feature of the system.

Epstein's reconciliation is ingenious but in my view totally fallacious. For a start, it is difficult to feel altogether satisfied with an argument which tacitly admits that it only applies to bad years which are not *too* bad, for when – as she disarmingly acknowledges – it comes to the crunch the master flexes his superior muscle and the specialist starves.

It is also difficult to see how a system of customary rewards geared at subsistence level can cope with demographic fluctuations. Given such fluctuations it is clearly impossible to fix *both* the individual contributions of the patrons and the total income of the servant. Epstein is mainly concerned with the latter; so presumably as the population of patrons and specialists expands and contracts, the scale of customary rewards due from each patron must be constantly re-adjusted to keep the aggregate receipts of the specialists fixed at the appropriate point just above the bread line. But when we take account of complicating factors like the servant's additional sources of income and the number of mouths he has to feed, it is hard to imagine how a large and diffuse body of patrons calculate their individual contributions to this finely adjusted total unless they are collectively guided by a divine hand with an adding machine. Moreover, if the total income of, for example, each carpenter is to remain fixed at subsistence level (and if factors like family size and landholding are held constant), we either have to assume that all carpenters have an equal number of patrons, or that their rates vary inversely with the size of their clientele. Both possibilities seem equally unlikely in the light of comparative data which clearly document the unequal distribution of both patrons and rewards between specialists of the same caste (cf. Lewis 1965:59; Reddy 1955). Even if we assume that Epstein means no more than that there are certain broad limits within which the craftsman's rates are set, it is not at all clear how these limits are maintained over time.

An even more serious problem is that the model depends entirely on the initial postulate that the rewards of the service castes are typically 'paid annually in the form of fixed quantities of farming produce' (p. 230). In striking contradiction of this is Orenstein's observation (1962:302) that one of the most distinctive – if not unique – features of the system is that 'payment is usually gauged not only with regard to the goods and services rendered, but also with regard for the amount of goods produced by the "purchaser" '. In line with this characterization we find that in many parts of India customary rewards are not in fact fixed as an *absolute* quantity but as a *proportion* of the total product; while elsewhere remuneration varies with the kind and amount of the service performed (e.g., Neale 1957; Beidelman 1959:53–4; Pocock 1962:84; Ishwaran 1966:40; Mayer 1960:67–8; Berreman 1963:58). In neither instance is it simply a case of unvarying customary payments guaranteeing minimum subsistence needs.

Lewis's table (1965:61) of customary rewards in Rampur provides a useful reminder that several different methods of payment may co-exist in the same village, some service castes receiving fixed quantities of grains, others a proportion of the crop, and others piece-work rates. But by lumping most of the service castes together it is precisely this diversity which Epstain fails to tackle; despite her preliminary remarks on the necessity of exploring variation within the system, and her contrast between the patrons' tied hereditary relationship with most types of specialist and the highly contractual relationship with, for example, the basket-maker and potter. Yet it is clear from her fieldwork monograph (Epstein 1962:208–9) that within the first undifferentiated category some specialists are more secure than others, and it would be surprising to learn that they are all rewarded at precisely the same rate irrespective of their status, bargaining position, type of work and so on.

In my view, Pocock (1962) has charted a more skilful course between the Scylla and Charybdis of the 'exploitative' and 'integrative' models of *jajmani* relations; and I believe that the Kangra material endorses his insight that it is analytically necessary to distinguish between different kinds of specialist, though it also perhaps implies that the distinction he draws may need some refinement.

As Dumont (1970) has elegantly and persuasively argued, the hierarchy of castes, their separation, the division of labour between them and the interdependence that results, all have a common (intellectual) basis in (as opposed to being caused by) the simple opposition between the pure and the impure. Hierarchy derives from the fact that purity is superior to pollution; separation from the need of the high castes to isolate themselves from polluting contacts with the low castes if they are to preserve their purity. But given that the pure can only maintain their purity if there is somebody to remove the pollution that they inevitably incur through involvement with the natural world, and especially contact with biological matter like faeces, blood and saliva-polluted substances, the ideology of pollution not only requires the separation of castes but also a division of labour between them.

Now this seems to invite the conclusion that the *jajmani* system is one in which specialists and their patrons are engaged in a perpetual exchange of purity for material goods (Gould 1967). The Brahman transmits purity down the ladder through the performance of his priestly duties; and the low castes transmit purity up the ladder by removing pollution. In order to emphasize that both priests and untouchables are dealing in essentially the same commodity – namely purity – Gould characterizes the latter as 'contra-priests'[23] (cf. Hogart 1968:11).

But one problem with this formulation is that there are many caste occupations which are religiously neutral. Carpentry, for example, is *per se* neither pure nor impure; the carpenter does not dispense purity to his inferiors, nor remove pollution from his superiors. There is then, Pocock argues, a useful analytical distinction to be made between caste occupations of an essentially religious nature and those of a technical-cum-economic kind. Within this second category we can distinguish the unskilled agricultural labourers from the artisans, who are again subdivided into those who provide a commodity and those who provide a service. But it is for the network of ties between the religious specialists and their patrons that Pocock reserves the term of '*jajmani* relationship'. The need for their services 'derives directly from the structure of the caste system (p. 84). . . . As long as there is a caste system there must be specialists whose business it is to cope with impurities arising from the natural course of life' (p. 85). The religious specialists, then, are essential to the status of their patrons; and consequently enjoy a comparatively secure and stable clientele. By contrast, 'it is nowhere reported that the relationship between any one of these artisan castes and the people they supply is of the tied, exclusive, status-governed nature which one associates with the religious, *jajmani* relationships' (p. 86).

But how, as Dumont (1970:104) asks, can we 'effectively distribute the facts among two such different categories as religion and economics'? Is leather-work to be regarded as a technical or ritual occupation? Pocock does not claim that his categories mirror collective representations, though he does suggest that 'they find their basis in popular ideas and language' (p. 89). Now, as I have already argued, the Kangra distinction between *purohit* and *kamin* does not discriminate between 'religious' and (in the strict sense) 'secular' specialists but rather between those specialists essential to the performance of life-crisis rituals and the artisan-type occupations. If we accept the distinctions with which the people themselves operate, and modify Pocock's thesis accordingly, then Dumont's difficulty disappears and the argument seems to fit the data rather closely. By contrast with the *kamin*, the *purohits* have a tied hereditary relationship of great durability. Within the *kamin* category, those who provide a service (the blacksmith, carpenter and barber) are still to a large extent paid in terms of *gadi-kalothi*, while those who provide a commodity (the potter, weaver, basket-maker and shoe-maker) have been virtually eliminated from the system of customary rewards. This last contrast is strikingly illustrated by the case of the Chamars, who as shoe-makers have been largely driven out of business by competition from factory-made products, while the need for their services as scavengers of dead cattle (their reward being the dead animal's hide) remains as great as ever.

The implication of all this for the wider debate about the nature of *jajmani* relationships seems clear. In the case of the *purohits*, the Leach-Wiser emphasis on the 'special privileges' of the service castes seems rather less Utopian than is often supposed. But when we come to talk about the artisan-type occupations, the inequality and instability of the patron/specialist relationship which Beidelman so emphatically stresses seems nearer the mark. I would refrain, however, from calling the latter relationship 'exploitative', since the precise meaning of this term is notably obscure in the literature under discussion. With its touching faith in the neutrality of the market, Orenstein's suggestion (1962) that the issue might be resolved by comparing the value of the specialists' customary rewards with the rates they could command on the open market entirely begs the question.

But obviously the relative security enjoyed by the different kinds of specialist is not simply a matter of the different moralities which are held to govern their relations with the dominant caste. Given the evaluation – based partly on ideological and partly on pragmatic considerations – that certain goods and services are indispensable while others are not, there is then the question of the availability of surrogates for them. So long as a *purohit* of the appropriate caste is considered essential to the status of his patron, his caste monopoly is in no way jeopardized by an extension of the 'economic frontier' since purity does not come in tubes. By contrast, most of the commodities traditionally supplied by the *kamin* are now readily available in the local markets; and at the same time the dramatic rise in the price of grain and the difficulty of buying it even if one has the cash, has made many patrons reluctant to part with their own produce in *gadi-kalothi*. So while the nature of their services renders the *purohits* virtually irreplaceable, specialists of this kind who supply a commodity have become highly expendable. Somewhere between these two poles are those *kamin* who provide a service, the demand for which tends to be immediate and therefore favours the craftsman on the spot. Here we can distinguish between the highly competitive and religiously neutral trades (like carpentry) which are open to interlopers from other castes, and the 'closed shop' which the Barbers and Chamars can more easily maintain on account of the religious evaluation of their occupations which discourages trespassing by opportunist outsiders. In short, we can order in terms of their relative security the *purohits*, the *kamin* who provide a religious service, those who provide a purely technical service, and those who provide a commodity; and this ordering – at least in part – reflects the extent to which the market economy can provide a substitute for the functions they perform.

Now by distinguishing within the *kamin* category between religious and non-religious services, I have of course slipped Pocock's analytical distinction in through the back door and am forced to confront the question which Dumont poses. For Dumont:

> functions in which the religious aspect is minimal are encompassed within a system that is decisively shaped by religious functions (the wheelwright is somehow assimilated to the barber or Brahman). . . . In every society one aspect of social life receives a primary value stress and simultaneously is made to encompass all others and express them as far as it can (1967:33).

The implication here would seem to be that there is no such thing as a non-religious caste occupation since all such functions are, as it were, contaminated by the encompassing ideology. In confirmation of this one might cite, for example, Stevenson's report (1954:51) that (at least in some areas) different degrees of purity are held to be inherent in different kinds of metal, and his claim that the various castes of metal-workers are ranked on this basis. But in spite of all this it seems to me that Pocock's analytical distinction is a valid one since Indians themselves clearly discriminate between occupations which are essential *to the status of the patron* and those which are not. While a Kangra farmer cannot remove the carcass of a dead buffalo without incurring pollution, there is nothing in the ideology of purity to prevent him from repairing his own ploughshare.

A wide range of material from other parts of India seems to conform to a broadly similar pattern to the one I have described for Kangra. There are at least echoes of the *purohit/kamin* distinction in, for example, Ishwaran's data on south India (1966), Mayer's data from central India (1960) and Berreman's data from the Himalayan foothills (1962; 1963).

The series of different prestations which Ishwaran describes embody a clear distinction between grains paid as *aya* to the craft specialists, and *ulipi* given (ideally without precise calculation, p. 126) to, for example, the priest, Barber, Washerman and Goldsmith for the performance of essential ritual roles. The inclusion of the Goldsmith here is at first sight perhaps surprising, but falls into place when we learn that such gifts are made in the context of the ear-boring ceremony over which he presides (p. 42), and on occasions when he supplies ornaments which signify the new social status which an initiate is about to assume – as, for instance, at marriage, when he provides the *tali* emblem which the groom ties around the bride's neck and which thereafter symbolizes her status as a married woman (pp. 60–2).

Mayer divides the Ramkheri specialists into three categories: the *mangat* whom he describes as 'priests' (though the category is not precisely comparable to the Kangra *purohits* since some of them do not appear to have any essential function in life-cycle rituals); the *kamin* who are artisans employed for seasonal grain payments; and a third category which has no generic name but which includes craftsmen who are paid on a piece-work basis usually in cash (p. 63). The only anomalous case are the Sweepers who rate both as *kamin* and as *mangat*

(p. 66), the second term relating perhaps to their traditional role as functionaries at mortuary rituals (p. 67). Most of the *kamin* castes provide a service, and significantly a substantial proportion of their members actually perform their caste-specific occupation. This is in marked contrast to the occupations in the third 'general' category, which are concerned with the production of a commodity and which 'have more or less been taken over by industrial processes' (pp. 76–8). Amongst the *kamin*, those who deal in polluting substances are, with the exception of the Barbers (pp. 68–9), the more secure. Unlike other specialists, the Sweepers have rights which can be bought and sold (p. 70); while the Tanner is highly remunerated for his 'inconsiderable services' since he is 'the only person who will undertake the polluting work of disposal of carcases' (p. 68).

Again, the villagers of Sirkanda (Berreman 1962; 1963:57–61) distinguish between the services of the Brahman priest who receives a gift, and the services of the artisans who receive a payment. In the one case the employer is a *jajman* and in the other *gaikh*. While the Brahmans enjoy considerable occupational security, the employment of the artisan is notably insecure. From the plains of Uttar Pradesh, Mahar (1972:19) contrasts the superior bargaining position of those untouchable castes who pursue a defiling occupation with those whose occupations are religiously neutral, while Lewis (1965:57, 64) describes a situation in which the Sweepers are secure enough in their rights to be able to sell them, but a Blacksmith who returned to the village after a year's absence had great difficulty in getting back his clientele. The Banking Enquiry Committee of 1923 recorded eighty-four cases in which mortgages of *jajmani* rights had been registered. Blunt (1969) notes that in nearly all of these, the rights belonged to the Sweepers and Funeral Priests – and that, I suggest, is no coincidence. In Konku, 'the barbers and washermen have stuck the most consistently to their traditional occupation' (Beck 1972:192). Epstein (1962:34, 84, 207), Mencher (1972:51) and Harper (1959:770–1) provide data which illustrates the comparative security of the Barber in his capacity as a functionary at life-cycle rituals and his insecurity as a specialist on profane occasions. Even when, as amongst the Sikhs, there is no question of the Barbers actually barbering, the importance of their ritual roles seems to ensure for them the continued patronage of the dominant caste (Mandelbaum 1970:166). As Pocock aptly notes:

The test which divides such religious specialists from others is finally what happens when their secular activities are replaced. The razor-blade may take away the barber's daily work, it does not destroy the barber caste. The weavers, for example, have on the other hand been eliminated by the introduction of mill-cloth (Pocock 1962:85).

3:5 Conclusion

The present chapter started out with a consideration of the remittance economy, moved on to outline the agrarian class structure, and has wound up with a discussion of *jajmani* relations. By way of conclusion I want to draw explicit attention to the striking disparity between the material significance of these different areas of the economy and the extent to which they are ideologically elaborated.

In the participants' ideal model, the social order is conceptualized in terms of an organic interdependence brought about by the division of labour between castes; and the local economy is represented as being based on this division of labour and on relationships which can – in the general sense of the term – be described as *jajmani*. But if *jajmani* relations are conceptually central, they are economically peripheral. More than half the male population of working age is employed outside; only a small proportion of those who have remained at home derive any part of their income from the pursuit of their caste-specific occupation; even those who are more or less full-time specialists usually have some other source of income, and of the latter only the Carpenter and the Blacksmith is really vital to agricultural production. These remarks refer, of course, to the present day; but in a less extreme form the same situation obtained throughout the British period.

The paradox, then, is that the economy tends to be represented in terms of a model of relationships whose pragmatic significance for most households is probably rather marginal. For the majority, the areas of activity which really count in the material sense are those which were discussed under the headings of social class and the remittance economy. But here the relationship with caste is of a much more indirect and tenuous nature. As we move along the continuum from 'true' *jajmani* relations (*purohit/jajman*) → quasi-*jajmani* relations (*kamin/zamindar*) → agrarian class relations → urban wage labour, the extent to which relations within each sphere are explicitly organized on the basis of caste is progressively attenuated, while (in rough terms) the material contribution to the total economy increases. To the extent, then, that the people themselves (and derivatively their ethnographers) represent the empirical economy of the village in terms of *jajmani* relations and the division of labour between castes, they misrepresent it.

4 The hierarchical aspects of caste

4:1 Introduction

In the previous chapter I made various marginal references to the hierarchical aspects of caste. The present chapter develops this theme in relation to the attributional and interactional criteria of caste ranking; a consideration of the nature of 'untouchability', and the case of an 'untouchable' caste who have made concerted and persistent efforts to attain clean-caste status.

I have already drawn attention to the concentration of Chadhiar's resources in the hands of the dominant Rajputs who own nearly ninety per cent of the land and occupy all the key positions of political influence. It is, however, clear that hierarchical status is not a simple reflection of the distribution of power and wealth. Of the 17 castes in the *mauza* 16 own a total of just over 10 per cent of its land; and it is hard to see how such a small proportion can form the basis for so many discriminations of rank. Nor, of course, does the distribution of resources explain why the Brahmans rank higher than the Rajputs, or why, for example, the Goldsmiths are considered superior to the Jogi-ascetics when both castes are completely landless. Neither the landholding figures for the district as a whole, nor figures on alternative sources of income, would help to resolve these difficulties. When people range the castes of their local area on a ladder of relative prestige, then, they make a number of discriminations which have no apparent material basis. This forces the analysis back into the realm of ideology. The system cannot meaningfully be divorced, as Dumont (1970) has forcefully argued, from the ideas that people have about it.

4:2 'Jat' as genus

The term *jat* (or *jati*) denotes a 'genus' or 'species' and is conventionally translated by the English words 'caste' or 'sub-caste'. In fact, of course, it also refers to other segmentary levels; but I will discuss these other referents at a later stage and for the time being confine myself to *jat* in the sense of 'caste'.

As the term itself suggests, members of different castes are conceived of as members of different species. A carpenter friend used the analogy of trees. Castes are as different as kinds of wood; and it is their *dharma* (religious duty) to live in harmony with their own particular nature. In quite a literal way their blood (*khun*) is held to be – as it were chemically – different from the blood of other castes. One acquaintance approvingly told me, for example, that in order to ensure that no cross-caste unions occurred, the Nazis (with whom many Rajputs closely identify[1]) always took blood tests before they would issue a marriage certificate. On an occasion when I cut myself, one of my companions expressed consternation on account of the fact that my blood is red. A proper Englishman, he was sure, had blue blood and this led to some light-hearted speculation about my parentage.[2]

The members of each caste are believed to have a special aptitude for their caste occupation and this aptitude is thought to be transmitted 'in the blood'. The Rajputs, for example, believe that the martial qualities associated with their caste are a matter of genetics, and I was repeatedly told that India's humiliation by China in 1962 could only be attributed to the large number of non-Rajputs now taken into the army. 'You can put these people in the same uniform', they say, 'but you can't make them fight in the same way. It is a question of the blood.'

But in some respects Rajput genetic theory has more in common with Lysenko than with the racist theory of the Anglo-Saxon world. Blood, it seems, is not an immutable substance but can – albeit within narrow and vaguely conceptualized limits – be transformed for better or worse. Thus skills acquired in caste-free occupations may be passed on 'in the blood' to the next generation. Master Inder Singh often expressed distaste for his life as a teacher and fretful resentment that a minor disability had prevented him from following his father into the military. But when a group of us discussed the matter, everybody was agreed that his unborn sons would take to teaching like ducks to water, because that was their father's profession. Their ability in this direction would be partly a matter of upbringing but also a matter of heredity.

The quality of the blood which flows in an individual's veins may be improved by a pure and wholesome diet, or impaired by an illness (medicines being prescribed to 'cleanse the blood'). But above all pure blood is a matter of pure parentage. Though at first sight heterogeneous, these ideas are at least implicitly connected. Health is in large measure a question of diet; a fat man is a healthy man. Food nourishes the body and is the source of blood; while concentrated blood is the source of semen (*virya*) and thus of procreation (cf. Carstairs 1957: 83–4; Inden and Nicholas n.d.; for classical precedents see O'Flaherty 1973:280–2). The sex of the child is determined by the relative quantities of semen and vaginal fluid secreted during intercourse, and this depends on the relative health of the couple.[3] As a consequence a woman who has conceived daughters but no sons can remedy this situation by denying herself nourishing foods. The connection between health, diet and procreation recurs in the complex of beliefs surrounding the incubus and succubus of Kangra folklore. Lethal wasting diseases may be caused by a *churel*, the malevolent spirit of a woman who has died in childbirth. Though to others either invisible or an ugly hag with breasts hanging over her back, she steals the life-force of her victims by regularly appearing to them in the form of a beautiful seductress. The succubus Paharia – generally depicted as a Gaddi shepherd – causes infertility and the symptoms of chronic undernourishment by ravishing his female victims. But however close the association between food and blood, the apparent implication that appropriate nourishment may elevate an inferior to the status of appropriate mate would be dismissed as absurd.

Since people of different castes are of qualitatively different kinds, and since bodily substance is derived (though in unequal measures) from both parents, eugenic considerations demand that a tight rein be kept on their sexuality; for how – as the Rajput aristocrat rhetorically asks – 'can a lion mate with a fox?' Castes, then, are ideally endogamous units; though it must be stressed that the real objection is to miscegeny with inferiors and not to unions with superiors. As Dumont (1970:123) succinctly puts it: 'The separation or closure of one group with respect to those above results fundamentally from the closure of other groups with respect to those below.' Attitudes to cross-caste unions vary significantly, however, according to whether the man is of inferior or superior status. The first case is heinous; the second – though still considered somewhat depraved – less so. In some cases, where the disparity of caste status is not too great, the justification that 'the semen is stronger' may be invoked to accommodate the offspring within the superior caste. As we shall see (chapter 7), this patrilineal bias in the inheritance of caste substance meshes in with the exigencies of hypergamy which, in the past, condemned the lowest ranking Rajput clans to recruit a proportion of their spouses from inferior castes.

4:3 The hierarchy in terms of attributes

That the customs and style of life of different castes should display wide variation is a natural consequence of the fact that they are members of different species. This is both an expression of their diverse natures and the prime justification for judgments of relative worth. Hence Kangra people often talk as if the order of precedence within the hierarchy is determined, or at least sanctioned, by the set of attributes with which each caste is associated. The high castes are considered to owe their superiority to the fact that they follow a style of life and a set of customs which are both prestigious and pure. By contrast, the low castes are associated with 'low' and polluting customs.

According to popular theory, the higher the caste the more fastidious it is in avoiding pollution. In ideal terms, for example, a Brahman or aristocratic Rajput woman is supposed to be completely segregated during her monthly course. During the four days that she is polluted, a married woman may not fetch drinking water or touch utensils which are in everyday use; and may not enter the kitchen, let alone cook. In hyper-orthodox households she will even be confined to a single side room of the house. Here she sleeps on the floor and uses separate bedding and utensils which are specially set aside for such times. Temporarily, then, she acquires the characteristics of, and is treated like, an untouchable. During three of the months of the Hindu calendar she should take neither food nor water after sunset while she is menstruating. On the fifth day after her period started she has a purificatory bath but it is not until the eighth day that she can again participate in rituals or approach the gods. In the case of a widow, however, the whole set of these restrictions should apply throughout a full seven days.[4] Women of the lower status Rajput clans and of the other 'clean' castes are said to observe some but not all of the rules; while low-caste women ignore the lot.

Similarly, Brahman and aristocratic Rajput men who wear the sacred thread are supposed to eat boiled foods only when they are in a ritually pure state. Before eating they should have bathed and the area in which the food is to be consumed (the *chauka*) should have been freshly purified with cow-dung (*gobar*). While they are eating they should be naked except for a *dhoti* (loin-cloth). Low-caste people are held to be unconcerned with such precautions against impurity.

In practice, however, the hierarchy is really rather more homogeneous in terms of these observances than all this would imply. Most high-caste households fall some way short of the ideal standards I have described, and some low-caste households are stricter than the high castes would care to admit.

Among the most important of the attributes which may be held to influence a caste's position in the hierarchy is its occupation. This is clearest in the case of the castes at the two poles of the hierarchy who deal in purity and pollution. The Brahmans are said to be the highest because priesthood is the purest of all occupations. The Leatherworkers and Sweepers are lowest because they pursue unambiguously polluting occupations. Again, people explicitly associate the low status of the Basket-makers with the fact that they take the shroud off the corpse before it is burnt; while the inferiority of the Weavers is sometimes attributed to their side-line as butchers, from which they acquire the sobriquet *bakra-bad*, 'goat-killers'.

People also explain the status of a caste by reference to its marriage customs and diet. In the most prestigious form of marriage a virgin is handed over, along with her dowry, to her husband's family as a completely free and sacred gift for which no return whatever should be accepted. Marriage is regarded as an indissoluble union – which as far as the woman is concerned is also a monogamous union. As a corollary of this, widow remarriage and divorce are absolutely forbidden. In flat opposition to these ideals, the low castes – as well as low-status Rajput and Brahman clans – sanction the inheritance of a deceased elder brother's wife, as well as other forms of widow remarriage. They also allow various types of exchange marriage which are considered to run counter to the notion of the gift, accept bride-price payments, tolerate divorce, and when expedient turn a blind eye to casual sexual liaisons.

The sacred scriptures divide Hindu society up into four hierarchically ranked *varnas*, each associated with a particular hereditary function. Within any local area each caste is likely to be identified with one or other of these categories. Dumezil (1940) – and following him Pocock (1957) and Dumont (1962) – have shown that this *varna* scheme is more appropriately seen as a set of dialectically related models rather than as a single linear series. Thus the Brahmans, Kshatriyas and Vaishyas are opposed to the lowest *varna* – the Shudras – in that they are entitled to study the Vedas and to offer sacrifice. Brahmans and Kshatriyas stand in opposition to the last two as the rulers of all creatures; but are themselves opposed as rulers of the spiritual domain and rulers of the temporal domain. Associated with these oppositions are radically opposed styles of life and radically opposed ethics. The ethos of the Brahman is in many respects the inverse of that of the Kshatriya. 'The commonly understood Brahman ideal,' says Marriott (1968a:110), 'stresses intellectual refinement, ascetic standards of consumption, and non-violence, while the Kshatriya ideal stresses on the other hand, strength, readiness for violence, luxurious consumption, including meat-eating, etc.' Kshatriya and Vaishya values are again opposed, the Vaishya model being much closer to that of the Brahman.

Since there is a sense in which a man *is* what he eats, it is not surprising that opposing dietary habits are associated with these opposing ideals. The crucial distinction here is between 'hot' (*garam*) and 'cold' (*thunda*) food. 'Hot' food includes meat, eggs, alcohol, groundnuts, carrots, onions and garlic. Rice, milk, honey and *ghee* fall into the category of 'cold' food. Each of these categories is linked with contrary personal qualities: the one with lust, aggression and courage; the other with continence, meekness and tranquillity – that is, with the qualities of the carnivorous Kshatriya and the vegetarian Brahman of the great traditional model.

In practice most people in Chadhiar, including the Brahmans, are meat-eaters. One Brahman I knew had even set himself up as a distiller of illicit country liquor; and though he was not considered altogether respectable he was still regularly employed as a ritual cook at 'clean'-caste marriages. These days only high-caste widows are really expected to avoid all 'hot' foods, but it is said that a generation ago such food was more widely shunned. Though a more prosaic explanation would be in terms of Rajput dominance, the Brahmans themselves are apt to explain their self-acknowledged lapse from orthodoxy by reference to winter in the hills; for 'hot' food not only produces hot passions, but also warmth in the body which enables one to withstand a cold climate. (It is on account of the English climate that Englishmen eat so much meat, an excessive indulgence in which is responsible for their deplorable sexual morality.) While by scriptural standards themselves lax on matters of diet, the Brahmans cite the Temple priests' willingness to eat grains offered at temples dedicated to Siva and Durga as irrefutable evidence of the latter's inferiority.

Although a majority in all castes are prepared to eat meat, there are differences in the kinds of meat they regard as acceptable. Goat is the most widely consumed, but chicken and wild boar (rarely available) are also unexceptionable, though it is said that in the past the Rajputs and Brahmans entertained a strong prejudice against both poultry and eggs. Mutton is regarded as a poor quality 'soft' (*naram*) meat, and is avoided by the high castes. But some of the untouchables are reputed to eat even the flesh of a sheep which has died a natural death. The Leather-workers are the only caste associated with the consumption of beef, and although the consensus is that they gave it up a long time ago, they have never managed to rid themselves of the stigma.

The inferiority of the low castes, then, is attributed to the fact that they follow a 'low' and 'degrading' style of life. But there is a good deal of circularity in the whole situation since many attributes seem to be regarded as 'low' merely because the people with whom they are associated are low. More importantly, the situation is circular in the sense that the castes at the bottom of the ladder have 'low' customs because their freedom to acquire prestigious ones is curtailed. In other words, they have traditionally been prevented from acquiring the symbols of high status by a set of sumptuary regulations backed up by the authority of the raja and the power of the dominant caste.

In addition to numerous other restrictions, they were forbidden to perform certain rituals, to keep moustaches, or to use distinctively high-caste personal names with suffixes like 'Singh' or 'Chand'. Nor, of course, do they have the privilege of wearing the sacred thread. Before entering high-caste courtyards people of low caste have first to remove their shoes. Of the most inferior castes in the hierarchy Barnes (1889: 40) wrote:

> In the hills (their) depression . . . is more marked than I have observed elsewhere:– their manner is more subdued and deprecatory; they are careful to announce their caste, and an accidental touch of their persons carries defilement, obliging the toucher to bathe before he can regain his purity. If any person of this caste has a letter to deliver, he will throw or deposit his charge on the ground, but not transmit it direct from hand to hand. . . . Under the rule of the Rajas they were subjected to endless restrictions. The women were not allowed to wear flounces deeper than four inches to their

> dress, nor to use the finer metal of gold for their ornaments. Their houses were never to exceed a certain size, nor to be raised above one floor; the men were interdicted from wearing long hair, and in their marriages, the bride was forced to go on foot, instead of riding in a *jhampan* or chair, as allowed to every other class. Certain musical instruments . . . were positively prohibited. Many of these restrictions are still maintained, although, of course, there has been no sanction given or implied by the officers of Government.

Since Barnes's time, however, many of the diacritical markers which distinguished superior from inferior castes have disappeared, and the adoption of high-status attributes by low-status people has been widespread. By removing the legal sanction behind the sumptuary laws, and curtailing the legitimate coercive powers of the dominant caste, the British gave those with aspirations to a higher status a freer hand in the pursuit of their ambitions, while increased contact with the sources of the great tradition fostered these ambitions (cf. Srinivas 1962). As a result, the trend over the last hundred years or so has been for the hierarchy to become increasingly homogeneous in terms of customs and styles of life.

This, of course, raises the problem of how the rank order is maintained once those lower in the hierarchy have brought their customs and style of life into line with those above them. In Kangra, as in many other areas, a number of different castes share an almost identical set of attributes, but are nevertheless distinguished in rank (cf. Marriott 1959). Another difficulty with this attributional model of caste ranking is that Rajput and Brahman clans are themselves arranged in a hierarchy, and the different ranks *within* the caste are associated with different sets of attributes. This creates a situation in which the aristocratic Rajput clans have 'higher' attributes than many low-status Brahman clans; yet people clearly and unambiguously state that all Brahmans rank higher than all Rajputs. Marriott (1959; 1968b) draws attention to several other problems: the presumed hierarchy of attributes often seems to bear little relation to the observed order of precedence (as when a meat-eating caste ranks higher than a vegetarian caste); there are no criteria for measuring the *degrees* of impurity inherent in different polluting substances (e.g., leather and faeces) and thus no systematic principle for ranking the occupational groups associated with them (the Leather-worker and the Sweeper); and there is no way of scoring the aggregate of one caste's attributes against another and so of ranking, for example, a vegetarian caste with an impure occupation *vis-à-vis* a meat-eating caste with a pure occupation.

Such considerations prompt Marriott to argue that attributional evaluations are secondary rationalizations of a rank order which is primarily determined by other considerations; and to suggest that 'castes are ranked according to the structure of interactions among them' (1959:96). It follows from this that in order to raise its status in the hierarchy it is not sufficient for a caste to change its attributes; it must also validate its claims by changing its interactional relations with other castes. Such relations maintain the hierarchy, despite the trend towards a greater homogeneity in customs and styles of life.

4:4 Interactional relations

Logically, exchanges may be either symmetrical or asymmetrical; and the two possibilities have rather different structural implications. Symmetrical exchange posits an initial equality between the parties to the exchange, but may be used to express rivalry and generate discriminations of rank in competitive potlatch-type situations. Inequality is established by making a prestation which – precisely because the same items are exchanged – is demonstrably larger or smaller than one's partner's. Where status positions are open to competition and are primarily a matter of achievement rather than ascription (as, for example, in the New Guinea Highlands) competitive exchanges of this sort often provide the main mechanism for their allocation; and there is a tendency towards an extreme elaboration of the exchange system which becomes the route by which inequalities of rank are established or validated.

Asymmetrical exchanges may also be used to express or establish inequality. But, by contrast, they do not start from the premise of equality and do not therefore carry the same potential for expressing competition; for one cannot compete with those who are self-evidently superior or inferior to oneself. Such exchanges may also preclude competition in that the values exchanged are commonly incommensurate with each other, and there is consequently no way of calculating an equivalence between them. There is, for example, no means by which the *jajman* can balance the account with his *purohit* since there can be no measure of equivalence between the grain payments he offers and the purity which the *purohit* confers through his priestly ministrations. In such a transactional context, then, there can be no winners or losers, and no competition between the parties to the exchange.

While the elaboration of symmetrical exchange is most highly developed in systems in which positions of power and prestige are open to achievement, asymmetrical exchanges are characteristically associated with non-competitive social relations in which status is non-negotiable and ascribed. In both cases, however, superiority is established by making the greater prestation. In the first instance it is acquired by giving more of the same thing. In the second, to take the Indian example, it is again the superior who makes the greater gift, for the Brahman's actual (material) dependence on others is transformed by the ideology into their dependence on him for the infinitely more valuable merit they acquire by his acceptance of their charity (cf. Van der Veen 1972: 223; 1973).

In Indian society transactional relations between castes are predominantly asymmetrical. Since castes are by their very nature unequal, they do not play, as it were, in the same league. On the *conceptual* level, then, Leach (1960:7) is perfectly correct in concluding that 'there can therefore be no possibility that they should compete for merit of the same sort'. (What is more questionable is his assimilation of this conceptual impossibility with past empirical reality.) While it may be appropriate to liken the interactional *strategies* of castes to games or tournaments (cf. Marriott 1968b), such similes – with their connotations of competition – are quite inapposite to the way in which the *ideal* system is perceived.

It is by reference to a variety of asymmetrical exchanges that Kangra people are able to distinguish a rank order between corporate groups which could not be ranked consistently on the basis of their attributes. Such exchanges are typically 'transitive' in the sense that if the exchange defines A as superior to B, and B as superior to C, then A is superior to C although there is no exchange between them (ibid., p. 142). The principal rank-defining transactions between castes involve the exchange of food, services, greetings and tobacco. Exchanges of women – which establish a hierarchy of Rajput and Brahman clans – have no relevance to the ranking of castes. Castes are in theory endogamous, while in practice there are no systematic exchanges between them by which the hierarchy as a whole might be ordered.

The exchange of greetings, on the other hand, does serve to distinguish castes of different status. The rule is that a man of an inferior caste should offer salutations to his superior first (though none is appropriate when the latter is eating, bathing, shaving or suffering from death pollution, *patak*). Superiors should always be addressed by an honorific or title and the respectful plural pronoun forms employed; inferiors may be called by name and for them the singular pronoun forms are appropriate. In some cases the greetings themselves are asymmetrical. A non-Brahman, for example, will greet a Brahman with '*matha tekna*' ('I bow my forehead') and the Brahman will reply '*ashirbad*' ('blessings'). All except the Brahmans will greet the aristocratic Rajputs, and today more generally all Rajputs, with '*Jai Dewa*'.[5] People of low caste may alternatively greet both Rajputs and Brahmans with '*pairi poana*' ('I touch your feet') to which the appropriate acknowledgement – if the high-caste person deigns to reply at all – is '*Ram Ram*' or '*raji raho*' ('Stay well'). These days, however, many young men of low caste will only use greetings – like '*Jai Hind*' ('long live India') – which are symmetrical in form.

When the menfolk smoke together they may share either a cigarette, a hookah or a small stemless clay pipe shaped rather like an inverted cone and known as a *chillum*. Since saliva is a source of defilement, it would however be gross to put the mouth directly into contact with the object smoked. A cigarette or a hookah stem is held in the clenched hand through which the smoke is drawn. A *chillum* is held in cupped hands with a piece of cloth, or a bunch of grass, clasped to its base as a filter.

In theory the members of any clean caste may smoke a common *chillum*, while in practice those who get together to smoke *bhang* (hemp) often include low-caste men as well. Where disparate statuses are represented within the same smoking group, however, smokers of different caste will each apply their own filter.

The rules about smoking from a common hookah are a good deal stricter, but do not define a consistent hierarchy of status since smoking together is necessarily a reciprocal act. But although you cannot tell whether A ranks higher than B by merely observing their smoking patterns, you can tell whether they are of equal or unequal status. If they do not smoke together then there is probably a significant difference in status between them. If they smoke together, but first remove the stem (*nari*) of the hookah and draw the smoke direct from its base, then it can be reckoned that the difference in status between them is comparatively slight. Only people who are prepared to acknowledge a close equivalence of status smoke from the same *nari*.

All but the most impoverished Rajput and Brahman households keep two or more hookahs for guests of clean caste; and will probably also keep a *chillum* specially for low-caste people. Today most Brahman households will offer their hookah without the *nari* to Rajput visitors, and vice versa; though the aristocratic Rajputs tend to be more exclusive, the most conservative among them refusing to share the same hookah with anybody but their closest agnates. The rules governing hookah transactions between the top three castes are complex and open to rival interpretations; and will be discussed in more detail at a later stage. What is more straightforward, however, is that these castes will not smoke the same hookah as any of their inferiors; and that a high-caste household will generally reserve one of its hookahs for the exclusive use of the middle-order castes: the Carpenters, Blacksmiths, Goldsmiths, Barbers, Potters and Girth-cultivators. These middle-order castes are reckoned to be roughly equal in status, and this equality is signalled by the reciprocal exchange of cooked food (see below), and by their willingness to smoke together without the *nari*. But some of them – precisely which ones differs from area to area – are prepared to smoke from a common *nari*. In *mauza* Khera, for example, the Girth-cultivators, Potters and Water-carriers (Jhirs) smoke together on a basis of complete equality, but remove the *nari* when smoking with a Barber. In Chadhiar, however, the Potter and Girth-cultivator will not share the same *nari*, but the Potter and Barber will. Throughout the sub-division, Carpenters and Blacksmiths are considered to be of identical status. They intermarry, treat their occupations as interchangeable, engage in the symmetrical exchange of cooked food, and smoke together from a common *nari*. None of these middle-order castes will smoke with the Kolis and their inferiors, and neither will the latter smoke with each other.

The rules of commensality vary according to the kind of food served. The first distinction to note is between cooked and uncooked food. Uncooked food, which includes unheated milk, unmilled grains and fruit, can be taken from anybody without distinction of caste. Cooked food is divided into two types: *nali rasoi*, food boiled in water, can be eaten only if it has been cooked by someone of one's own ritual status or by a superior; whereas *suji rasoi*, food cooked in *ghee*, can be taken – within strictly defined limits – from inferiors. This, of course, corresponds to the distinction made elsewhere in India between *kacca* and *pakka* food (cf. Mayer 1960:33; Marriott 1968b).

Marriott (ibid., p. 144) reports that in Kishan Garhi festive food is *pakka* food. In Kangra, by contrast, the festive food *par excellence* is boiled rice accompanied by several side dishes of lentils and vegetables.

In the normal way there are two substantial meals in the day; a mid-morning meal of *bhat*, boiled rice with vegetables or lentils as a garnish; and an evening meal of *roti*, unleavened bread made of wheat (*chapati*) or maize flour (*challion di roti*), accompanied by a vegetable. Breakfast generally consists of little more than a cup of tea and a few cold morsels which have been set aside from the previous evening. In Chadhiar, however, availability continually modifies habit, and during lean times of the year some of the less affluent households may exist from one week to the next on a monotonous diet of maize bread (a poor man's food).

All the clean castes – from the Brahmans at the top of the ladder down to and including the Girth-cultivators – accept water and *suji rasoi/roti* at each other's houses. Though the acceptance of *nali rasoi/bhat* is much more restricted, the members of all these castes will sit in a single unbroken line (*painth*) to eat such food at a wedding feast, or on some other ritual occasion when a Brahman *boti* has been called in to prepare the meal. But those who are higher in caste will sit higher in the line – that is, nearer the kitchen – than their inferiors.

On ordinary everyday occasions clean-caste people may be invited to eat in each other's kitchens, though in Brahman and high-status Rajput houses there are certain restrictions about where they can sit. In its broadest sense, the term *chauka* refers to any area of purity from which (relatively) impure objects and persons must be excluded. The household deities, for example, are worshipped within a space freshly plastered with cow-dung (*gobar*), and this space is known as a *chauka*. The cooking hearths (*chulahs*) of the Brahmans and of the more fastidious Rajputs are surrounded by a *chauka*, an area some six to ten feet square raised slightly above the rest of the floor. This area is purified with cow-dung at regular intervals, and should be specially protected during the preparation and consumption of *nali rasoi.* Clean-caste guests who are lower in status than their host may eat in the kitchen, but may not go inside the *chauka* while *bhat* is being prepared; nor may they eat such food inside the *chauka*. Guests who are of equivalent status to their host will be invited to take *nali rasoi* inside the *chauka* provided that they are in a ritually pure state; while those of a higher status do not accept *nali rasoi* from their inferiors, so such considerations do not arise. The rules about *suji rasoi* are much less strict and this sort of food may be eaten inside the *chauka* by people of any clean caste.

The rank order is disputed at several points, and in these cases there tends to be a total embargo on all exchanges of cooked food. The Jogi-ascetics, for example, claim to be superior to the Kolis and the two castes will not eat together. But it is the Kolis who are assigned the higher status in the overall pattern of food transactions, since the Weavers are prepared to accept food from them but not from the Jogis, and since some clean-caste liberals, who would never dream of eating at a Jogi house, will surreptitiously accept *suji rasoi* from the Kolis. (The Kolis' position in the hierarchy is a somewhat ambiguous one and will be discussed in detail in the final section of this chapter.) The Basket-makers, Leather-workers and Sweepers all claim superiority to each other and never eat together. All three of these castes also assert that they will not eat with the Musicians. But since there is only one Musician household in the *mauza*, consisting of just one elderly widow, the matter is never put to the test.

In order to present the Chadhiar data on exchanges of cooked food in a systematic way, I have adopted Marriott's (1968b) technique of matrix presentation in Tables 12 and 13. Each of the diagonal numbers refers to the corresponding caste listed at the left of the table, and each cell stands for a potential exchange between two castes. The rows which correspond to each number represent that caste as a giver of food; the columns represent it as a receiver. A plus indicates that an exchange takes place; a minus that there is no exchange. For transactions between each pair of castes there are two cells and four possible outcomes; two symmetrical and two asymmetrical (though only one of the asymmetrical possibilities actually occurs). In Table 12, for example, all the exchanges of *nali rasoi* in which the Brahmans (number 1) participate are of an asymmetrical kind and serve to stress their superiority. The row of plusses shows that they give such food to all other castes in the hierarchy. The column of minuses below their serial number shows that they accept *nali rasoi* from no other caste. Symmetrical outcomes, represented by reciprocal exchanges, as between Carpenters (5) and Blacksmiths (6), or by the absence of any exchange at all, as between Kolis (11) and Jogis (12), do not distinguish rank.

Food which is left over on the plate after eating is classified as *jutha* and is considered to have been polluted by contact with saliva from the mouth. But the mere touch of somebody in a lesser state of purity is sufficient to convert food into *jutha*. Mata Ji, my adoptive Brahman 'mother', would exploit this fact to press her hospitality on a reluctant visitor. Her ploy was to touch a plate of food against the

TABLE 12 *Matrix of transactions in* nali rasoi

Caste		*Gives to* →																	*Given*	*Received*	*Net*
1 Brahman	↓	1	+	+	+	+	+	+	+	+	+	+	+	+	+	+	+	+	16	0	16
2 Temple priest		—	2	—	+	+	+	+	+	+	+	+	+	+	+	+	+	+	14	1	13
3 Rajput	R	—	—	3	+	+	+	+	+	+	+	+	+	+	+	+	+	+	14	1	13
4 Trader	E	—	—	—	4	+	+	+	+	+	+	+	+	+	+	+	+	+	13	2	11
5 Carpenter	C	—	—	—	—	5	+	+	+	+	+	+	+	+	+	+	+	+	12	9	3
6 Blacksmith	E	—	—	—	—	+	6	+	+	+	+	+	+	+	+	+	+	+	12	9	3
7 Goldsmith	I	—	—	—	—	+	+	7	+	+	+	+	+	+	+	+	+	+	12	9	3
8 Barber	V	—	—	—	—	+	+	+	8	+	+	+	+	+	+	+	+	+	12	9	3
9 Potter	E	—	—	—	—	+	+	+	+	9	+	+	+	+	+	+	+	+	12	9	3
10 Girth-cultivator	S	—	—	—	—	+	+	+	+	+	10	+	+	+	+	+	+	+	12	9	3
11 Koli		—	—	—	—	—	—	—	—	—	—	11	—	+	+	+	+	+	5	10	−5
12 Jogi-ascetic		—	—	—	—	—	—	—	—	—	—	—	12	—	+	+	+	+	4	10	−6
13 Weaver	F	—	—	—	—	—	—	—	—	—	—	—	—	13	+	+	+	+	4	12	−8
14 Musician	R	—	—	—	—	—	—	—	—	—	—	—	—	—	14	—	—	—	0	13	−13
15 Basket-maker	O	—	—	—	—	—	—	—	—	—	—	—	—	—	—	15	—	—	0	13	−13
16 Leather-worker	M	—	—	—	—	—	—	—	—	—	—	—	—	—	—	—	16	—	0	13	−13
17 Sweeper	↓	—	—	—	—	—	—	—	—	—	—	—	—	—	—	—	—	17	0	13	−13
Total received		0	1	1	2	9	9	9	9	9	9	10	10	11	13	13	13	13			

TABLE 13 *Matrix of transactions in* suji rasoi

Caste		Gives to →																	Given	Received	Net
1 Brahman	↓	1	+	+	+	+	+	+	+	+	+	+	+	+	+	+	+	+	16	9	7
2 Temple priest		+	2	+	+	+	+	+	+	+	+	+	+	+	+	+	+	+	16	9	7
3 Rajput	R	+	+	3	+	+	+	+	+	+	+	+	+	+	+	+	+	+	16	9	7
4 Trader	E	+	+	+	4	+	+	+	+	+	+	+	+	+	+	+	+	+	16	9	7
5 Carpenter	C	+	+	+	+	5	+	+	+	+	+	+	+	+	+	+	+	+	16	9	7
6 Blacksmith	E	+	+	+	+	+	6	+	+	+	+	+	+	+	+	+	+	+	16	9	7
7 Goldsmith	I	+	+	+	+	+	+	7	+	+	+	+	+	+	+	+	+	+	16	9	7
8 Barber	V	+	+	+	+	+	+	+	8	+	+	+	+	+	+	+	+	+	16	9	7
9 Potter	E	+	+	+	+	+	+	+	+	9	+	+	+	+	+	+	+	+	16	9	7
10 Girth-cultivator	S	+	+	+	+	+	+	+	+	+	10	+	+	+	+	+	+	+	16	9	7
11 Koli		—	—	—	—	—	—	—	—	—	—	11	—	+	+	+	+	+	5	10	—5
12 Jogi-ascetic		—	—	—	—	—	—	—	—	—	—	—	12	—	+	+	+	+	4	10	—6
13 Weaver	F	—	—	—	—	—	—	—	—	—	—	—	—	13	+	+	+	+	4	12	—8
14 Musician	R	—	—	—	—	—	—	—	—	—	—	—	—	—	14	—	—	—	0	13	—13
15 Basket-maker	O	—	—	—	—	—	—	—	—	—	—	—	—	—	—	15	—	—	0	13	—13
16 Leather-worker	M	—	—	—	—	—	—	—	—	—	—	—	—	—	—	—	16	—	0	13	—13
17 Sweeper	↓	—	—	—	—	—	—	—	—	—	—	—	—	—	—	—	—	17	0	13	—13
Total received		9	9	9	9	9	9	9	9	9	9	10	10	11	13	13	13	13			

latter's person, and then claim that since it was now *jutha* it would go to waste unless it were eaten. *Jutha* contaminates the utensils from which food has been taken, and both the leavings and the dirty utensils can be handled only by the eater, or by someone inferior to him. A younger brother may clean the utensils of his elder brother, but not vice versa; similarly with wife and husband, or low-caste person and high-caste person. When a man is fed in the house of somebody of higher caste he is expected to rinse his own dishes (though the rules are commonly waived for people of high achieved status). The inferiority of the Leather-workers and Sweepers is highlighted by the fact that until recently they would consume what was left over on the plates of the guests at high-caste feasts. This points to a fundamental aspect of pollution, its relativity: what pollutes the pure may even purify the impure. Just as the *jutha* of the high castes is pure enough to be consumed by the lowest castes, so the sacramental *prasad*, the food which is consecrated to the deities and is distributed after every *puja* (act of worship) to all the worshippers, is technically divine *jutha*.

It is important to recognize, however, that the semantics of food symbolism is by no means exhausted by a discussion of the relationship between food and purity. I have already drawn attention to the connection between diet and personal qualities. But more than this, 'to eat together signifies amity; to refuse, or to be prohibited from doing so, signifies its absence' (Fortes 1969:236). Where there is enmity it is dangerous to dine. An individual of any caste who considers himself wronged by another may invoke the retribution of Chano Sidh, the patron deity of the Leather-workers. But having once done so he must not eat or drink with the intended victim, or even sit in the same line of diners, lest the reprisal rebound on the supplicant. Precisely the same precautions are essential in the case of *jadu* (witchcraft). Again, the story is told of an internecine dispute in the distant past between the Rajput Khaurwal sub-clans of *mauzas* Droh and Thural. As the Thural version has it, their ancestors were invited to a feast by their agnates in Droh, who intended to poison them. Forewarned of the plot, the Thural Khaurwal massacred their hosts. From that time on there have been no commensal relations between the two sub-clans, and it is said that the very few individuals who have had the temerity to ignore this ban have died shortly afterwards as a result.

The other side of the coin is that the giving and receiving of food is an expression of diffuse solidarity. Invitations provide an opportunity to display one's hospitality, and to honour – in fine measure – one's guests. On their return the latter will be subjected to a minute interrogation by the women who have remained at home. How many dishes were served? Was there a sweet dish at the end of the meal? Were the *chapatis* moistened with *ghee*? The meal itself has, to borrow Tandon's metaphor (1972:74), the form of a chivalrous 'battle between the hosts and the guests, in which the latter must, after much seemly protesting eventually lose!' Continually replenishing their plates, the host protests that his guests have eaten nothing, while the latter vainly defend their plates with outstretched fingers and assurances of repleteness.

In the last resort, however, the principles underlying the commensal hierarchy are obviously founded on an ideology of pollution without which this hierarchy would be incomprehensible. Why else is it essential to refuse food from an inferior? But this is not to return to a purely attributional model by implying that in every case the reason why caste A will not take *nali rasoi* from caste B is because of its self-evidently purer life-style. In terms of attributes there may be little to choose between two castes which engage in the asymmetrical exchange of food, with the result that as far as purity is concerned the interactional rules sometimes appear to have an almost adventitious quality in their specific application. Nor is it to suggest that on the conscious level considerations of purity are always paramount. At the level of the underlying model, for example, the rules governing the disposal of *jutha* seem to be a means of protecting the purity of the superior partner in the transaction. But on the ground it often appears that the real reason why the people who come off best in such transactions attach such importance to them, is not so much on account of the purity they protect, but more on account of the inequality they express.

I remember, for example, an occasion when a Girth-cultivator friend came to visit me in the Brahman house where I lived, and Mata Ji was prevailed upon to make tea for my guest. As he was about to leave, my friend asked me for some water to wash his cup, but I insisted that he should not bother. When Mata Ji – normally the most amiable and even-tempered person – discovered that my guest had left without washing his own cup, all hell broke loose. I thought I should pacify her if I did it myself, but as it turned out it made not the slightest difference. It was not that she would have any qualms about washing the cup herself, she said. It was rather a question of the insult (*bejti*) implied by my guest. In other words, what was worrying her was not her purity, but rather the breach of interactional rules in which a Girth had failed to act out his subordination to a Brahman.

Clean-caste men who are employed in the cities, or in the army, will sooner or later find themselves sitting next to an untouchable for a meal in a restaurant or canteen. The chances are that the utensils in which the food is served have recently been used by people of polluting caste, and as often as not the diner has not enquired too closely into the caste of the cook. Everybody at home knows all this, but nobody really cares very much. But were the factory worker or the soldier to be equally undiscriminating while he is at home on leave, he would soon find himself boycotted. The point is that those at home can afford to be tolerant about his behaviour in the anonymous environment outside because abstract notions of pollution seem rather academic to most people once they are divorced from the maintenance of a local hierarchy of precedence.

Such considerations force me to clarify the nature of the data recorded in the matrices; and to acknowledge that there are various respects in which such representation is an oversimplification of a far more complex reality. An emphasis on the interactional criteria of caste ranking may appear to have the attraction of providing an objectively more realistic picture of the hierarchy, since interactions are immediately verifiable from direct observation. But, in fact, even the most sophisticated analyses of this kind rely rather heavily on rules extrapolated from the generalized statements of informants. Beck's matrices, for example, are entirely based on the expectations of the 25 informants she systematically interviewed on this topic (1972:157). While Marriott's analysis combines his own observations of actual behaviour and reports about actual behaviour, a significant proportion of the cells (over half) have been completed 'according to villagers' general statements as to what would normally be expected to occur between these two pairs of castes' (1968b:150). The results I have presented in Tables 12 and 13 are obtained in precisely the same way as Marriott's. One reason why the empirical observations are incomplete is that in practice there may be no circumstances under which the general expectations of appropriate interactional behaviour will be put to the test (cf. Pocock 1972:45; Dumont 1970:83). I know of no occasions, for example, when either of the two Trader households in the *mauza* was invited by the one Potter household. This is partly because they live in different hamlets and partly because the Potters do not possess the financial wherewithal to entertain on a lavish scale.

One further reservation which might be registered here is that it cannot simply be assumed that all the castes in any local area belong to the kind of linear hierarchy suggested by my Tables. In Kangra there are, in fact, some castes which cannot be appropriately ranked against the others. Before Partition there were three fairly numerous Muslim castes in Chadhiar. My informants were perfectly prepared to rank these three castes in relation to each other, but I could never get them to say whether they were higher or lower than any particular Hindu caste. Similarly with the Gaddis, a tribal group of transhumant shepherds who drive their flocks through Chadhiar on their seasonal migration. The villagers know that there are different castes of Gaddi and have a fairly clear picture of the Gaddi hierarchy. But again it does not occur to them to rank these castes in relation to village castes.

More importantly, I have over-simplified my data by ignoring both the context of the encounter and a certain amount of individual variation. In general, the women tend to be rather more punctilious in their observance of the rules than the men (cf. Mayer 1960:40; Mandelbaum 1962:311). On a trip to town, some men will eat in restaurants with people they would never dine with at home; while Rajputs who would readily accept *roti* from Kolis in the discreet privacy of their houses would never do so on a public occasion. But an element of personal rank also enters the picture here, for many Rajputs who were prepared to eat openly with Chadhiar's Koli sub-Postmaster were not prepared to do so with his run-of-the-mill caste fellows. For many people, it seems, the real sin is not that the forbidden contact took place at all, but that it did so with a blatancy which forced public opinion to take cognizance of it. One of several incidents I noted which illustrates the pragmatic spirit in which the rules are commonly translated into practice was the occasion when my Brahman 'uncle' and a Rajput neighbour were sitting outside our house convivially smoking a hookah from the same *nari*. Babu Kanshi Ram, a Rajput aristocrat with a reputation for being something of a stickler on such matters, happened to pass by, and as soon as he came into sight the offending *nari* was guiltily whipped off the hookah, and the appropriate interactional pattern re-established. More generally, my data would support Beck's observation (1972:172) that there is greater liberality in informal than formal contexts, and that the latter are the more resistant to change (cf. Pocock 1972:45).

Leaving individual peccadillos aside, there are certain important exceptions to the general assumption that each caste can be treated as a single undifferentiated unit in the matrix; that exchanges of cooked food take place on a reciprocal basis within the caste; and that all the sub-divisions of caste A either accept or reject a given type of food from all the sub-divisions of caste B without discriminating between them.

Both the Rajputs and Brahmans are internally stratified and the clans of each caste are grouped into four hypergamously ranked categories, or *biradaris*. The clans of a single *biradari* are reckoned to be roughly equal in status, exchange women on a symmetrical basis and share, broadly speaking, in a common set of customs and a common style of life. The hierarchical ordering of *biradaris* is largely defined by the asymmetrical exchange of women. Wives are taken from the *biradari* immediately inferior to your own, but preferably from your own *biradari*; daughters are given to your own *biradari* but preferably to the *biradari* above.

In addition to the four 'pure' Brahman *biradaris* there are several other endogamous 'castes' which are also recognized as belonging to the Brahman *varna*: the three types of Funeral priest (Sanyasi, Charaj and Parcharaj), the Temple priests, and a caste of mendicant Brahmans known as Bujurus. Of these only the Temple priests are resident in Chadhiar, though their *purohitchari* duties bring the Charaj and Sanyasi to the *mauza* as occasional visitors.

In terms of the ideal model not all Brahmans or Rajputs can accept *nali rasoi* from all clans of their own caste. The aristocratic Rajputs, for example, should not eat *nali rasoi* in the houses of people who belong to clans which fall into any of the lower *biradaris*. The Rajputs of the second *biradari* can eat with the third *biradari* but not the fourth; while the third and fourth may eat together. Commensal relations between the four Brahman *biradaris* should, in theory,[6] conform to a broadly similar pattern. In addition none of these 'pure' Brahmans may accept *nali rasoi* from the Funeral priests, Bhojkis or Bujurus. In the case of the Charaj and the Parcharaj they cannot take even *suji rasoi.*

As far as the more orthodox Brahmans are concerned the rules are yet more exclusive. While the Rajputs do not discriminate on the basis of the sex of the cook, the Brahmans do. A Brahman who wears the sacred thread should only accept *nali rasoi* if it has been cooked by a man who is equal or superior in status, who also wears the sacred thread, and who has purified himself before preparing the meal by bathing and dressing in a *dhoti*. He will not take *nali rasoi* which has been cooked by a woman, even if she happens to be his own wife.[7]

For the purposes of the present discussion, however, the essential point concerns transactions in *nali rasoi* between the different strata of Rajputs and Brahmans. My entry in Table 12 is somewhat misleading as to both theory and practice here. The theory is that the two lowest of the Rajput *biradaris* take boiled food from all four 'pure' Brahman *biradaris*; and this is in fact what actually happens. But second-grade Rajputs claim that they are prepared to accept boiled food only from first- or second-grade Brahmans, who traditionally do not plough. The aristocratic Rajputs are fussier still and theoretically refuse boiled food from all but the highest *biradari*, who are the only people they will employ as ritual cooks.

The practice of the high-status Rajputs, however, tends to be less exclusive than the theory. As one would expect, the most competitive and status conscious of the high-ranking Rajput sub-clans are the most uncompromising champions of the ideal. Others may only be really particular about the status of the Brahman cooks they employ at weddings or on other festive occasions.[8] But in Chadhiar even this minimum is commonly compromised in practice since hardly any Brahmans of the highest *biradari* are resident in the *mauza*. Short of importing them from outside, the aristocratic Rajputs have to employ ritual cooks with less impeccable credentials; and the real test which they apply is whether members of the Brahman sub-clan are known to plough. In *mauza* Khera, on the other hand, I found that the aristocratic Katoch, who take an immense pride in being a closely related collateral branch of the Raja of Lambagoan's family, were much more discriminating, and did in fact insist on employing ritual cooks of only the highest status.

No Rajput will take *nali rasoi* from the Temple priests, Bujurus or any kind of Funeral priest. In fact, none of the clean castes take boiled food from the Sanyasis, and none of them will accept either sort of cooked food or water from the Charaj.

As in the case of transactions in *nali rasoi*, not all Rajputs or Brahmans are equal for the purposes of smoking a common hookah. Fifty years ago the rule is said to have been that you could smoke only with the clans of your own *biradari*. But some of the aristocratic Rajputs were undoubtedly even more exclusive and would smoke only with the members of their own sub-clan (cf. Chapter 7:3). As a result of events which I will discuss in Chapter 8, standards have since been modified and the general consensus is that all Rajputs may now legitimately smoke together from the same *nari*, as may all Brahmans. But in fact the aristocratic Rajputs still retain much of their old exclusiveness; many of them will not smoke from the same *nari* as Rajputs of lower status, and some will not smoke with them at all.

These days, though not I think in the past, Rajputs and Brahmans are generally prepared to share a common hookah once the *nari* has been removed. But the most superior Brahmans may refuse to smoke with the most inferior Rajputs, while Rajput aristocrats with conservative inclinations – those who will accept *nali rasoi* only from the highest Brahmans – apply the same limits when it comes to smoking relations. No Rajput with any pretensions to respectability will smoke with either the Temple priests or the Funeral priests.

All this poses some difficult problems for an interactional analysis. By refusing to accept *nali rasoi*, or to smoke with any but the highest-status Brahmans, the aristocratic Rajputs might appear to be asserting the inferiority of most Brahmans. Similarly the Rajputs' interdiction on smoking with the Temple priests and on accepting their *bhat* would seem to amount to a claim to superiority. The same goes for the refusal of the clean castes to accept any sort of food from the Charaj Funeral priests. In none of these cases, however, does either party accept *nali rasoi* from the other, while those who exchange *suji rasoi* do so on a reciprocal basis. The structure of interactions does not therefore set up any explicitly acknowledged order of precedence. The indirect inferences that might be extrapolated from the overall pattern of interactions about the mutual ranking of these units are equivocal and somewhat contradictory. It might, for example, be inferred that the top Rajputs rank higher than the bottom Brahmans because it is the former who refuse to smoke a common hookah, while the latter are for their part perfectly prepared to smoke with inferior Rajputs (provided that the *nari* is first removed). If, on the other hand, we consider transactions in *nali rasoi*, and adopt Marriott's method of scoring the matrices (as in the right hand columns of Tables 12 and 13), then the low-status Brahmans rate the higher score since they give *nali rasoi* to one more caste (the Temple priests) than any of the Rajputs. By the same reckoning the Temple priests and Rajputs score equal points and would not be distinguished in rank; while the Charaj Funeral priests would rank low in the hierarchy since none of the clean castes will accept any cooked food from them.

By contrast with this complex and somewhat confusing interactional pattern, informants' statements on how the pairs are ranked are clear and precise. For them it is self-evident that all Brahmans, Temple priests and Funeral priests are superior to all Rajputs no matter how aristocratic; and the basis for their certainty has little to do with either attributes or interactions, and even less to do with the arithmetic by which Marriott scores the matrices. When asked to decide, for example, whether the Temple priests rank higher or lower than the Rajputs, my informants would first identify them with the *varna* category to which they belong, and then derive their rank from the status of the category as a whole. In other words, they would argue that the Bhojkis are a variety of Brahman, that the Brahmans are the most superior of all kinds of men, and that therefore the Temple priests must rank higher than any non-Brahman. On this argument, then, the fact that the Charaj Funeral priests are treated much like untouchables in their interactions, and the fact that low-status Brahmans have lower attributes than high-status Rajputs is quite irrelevant. Brahmans are Brahmans and as such superior to everybody else.

Such reasoning has much in common with the twin processes of 'inclusion' and 'exclusion' which Pocock (1957) has described for Gujarat. The Patidars and their subordinates the Barias are two large, amorphous and highly differentiated castes. In terms of customs and styles of life there is little to choose between the leading Baria families and the average Patidar; while the lowest Patidar have less in common with the Patidar aristocrats than do the richest Baria. But in spite of this the Patidars as a whole are said to rank higher than the Barias. Pocock argues that this comes about because the low-status Patidars arrogate to themselves the superiority of the middle and highest sections of the caste – a situation which the latter have to put up with since outsiders treat the whole caste as an undifferentiated unit of status. Were they to treat high-status Barias as superior or equal to low-status members of their own caste, they would be bringing their own superiority into question. All Patidars, then, are included within the same category, while at the same time they exclude the higher levels of Baria by including them with the lower.

To put the Kangra situation in Pocock's terms we can say that all representatives of the Brahman *varna* arrogate to themselves the superiority of the high-status Brahmans. Since it has to be a Brahman who officiates at mortuary rituals, and since Brahmans are the only appropriate intermediaries with the gods of the great tradition of Hinduism, it is not difficult to see how the Temple priests and Funeral priests come to be included within the same category. At the same time as these castes are included with the high-status Brahmans, the Brahmans as a whole collectively exclude and stand opposed to the non-Brahmans.

Much the same process is repeated at other levels in the hierarchy.

Low-ranking Rajputs are associated with a style of life and a set of customs which are indistinguishable from those of all but the very lowest castes. Yet this does not put their superiority in question, as they are included in the same category as the aristocratic Rajputs. Their identification with the highest-ranking clans, and repudiation of the pretensions of the lower castes, allows the Rajputs as a whole to stand opposed to those lower in the hierarchy. But while the superiority of the low-status Rajputs over castes with similar attributes is backed up by a series of asymmetrical exchanges, the superiority of the low-status Brahmans and Temple priests over the high-status Rajputs is established by the mere fact of their Brahmanical status, and is not unambiguously reflected in their interactions.

The moral would seem to be that, although an interactional analysis may provide a clearer and more precise picture of the way in which the people order the hierarchy than does any attempt to see castes as ranked simply on the basis of their attributes, there are certain respects in which such an analysis is incomplete. In his 1968 paper Marriott emphasizes the importance of food transactions in establishing rank. But in fact such transactions serve to discriminate only a proportion of the ranks which people actually distinguish. In Marriott's own material, for example, the structure of these exchanges establishes only 12 ranking positions between 24 castes (1968b). But when informants were asked to rank these 24 castes in a single series, some of them distinguished 24 ranks, while the average was 18·5.

There are 17 castes in Chadhiar and, assuming for the moment that each caste can be treated as an undifferentiated unit, there are potentially 17 ranking positions in the hierarchy. In practice, informants generally distinguish between 16 and 12 ranks. Those who distinguish the largest number assign each caste, with the exception of the Carpenters and Blacksmiths, to a separate rank. There is no general agreement about the relative ranking of the 5 middle-order castes (who exchange *nali rasoi* on a symmetrical basis), and those who distinguish the smallest number of ranks assign them all to a single rung of the ladder. By comparison, reference back to Tables 12 and 13 shows that transactions in *nali rasoi* discriminate between 8 ranks, while transactions in *suji rasoi* discriminate between 5 ranks. But all of the distinctions made by transactions in *suji rasoi* duplicate distinctions made by asymmetrical exchanges of *nali rasoi*. In other words, Table 13 is redundant in that it introduces no new distinctions, and transactions in both types of cooked food serve to discriminate only 8 of the 12 to 16 ranks which the people themselves discern. They fail to differentiate between the Rajputs and Temple priests, between the 5 castes in the middle ranges of the hierarchy, and between the 4 lowest castes.

As far as the ranking of Rajputs and Bhojkis is concerned, I have suggested that the *varna* categories intervene to establish a measure of precedence where food transactions fail to do so. In the case of the castes in the middle of the hierarchy there seems to be absolutely no interactional or attributional basis for such discriminations of rank as people make. The fact that not all of these castes will smoke from the same *nari* suggests some slight inequality, but provides no basis for saying which of them rank the higher. Consistent with this, there is no general consensus on ranking in this part of the hierarchy, and many people refuse to order these castes at all. There are no food transactions between the 4 castes at the bottom of the ladder; nor amongst themselves do they engage in other sorts of exchange by which they might be ranked. But even so, the relative status of these castes is established by an interactional logic of a sort, for they are subjected to different degrees of exclusion by their clean-caste superiors.

4:5 Degrees of untouchability[9]

In the local dialect castes are divided into *andarke* and *baharke*, those 'of the inside' and 'of the outside'. Not everybody agrees what the terms 'inside' and 'outside' refer to in this context. The majority view is that *baharke* castes are outside in the sense that they were traditionally not allowed to enter the temples. But more sophisticated informants sometimes derive the terms from the fact that the untouchables are outside the *varna* hierarchy of the sacred scriptures; though it should be emphasized that this is not part of popular taxonomy and that usually all the castes below the Traders are lumped together into the undifferentiated category of Shudra. In Table 14 the *andarke* castes are those of the first 5 categories, while those below Koli are *baharke*. The Kolis themselves are currently in a somewhat indeterminate position.

The Hindi word *achhut* is used in everyday conversation for those castes which in Pahari would be described as *baharke*. Literally *achhut* means 'untouchable' but in Kangra not all castes which are described by this adjective pollute clean-caste people by physical contact alone. Writing of a village in eastern Uttar Pradesh, Cohn (1955:62) reports that:

TABLE 14 *Categories of untouchability*

Caste	Varna	*Inside/outside* (andarke/baharke)	*Touchable/untouchable (by physical contact)*	*Backward Class Status*[1]
1 Brahman – Landowners and priests	Brahman	Inside (*andarke*)	Touchable	Nil
2 Bhojki – Temple priests				
3 Rajput – Landowners and Warriors	Kshatriya			
4 Mahajan – Trader	Vaishya			
5 Turkhan – Carpenter; Lohar – Blacksmith; Sonyar – Goldsmith; Nai – Barber; Kumhar – Potter; Girth – Cultivator	Most people would say that all these castes are Shudras. But on occasion castes of categories 5, 6 and 7 will claim to be either Kshatriya or Brahman			Other Backward Class except Turkhan (nil); see note
6 Koli – Cultivator		Inside/outside?		Scheduled Caste
7 Jogi – Beggar and ascetic				Other Backward Class
8 Jullaha – Weaver		Outside + (*baharke*) *achhut*		Scheduled Castes
9 Sanhai – Musician				
10 Dumna – Basket-maker			Untouchable	
11 Chamar – Tanner				
12 Bhangi – Sweeper				

[1] In terms of the Chadhiar hierarchy the Backward Class classification is anomalous at certain points. The Kolis are generally reckoned to be of superior status to the Jogis. But the Kolis are Scheduled and the Jogis an Other Backward Class. The Turkhans and Lohars are of equal political, economic and ritual standing and intermarry. The Lohars are classified but the Turkhans are not.

> The status of the Camar has generally been described as untouchable . . . they are often dubbed with the vernacular term *achut* which means just that. Elsewhere, too, their status has been said to be actually untouchable. . . . In Madhopur at the present time however a Camar's touch does not ordinarily carry defilement to the body of another. When most high-caste persons refer to a Camar as 'untouchable', they mean only that they cannot take food or water from him, and that his touch will pollute food, water, and the utensils used for food or water.

In Kangra matters are somewhat more complex, for within the wider category of people who are 'untouchable' in this loose sense, there are several castes which are 'untouchable' in the stricter sense of polluting others by their touch. The Basket-makers, Leather-workers and Sweepers of the Chadhiar hierarchy are in theory 'untouchable' in this more rigorously defined way. Even the shadows of Leather-workers and Sweepers, but not of Basket-makers, are said to transmit pollution to a widow, or to a Brahman who wears the sacred thread. But today, in fact, only those who are excessively fastidious about such matters will actually bath after touching a person of one of these defiling castes. Yet this does not mean that the rules can be regarded as pure fiction. People over thirty recall a time when they were much more strictly observed, and the historical sources lend some credence to their recollections (e.g., Barnes 1889:40, quoted above).

Baharke or *achhut* castes are not allowed to take water from the same wells as the clean castes. In Palampur this regulation has little practical application, however, since the water-source is generally a mountain spring, which can be used by all except the Leather-workers and Sweepers. Nowadays Chadhiar people of every caste draw water from a tapped supply provided by the Government. Everybody uses the same cremation ground on the banks of a small stream, but the Leather-workers have to burn their dead some way downstream from the spot frequented by other castes, and they expect the Sweepers to go downstream of them.

The distinctions between the untouchable castes who pollute by physical contact alone, and those whose touch contaminates only food, water and utensils, corresponds with the distinction between those castes whose duties involve handling impure substances, and those with caste occupations which are relatively neutral in terms of purity and pollution. The Leather-workers remove and skin dead cattle and tan hides; the Sweepers remove human excrement. The Basket-makers are also considered to be polluted by their caste's duties since they drum at mortuary rituals and take the shroud off the corpse as payment. But the Kolis, Jogi-ascetics, Weavers and Musicians are not associated with caste occupations which are considered to be intrinsically polluting.

In terms of customs, diet and style of life there is very little to choose between this second category of untouchable and the clean castes in the middle ranges of the hierarchy. In fact there is less to distinguish the Kolis from those Rajputs who are on the bottom rungs of the hypergamous ladder, than there is to distinguish the latter from the aristocratic Rajputs. Neither attributes nor pollution values, then, will explain why the line between *andarke* and *baharke* castes is drawn in one place rather than another; though purity considerations do provide a justification for the literal untouchability of the lowest castes. The only reason, it seems, for the untouchability of the others is that they are defined as untouchables by their interactions with the clean castes. Discrimination becomes 'proof' of the inferiority of its victims, and again we encounter the kind of circularity I noted earlier with regard to the acquisition of more prestigious attributes. The only escape from this vicious circle lies in the laborious and formidable task of establishing a new interactional pattern.

Largely as a result of a lengthy and not entirely unsuccessful campaign of this sort, the position of the Kolis is today an ambiguous one. Sometimes they are said to be an *andarke* caste, but more often they will be described as *baharke* or *achhut*. It all depends on whom you are talking to and when. Like other untouchables they were not traditionally allowed to enter the local temples; but unlike the other untouchables Brahmans and Barbers have acted as *purohits* at their rituals as far back as living memory goes. The anomalous position of the Kolis is at its most striking in the pattern of commensal relations. Conservative opinion is that clean-caste people should on no account eat with a Koli or accept food or water from a Koli house. But, as I have already noted, there are today a number of clean-caste liberals who are prepared to accept a clandestine meal of *suji rasoi* at Koli houses; while some Koli individuals of high achieved position may even be invited to sit down to eat with the clean castes on festive occasions.

The utensils given to members of the *baharke* castes should be quite separate from those used by clean-caste people. In the past low-caste individuals who were fed in high-caste houses were given rough earthenware dishes which were thrown away after use. But current practice is to keep a separate set of brass utensils for their exclusive use. The orthodox position is that Koli food should be served in these separate utensils. But when my friend the Koli sub-Postmaster brought his schoolteacher cousin for a meal in the Brahman house where I lived, they were given the same dishes as clean-caste people.

The law says that shops, like other public facilities, should be accessible to everybody without distinction of caste. The law is one thing, however, and its enforcement another. With evident satisfaction, one of the principal Brahman protagonists told me of the aftermath of an attempt by a Leather-worker schoolmaster to stand by his rights. The master had been posted to my informant's village in a different part of the sub-division, and immediately insisted in drawing water from a spring used by the clean castes. The latter remonstrated, and when he failed to desist, some high-caste youths endeavoured to discourage him with some rough manhandling. A complaint was lodged with the local police, who proved quite unsympathetic and who allegedly took steps to ensure that the troublemaker was hastily transferred out of the area.

For the tea-stall owners in Chadhiar, however, it would be neither profitable nor expedient to circumvent the law altogether. But nevertheless they will only serve tea to untouchables in separate cups which these customers are expected to wash themselves. Partly for this reason, but also because they live at some distance, most Kolis never take tea at the shops. Those who do tend to be those with some standing in the community. They are served in the same cups as high-caste customers and it is the shopkeeper, or his helper, who washes up.

In conflict with Pocock's observation (1972:65) that 'a wealthy untouchable has no standing outside his own caste', in cases like these the high standing of individual Kolis seems to mitigate their low-caste status.[10] But it should be emphasized that this was not generally the case with high-ranking individuals of other untouchable castes, for whom the rules cannot be modified with impunity (as the example of the Leather-worker schoolteacher illustrates). The difference between eating with Kolis and eating with other untouchables was forcefully brought home to me on my first encounter with the local Malaria Inspector shortly after my arrival in Chadhiar. During the course of our conversation I asked him whether he would take food at a Koli house. My question was met with indignant self-righteousness. 'Naturally,' he said, 'I eat with Kolis. As an educated man and a graduate of the Punjab University it would be against conscience to refuse.' Impressed by his high moral stand and a lengthy reference to egalitarian values I asked him what his family thought about it. Apparently in matters of conscience he did not give a damn what they thought. But five minutes later he was telling me that he would never dream of eating with a Leather-worker. 'After all, I am an Indian. What would be the condition of my family then? It is not that we hate them, but they are so dirty.'

The general point which emerges from all this is that there are various well-marked gradations of status among the untouchables. These are important not only from the point of view of the low castes themselves, but also for the clean castes too. Writing of a village in Andhra Pradesh, Hiebert (1969:446) by contrast reports that people tend 'to lump together castes that are farthest removed from themselves in the hierarchy' and that social distance 'leads to ignorance of the finer distinctions of ranking'. Again, Berreman (1963:213) records that in Garhwal 'high-caste people know the distinctions among the low castes but consider them unimportant or irrelevant. . . . All low castes are considered by them to be approximately equally polluting.' The Chadhiar data accords rather better with Marriott's finding (1968b) that in Kishan Garhi the high castes make as many discriminations amongst the low castes as the latter do themselves.

The relative status of the untouchable castes is partly expressed in the commensal hierarchy; but also by the degree of exclusion to which they are subjected by the high castes. At the top of the ladder of the 'outside' castes are the Kolis and it is an open question whether they can be legitimately described as 'untouchable' at all. In their capacity as *purohits* the Barbers and Brahmans will serve them, but will not serve other *baharke* castes. At the most they – along with the Jogi-ascetics, Weavers and Musicians – are polluted only in the sense that the clean castes may take neither food nor water from them, and that their touch contaminates the food, water and utensils of the clean castes. While the structure of food transactions does not elevate the Musicians above the Basket-makers, Leather-workers and Sweepers, their superiority is marked by the pattern of interactions between clean and untouchable castes, for it is only the lowest three castes who convey pollution by physical contact alone, and whom the Barbers categorically refuse to serve no matter what the occasion (cf. Chapter 3). Within this last category the Basket-makers are differentiated from the others by a lesser degree of exclusion. Unlike the Leather-workers and Sweepers they are not associated with the consumption of *jutha* left over after high-caste feasts, their shadows are not polluting, they cremate their dead in the same place as other castes, and they are entitled to use the same springs for drawing water. But all the castes from Koli down to Sweeper are described as *baharke* or *achhut*. 'Untouchability' then, is something relative and a matter of degree.

Some ethnographic accounts suggest that the line between touchable and untouchable castes is 'clear, precise, immutable' (Rosser 1966:88), and is 'an insuperable obstacle to mobility' (Bailey 1958: 275). Srinivas, for example, concludes that:

> However thoroughgoing the Sanskritization of an Untouchable caste may be, it is unable to cross the barrier of untouchability . . . an Untouchable caste is always forced to remain Untouchable. Their only chance of moving up is to go so far away from their natal village that nothing is known about them in the new area (1962: 58–9).

There is now, however, a good deal of data which throws grave doubt on such generalizations (e.g., Aiyappan 1965; Hardgrave 1969; Harper 1968a:45; Marriott 1968b; Rowe 1968:69; Rudolph and Rudolph 1967). The Kangra material – in particular the indeterminate status of the Kolis – provides a case in point, and supports the Rudolphs' conclusion (1967:132) that:

> the distinction between 'clean' and 'unclean' castes is not so definitive as is often assumed. There is an indeterminacy in their distinction as in other symbolic and behavioural aspects of social distance. 'Polluting castes' are not so much a separate category below a self-evident line as they are units on a continuum that extends between 'clean-castes', on the one hand, and those that deal with death, blood, feces and other polluting substances, on the other.

4:6 The politics of social mobility: the Koli case

The anomalous position in which the Kolis now find themselves is largely a product of their upward mobility. But it also has to be seen in the light of the policy of 'protective discrimination' laid down by the Indian Constitution. The phrase 'protective discrimination' refers to a fixed quota of vacancies and promotions in Government departments, and reserved seats in Parliaments and the State Assemblies, for the Backward Classes.[11] It means reservations in state-run educational institutions and scholarships for Backward Class students, as well as a host of other measures designed to enable the traditionally under-privileged to gain economic and social equality with the more advanced sections of society.

The Backward Classes are a vast, amorphous and highly differentiated collection of people. Together they add up to more than a third of India's population. In this context the word 'classes' is a misnomer for 'castes' or 'tribes', and the word 'backward' a polite shorthand for those who were low in the traditional social hierarchy. Membership in the Backward Classes, then, is ascribed by birth into a caste or tribe occupying a more or less inferior position in the caste system. Doctors and lawyers are as eligible as sweepers and shoe-makers.

There are four varieties of Backward Class: the Scheduled Tribes, the Denotified Tribes (known as the Criminal Tribes in the less delicate days of the British Raj), the Scheduled Castes and the Other Backward Classes. Each of these has its own quota of reservations which vary in size for each category and for which only the members of the appropriate category are eligible. For example, a member of the Scheduled Tribes cannot contest for an Assembly Seat reserved for a Scheduled Caste representative, nor vice versa. (No political offices are reserved for members of the Other Backward Classes.) Government jobs are thrown open to other categories of Backward Class only if there are not enough qualified candidates in the category for whom they were reserved. In terms of the present discussion it is the Scheduled Castes and the Other Backward Classes which are of interest. They account for roughly four-fifths of the Backward Class population.

Before the First World War special treatment for the Scheduled Castes, at that time known as the 'Depressed Classes', had been adopted on a small scale in education by a few provincial and State Governments. This was later expanded and extended to include other fields as a result of the Montford reforms. But it was not until the Government of India Act of 1935 that the first formal lists of the Depressed Classes were drawn up. Castes were included on the basis of their traditionally polluted status. Although attempts to apply an all-India set of criteria for determining untouchability ran into difficulty and additional criteria of poverty and illiteracy had to be added, it was untouchability, more or less rigorously defined, which was the basis on which castes were listed (Galanter 1966). Today lists of the Scheduled Castes are drawn up by the Central Government and can be revised only with the authority of the President.

There is no all-India list for the Other Backward Classes. State

Governments are given discretion to decide the basis on which people should be included, although in recent years the Central Government has been pressing the States to drop caste as the operative unit and adopt instead economic criteria. Caste groups included in the Other Backward Classes vary enormously in size and social status. More heterogeneous than the Scheduled Castes, they are more difficult to characterize. On the one hand there are the powerful Lingayats of Mysore and Iravas of Kerala; on the other a number of small, politically impotent and poverty-stricken artisan castes isolated in various parts of the country. Typical perhaps are the peasant-cultivator castes with a low position in the *varna* hierarchy who lack a tradition of literacy and are consequently poorly represented in government and white-collar jobs. Often they are small landowners and sometimes the dominant caste of a village, or if numerically strong enough, even of a whole district.

The situation created by the Backward Classes legislation is fraught with paradoxes. One of these is that many castes have developed a vested interest in being backward and in some cases have become powerful enough to resist attempts by the State Government to remove them from the Backward Classes list (Srinivas 1962). Another is that 'protective discrimination' defeats its own ends, as Dushkin notes, in direct proportion to its success. As the congruence between caste, class and occupation breaks down, untouchables increasingly enter white-collar jobs and the professions. The concessions of which they made use are still available to their children, but are not available to the children of agricultural day labourers who are clean-caste Hindus.

But perhaps the most obvious of these paradoxes is the idea of separating off the Backward Classes in order to destroy their separateness. This leads to a situation in which 'the individual who seeks help in getting rid of his identity must proclaim it' (Isaacs 1965:114; cf. Rudolph and Rudolph 1967:150). Béteille (1969:133–4) puts it like this:

> Whereas the Backward Classes are prompted to merge their identity with the higher strata to enhance their status, considerations of power and economic advantage lead them to define their identity in opposition to the advanced sections of society. This is the dilemma of Backwardness. A low caste would like to acquire a high-sounding title, claim Kshatriya status, and assume the symbols of high-caste status; at the same time it would insist on its right to be officially classified as backward.

The Kolis, who are concentrated in the eastern part of the Kangra Valley and in the adjacent area of districts Mandi and Bilaspur, face just such a dilemma.

The evidence suggests that a hundred years ago their position in the hierarchy was more clear-cut than it is today: they were unambiguously untouchable. Writing of the 1870s, Lyall was quite explicit on this point (cf. Kangra District Gazetteer, 1926:183); and the Kolis admit as much themselves though they would see it as a temporary fall from grace rather than their natural state. Their story is that originally they were of clean caste but were demoted to untouchable status as the result of a minor breach of caste orthodoxy and the irascible whim of the Raja of Kangra. The offence which led to their collective downfall was that of a Koli woman who was discovered eating *chapatis* as she carried water to the Raja's palace. The Koli claim is that originally they were Rajputs. High-caste people generally concede the story in outline but contest the claim to Rajput origin. As they see it, the Kolis were once Girth-cultivators or 'like Girths'.

In their endeavour to regain their 'true' status, the Kolis have tried to approximate their customs and style of life to one regarded as acceptable by local Rajputs of standing. This has involved attempts to eliminate such dubious practices as widow-inheritance, bride-price payments and exchange marriages in which a brother and a sister marry a brother and a sister. In this the Kolis have had less far to go than the other 'outside' castes. Even in the nineteenth century they had a developed clan system and a set of exogamic rules much like those of the Rajputs. This is in marked contrast with, for example, the Leather-workers.

In the process of Sanskritization the Kolis have often had to defy the numerous restrictions imposed on them by the high castes. Traditionally, for example, they were not allowed to play musical instruments in their weddings, to use distinctively high-caste personal names, nor were their women allowed to wear gold ornaments. The Brahmans could not blow the conch shell (*sankh*) at their rituals, nor, of course, could Kolis assume the sacred thread. In the face of bitter high-caste opposition they have attempted to do all these things with varying degrees of success. When the Kolis of one of the Chadhiar hamlets wanted to perform the sacred thread ceremony the Brahmans refused to co-operate, and the Kolis were reduced to stealing the sanctified threads with which the high-caste women festoon the sacred *bar* tree. The first Brahman to blow the *sankh* in a Koli ritual was summarily boycotted.

Sanskritization, and the increasing independence of the Kolis in their relations with the high castes, has been the accompaniment of a widening range of economic opportunities and greater economic security. As tenants, recent land legislation has given them at least a measure of security of tenure. Although, in Chadhiar, there has been little general redistribution of the land in favour of the lower castes since the end of the last century, such as there has been seems to have favoured the Kolis. In 1915 the Rajputs owned 99 per cent of the land falling within the hamlet of Salehra, the population of which is entirely Koli (Tika Assessment Notes, 1915). By 1968 they had sold all but 39 per cent of this to the Kolis. But more significant still is the fact that over the last fifty years employment opportunities outside Kangra have increased dramatically, while the range of jobs for which the Kolis can now compete has widened enormously. Early British army recruiting policy, for example, was to accept only Rajputs; and to some extent Koli claims to Rajput status were directed at entering the military. During the First World War they succeeded in getting themselves recruited to the ancillary services, but it was not until the Second World War that they were allowed to join the infantry. Now out of 207 men between the ages of fifteen and fifty-five in the large all-Koli hamlet of Salehra, 117 are employed outside and over half of these are soldiers. A further 43 out of 90 adult men living at home were previously employed outside.

In view of British army recruiting policy and the prestige attached to military service, it is not altogether surprising that the conscious model for emulation of most castes which aspire to a higher status has been a Rajput rather than a Brahman one. Another reason, perhaps, is that the Brahmanical ideal with its emphasis on vegetarianism, teetotalism and asceticism, seems rather more remote and unattainable to the low castes than does the Kshatriya model with its tolerance of meat-eating and the consumption of liquor, and with its less obsessive insistence on the rules of purity. But the most important reason why these castes claim Rajput rather than Brahman status is that, although Brahman values are unquestionably superior, it is the Rajput style of life and its associated martial ethic which has the greatest kudos in the eyes of most Kangra people.

Most of the clean castes with artisan-type occupations also advance claims to a Kshatriya origin.[12] But their account of how they lost their Kshatriya status is different from that of the Kolis. There was once, they say, a Brahman possessed of miraculous powers called Pars Ram who was sworn to the systematic extermination of all Kshatriyas. In order to escape his notice their ancestors had been forced to deny their true status, had adopted the disguise of working as potters, goldsmiths, blacksmiths or whatever, and had thus founded new castes associated with the occupations they had taken up as a matter of expediency.[13]

Hand in hand with their campaign of Sanskritization the Kolis have endeavoured to advance their cause by appeals to an external political authority: first to the rajas and subsequently to the British courts. The Sanskrit texts give the raja wide powers to legislate on caste matters, and to prevent – as Kautilya puts it – 'the confusion of castes and duties'. Evidence from many parts of the sub-continent suggests that the king did in practice use his powers to manipulate the caste hierarchy, and to legitimize a change in caste status (cf. Maynard 1917; Srinivas 1966, 1968; Aiyappan 1965:138; Rosser 1966:110; Furer-Haimendorf 1966:23). In the Kangra region the intervention of the local rajas in caste organization seems to have been commonplace. Lyall (1889:70), for example, reports that:

> The Raja was the fountain of honour, and could do as he liked. I have heard old men quote instances within their memory in which a Raja promoted a Girth to be a Rathi, and a Thakur to be a Rajput, for service done or money given; and at the present time the power of admitting back into caste fellowship persons under a ban for some grave act of defilement is a source of income to the *jagirdar* Rajas.

The Raja of Kangra is reputed to have created the different grades of Brahman and to have given certain Gaddis the right to wear the sacred thread. He also played a key role in legitimizing Koli claims to clean-caste status, though perhaps because his real power had by that time been seriously eroded his authority did not prove decisive.

Koli efforts to enlist the raja's aid go back at least a century. Lyall recorded that they have 'several times attempted to get the Raja to remove the ban but the negotiations have fallen through, because the bribe offered was not sufficient' (quoted in Kangra District Gazetteer, 1926:183). But by 1913 the Kolis had won the raja round. Maynard (1917), an official of the Punjab Government, was a witness when purificatory rites were performed at the palace by the Brahmans; the raja proclaimed the Kolis a clean caste whose temporary degradation had come to an end, and the assembled high-caste dignitaries accepted *prasad* (consecrated food) from the Koli leaders.

The impact of this formal recognition of clean-caste status does not seem to have been as far-reaching as the Kolis must have hoped. It was to have been followed up at the local level by a series of repetitions of the symbolic acceptance of food from Kolis. But in Chadhiar, at least, the affair was a fiasco since practically all the high-caste people who turned up refused to eat, and the few who did were boycotted.

The immediate results of the raja's initiative were negligible. But in the late 1920s and early 1930s circumstances were more favourable and the Kolis renewed their pressure. It was at this time too that the Girth-cultivators were vigorously pushing their claim to a higher status and rejecting Rajput and Brahman authority. The 1925 edition of the District Gazetteer (pp. 173–4) says that:

> At present a fierce struggle is going on between the Girths and the Rajputs. The former have risen up in revolt against the restrictions imposed by the latter and accepted by the former in the past. The Girths assert their right to beat their drums when passing in front of the Rajputs' houses, they often refuse to cleanse the vessels in which the Rajputs have taken their food and to carry the palanquins of the latter. Many of them anxious to assume a higher status have begun to wear the sacred thread though the Brahmans refuse to perform the sacred thread ceremony. In several places the Rajputs and Girths have come to blows as the Rajputs still refuse to admit them to a footing of equality. The trouble has also assumed an economic aspect. The Girths have asserted claims to a better share of the produce, which the Rajput landowners do not recognize . . . Numerous fields have been left uncultivated owing to this friction.

In those parts of Kangra where there are both Kolis and Girths, the Rajputs used Koli pretensions to clean-caste status to blackmail the Girths into a more submissive attitude. In this the Kolis acquiesced. The Girth revolt left many Rajputs in something of a quandary since traditionally Girths had been their domestic servants. Because they were a clean caste they could perform various duties – like fetching water or cleaning cooking utensils – which could not be done by servants of the lower castes. But in their attempts to claim a higher status the Girths refused to do this sort of menial work. They opted out of the most demeaning of their interactions with the Rajputs, and they boycotted those of their members (among them a number of Chadhiar Girths) who continued to work for the Rajputs on the same old basis. The Kolis saw their opportunity and cashed in on it. Their leaders approached the council of royal Rajput clans and pressed for recognition of their claims to Rajput origin. The deal was that the Rajputs were to recognize the Kolis as a clean caste and a sort of inferior Kshatriya, and the Kolis would then be eligible to do the work the Girths had just left off. For the Rajputs this not only had the advantage of solving their labour problems but also of curbing Girth pretensions with the threat of recognizing the Kolis as superior to them.

The reaction of the Girth leaders was to try to come to terms with the Kolis. One of the palliatives adopted by the lower-ranking Rajput clans in response to the shortage of women they experience as a result of hypergamy has been to recruit wives from the Girths. The Girth manoeuvre was to offer the Kolis a relationship of hypergamy like that linking themselves and the most inferior Rajputs. This was a compromise which expressed Girth superiority at the same time as acknowledging the clean-caste status of the Kolis and a small ritual distance between the two castes.

At this point the leaders of the Koli caste council seem to have played their cards rather badly. They turned down the hypergamous marriage offer. Perhaps this was because they doubted the good faith of the Girth leaders, or their ability to get the new marriage regulation accepted by more than a handful of Girths; or perhaps it was because they were playing for bigger stakes and thought that the Rajputs were about to recognize them as Kshatriyas and superior to the Girths, a status which would not have been tenable had they accepted the position of wife-givers in a hypergamous relationship. Whatever the reason, they wound up by missing their opportunity altogether. Representatives of the royal Rajput clans consulted the raja and eventually organized a large meeting at which the Kolis again served food to a gathering of prominent high-caste notables; but again this seems to have had little practical effect. Seeing that the Kolis' position was not substantially improved, the Girths then repudiated their offer of a marriage link.

This sort of calculated wheeling and dealing over whether the Kolis were a 'clean' of 'untouchable' caste seems to have had precedents in the neighbouring state of Bilaspur. Rose (1919:I:iv) reports that there:

> the Raja probably promoted the outcaste Koli to a recognised status within the pale of the caste because he needed his services as a soldier; whereas the Katoch Raja (of Kangra) refused to remove the

ban on the Kolis of a tract like Rajgiri, where the clan is pretty numerous because he had no need of their services in a military capacity.

The Koli cause received a serious setback in 1936 when they were included in the first lists of 'depressed classes' drawn up for the coming elections. Since castes were included on the basis of their traditional untouchability this was a considerable embarrassment. That year they filed a civil suit against the Government classification and they eventually won their case after a series of appeals up to the High Court in Lahore. Koli witnesses claimed in evidence that as a result of their appearing on the list high-caste people were now reluctant to eat with them or employ them as domestic servants. I doubt whether this is strictly accurate, for it implies a willingness to eat with them before. But it is certainly the case that it imposed an effective brake on their mobility. The Judge's verdict was that they were not an untouchable caste and could not therefore be listed as a depressed class.

But that was not the end of the story. The Kolis won the case but have never been able to enforce the decision. Through some inexplicable bureaucratic tangle which some people attribute to the machinations of high-caste politicans and government officials determined to keep the Kolis in their place, they have appeared on every subsequent Scheduled Caste list. With the object of getting off the list the Koli caste council has devoted enormous energy to petitioning politicians, Cabinet Ministers and senior bureaucrats. During the period of my fieldwork several meetings of the caste council were taken up with this issue alone. Representatives have also been sent to sessions of the All-India Koli Sabha, an organization which purports to represent the caste on a national level but which actually seems to be dominated by Kolis from Gujarat and Rajasthan. Local Kangra politicians know that, if they are to win Koli votes, they must endorse Koli pretensions to clean-caste status, at election times at least.

For the Kolis, however, the issue is no longer as simple as it used to be. Since Independence the increasing advantages of being a Scheduled Caste have created a bigger and bigger dilemma for them. On the one hand their Scheduled Caste status means scholarships, reserved seats in colleges, better job opportunities and perhaps a representative in Parliament or the State Assembly. But on the other hand it implies that they are untouchables and of low social standing. As they see it, and as other people tend to see it, it equates them with the Leather-workers and

Sweepers. At caste council meetings the issue now splits the Kolis into two hostile camps. On one side are the older and more conservative leaders – men without formal schooling – who want, as a matter of self-respect, to drop out of the Scheduled Caste category regardless of the consequences. Opposed to them are a handful of young educated men in white-collar jobs, most of whom have personally benefited from the Government's policy of protective discrimination. Those people are determined that the Kolis should remain a Scheduled Caste. Their attitude would seem to mirror a much broader trend, in which the low castes are becoming less concerned with Sanskritization as a strategy for winning higher ritual status, and increasingly concerned with political power as a way of opening up new opportunities for individual advancement based on educational and occupational criteria (cf. Bailey 1958; Cohn 1959; Rudolph and Rudolph 1967; Srinivas 1966, 1968 and Zelliott 1966).

The Koli dilemma was particularly apparent during the 1967 General Elections, when the Assembly constituency in which Chadhiar is located was unexpectedly declared a reserved seat for a Scheduled Caste representative. This created something of a power vacuum in the constituency since all the established leaders were Rajputs and they were forced to contest outside their home constituency. Numerically the two largest of the Scheduled Castes in this area are the Kolis and the Leather-workers. Since in Kangra people normally prefer to vote for a candidate of their own caste it was all along obvious that the major political parties would put up either a Koli, or a Leather-worker, for they would have large caste-based 'vote-banks' behind them. It was also a fair bet that most parties would prefer a Koli over a Leather-worker, since the Leather-worker had little chance of roping in high-caste votes.

High-caste people generally resented the reservation of their constituency and many of them reacted by losing interest in the election altogether. But in so far as they did continue to participate they were in favour of a Koli and were strongly antagonistic to the idea of a Leather-worker representative. As one Rajput friend of mine put it: 'If we have a Koli, then at least we will be able to sit down beside our MLA.' To emphasize their preference for a Koli and the difference between Kolis and Leather-workers, Rajputs discussing the campaign would refer to the Kolis as *chotte Rajput* – 'small' or 'junior Rajputs'. Provided that there were not too many Kolis in the field so that their vote would be split, the constituency looked like a walk-over for a Koli candidate.

The weeks before nomination were a frantic time for the Koli leaders. Their main concern was to reach a unanimous decision on a candidate for the Congress ticket who would contest the election with the united support of the whole caste. But initially their problem was whether they should contest the election at all. To do so would look like a clear admission and acceptance of Scheduled Caste status. But to have failed to do so would have been to deny themselves of an enormous amount of patronage controlled by an MLA of their own caste. This might mean a water-supply scheme or electricity for Koli majority hamlets, or jobs for Koli boys. In spite of a vociferous lobby against it, they opted in favour of contesting the election, though they never did manage to agree on a single candidate. On polling day, however, a section of the caste abstained from voting because they disapproved of Kolis standing. One of the candidates, who eventually stood for the Jan Sangh, but who had earlier been putting out feelers for the Congress ticket, told me that as far as he was concerned the party tag was quite irrelevant. What was really important, he said, was to get a Koli into the Assembly to agitate for their removal from the Scheduled Castes. The irony of doing this from a reserved seat did not appear to strike him.

When nominations were filed a Leather-worker candidate challenged those of the four Kolis who were standing. His case was that the Kolis were not eligible to stand since the High Court had decided that they were not an 'untouchable' caste and should not have been included in the depressed classes. They could not therefore be said to be a Scheduled Caste. This objection was overruled by the presiding officer on the grounds that they nevertheless appeared on the Government Scheduled Caste List. But after a Koli had won the election the Leather-worker framed an election petition based on the High Court order, although in the end it came to nothing as he did not have the resources to pursue it through the courts.

The Leather-workers felt cheated by the whole episode, for, as they saw it, the reserved seat should have been theirs. Their complaint is that the Kolis are a Scheduled Caste when it suits them, and a clean caste when it does not. But the Kolis are not the only ones who want the best of both worlds. In everyday interaction the Rajputs insist on deference from the low castes and the maintenance of their traditional privileges. But when it comes to the Backward Class legislation, which they bitterly resent, they assert that in modern India, as is only right and proper, all men are equal before the law, and that protective discrimination flatly contradicts this fundamental principle. But although the

Rajputs resent protective discrimination, they have managed to capitalize on the Kolis' use of it. During the election campaign the Kolis were 'small Rajputs', but subsequently the Koli MLA became irrefutable evidence of their untouchable status. One of the reasons why so many clean-caste people were anxious to vote for a Koli was that a Koli MLA representing a reserved constituency was incriminating beyond doubt.

Shortly after the election the Koli caste council renewed the discussion about their Scheduled Caste status and addressed a series of resolutions to the Government calling for their re-classification. This was initiated by one of the unsuccessful candidates and was supported by the others. If anybody had taken any notice and the Kolis had been removed from the list, it would have meant, of course, that the man who had won the election would have had to resign.

Although the Kolis are anxious to move out of the Scheduled Caste category they are reluctant to give up Backward Class status altogether. Their aim is to be incorporated into the Other Backward Classes so that they would still be able to claim some of the concessions available to them as a Scheduled Caste. To be classified as Scheduled Caste has distinctly pejorative connotations, whereas to be an Other Backward Class has not. This difference is neatly illustrated by the case of the Girth-cultivators who belong to the Other Backward Class category and who would strongly resist any attempt to remove them from it. Now they are one of the most powerful castes in Kangra politics and are well represented in white-collar jobs. Originally, it seems, they were included in the list of Other Backward Classes in an attempt to persuade them to vote for the Congress party. During the 1952 elections a close associate of Pratap Singh Kairon – the then Chief Minister of the Punjab – was being run very hard by an influential Communist in one of the Kangra constituencies. A significant proportion of the electorate were Girths, and most of them supported the Communist. But shortly before polling day the Girth leaders allegedly did a deal with Congress by which they traded Girth votes for Other Backward Class status.

The recent history of the Kolis just across the border in district Mandi is strikingly similar to that of Kangra. Traditionally they were 'untouchables'. Like the Kangra Kolis their ambition was to get accepted as a clean caste and they tried unsuccessfully to persuade the Raja of Mandi to support their claim. After Independence five Koli families fought a civil case against their inclusion in the Scheduled Castes. They won the case, but the decision applied only to the individuals who had fought it, and the position of the caste as a whole remained unaffected. Shortly after this a new case was initiated on behalf of the Kolis of 8 *panchayat* areas and this was decided in their favour in 1967. Posters headed with the slogan 'Truth is Victorious' announced the verdict and claimed that the court had found that they were Rajputs.

Reaction among the Koli students from the area at Baijnath College was predictably hostile. They lost their stipends. More surprising at first sight was the coolness with which the Koli leaders in Kangra received the news. A network of intermarriage connects the caste in Kangra with Mandi. What the Kangra people were worried about was that it would not be long before the Mandi Kolis started to reckon themselves rather superior, and refuse to marry with them, on the grounds that they were still a Scheduled Caste.

In the 1962 General Elections, Jogindernagar constituency in district Mandi was a reserved seat. Within a given region the decision to reserve one constituency rather than another is made primarily on the basis of its having the higher percentage of Scheduled Castes. There was an appeal by a Rajput politician to the Election Commission against this particular reservation on the grounds that the Kolis had been included as a Scheduled Caste when the calculation of percentages had taken place. But the Kolis, so the argument ran, are not properly a Scheduled Caste, and if their numbers were discounted, then the constituency had a lower percentage than its neighbours. The appeal was rejected and a Koli candidate, in the face of strong opposition from influential Koli leaders who were then manoeuvring their case through the courts, contested the election. I am told that a large number of his caste fellows resented his candidature and that few of them voted for him.

The Kolis are not, of course, alone in their dilemma. Many members of the neo-Buddhist movement, which has been particularly influential among the Mahars of Maharashtra and the Jatavs of Agra, have been faced with a similar choice (Dushkin 1961; Zelliott 1966; Galanter 1966, 1968 and Lynch 1968). In each of these cases the dilemma is largely a product of the Government's policy of 'protective discrimination'. But in a slightly different form the problem is an old one. Those low castes who pursue polluting occupations have always been in a position in which they have either had to opt for the economic advantages of their caste specific duties, or renounce the profits and their traditional occupation in an attempt to enhance their status through Sanskritization. Whether they decide to abandon their traditional occupation or not will obviously depend, to some extent, on how profitable it is. The Chamars of Rajasthan, for example, were in 1958 attempting to dissociate themselves from leather-working. But the Rudolphs' report (1967:134) that as a result of new market opportunities and Government subsidies, they were ten years later trying to exclude '"opportunists" from invading their ancient monopoly'. The general point here is that, as so often in the caste environment, high status and material gain stand, as Marriott (1968b:146) puts it, 'in a relation of complementarity'.

The Kolis' position at the top of the ladder of 'outside' castes, and the fact that they are not associated with any polluting occupation, has made it realistic for them to attempt to transcend their untouchability. The Leather-workers, by contrast, start with no such advantages. While the traditional aim of the Kolis has been to change their own position within the system, rather than the system itself, the latter have tended to adopt a more radical approach, and some have marked their complete rejection of the hierarchy by embracing a new religion.

In the late 1930s and early 1940s, the Ahmadiyas, a proselytizing Muslim sect, made a concerted attempt to convert the low castes in the western part of Kangra. With the partition of India imminent, and with the proximity of this area to the present border of Pakistan, the percentage of Muslims in the population was locally considered to be of crucial political importance. Quite apart from the fact that the Muslims were not subjected to the same degree of exclusion by the high castes, and could take water from the same wells, the egalitarian ideology of Islam had obvious attractions for the Leather-workers. In Nurpur subdivision their leaders were able to exploit this situation to bring about a confrontation with the high castes, and to wrest certain concessions from them. They threatened to lead their community into Islam unless the Chamars were allowed to use the same water sources as the high castes. The tank at Jawali became the *cause célèbre*, and under pressure from Hindu political leaders and particularly from the reformist Arya Samaj movement, the high castes of the village were forced to concede.

Part two

The internal structure of the caste

5 Clans and their segments

5:1 Introduction

The previous two chapters discussed the economic and hierarchical aspects of relations between castes. The rest of this study is concerned with relations within the caste. But this division between the internal and external aspects of caste is intended simply as a convenient way of presenting the data, and is in no sense meant to imply a rigid distinction between the two levels. No such distinction is possible, for the principle of hierarchy not only pervades the realm of inter-caste relations, but also orders relations within the caste. 'There is', as Dumont (1957:4) succinctly puts it, 'no absolute difference between what happens inside and outside a caste group, and we may expect to find in its internal constitution something of the principles which govern its external relations.'

The caste system, as Dumont (1970) and Béteille (1964) have clearly shown, is segmentary in nature; and the participants' categories make no clear-cut distinction between *varnas*, castes and grades within a caste. Typically the same word is used to describe groups at all these levels of segmentation, and those who operate the system see no radical difference in kind between them. In Kangra, for example, the term *jat* may be used to designate a *varna*, a 'caste' or a clan, and it is only the general context which indicates the sort of unit under discussion. The principles which organize relations within the caste, and the idiom in which these principles are expressed, are (*pace* Pocock 1972:65) homologous to those which govern relations between castes. Just as each caste is conceptualized as a different genus, so the constituent units within a single caste are in certain contexts seen as being of qualitatively different kinds (Chapter 7). An apt analogy here would be the Linnaean taxonomic hierarchy in which orders are divided into families, families into genera, and genera into species.

The clan, however, is not only a *jat* of the least inclusive order of segmentation but also a *khandan*, or patrilineal descent category, of the most inclusive order. The present chapter outlines this agnatic descent ideology and the uses to which it is put.

The task of providing a general description of the internal structure of the caste is complicated by a certain amount of significant variation between castes. One obvious distinction to draw is between the top three castes of the Chadhiar hierarchy where marriage is explicitly hypergamous, and their inferiors for whom marriage is isogamous. My analysis of affinal relations in subsequent chapters relates primarily to the former. But in broad outline the present discussion of patrilineal descent is valid for all but the very lowest castes in the hierarchy. The latter seldom reckon agnatic ties beyond a lineage of shallow depth, and a recognition of common descent does not long survive the dispersal of the group. The widely ramifying and geographically scattered clans of the aristocratic Rajputs, the grouping of clans into *gotras*, the proud identification with a common patronymic and a common clan deity, and the elaborate rules of exogamy, have a somewhat attenuated significance at other levels of the hierarchy; they disappear altogether at the bottom of the ladder.

5:2 Clans and 'gotras'

With this qualification, each caste is divided into a large number of named exogamous patriclans. For Palampur sub-division alone I have a list of 176 Rajput clans, and my records are by no means exhaustive. The clans of the hypergamous castes are ranked; those of the other castes are not. Most are scattered over a wide area, though in some cases all known clan members are confined to a group of adjacent hamlets. Broadly speaking, the Rajputs and Brahmans have the largest and most widely dispersed clans; and the most aristocratic clans of these castes are the most numerous and have the greatest geographical scatter. Representatives of most of the royal Rajput clans are found throughout Kangra and the neighbouring districts, though the bulk of their population is concentrated within the area of its own traditional kingdom. In population the largest clans number several thousand members.

The people of one clan belong to a single *kul*, or line of patrilineal descent, the founding ancestor of which is their *bans.*[1] They are of 'one blood', the theory here being that blood comes from the father and milk from the mother, and that the mother's womb is the field in which the seed is sown (cf. Mayer 1960:203–4).[2] Although all members of a single caste who share a common clan name are putatively assumed to be descended from a common agnatic ancestor, the vast majority of them are not able to trace precise genealogical links with each other.

The same clan names sometimes occur in different castes. Several different explanations are offered for this. According to one theory, the lower-caste clan must have been founded by a high-caste individual who had for some reason or other been deprived of his caste status. His progeny could arrogate their father's clan name but not his natal caste status. A second theory suggests that clans pre-date the origin of the caste system which was created by Manu, the lawgiver, who assigned different segments of the same clan to different castes on the basis of their different occupations. The more worldly-wise of my informants, however, noted that those names which recur most frequently are the names of the royal Rajput clans; and speculated that these had simply been usurped by their inferiors out of motives of snobbery.

In theory all members of the clan, no matter where they live, owe allegiance to a common clan deity, or *kulaj*. The *kulaj* is propitiated by the principal celebrants at all important life-cycle ceremonies; but there are no rituals at which the whole clan, or even the whole of a localized segment of the clan, unites in common worship of its deity. In theory too, all clan members recruit their *kul-purohits* (household priests) and *guru-purohits* (spiritual preceptors) from the same two Brahman clans. Although few people are aware of it, in fact different localized segments of the same clan often worship different deities and call on different clans of Brahmans as their *purohits*. An additional complication is that some localized clan-segments recognize more than one *kulaj*, and the chances are that not all the members of the group will offer allegiance to precisely the same set of deities. One of these may be distinguished as the 'true' *kulaj* – which in theory belongs to the whole clan – while the others are considered to be subsidiary *kulajs* and are worshipped only by a particular segment of the clan. These subsidiary clan deities and their shrines are sometimes used as diacritical markers which indicate structurally significant points of segmentation within the clan.

Some but not all high-status Rajput and Brahman clans have their own particular myth of origin. Such myths often associate the origin of the clan with the clan deity. For example, the Katoch, the clan of the Raja of Lambagoan, trace descent from a founding ancestor called Bhumi Chand. The myth recounts how Bhumi Chand was born fully-formed out of the earth (*bhumi*) which had been fertilized by sweat from the brow of the goddess Ambika Devi as she fought with the *dewtas* (deities) against the *dait* (demons).[3] Ambika Devi is one of the thousand incarnations of Siva's consort Parvati, and is worshipped as the *kulaj* of the Katoch. In another form she is known as Bhawani, and the Katoch are known as 'Bhawani *putr*', 'sons of Bhawani'.

I have little concrete data on the foundation of new clans, but according to popular theory some clans came into existence as a result of a process of clan fission brought about by the spatial separation of clan-segments coupled with the lapse of generations. It is claimed, for example, that the royal clans of five of the small Kangra states were originally founded by younger sons of the Katoch rajas. Over the centuries their connection with their parent stock became more remote, while their association with their own states became more complete, and as a result each of these clan-segments started to call itself by a new patronymic derived from the name of its own territory. Eventually these patronymics came to be reckoned as the names of independent clans, and the tradition of a common origin was perpetuated only in a common *gotra*.

As a theory of clan fission all this is perfectly plausible since many clan names have an obvious association with place names. Such claims cannot always be taken at their face value, however, for the shared pedigree may sometimes be little more than a charter for the contemporary pattern of political alliances. More importantly, connections of this sort are often manufactured by an upwardly mobile Rajput or Brahman clan-segment in an attempt to assert a higher status on the hypergamous ladder by associating itself with a higher ranking clan (a process I discuss in detail in Chapter 9).

In some areas of northern India the clan is designated by the term *got* or *gotra* (Pradhan 1966:ix; Tiemann 1970); but elsewhere the *gotra* is a phatry or grouping of clans (Sharma 1973). In Kangra the term is used in this second sense. Though in the limiting case a single clan is said to be the only representative of its particular *gotra*, in general several clans of the caste share a common *gotra*.

Clans are exogamous, but they are not – in ideal terms at least – the widest units of exogamy. Theoretically, those who share a common *gotra* may not marry, though in practice this restriction is honoured more in the breach than in the observance by all but the Rajputs.[4] Even in their case the *gotra* has recently lost most of the importance that it once had in the regulation of marriage (for reasons I discuss in Chapter 8). Many non-Rajputs cannot even name their own *gotra*, let alone being able to identify the other clans which belong to it. That they pretend to a *gotra* organization at all seems only to reflect the fact that *gotras* belong to a prestigious Sanskritic way of life, and are embodied in the repertoire of the dominant caste. This applies as much to the Brahmans as to the other clean castes, so that paradoxically it is the Rajputs who are the guardians of an institution associated primarily with a Brahmanical tradition.

Kangra people entertain two distinct theories about how several clans came to share a common *gotra* (cf. Berreman 1963:187); and both of the rival theories have their advocates amongst the classical Indologists (Madan 1962a:62–3). What is generally agreed is that each *gotra* is named after a *rishi*, a holy sage of a former epoch. But according to the first school of thought the founding ancestors of the clans of the *gotra* were the *rishi*'s unrelated disciples (*chelas*). The *gotra* was therefore a kind of ritual college to which members of any of the twice-born castes might have belonged, and this explains why clans of different castes or of different *biradaris* within the caste may claim allegiance to the same *gotra*. The second theory is that all the members of the *gotra* are the *rishi*'s lineal descendants, who have become differentiated into a number of clans as a result of a process of clan fission. On this theory the recurrence of the same *gotra* name in different castes may be accounted for in exactly the same range of ways as the recurrence of the same clan names in different castes.

But whichever theory is subscribed to, all the members of a single clan ought to belong to a single *gotra*. In practice, however, different localized segments of the clan often identify themselves with different *gotras* and list a slightly different set of clans as members of their own *gotra*.

In summary, both clan and *gotra* are more accurately described as social categories rather than as corporate groups in Radcliffe-Brown's (1950:41) sense. They hold no material property in common; there are no occasions on which all their members participate in any joint activity, and only briefly during a period of upheavals in the hypergamous hierarchy (described in Chapter 8) did some Rajput clans acquire leaders and a council representative of the group as a whole.

5:3 Sub-clans and lineages

A localized segment of a clan – those clan members who live in a single hamlet or a group of adjacent hamlets – I shall call a sub-clan. In population the sub-clan may number as many as six or seven hundred persons, though at the other end of the scale it might consist of a single household. Normally it is only with this group of agnates that an individual has much contact. In spite of the ideal theory, two different sub-clans of the same clan may, as we have seen, worship a different *kulaj*, claim membership of a different *gotra*, and call on different clans of Brahmans as their *purohits*.

In some cases the clan and the sub-clan are coterminous since all recognized clan members live in a single group of adjacent hamlets. In other cases, the sub-clan consists only of a shallow lineage which traces descent from a recent ancestor who first settled in the locality. Most sub-clans, however, are made up of one or more maximal lineages, defined as the most extensive group of agnates between whom precise genealogical links can be traced. These are in turn segmented into less inclusive lineages by reference to more recent ancestors. Maximal lineages display a certain variation in depth. In the case of the Rajputs and Brahmans they generally consist of those agnates who are descended from a common ancestor between five and eight generations removed from the present set of household heads. In other castes they tend to be slightly shallower.

The maximal lineage often coincides with the group of agnates who live in a single house-cluster. When a joint household partitions, a new house will eventually be constructed as close as possible to the old one, with the result that a man's nearest neighbours are typically also his closest agnates, and spatial distance within the house-cluster is commonly a rough measure of genealogical distance. But although members of the maximal lineage are usually members of the same local group, this is not invariably the case. Precise genealogical links are only likely to be remembered between distantly related agnates who belong to the same sub-clan, however, since ties of neighbourhood give rise to joint interests and frequent interaction.

For this reason distant agnates who live in the same house-cluster may have much closer ties than relatively close agnates who live in different house-clusters. The Manhas Rajputs of the hamlet of Matial, for example, belong to two different maximal lineages which are said to have migrated to Chadhiar at different times and from different places. The sub-clan segments of the *lambedar* and of Captain Gian Chand belong to the same maximal lineage but reside in different house-clusters separated by a patch of waste ground no more than thirty yards wide. All the members of the other maximal lineage live in the same house-cluster as Captain Gian's lineage segment. Even in the matter of birth and death pollution, the latter treat these other Manhas of their *narar* as if they were closer agnates than the members of their own maximal lineage who live in the *lambedar*'s house-cluster.

The term *al* refers to a nickname or title applied to a clan or clan-segment of any generation depth. Some *als* derive from a notable characteristic of a structurally significant ancestor or from the office he occupied. Others derive from the name of the place in which the clan-segment resides, or from which it had originated. Thus the sub-clan itself, and/or its constituent lineages, may be known by an *al*, though the majority are not named groups at all. As I will explain in Chapter 9, the manipulation of *al* names is part of a much-used strategy for social climbing within the clan hierarchy of the hypergamous castes.

The people themselves may describe either a clan, or a small-scale lineage, or any intermediate grouping of agnates as a *khandan*. The distinctions that I have drawn between the clan, sub-clan and maximal lineage are only therefore those of the observer. My use of this sequence of conventional anthropological labels also requires the caution that the technical terms normally denote all the agnatic descendants of a given ancestor and these alone; while the *khandan* includes wives and excludes married daughters and sisters. At marriage a woman is transferred to her husband's clan and *gotra*. Before her marriage she rates as a *dhi* to her natal clan, but after marriage she becomes their *dhyan*.

A married woman never entirely renounces her moral right to the help and protection of her parental household (her *piochiyon*), however. They observe mourning for her death and her brothers have their heads shaved by the family Barber at *kapar-dhuai* (literally 'washing the clothes') which they hold on the seventh day and which marks the end of their pollution. But the responsibility for performing the mortuary rituals and for making offerings to the departed falls on her *sohriye* (her father-in-law's household) who celebrate *kapar-dhuai* on the tenth day, when all the men of the *khandan* who are junior to her husband have their heads shaved. Ideally it is her son who is the chief mourner, but in the absence of a son her husband may perform the obsequies. *Kapar-dhuai* is also held on the tenth day for a *dhi* of the *khandan* as for a male agnate. In the first case all men of the girl's own generation and of junior generations have their heads shaved irrespective of relative age.[5] In the second case, only those younger than the deceased in his own generation (plus men of junior generation regardless of age) have their heads shaved.

People who are of one *khandan* are *gret*, which I translate as 'patrikin' (with the proviso that it includes wives and excludes married daughters). Those *gret* who are genealogically close are distinguished as *succa gret*, or 'real' *gret*. But the closest agnates of all are categorised as *srik*. The range of clan members described as *succa gret* or *srik* depends a good deal on the context, and on the advantages and disadvantages of the connection. While a highly placed individual – a clerk, an army officer, a schoolmaster – may be claimed as *srik* though he comes from a different maximal lineage or even a different sub-clan, the epithet is unlikely to be applied to a close but disreputable lineage 'brother'.

Although far less commonly used than *khandan*, the term *kutumb* also refers to a segmentary grouping of patrilineal kinsmen. But while *khandan* describes a descent group of any order of segmentation, *kutumb* generally refers to the less inclusive orders. The widest group of agnates which is likely to be described as a *kutumb* is the maximal lineage, but more commonly the term applies to a lineage of narrower span. It never includes the non-agnatic cognates and affines of the Malwa *kutumb* (Mayer 1960:170; cf. Gupta 1974:47).[6]

For Malwa, Mayer (1960:169) draws a sharp distinction between the 'lineage of co-operation', those agnates who attend each other's social functions, and the 'lineage of recognition' which 'is based simply on recognition of a previous agnatic link'. No such distinction is possible in the Kangra case since the 'lineage of co-operation' varies widely according to context. Marriages and other major life-cycle rituals require the participation of a wide range of agnates, perhaps even of the whole sub-clan. But on lesser occasions – birthdays, *pujas* to particular deities, and so on – only one's nearest agnates are involved. The number of such occasions which are celebrated and the range of kinsmen invited will obviously depend on the state of the household's finances.

A sub-clan may emerge as a political faction, or as one of the constituent units of a political faction. At election time there is likely to be strong pressure on sub-clan members to display their solidarity by voting as a block, and this pressure is particularly strong if the sub-clan itself has a candidate in the field. When a candidate is standing from a constituency which includes members of a number of different sub-clans of his own clan, he can count on winning a substantial proportion of their votes by appealing to a wider clan loyalty.

But agnates are not invariably political allies, and the ideal unity of the sub-clan is often disrupted by competing property interests, or by the bitter legacy of such competition. Many of these disputes stem from quarrels over the division of the joint estate. Others begin with accusations of encroachment on each other's land, a major cause of conflict between close agnates, who tend to own neighbouring fields. But whatever the cause of the acrimony, close lineage kin with a long-standing quarrel sometimes give allegiance to rival factions. In the 1967 General Elections and the 1964 *panchayat* elections, there were a few defectors from even the most united sub-clans. But despite a handful of renegades, it is still broadly true to say that most members of the sub-clan tend to belong to a single faction, and that the basic pattern of Chadhiar factionalism is one of competition between loose coalitions of Rajput sub-clans and their dependants.

I have already noted that the maximal lineage tends to correspond to that group of agnates who live in a single house-cluster. All the households of such a group will probably be invited to send a representative on the marriage party (*janet*) of a groom of the lineage, and will have *bartan* with each other: that is, they attend the most important life-cycle rituals in each other's houses, make reciprocal gifts of money and cloth on these occasions and may lend a hand with the preparations. An individual will also have *bartan* with a wide range of non-agnatic kin, and with friends and neighbours.

A man's close patrikin are polluted by birth or death in his household. Birth pollution (*sutak*) and death pollution (*patak*) last the same number of days. As a rule of thumb it is said that Brahmans are purified on the eleventh day when the *panjap* ceremony releases them from *sutak* and *karam-kriya* from *patak*. Other castes celebrate *panjap* and *kriya* on the thirteenth day; but for those below Rajput this is a recent innovation, and the high castes consider that they should all, except the Traders, properly wait until the twenty-second day (though the conventional Shastric formula is that as Shudras they are polluted for thirty days). It would, however, be more accurate to say that these rituals terminate the period of quarantine for agnates outside the afflicted household, and mark the end of a phase of severe pollution within it. Impurity has a tendency to decrease over time and there are, as Dumont and Pocock (1959:14) note, 'successive "ends of mourning", each marked by a certain diminution of impurity'. The intensity of pollution also depends, as we shall see, on what Orenstein (1970) calls 'the proximity of kinship premise'.

The ideal is that no person of clean caste should eat with somebody who is contaminated by *sutak* or *patak*. Their impurity makes it inappropriate for them to approach the gods, and consequently they should not participate in any auspicious ritual. In practice, only orthodox Brahmans and high-caste widows refuse to eat with those affected by *sutak*, and I never heard of any important life-cycle ritual being postponed on account of a birth in the lineage, though the parents of the new-born child would be debarred from playing any role in the ritual itself. *Patak* is taken less lightly, however, and there would be strong pressure to postpone a marriage if there had been a recent death within the maximal lineage. Birth pollution, then, seems to be less polluting than death pollution, and consistent with this, it is in some cases observed by a narrower range of agnates.

For example, a Manhas woman of the *lambedar*'s house-cluster had a child in hospital in Delhi. Mata Ji was at the time preparing to perform Hariali *puja* which commemorates the marriage of Siva and Parvati, and all the Manhas women had been invited to participate. Those of the *lambedar*'s house-cluster now had to decline the invitation; but most of the women of Captain Gian's house-cluster felt that it was perfectly proper for them to attend because, they reasoned, the birth had been in hospital. One or two of the older women saw this as a piece of special pleading, however, and stayed away. When Lachman Manhas died there was, by contrast, absolutely no question but that all the Manhas of Matial were afflicted by *patak*.

During *patak* those who meticulously observe the regime of mourning sleep on the floor, take only one meal in the day, and abstain from any kind of 'hot' food. They should not wash, shave or have sexual intercourse. The women wear no jewellery and put on a *ghaggri*, a long full-skirted dress worn on all sacred occasions, instead of everyday clothes. These restrictions are lifted for everybody but the household of the chief mourner at *kapar-dhuai*, when all the mourners take a purificatory bath and wash their clothes, and when the male mourners have their heads shaved if they are junior to the deceased, and their beards shaved and hair cut if they are his seniors. The *khandan* does not celebrate the first festival after the death.

Neither my observations of actual behaviour nor people's ideal statements of the rules allow me, however, to isolate a substantive pollution-cum-mourning group to whom all these restrictions apply. The rule is formulated as a requirement that all members of the *khandan* should mourn; but the segmentary level of *khandan* to which this precept applies is never clearly specified. In practice some sub-clan members punctiliously observe the whole gamut of proprieties, some content themselves with the decent minimum, while others ignore the death altogether. My impression is that the more visible the symbol of mourning the more widely it is observed (the exception being that some white-collar *babus* regard a shorn head, the most visible sign of all, as the epitome of ridiculous rusticity and therefore search for any excuse to absent themselves from a *kapar-dhuai* which they are not absolutely required to attend).

This kind of variation is not, however, simply a matter of individual whim. 'Relational' pollution incurred at birth and death is treated as if it were to some extent proportional to the individual's proximity to its source and the more distant the agnate the less binding his obligations are felt to be. Only those descended from the same father's father's father (*pardada*) are expected to be very literal-minded about the whole set of rules. Beyond this range their observance has an increasingly optional quality. While most members of the maximal lineage will purify themselves at *kapar-dhuai*, this does not mean that they are all expected to modify their diet or spend uncomfortable nights on the floor. More remote agnates of different maximal lineages of the same sub-clan may shave their heads for an elderly and respected figure, or for a member of a rich and powerful household, while the death of a closer but less consequential agnate – or of an agnate with whose household one has a quarrel – may go unnoticed.

According to the classical theory of the Sanskrit texts, death pollutes a bilateral grouping of *sapinda* relations who are defiled by virtue of sharing the same body particles as the deceased. Not all *sapinda*, however, are equally affected. Orenstein's 'proximity of kinship premise' refers not only to the tendency we have just encountered for relational pollution to decrease with genealogical distance, but also to the fact that an inequality of 'normal' pollution weakens the bonds of kinship between *sapinda* and thus shortens the period of mourning prescribed. So, for example, children start out less pure and are therefore less mourned by adults; but as the gap is closed by purification at successive *rites de passage* they are mourned for longer periods. Or again, *sapinda* of different *varna* mourn for shorter periods than those of the same *varna*. But there is an asymmetry here, for 'the reduction in duration of pollution for the lower *sapinda* on the demise of the higher is disproportionately smaller than the other way round' (Orenstein 1970:1367; cf. Tambiah 1973b:211).

In line with classical theory, and indeed with Hertz's (1960:84) general proposition that children have not yet fully entered society and that there is therefore 'no reason to exclude them from it slowly and painfully', the death of a small child entails only the most attenuated mourning. In Kangra an infant of less than 22 months (some people say 27 months) is buried and not cremated. No *pind* (flour balls) are offered to the departed spirit, no *kriya* is performed, and the mother alone is afflicted by *patak* – and then only for a period of five days. The principle that an inferior is more polluted by the death of a superior than vice versa is perhaps reflected in the relative stringency of the purification required on the death of a senior agnate. As we have seen, a junior agnate may remove the *jutha* of his senior, and this suggests that he is relatively less pure. Consistent with this, a more thorough purification – expressed by shaving the whole head – is necessary on the latter's death than would be called for on the death of a junior agnate. Though it more properly belongs to the subject matter of Chapter 10, I note in passing that the same principle is even more clearly reflected in the extent of the mourning observed for members of wife-giving and wife-taking lineages. For a married sister or father's sister, *kapar-dhuai* is celebrated after seven days, and for their husbands on the fifth day. The death of one of these superior individuals obliges one to be tonsured. But for inferior wife-givers like the wife's brother or mother's brother, *kapar-dhuai* is held after only three days, and there is no obligation to shave.[7] By contrast with *patak*, which to this extent afflicts non-lineage kin and affines, *sutak* does not appear to spread outside the *khandan*: it falls – as my informants put it – on the mother's *sohriye* and not on her *piochiyon*.

As we have already seen with regard to mourning, those patrikin who are the descendants of a common great-grandfather (*pardada*) share a special sense of identity; and this identity is stressed in a number of other contexts (cf. Madan 1965:81; Sharma 1973:87; Pocock 1973:17; Tiemann 1970). Offerings are made to the ancestral spirits of one's male and female patrilineal ascendants up to and including the father's father's father and mother.[8] According to one school of thought, only agnates within this range have ever had unconditional reversionary rights of inheritance in each other's ancestral property in preference to other categories of kin. I elaborate on this statement in

Chapter 6:4; while in Chapter 7 I try to show that the rules of exogamy, and one of the prevalent theories about the genetic make-up of the child, again single out the great-grandfather as an ancestor of major structural significance. In this context it is also worth noting that the formal kinship terminology – that is, the terminology of reference – covers a range of three ascending and three descending generations from ego's own generation. On ritual occasions a group of close agnates, typically those descended from a common *pardada*, may symbolically be identified in some obvious and striking way. When accompanying a boy's marriage party, for example, the men who are most closely related to him will wear distinctively coloured identical turbans.

The senior members of a small-scale lineage – again characteristically defined as those descended from a common *pardada* – can invoke the ancestral curse (*pitr kop*) against any member of a junior generation who flagrantly fails to fulfil his kinship obligations. Its result is that the victim suffers a whole series of misfortunes, ranging from the loss of livestock to continual poverty, or even disease and death in his household. On all this there is general consensus; but what people are less clear about is whether *pitr kop* can be given only by a senior living agnate or whether dead ancestors can curse too. There is also disagreement as to whether the curse can be removed after the death of the offended agnate. The majority view is that only a living agnate can pronounce *pitr kop* and that there is no undoing its effect once he or she is dead. *Pitr kop* is only effective against one's *gret* and cannot touch an affinal or uterine relative. Hence a married father's sister can neither curse her nephew nor remove her brother's curse, since she loses full membership rights in her natal lineage once she is married.

An individual is held to be so closely identified with his nearest agnates that supernatural forces may not discriminate between them. When Rattan Singh quarrelled with, and assaulted, one of his tenants, the tenant is said to have invoked the Leather-workers' deity, Chano Sidh. Chano Sidh did not punish Rattan directly, however, but first attacked his son's wife and then his father's brother's son's son. In the same way death itself may treat close agnates as if they were interchangeable. During the period of my fieldwork, old Prema was predeceased by two much younger members of his lineage. At the time of the second death there were mutterings that both men had been taken as surrogates for Prema, who obstinately clung to life though he had outlived his allotted span.[9]

By way of anticipating a more detailed discussion in the next chapter, I note here that neither the sub-clan nor the maximal lineage holds any corporate property; though popular sentiment would generally accord any member of the maximal lineage a reversionary right to inherit in preference to non-agnatic kin. Actual co-owners of undivided property are almost invariably the members of a single domestic group. But in some rather rare instances brothers may continue to manage their land jointly after they have set up independent households. In the case of land which has been given out on tenancy, the shares of the co-parceners may occasionally remain undivided between more distant agnates, with the result that all the households of a small-scale lineage may sometimes have a joint interest in certain fields. Those agnates who live in a single hamlet may be associated – together with people of other castes and clans – as right-holders in the wasteland of the *tika*. But title here does not derive directly from a genealogical charter. It is now contingent on being a resident of the hamlet, while formerly it derived from the ownership of arable land located within the *tika* boundaries.

5:4 Clan-segments, deities and shrines

I noted earlier that in theory clan members share a common *kulaj*, or clan deity; but that in practice a clan-segment sometimes owes allegiance to a whole set of deities, and that the set of deities worshipped by one clan-segment only partially overlaps with that of another clan-segment. In some cases this multiple allegiance reflects a pattern of segmentary opposition between clan-segments and mirrors important cleavages in the internal structure of the clan. Segments of a single clan which are united in their common allegiance to a single deity are simultaneously differentiated by reference to the shrines at which they worship this deity, and sometimes by reference to other deities to whom they owe allegiance. The pattern is best illustrated by a concrete example.

The only two sub-clans of Kanthwal Rajputs in Palampur sub-division are those of *mauzas* Chadhiar and Khera, though there are also Kanthwals in other parts of the district. In Chadhiar the 52 households of the sub-clan belong to 5 separate maximal lineages which are concentrated in 4 neighbouring hamlets. Four of the maximal lineages are characterized by an *al* name which is supposed to have been acquired by the lineage's founding ancestor. The members of these four lineages are known as Bakshis (Paymasters), Wazirs (Ministers), Roos (Strong

Men) and Vaids (Ayurvedic Doctors). The members of the fifth maximal lineage – the Kanthwals of *tika* Khooh – do not possess an *al* and are just plain Kanthwal.

The Bakshis, Wazirs, Roos and Vaids claim to be the descendants of the first Kanthwal to settle in the *mauza*, while the Kanthwals of Khooh are reputed to belong to a different branch of the clan and to be later immigrants to the area. Although no precise links are known, the Bakshis and Wazirs believe that they are more closely related to each other than they are to members of the other two *als*. Of the latter the Roos are said to be the less remote. When Bakshi Sukh Ram died, none of the Vaids or Roos mourned for him, while by contrast a number of Wazirs had their heads shaved at *kapar-dhuai*. Since there is some difference in status between those lineages and since this difference corresponds to the supposed genealogical distance between them, it seems likely that genealogical distance is in such cases merely one of the idioms in which claims about current status positions are couched.

The pattern of allegiance to clan deities and to the particular shrines in which these deities are worshipped has a structure roughly homologous to that of the clan itself. Members of the Kanthwal sub-clan of *mauza* Khera worship Balak Sidh whom they describe as the *kulaj* of all Kanthwals everywhere. But the Kanthwals of Chadhiar make the same claims for Chori Sidh, who is sometimes said to be Balak Sidh's brother and who is acknowledged by all the members of the sub-clan as their 'true' *kulaj*. Allegiance to two other deities, however, divides the Chadhiar Kanthwals into two blocks: the Bakshis, Wazirs, Roos and Vaids on the one hand, and the Kanthwals of Khooh on the other. The former worship Kapalmani Sidh, the latter Roi Shoi.

In the congregations of the different shrines dedicated to Kapalmani Sidh we find a reflection of a further series of structurally significant discriminations between sub-clan members. Located on the periphery of one of the Wazir house-clusters is a small stone temple to the deity, and it is here that both the Wazirs and the Bakshis make their offerings on all the most important ritual occasions. On less significant occasions, however, the Bakshis worship at a small shrine in their own house-cluster. The Vaids and Roos have their separate shrines and do not attend the temple where the Bakshis and Wazirs worship. The Vaid lineage have a single shrine of their own, and up until a few years ago so did the Roos. These days, however, two Roos lineages – each descended from a different great-grandfather – worship at two different Kapalmani Sidh shrines. The second of these was built within the last few years after a peculiarly bitter land dispute between the *gret*.

I should emphasize, however, that this neat pattern is not repeated throughout the hierarchy, but seems to be associated with the larger and more affluent Rajput sub-clans of the higher *biradaris*. Less elevated groups often do not appear to identify strongly with any particular *kulaj*; and when members of the same sub-clan volunteered alternatives this seemed to reflect the lack of any firm opinion on the subject rather than the kind of consistent segmentary pattern displayed by the deities and shrines of their superiors.

5:5 Deference within the sub-clan

Deference is due to all members of the *khandan* who belong to a senior generation. Within a single generation the order of precedence between siblings of the same sex follows age. A real or classificatory elder brother (*barka bhau*) is one's senior and should be respected; a younger brother (*halka bhau*) is one's junior and must pay respect. In the royal Rajput clans those collateral lines of descent most closely related to the ruling line are lent a certain lustre by their genealogical proximity to the raja. But there is nothing so systematic as the 'principle of sinking status' described for the Balinese Gentry (Geertz and Geertz 1975: 124-31) or the Tswana royals (Schapera 1950, 1957), whereby lines descended from brothers of more recent kings are consistently ranked above lines descended from brothers of earlier monarchs. Amongst commoners there is obviously no mileage to be extracted from proximity to a line of succession, and there is absolutely no notion that the whole of an elder brother's line is senior to the whole of a younger brother's line.[10] Respect is due to those who are older in age or senior in generation. Where these two principles conflict, as for instance when a classificatory 'father's brother' is younger than his 'brother's son', it is the generation principle which counts. Whatever their relative ages it is the 'brother's son' who owes formal deference to his 'father's brother'.

The principles which govern the expected pattern of deference between real or classificatory siblings of opposite sex are less straightforward. As one would expect in this hypergamous milieu, gestures of respect and subordination are appropriate to a married sister whether older or younger. But an unmarried sister seems to be defined as an inferior in certain contexts and as a superior in others. On the one hand she – along with all other women of the *khandan* regardless of generation – can remove the *jutha* of her brother. But on the other hand the brother touches her feet on a number of symbolic occasions or after a period of separation, and shaves his head in mourning for her death whether she is older than him or not. This respect may perhaps be seen in the light of the fact that she is destined for higher things, for she will marry a man whose status is defined by the very existence of the transaction as superior to that of her brother. But it also has to be understood in the context of the aura of sanctity which surrounds all pre-pubescent girls and which makes them an appropriate gift (*dan*) to a superior. *Kanya puja* ('virgin worship') is performed at almost all auspicious rituals. Offerings of cloth, consecrated food and money (*kanya puja di avarni*) are made to an odd number of small girls – typically five or seven – who may be recruited from inferior castes but who are nevertheless described as *kanya devis* ('virgin goddesses') and worshipped as divine. Because they are themselves *devis*, pre-pubescent girls do not touch the feet of the family *purohit*, and may, until their menarche, minister to the household gods (*thakurs*).

In certain symbolic contexts a man should make obeisance to the wives of all agnates who are senior to him, and is offered obeisance by the wives of those who are his juniors. Amongst themselves the wives of the lineage are ordered by reference to the seniority of their husbands, and not by reference to their own ages. Thus the husband's elder brother's wife (*jethani*) is superior to the younger brother's wife (*darani*) whether she is older or not. So completely does a woman become identified with her husband's status that she acquires a feminine form of the honorific title by which he is addressed. For example, the wife of a clerk (*babu*) will be called *babuani*, of a sergeant (*havaldar*) *havaldarni*, of a schoolmaster *masteraini*; while the wife of an army officer may eventually be placed on the dizzy pinnacle of *Mem Sahib*. At the time of Ajit Singh's promotion to Lieutenant, however, his wife's meteoric rise provoked only mild ridicule. When one of their agnates grandly announced in the Post Office that *Mem Sahib* would be along soon for some stamps, a member of the company quizzically muttered: '*Mem Sahib*? *Mem Sahib*? Is that the little girl who was yesterday reading in the ninth class?'

Regardless of their relative ages, a wife of the lineage is always inferior to her husband's real or classificatory sisters (her *nanan*). When a young bride returns home for the first time after her marriage she is made to stand in a square purified with cow-dung (a *chauka*) and is worshipped as a deity by her brother's wives. Indeed the husband's sister, or his father's sister, may sometimes be addressed as *Devi Ji* as though an incarnate goddess. By sitting in strict order of seniority at *dham*, the final meal of the wedding just before the guests depart, the women of the group act out for the benefit of a wide audience the whole order of precedence between themselves, and by implication between their husbands. (Widows are excluded from the *painth*.) It is significantly an unmarried sister of the groom who takes pride of place at the very head of the line.

There are a large number of ways in which an individual expresses deference to senior lineage kin, and many occasions on which he is expected to do so. He should never appear before a senior male agnate without some head-covering (except at death when the younger men go bare-headed to the cremation ground and elders cover their heads); while amongst people of high caste his wife should never appear unveiled. As a consequence many Rajputs of 'good' *khandan* report that unless they chance to hear her speak they are quite incapable of recognizing the wife of a close younger agnate if they encounter her away from home. When two *gret* meet after one of them has been away from home for a time, the junior touches the feet of his senior; and on all ritual occasions the chief celebrant will touch the feet of all senior lineage kin who are present. Though in reality often impractical, the ideal is that a younger brother should never build a new house at a higher elevation than that of his elder brother. The ruins of a substantial building on the crest of a hill in *tika* Doli are said to be those of a mansion which was razed to the ground by an irate Rajput incensed by his younger brother's temerity in ignoring this courtesy. At the *seri* festival a man presents walnuts to senior members of his *khandan*; and as we have seen he may remove the *jutha* and must shave his head on the death of a senior.

Again, superior agnates should be greeted first, are never addressed by their personal names but always by a kinship term or by an honorific, and the respectful second person plural pronoun *tussan* is employed. Juniors are called by name and addressed with the familiar second person singular *tu*. (A younger sister is *tu* before her marriage and *tussan* after it). For a wife of the lineage the rules of address are still more exacting, for there is an absolute ban on pronouncing her husband's name, or the name of any of his senior agnates. Even words which resemble her husband's name should ideally be dropped from her vocabulary. If, for example, her husband is called Pancham, she should never use the word *panch* meaning 'five' but always signify the number as 'four plus one'. No child may be given the same personal name as any of its senior kin who are descended from the same great-grandfather (cf. Karve 1965:129; Stevenson 1920:14).

All these symbolic gestures of subordination will, I hope, have a familiar ring about them, for there is little here that has not already cropped up in the context of my discussion of other sorts of relationship between individuals of unequal status. We have seen, for example, that house-tenants should never appear before their landlord without some form of head-covering, should touch his feet, present him with walnuts at *seri*, be tonsured on his death, and avoid giving their children the same name as any member of his lineage; and that the same gestures of subordination are theoretically due from a *kamin*. We have also seen that the expectation that inferiors should not build their houses at higher elevations than their superiors, and that the regulations governing the disposal of *jutha*, the exchange of greetings and the use of honorifics have their counterparts in the realm of inter-caste relations. As I point out in the next chapter, even the domestic group is invaded by the hierarchical principle; while in subsequent chapters I show that the asymmetrical status of affines is again expressed in precisely the same idiom. The general point is that just as the axiom of inequality pervades the spheres of caste and class relations, so it pervades the spheres of agnatic and affinal kinship, and is expressed in the same symbolic language throughout.

6 Households and their partition

6:1 The decay of the joint family system

Until comparatively recently there was a widespread assumption – deriving partly from an evolutionist perspective and partly from a functionalist one – that a modern economy is incompatible with an extended family structure. The extended families of 'traditional' societies were thought to be disintegrating under the impact of industrialization and urbanization; and change was assumed to be in the direction of the sort of elementary family typical of industrial Western society. Different writers suggested different reasons why this should be the case. Parsons, for example, argues that a modern economy demands a mobile labour force and that the type of family best adapted to this requirement is 'an isolated conjugal family which (is) not bound to a particular residential location by the occupational, property, or status interests of other members' (Parsons 1949:189–90). Other versions of the same general theory stress the occupational diversification which accompanies the new economy, and which creates disparate interests among the members of the extended family (e.g., Linton 1952). It is felt that this puts an intolerable strain on the unity of the group and almost inevitably leads to its dissolution.

Where extended families have demonstrably persisted in the context of industrialized urban communities, there has been a tendency to see them as an example of the obdurate persistence of traditional values and, by implication, of an almost perverse conservatism.

Adopting this sort of approach, a number of students of Indian social life have discerned a current undermining the Hindu joint family and have cited evidence of its decay. Amongst the earliest of these is

Mandelbaum (1949), and his general view is reiterated by Ross (1962). But in the Indian context the argument has been presented most forcefully in the monographs of two Manchester anthropologists (Bailey 1958; Epstein 1962).

Bailey notes a distinct trend towards the disintegration of joint families in Bisipara. Now they are the exception where previously, he says, they had been the rule; and this he attributes to a diversification and expansion of the economy. Before the village had been drawn into the wider economy all the members of a joint family were engaged in subsistence agriculture. But as the economic frontier expanded, new opportunities for earning an income outside the subsistence sector presented themselves. As cultivators the members of the joint family worked as a team, but in the commercial economy many of them now participate as individuals.

> Whatever the rivalries and tensions between brothers their economic interest is directed to the same end – making the estate produce as much as possible. But when one brother gets an income from trade and another is a policeman and a third is a carter and the fourth and fifth remain on the land; and when the trader and the policeman and the carter refuse to put their earnings into a common pool, as they are permitted to do in certain conditions; and when they demand a share in the estate so that they may sell it and use the money to finance other undertakings – then all the brothers are glad to partition and go their own way. The joint family cannot survive divergent interests and disparate incomes among its members (Bailey 1958:92).

Epstein (1962) also interprets her material to suggest that the joint family is fast disappearing in the two Mysore villages she studied. But against Bailey she argues that the root cause of this is not economic diversification *per se*, but an extension of the cash economy. One of the villages she describes has experienced little in the way of diversification. Rather an apparently rapid decline in the number of joint families has gone hand in hand with the switch from subsistence to cash crops. Her argument is that:

> If a cash crop is introduced into a society of subsistence farmers holding estates on the basis of joint families, the conversion of the subsistence into a cash economy will necessarily produce competition between the component families and lead to the breaking of wider kinship ties (Epstein 1962:178).

While there was little scope for initiative or competition in the subsistence economy, competition accompanies incorporation into the market economy.

> The new opportunities to earn cash induce young men to seek independence from the parental productive unit; they want to be able to work and save money for new equipment or such items as watches and bicycles, or to buy jewellery and costly saris for their wives (Epstein 1962:177).

A good deal of the more recent literature, however, cites evidence which opens the way to a radical reappraisal of such hypotheses. The empirical basis for generalizations which posit the inevitable decay of 'traditional' kinship organization when confronted with a modern market economy turns out to be, at best, rather shaky. Many of those who have studied the effects of far-reaching economic changes on tribal communities in Africa have – like Watson (1958) and Hill (1963) – been more impressed by resilience and continuity of kinship institutions than by any evidence of change.

In the Indian case, there is now a substantial body of material which suggests the widespread prevalence of joint families in an industrial urban environment, as well as in villages which produce cash crops or which have highly diversified economies. Today few students would feel confident enough to go all the way with Mandelbaum's bold generalization of 1949 that the joint family

> is more characteristic of rural than of urban families; of the upper and wealthier strata of society than of the lower and poorer strata, of the more orthodox sectors than of those which have taken over western traits, and of Hindu than of Muslim communities (Mandelbaum 1949:93).

By contrast, Kolenda (1968) has concluded from a review of the recent literature that there is no evidence of a close relationship between caste rank and the proportion of joint families, nor any striking correlation between land-owning castes and castes with a high proportion of joint families. A study of two different neighbourhoods in Calcutta found that 58 per cent and 45 per cent of the high-caste population live in joint families, figures which indicate a higher proportion of joint families than those for comparable castes in many rural areas (Sarma 1964). Nor does Vatuk's (1972) meticulous analysis of kinship in two predominantly white-collar neighbourhoods of Meerut indicate any radical transformation in family structures; though the growing incidence of neo-local residence does necessitate new ways of caring for the aged, allows for a relaxation of the traditionally rigid separation between a woman's natal and affinal relationships, and thus promotes an increasingly bilateral emphasis in the kinship system. On the basis of his research in Howrah city, Owens (1971) has emphasized the complex nature of the relationship between industrialization and the pragmatic incentives for joint living, and has suggested that industrialization cannot be assumed to have a uniform effect on all families.

> Within the same industrial context, individual and group 'self-interest' (i.e. what was economically rational) varied widely. As a result, the economic value to an individual of living within a joint family or of making use of the authority structure and role relationships of a joint family (as the basis for a business, for example) also varied widely (Owens 1971:223).

Rao (1968) has subjected both the Bailey and the Epstein hypotheses to the test of data drawn from his own fieldwork in a village near Delhi. The most numerous caste in the village are the Ahirs, who own nearly all the arable land, a large proportion of which is devoted to market gardening. The village has been within the sphere of the cash economy since the 1920s when market gardening was first introduced. On the Epstein hypothesis one would predict a very low incidence of joint families; but in fact 56·6 per cent of households are joint. Nor is Bailey's formulation any closer to the observed facts, for of these roughly three quarters show occupational diversity of various sorts.

Rao points out that diversification of the economy may work in the opposite direction to the one predicted by Bailey, and that outside employment may provide the absentee earner with a positive incentive to remain in the joint family longer than he would otherwise be inclined. Often he will find it either impossible or uneconomic to maintain his wife and children in the city and will be glad to leave them behind in the care of his parents and brothers. What's more, partition of the joint estate would only force him to face a whole new set of problems about managing his share of the land. Madan (1965:153), Cohn (1961) and Owens (1971) make much the same point in the context of their own ethnographic experience.

Given all this evidence to the contrary, how are we to assess the reports of Bailey and Epstein that the incidence of joint families in their respective field areas is fast declining? The first point to note is that their evidence is remarkably imprecise. Nowhere, for example, do we learn how many of the elementary household heads have living brothers or fathers. In other words, we have no way of knowing what proportion of them have the option of being anything else but nuclear (Shah 1964).

Second, their analysis rests, as Shah (1964) points out, on rather doubtful assumptions about the past. The present situation, in which there is an observably high proportion of nuclear households, is viewed against a background of a past in which joint families were the rule. But the evidence for such a past is pretty scanty, and such evidence as there is, suggests that joint families were by no means universal. Several students have recently re-examined the census data, and on the basis of their work Abbi concludes 'that the size of the traditional family was small and that the strength of the norm relating to residential unity of male agnates and their wives showed wide variations' (Abbi 1969:124). Kolenda (1970) has analysed statistics collected by Surgeon Coats in 1819 in the village of Lonikand, Poona District, and has compared his figures with two recent surveys of the village. Her conclusion is that there appears to be as high a proportion of joint families at the present time as there were at the beginning of the last century.

What Bailey and Epstein fail to take into account is the fact that a normal developmental cycle will inevitably produce a certain number of nuclear families. Gould sums all this up when he writes:

> Perhaps the greatest deficiency in most early attempts to understand developmental trends in the Indian joint family was the tendency to view the family as a series or variety of static entities and then to apply to these entities criteria of change that had been devised in the context of the West's experience during the early stages of the industrial revolution; that is, Indian families were generally characterised as either 'nuclear' or 'joint', and then some statement was made about change based on the proportion of nuclear to joint families (Gould 1968:413).

But if the Bailey-Epstein thesis fails to hold good,[1] are we then to assume that the transformation of a subsistence peasant economy into a diversified cash economy is quite irrelevant to the structure of the joint family? I think not. Gould (1968), Madan (1965) and others have rightly emphasized that partition is a normal phase in the developmental cycle of the joint household. But by itself this formulation only describes the facts. As Barth (1966:2) puts it:

> Explanation is not achieved by a description of patterns of regularity, no matter how meticulous and adequate, nor by replacing this description by other abstractions congruent with it, but by describing what makes the pattern, i.e. certain processes.

In any single instance partition takes place because individuals decide that it should, and this decision is made within the context of certain demographic, economic and moral constraints. It is these constraints on choice which generate regularity or frequency in the empirical form. In general terms, Fortes (1949a) interprets the observed frequencies of household 'types' as a compromise between the competing moral demands of a man's loyalty to his lineage kin on the one hand and his conjugal family on the other. In his second Tallensi monograph (Fortes 1949b), however, he lays particular stress on economic and demographic pressures which combine with these 'structural cleavages' to disrupt the solidarity of the co-resident group of male agnates; while 'religious and jural sanctions (are chiefly responsible) for the reintegration of an expanded family' (p. 77).

Following the analytical path charted by Fortes, the present chapter attempts to understand both the composition of Chadhiar households and the timing of partition in terms of a developmental cycle model. More specifically I will try to show that decisions about partition are structured by a set of constraints imposed by an economy which relies heavily on remittances from villagers employed away from home.

6:2 The problem of definition

Discussion of the Indian joint family has been hampered, as Shah (1964) points out, by a lack of precision in the terminology. What we have to be clear about is just what makes the joint family joint, and for whom. A good deal of the analysis, however, sets out with a definition of a rather hazy multi-functional group. Thus for Karve:

> A joint family is a group of people who generally live under one roof, who eat food cooked in one kitchen, who hold property in common, participate in common family worship and are related to one another as some particular type of kindred (Karve 1965:81).

The difficulty here is that there are many instances in which groups of kin are divided into separate households yet hold property in common and participate in common rituals. Further some sorts of property may be held separately and others jointly; or alternatively rituals may be held jointly although there is no common property (Shah 1964).

To avoid this sort of ambiguity Mayer (1960:182) and Madan (1962b) have made a distinction between the property-holding and residential groups. Mayer, for example, distinguishes the joint household – defined as those who 'share a cooking hearth, pool their incomes and have living expenses in common' – from the joint family, which is 'a corporate property group of patrikin, not necessarily a discrete living unit'. In Ramkheri the division of the household is usually also the occasion for the division of the property, so that the joint family is in most cases – but not always – a joint household too. But among the Brahmans of rural Kashmir this is seldom the case. Partition of the household, Madan tells us, occurs invariably between brothers, yet 'co-parcenary rights in walnut trees, granaries and, sometimes land may exist between first (rarely second) cousins' (Madan 1962b:13).

In Chadhiar, as in Ramkheri, the division of the household is normally accompanied by a *de facto* – if not always a *de jure* – division of the land. In most but not all cases, then, the joint family and the joint household turn out to be the same set of people. But having said that, we should note that there are certain circumstances under which the property will be left intact when the household partitions. The first of these is when a son decides to set up an independent household during the lifetime of his father and in the face of the father's opposition. The father may then refuse to give him a share of the land, and the estate will remain undivided. Second, a division of the household may be decided upon after a series of quarrels between the wives of brothers. If, in spite of this, the brothers remain on good terms, they may continue to hold and cultivate their land in common. But it should be emphasized that this is an atypical solution which normally turns out to be rather short-lived.

The third case in which land may be held by a joint family which is not also a joint household is rather more complicated. When the division of the household occurs the shareholders may for various reasons – for example, the absence of one of their number in the city – be unable to decide on any permanent division of the land. In such instances the official revenue records will continue to show their land as *moustrika* (corporate and undivided property) although in practice each household will be cultivating its own share on the basis of an informal and temporary allocation. This is what I meant when I noted above that there is usually a *de facto*, if not always a *de jure*, division of the land at the time the household partitions.

But when the land is cultivated by tenants, the actual fields which constitute the joint property are likely to remain undivided for several generations, although shares in the produce of the land will be clearly specified. Under these circumstances, there is little incentive to partition the land itself, because the shareholder is primarily interested, not in who has the rights in which field, but in the amount of grains that his household receives. From the point of view of the shareholder this is a much simpler and more convenient arrangement since partition normally involves a complicated and contentious evaluation of the quality of every field; and since, now that he has legal security of tenure, it spreads the risk of being landed with an incompetent or unco-operative tenant. That part of the ancestral estate which is cultivated by tenants, then, may remain a joint holding for many years, while the rest of it will be cultivated by individual households of shareholders – though legally it may still be the corporate property of all of them.

A large amount of land in the hamlet of Dangaur is held as undivided *moustrika* by a 21-member corporation of Rajputs, descended from a common great-great-grandfather (*lakardada*). Internally, the corporation is divided into three lineages tracing descent from a common great-grandfather (*pardada*). A senior member of each of these lineages is appointed, on an informal basis, as the 'manager' of the interests of the other members. The land itself is cultivated by 20 low-caste tenants, each of whom is the tenant of the corporation as a whole. The individual tenant divides the landlord's share of the produce into three equal parts and gives one part to each of the three 'managers'. When a manager has received a share from all the tenants, he divides the total among the different households of his lineage on a *per stirpes* basis.

In ideal terms, Kangra people conceptualize the household in terms of the three criteria Mayer (1960:182) notes as characteristic of Ramkheri households. The dialect word *tol* translates as household in almost exactly this sense, and is used to refer to both the joint and the nuclear 'types' (the distinction between them being that of the observer only). It should be noted that a household does not necessarily require a separate house (*ghar* or *tabar*), and that there may be more than one *tol* in a *ghar*. As Kangra people see it, the most essential characteristic of a household is that its members should cook on a single hearth (*chulah*). The standard formula is that if there is more than one *chulah* there is more than one *tol*. They are *bak*, or 'separate'.

Those who share a common *chulah* are treated as a single unit for certain administrative purposes. The house-tax levied by the *gram panchayat* is paid by the *chulah* and not by the house, and in British days the amount of *begar* (labour service) due to the government was calculated per *chulah* and not *per capita*. Each *chulah* took its turn in the rota regardless of its size and composition (Lyall 1889:148).

But in practice things are rather more complicated than all this would imply, and my description turns out to contain exactly the same sorts of ambiguity as those which are built into the Karve definition of the joint family. When it comes down to it, it sometimes is not at all clear – even to the people concerned – just who belongs to which household. This is most obvious in the case where a man takes his wife and children with him to the city. If he does this, then it is unlikely that he will be in a position to send regular remittances to the village. In such circumstances none of the criteria definitive of the joint household (a common cooking hearth, pooling of incomes or common living expenses) will be met. Yet when the employee comes home on leave he may share a *chulah* with his brother's conjugal family and contribute a lump sum to their household funds. If a man has been away for some years without contributing significantly to the joint economy, and if his wife and children are with him, then nobody really knows quite where they stand. In a case like this, the general tendency would be to attribute joint membership to the two nuclear families unless there had been some specific decision about partition or unless the women had cooked at separate hearths when the family from outside had last returned on leave. But it is clear that in such circumstances jointness is often purely nominal, for the returning employee may well demand partition as soon as he is back in the village permanently.

Another common distortion to the ideal scheme occurs when an employee, having left his wife and children at home in a joint household with his brothers and parents, does not pool his income with them. He may do this with the consent of the other members of the household – consent which may readily be given if the household can meet its own subsistence requirements from the land or even produce a surplus for sale – or against their wishes and as a prelude to partition. In this case, then, the cooking hearth is common but the total income of the household members is not paid into a common pool.

Even if we take only the criteria of sharing a common *chulah*, a certain amount of ambiguity remains. If, for example, there is a quarrel between the members of the two elementary families which constitute the joint household, the women may start to cook on a common *chulah* at different times. In other cases a new *chulah* may be constructed, yet some members of the household may eat from either almost indiscriminately. Mangtu's mother and father's brother's wife, for example, had a violent row after which they refused to cook together, and his mother built a new hearth. But although the two women will never eat together, all the other people in the house are prepared to eat from either hearth, and in practice they often do so. The father and his brother continue to manage their land jointly and to pool their incomes. General experience, however, is that once a new hearth has been constructed things have gone beyond the point of no return, and formal partition is imminent. But while the women are cooking on a single hearth, even though at different times, the situation can still be remedied. Again, there are instances where two brothers live separately in the same area of the same city in which they are employed, but maintain a joint household at home. The general point that I am concerned to stress, then, is that household arrangements are rather variable and that their composition is not always unambiguous.

6:3 The ideal of joint living

It is a strongly sanctioned ideal in Kangra society that a man should remain in a joint household with his father. This is a binding obligation on the son because it was the father who provided for and protected him as a child. A man who initiates partition during his father's lifetime will be labelled as a moral reprobate. As public opinion tends to interpret it, partition in such cases amounts to a denial of his filial obligations, even perhaps to desertion.

Although sons also have a strong obligation to support their widowed mother, 'because she had to clean up the excrement when they were children', partition during her lifetime is not nearly such a serious matter. It is not regarded with such moral distaste, nor – as we shall see – does the mother control the material sanctions which the father can use to buttress the unity of the household. As a result, partition during the lifetime of a widowed mother is much less of a drama and is more common than partition during the lifetime of the father. The death of the father then, has much greater structural significance for the developmental cycle of the household, than that of the mother (cf. Madan 1965:64).

But although it is not especially shameful for brothers to divide the household during the mother's lifetime, people would take a decidedly dim view of them if they were to leave her to live by herself. Normally she will join up with the son with whom she gets on best, but in rare instances she might take turns to live with each of the newly independent households for a few months at a time. Among the 472 households in my census of 8 Chadhiar hamlets, there were just three cases in which a widow was living alone although she had one or more sons with whom she might have lived. There was one other instance in which a man had separated from his childless and widowed stepmother. But people did not find this partition so surprising or shocking as those between real mother and son, since the cultural stereotype for the relationship between stepmother and stepchild is one of mutual hostility.

If the father had remained in the same household as his brothers and their children, his sons may be expected to continue the arrangement until the death of the men of the senior generation. But it is the death of the father which is really crucial, and after this it no longer creates a scandal if his sons go their own ways, though the ideal is that they should remain joint. It is sadly recognized, however, that brothers rarely stay together once their own children are mature. The pressure on cousins to maintain the joint household once their seniors are dead is much weaker, and in fact there is only one such case among the 472 households of my census. Madan sums all this up when he writes:

> As we move from the parent-child (father-son) to the sibling (brother-brother), to the cousin relationships, the ideal of joint living becomes gradually weaker as a cultural compulsion, and personal interests and the interests of those who are closer (as against the interests of those who are remoter) kin gain ascendance (Madan 1962b; cf. Fortes 1949b:68).

During the sacred thread ceremony the novitiate goes in turn to beg from each of his assembled kin. Because the mother is a loving and indulgent figure she is the first person he is expected to approach. A son can sit and chat with his mother. They can laugh and joke together.

By contrast, the stereotype of a father is of a rather stern, authoritarian and remote figure who must be treated with the greatest deference and respect, and who must be obeyed even in matters which, like the choice of his bride, concern the son most intimately. In certain contexts there is an element of avoidance in the relationship. For example, the groom's father may not sit near his son under the marriage booth (*ved*) to eat the wedding feast (*dham*). At the time of his birth the

1 Thatched houses of an Untouchable house-cluster

2 Untouchable woman harvesting

3 A Brahman kitchen

4 Preparing 'roti'

5 A Brahman at home

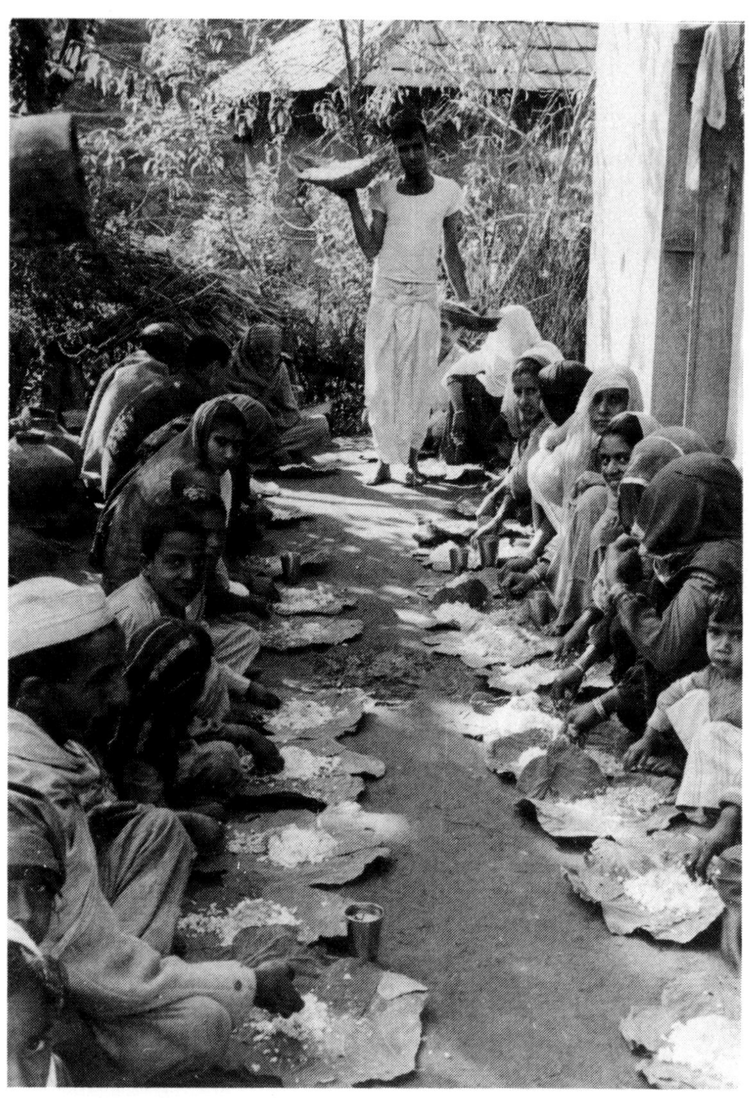

6 Feeding the relations at a sacred thread ceremony

astrologer (*jyotshi*) may discover that the son is a *tungu*, an inauspicious child who is 'bad' for his father, and may even be the involuntary cause of his death unless appropriate measures are taken. As a precaution a period of total avoidance will be prescribed, during which the father may not even set eyes on his child. There is something incongruous about paying elaborate deference to a man in the presence of his father. At *chabarakh* on the fourth anniversary of death the chief mourner makes gifts (*nimantran*[2]) to, and worships, an odd number of Brahmans (typically thirteen). On one such occasion I recall a lengthy debate about whether Pt Gyan could be the recipient of these attentions in the presence of his father, the *purohit*. Since the family were hard up they were naturally not averse to receiving the *namintran*, but others present insisted on the impropriety of worshipping the son in front of his father. The outcome was a characteristic compromise. Gyan received the gifts, but some sacred *drub* grass was worshipped his place.

Although the son may be a grown man with children of his own, the pattern of deference will remain substantially unmodified. As time goes on he may take more and more of the day-to-day management of the house and the fields into his own hands, but all the important decisions should still be referred to his father. In theory, if not always in practice, it is not until the father's death that a man can become an independent householder.[3]

Even after his father's death a man is not entirely free of his filial obligations. He must perform the lengthy and costly mortuary rituals which are completed only on the fourth anniversary of the death. For the rest of his life he must make offerings to his father's spirit at *kanyaktu* or *solha saradh*, which takes place each autumn during the 'fortnight of the ancestors' (*pitr paksh*) when collective offerings are made to his forebears; at *maritu saradh* celebrated on every anniversary of the death, and at *nandi mukh saradh* which precedes every important life-cycle ritual in his house. He should fast on the day of the month when his father died and every time he eats rice he should put a little aside in token offering to his father's spirit.

The relationship between elder and younger brother is also a highly asymmetrical one.[4] Even very old men are apt to take a high-handed and authoritarian line with brothers a few years younger than themselves. In many symbolic contexts the elder brother is identified with, and treated as though he were, a member of a senior generation. Just as one should never smoke in front of one's father, so one should not smoke in the presence of an elder brother; while all the other forms of deference noted in the previous chapter as appropriate towards senior lineage kin apply automatically to the elder brother. Again, the ideology of *kanya dan* ('the gift of a virgin') prevents a high-status Rajput or Brahman from eating in the house of his married daughter, or married younger sister. The identification between the elder brother and the father is once more reflected in the kinship terminology, for the younger brother's wife belongs to the same category as the daughter-in-law. Both rate as *nunh.*[5]

Aside from the pressure of public opinion and a highly structured superordinate-subordinate relationship between father and son, the father controls two important sanctions which he can use to maintain the unity of the joint household. The first of these is supernatural. As we have seen (Chapter 5), he can threaten a disloyal son with *pitr kop*, the ancestral curse. The second, and perhaps more important, of his sanctions is a material one. The Hindu Code Bill of 1948 gives him the right to dispose of his property as he likes. In other words, he can exclude a recalcitrant son from the inheritance; and, in fact, I recorded a number of instances in which fathers had done just that. But these were cases which achieved a certain amount of notoriety, and such drastic action was not the norm. Just as often fathers would make the best of a bad job, recognize the inevitability of the eventual division of the estate, and acquiesce in it.

Despite the ideal theory, partition between father and son is in practice by no means unknown. In Table 15, I have categorized the relationship between the heads of the new households resulting from 126 cases of partition drawn from the 8 hamlets of my census. These figures refer to the partition of households and not to the partition of estates. While in most instances the two took place simultaneously, this was not invariably so. It might also be noted that in many of these cases partition did not mean that all the constituent families of the joint household split up to form independent units. In a case, for example, where three married brothers partition their household, two of them might decide to remain joint while the third sets up on his own. In 35 (28 per cent) of the cases in the table the split had been between father and son; while in another 75 cases (60 per cent) it was between brothers. But out of the 35 father-son partitions, 21 concerned low-caste households, nearly all of whom were completely landless. In 8 out of the 14 cases involving high-caste households (all of them Rajputs) the undivided property amounted to less than two acres. The evidence, then, suggests that a high incidence of this type of partition is correlated with

TABLE 15 *Relationship between the heads of the newly independent households in 126 cases of partition*[1]

Relationship	*Rajput*	*Brahman*	*Temple priest*	*Leather-worker*	*Koli*	*Girth-cultivator*	*Barber*	*Weaver*	*Jogi-ascetic*	*Total*
Father/Son	14			7	11	2		1		35
Brothers	34	3	3	11	17	2		4	1	75
Widow/Deceased Husband's Brother	2									2
Brother's Son/ Father's Brother	2				2		1	1		6
Cousins	1				1	1				3
Widow/ Parents-in-law	1									1
Stepmother/ Stepson	1									1
Mother/Son	1				1			1		3
Total	56	3	3	18	32	5	1	7	1	126

[1] Two points which may affect the validity of these figures should be noted. First, these cases cover a considerable time span. Some of them took place as long as thirty years ago, though the majority of them are much more recent. Second, the table includes all the cases of partition from these hamlets for which I have the relevant details in my notebooks and on census forms. It does not represent a rigorously devised random sample.

landlessness or very small holdings; and conversely that the stability of the joint household during the father's lifetime is associated with his control of the land.

I have described all the cases of household fission in Table 15 as 'partition'. But where the decision to break up the joint household of father and son is a unilateral one, and where the father refuses to give his son a share of the property, it has – from the actor's point of view – a very different character, as well as different consequences, from cases in which the split occurs between brothers. Seen from their point of view, such cases are often more accurately described as 'desertion' (by the son) or 'expulsion' (by the father). Although it is usually the son who initiates the move, occasionally an exasperated father will turn his son out of the house and refuse to give him any land. Ajit Singh – like most of the Manthwal Rajputs in Chadhiar – is a member of the Congress faction which is headed by his fellow clansman, an ex-Minister of the State cabinet. When his son Karam Chand became an active worker for the Communist party, Ajit Singh told him never to darken his doors again, and refused to allocate him a share of the land.

6:4 The rules of inheritance

Medieval commentaries on the *Smrtis* set out two different principles for the devolution of property. The essence of the Dayabhaga system of the texts is that a man's heirs acquire their rights only by virtue of his death. During his lifetime they have absolutely no rights in his property, and the owner has complete freedom to do exactly what he likes with it. He can give it away, or sell it, and there is nothing that they can do about it. All his property is of the same kind and there is no distinction between the property which he inherited and the property which he acquired himself.

All this is in radical contrast to the Mitakshara system. Fundamental to this system is a distinction between self-acquired and ancestral property. By contrast with the Dayabhaga rule that the heirs only acquire their rights on the death of the owner, the basic principle here is that they have rights in the ancestral property from the moment of their conception. This difference generates a number of other differences. It means that ancestral property is held in common by a man and his descendants as co-sharers, and any one of them can demand partition at any time. The members of the senior generation are trustees rather than absolute owners of the joint property, and have no right to sell or give away the joint capital to the detriment of the other shareholders. But a man has full rights of ownership over his self-acquired property and can dispose of it as he likes (Karve 1965:341ff).

Before the introduction of the Hindu Code Bill in 1948, the inheritance rules in Kangra corresponded broadly – though with certain important modifications – to the ideal-type Mitakshara system set out in the medieval texts. In line with the Mitakshara rules, a distinction was made between ancestral property, or *jaddi*, and self-acquired property, or *jar kharid*. The *jar kharid* of the original owner became the *jaddi* of his heirs. *Jaddi* had to be passed on in an almost mechanical way to a man's heirs, and his rights to sell it, or give it away, were limited by their claims. Consistent with the Mitakshara notion that a man acquires rights in the ancestral property from the moment of his conception, a son born to a widow within a year of her husband's death was presumed to be legitimate and was entitled to inherit. By contrast with *jaddi, jar kharid* could be disposed of as its owner liked either by will (*vasiyat*) at his death, or by deed of gift during his lifetime (*hewa*). But in the absence of any specific provision to the contrary, *jar kharid* would be allocated in the same way as *jaddi* when he died.

The first in line to inherit were a man's legitimate sons. If a group of brothers were sons of a single father by different mothers, then the property would be distributed according to the rules of *chundabandh* or *pagbandh* (cf. Pettigrew 1975:240). The etymology of these terms provides the clue to their meaning. *Bandh* is the root of the verb *bandhna*, 'to divide'. *Chunda* and *pag* derive from the words for a woman's head shawl and a man's turban respectively. *Chundabandh*, then, is a (uterine) *per stirpes* division, and *pagbandh* an (agnatic) *per capita* division. Suppose, for example, that a man had married twice, that by the first wife he had only one son and that by his second wife he had four sons. If the *chundabandh* system was followed, the ancestral property would be divided into two halves. The only son of the first wife would get one half, and the other half would be divided equally between the four sons of the second wife. But if the division was according to the rules of *pagbandh*, then each would get an equal share irrespective of his mother. *Chundabandh* was followed by the vast majority of the population; *pagbandh* only (so far as I know) by some royal Katoch sub-clans and by Gosains and Gaddis. During the British period there seems to have been a good deal of dissatisfaction with the *chundabandh* system, and several castes tried to change over to *pagbandh* (Kangra District Gazetteer, 1926:139; Middleton 1919a:53).

If a man's sons died before him, and if the estate had not already been partitioned, then their sons (if any) would inherit direct from their grandfather. In such cases, the shares of the grandsons would be calculated on the basis of the shares which their respective fathers would have received, had they been alive. In other words, the size of their shares bore no relation to the total number of grandsons (cf. Middleton 1919a:64).

At least on the face of it there seems to be a certain contradiction between the ideal-type Mitakshara system of the texts – which implies a high degree of equality between the shareholders in the joint estate – and the highly asymmetrical and inegalitarian relationship between agnates of successive generations which exists throughout most of patrilineal India, and which demands the absolute subordination of a man to his father. It might be argued that this contradiction is more apparent than real since the inheritance rules are concerned with the level of legally enforceable jural rights, while the ideal of strict subordination of the son to his father relates to the level of moral obligations. But it seems to me that this formulation does not dispose of the problem but merely restates it. The fact remains that there is an uncomfortable incongruence between their jural equality as co-shareholders, and the inequality that is held to exist between them on another level.

I suggest that this conflict accounts for, and is resolved by, an important departure which the traditional Kangra inheritance system made from the ideal-type Mitakshara rules. Although the son had an indisputable right to inherit his share of the ancestral property on his father's death, and there was nothing that a father could do to exclude him, he could not enforce the partition of the joint estate during his father's lifetime without his father's consent (cf. Middleton 1919a:161; and Tambiah 1973a:77, who notes that popular opinion has always been averse to a son exercising his theoretical right to sue for partition). If he did insist on setting up a household independent of his father, and against his father's wishes, then the latter could refuse to allocate him a share of the property, though the son would still be automatically entitled to inherit his full share at his father's death. By this device of holding the son's right to claim his share of the ancestral property in abeyance till his father's death, the jural rules of the Kangra inheritance system reinforced the son's moral obligation to live in the same household as his father.

In the same way as there is an in-built contradiction between the equality implicit in the ideal-type Mitakshara system and the highly structured superordinate-subordinate relationship between father and son, so there is a degree of conflict – though far less marked than in the former case – between the idea that the elder is superior to the younger brother, and the rule that all the sons of the same mother are equal when it comes to inheritance (cf. Mandelbaum 1970:64). Again the strict equality between shareholders in the Mitakshara system is compromised in Kangra customary law, for the respect due to the eldest brother may receive symbolic recognition at the time of partition by the payment of *juthunda*. If the partition is amicable then the eldest brother may receive an extra, though usually nominal, share of the inheritance as *juthunda*. At most, however, this is his moral right – a right which has never been legally enforceable. *Juthunda* has always represented a minute fraction of the total value of the estate. In the richest families it may consist of a field or two, but in the case of the less well off it is unlikely to be more than a cow or a few utensils. Even in the past, however, *juthunda* was in practice very seldom given, and today many people have never even heard of the custom.

Unlike the father, a widowed mother had no material sanctions by which she could maintain the unity of her sons' joint household, since her rights in the deceased husband's estate were only those of maintenance and she could not obstruct the inheritance of the sons. Her claims to both the *jaddi* and the *jar kharid* of her deceased husband were of a limited and conditional nature. If a man had no sons, or sons' sons, then his widow could dispose of her husband's movable property as she liked. But her rights over his immovable property were much more limited. She could not sell any part of the estate but only mortgage it temporarily and then only for certain special reasons: to pay off her husband's debts, to meet the land revenue demand, or to finance a daughter's marriage. In such cases the widow had first to offer the mortgage to those right-holders (*hukdars*) who were in line to inherit the property after her death, and only if they refused could she alienate to an outsider. Among the aristocratic Rajputs and the Brahmans, her rights were conditional on her chastity. In all castes they were conditional on her not remarrying and on her continuing to live in her deceased husband's house. The widow of a man who had predeceased his father would inherit as the representative of her deceased husband, though again only on the same limited and conditional basis (Middleton 1919a:65).

In the Dayabhaga schema of the texts, non-agnatic kin are mixed with agnates in the order of precedence amongst the heirs. The Mitakshara system, on the other hand, is more consistently agnatic, though it compromises strict patrilineal principles by allowing a daughter or a daughter's son to inherit in preference to a collateral (Karve 1965: 348, 353–5; Tambiah 1973a). The Kangra inheritance rules went even further than the Mitakshara rules in their agnatic bias, for – as far as ancestral property was concerned – close collaterals were always preferred to married daughters or daughters' sons.[6] An unmarried daughter had conditional rights in her father's estate identical to those of a widow, but these rights lapsed on her marriage, with – as my high-caste informants stressed – the payment of her dowry (cf. Tambiah 1973a). She could, however, inherit full title to the *jar kharid* of her father if there was a will in her favour; but in the absence of such a document this land too would go to the heirs of the ancestral property.

If the deceased left no sons, sons' sons, or sons' sons' sons, then the property would be inherited by his nearest lineal ascendant or the latter's heirs. In the absence of a direct line of male descent, then, the deceased's heirs in order of priority were his father, brothers, brothers' sons and their sons; followed by his father's father, father's brothers, father's brothers' sons and their sons; followed by the father's father's father and those descended from him.

From the historical literature, however, it is not at all clear how far this principle should be taken before agnates became too remote to inherit, and precedence was given to a daughter or a daughter's son. According to some of the sources (Kangra District Gazetteer, 1926: 143; Cunningham 1932:87; O'Brien 1900), the inheritance of ancestral property did not automatically pass to collaterals who were descended from an ancestor more remote than the father's father's father of the deceased. A manual of Kangra customary law (Middleton 1919a:95), on the other hand, records that a daughter would only be eligible if there were no male agnates who shared with the deceased a common ancestor no more remote than seven generations; though it notes that some people put the limit at five generations. The District Gazetteer (p. 143) provides yet another theory: that any agnate, no matter how distant in genealogical terms, should inherit in preference to a daughter or a daughter's son. My own informants were no more precise or consistent about the exact limits, though the ideal was held to be that a daughter should never take precedence over a collateral of the sub-clan. This lack of precision is not perhaps so puzzling as it might at first sight appear, for in the pre-British period – as we saw in Chapter

2 – all land theoretically reverted to the raja on the death of the holder and he could therefore set the limit wherever he liked. In practice, the only pre-1948 cases I recorded in which a non-agnate had inherited in preference to an agnate concerned *ghar-jamwantru*.

The term *ghar-jamwantru* ('a son-in-law of the house') refers to a man who marries uxorilocally on the understanding that he will inherit his father-in-law's property.[7] A father with daughters but no sons, and with land to inherit, is likely to marry one of them to a *ghar-jamwantru*. The latter's inheritance prospects from his own father are typically poor and his position in his wife's house is a rather inferior one. Not only does he bear the stigma of poverty, but he is also likely to be accused of abandoning his own parents in the pursuit of a purely selfish material advantage. Another difficulty with which the *ghar-jamwantru* has to contend is that he is considered a usurper by his father-in-law's agnates, whose hostility can be taken for granted.

In my census of eight hamlets of Chadhiar there were two men who were living in their father-in-law's house as *ghar-jamwantru*, and four others who had already inherited his estate. In none of these instances did the father-in-law have sons. In two of the four cases in which he was already dead, the rights of the *ghar-jamwantru* had not been challenged – in one case simply because there were no collaterals, and in the other because there was very little land to squabble about. In the other two cases, however, there had been open and bitter hostility over the inheritance.

As a result of the Hindu Code Bill, the Kangra inheritance system has – on paper at least – changed radically since 1948. In both the ideal-type Mitakshara rules and the modified Kangra version of them, the basic premise is that a man holds his ancestral property in trust for his male lineal descendants, who become co-sharers from the moment of their conception. By re-defining the trustee as the absolute owner, the Bill cuts right at the roots of the system, and it is transformed into something which corresponds much more closely to the Dayabhaga model of the texts. Because all property is now owned absolutely, the distinction between that which is ancestral and that which is acquired has become irrelevant. Both can be disposed of as their owner likes and the son no longer has the unconditional right to inherit his father's ancestral estate. It seems likely that the effect of this has been to strengthen a father's authority over his sons, and thus to contribute to the stability of the joint household during the father's lifetime.

If a man dies intestate, the legislation provides a set of rules very different from those which governed the traditional system. His estate is divided on a *per capita* basis between his sons, daughters and widow, the daughters and widow inheriting rights of the same kind as the sons, and not just the temporary and conditional rights to which they had been limited in the pre-1948 system. Since all of the deceased's children are entitled to equal shares, the *chundabandh* system of dividing the property has become obsolescent. If there is no widow, and no sons, sons' sons, or daughters to inherit the deceased's property, a daughter's children or her children's children inherit in preference to the deceased's brother or brother's sons. Uterine kin, like the mother's brother, take preference over distant collateral kin. The effect of all this, then, is to destroy the agnatic bias of the traditional Kangra system.

These, at any rate, are the formal rules, though every effort is made to ensure that they aren't actually applied, for the Hindu Code Bill is the most bitterly resented piece of legislation which has been thrust upon Kangra since Independence. What goes most against the grain is the provision by which a married daughter inherits on the same basis as a son. Not only does this deny what are considered to be the legitimate rights of the collaterals in the ancestral estate, but it is also said to sow dissension between a brother and his sister. People sadly recognize that between themselves brothers have always had conflicting interests in their father's estate. But under the old inheritance rules this element of potential rivalry and competition is held to have been totally absent between a brother and sister. In ideal theory the intensity of this relationship and the mystique which surrounds it is only rivalled by the mother–son relationship. It should be one of pure affection and mutual respect bordering on the reverential, and should be completely unsullied by any material considerations. But the Hindu Code Bill is said to create divergent interests between them and so to put the realization of this ideal in jeopardy.

In order to forestall the possibility of daughters inheriting along with their brothers, many men now make wills. When the deceased has not left a will, it is not regarded as being in the least bit immoral to forge one in favour of the sons. Where there are brothers to inherit, moral opprobrium attaches rather to the daughter and her husband if they claim her legal share in the patrimony. Because of the pressure of public opinion and because of the possibility of making or forging wills, it is still rather uncommon for a daughter who has brothers to inherit a share of the ancestral property. But the pressure on a woman to renounce her claims in favour of anybody else will be far less strong; and though in abstract people will always assert the superior moral rights of even distant collaterals, in practice it is nowadays the daughter who is – in the absence of sons – the more likely to inherit. Since the chances are that she is married some way from home, and since recent legislation means that a share-cropping arrangement does not offer particularly attractive returns unless the landlord is on the spot to coerce his tenants into paying over the odds, there is a strong probability that the land inherited by a daughter will eventually be sold.

As far as my analysis of the timing of household partition is concerned, the key points about the inheritance rules which ought to be kept in mind are: that full brothers have equal jural rights in the ancestral estate; that paternal half-brothers may either inherit on a *per stirpes* or a *per capita* basis (depending on their caste or clan); that recent legislation has given daughters the legal right to a share in their father's estate; and that the father has a powerful material sanction against disloyalty in his children. Under the old inheritance system, it was only through the father that the sons had access to land during his lifetime. By re-defining the trustee of the ancestral property as its absolute owner, and by giving him the right to dispose of it as he likes, the Hindu Code Bill has further strengthened his hand.

6:5 Household composition

With a view to presenting my data in a form which can be readily compared with as much of the existing Indian evidence as possible, I have adopted – in Table 16 – Kolenda's twelve categories to classify the 472 households of my census (Kolenda 1968). Of the total number of households 40 per cent, accounting for roughly 30 per cent of the population, live in nuclear families consisting of a married couple and their children. Another 28·3 per cent of households (with 48 per cent of the population) are joint families of various sorts. The rest of the sample consists of households in various intermediate stages of growth or dispersal.

Only a small proportion (5·9 per cent) of all households contain non-lineage kin; and the actual number of individuals who do not belong to their households either by virtue of being agnatically related to the household head, or by virtue of being married to a man who is so related, is only about 1 per cent. Table 17 shows the incidence of particular types of relationship between these non-lineage household members and the household head. Broadly speaking, they fall into two

TABLE 16 *Household composition*

Caste	Brahman	Temple priest	Rajput	Blacksmith	Goldsmith	Barber	Potter	Girth-cultivator	Koli	Jogi-ascetic	Weaver	Musician	Leather-worker	Total number of households	%	Total population	%
1 Nuclear	3	7	75		1	1	1	7	49	2	12		31	189	40·0	908	29·7
2 Supplemented nuclear	4	1	31			2		3	18	1	4		8	72	15·5	443	14·5
3 Sub-nuclear	1		19			1		4	11		3		4	43	9·1	163	5·3
4 Single person	5		11		1				4		1	1	2	25	5·3	25	0·8
5 Supplemented sub-nuclear	3		2							1	1			7	1·5	34	1·1
6 Collateral joint			9	1				1	1				1	13	2·75	135	4·5
7 Supplemented collateral joint		1	17						20		2		3	43	9·1	515	16·8
8 Lineal joint			12		1				10		2		5	30	6·35	204	6·6
9 Supplemented lineal joint			3						1		1		1	6	1·3	51	1·6
10 Lineal collateral joint	2	1	14					2	5	1	1		5	31	6·6	389	12·7
11 Supplemented lineal collateral joint			3						3		1		3	10	2·1	176	5·7
12 Other	1		2											3	0·6	18	0·7

TABLE 17 *Showing the number of households containing different varieties of non-lineage kin*

Relationship to household head	*Number of households*
1 Married or widowed daughter or sister (with or without children)	11
2 Daughter's son or daughter	7
3 Uxorilocally resident son-in-law (*ghar-jamwantru*)	2
4 Sister's daughter	1
5 Mother's mother	1
6 Wife's mother	2
7 Wife's brother or sister	2
8 Wife's brother's daughter	1
9 Wife's mother's brother's daughter	1
Total	28

main categories. First, there are married daughters or sisters who have returned to their parents' or brothers' house because they have been left alone after their husband's death or because they do not get on with their in-laws. The second main category are children or adolescents who have been given to close uterine or affinal kin to foster.

6:6 Partition as the outcome of personal conflict

No ritual marks the partition of the household, though various symbolic acts announce to the world at large that it has taken place. The most obvious of these are the construction of new *chulahs*, and the separate offerings made to the ancestors by the heads of the newly formed households at the *saradh* ceremonies. (In the joint household the senior man makes these offerings on behalf of everybody else.)[8] Partition is seldom accompanied by an immediate shift to a new house; the rooms of the old house will be allocated for the exclusive use of each separate unit. In most cases, as we have seen, the land is divided at the same time as the household. Only the household deities (*thakurs*) are not divided but are taken over *in toto*, preferably by the eldest brother, but usually in fact by any of the new households which happens to have a man at home to perform the appropriate rituals.

Partition is frequently the occasion of much bitterness and acrimony, and sometimes even leads to violence. Nearly all the murders I ever heard about in Kangra were those of close lineage kin and had been foreshadowed by a series of quarrels about the division of the estate. The most contentious part of the distribution often concerns purchases made out of earnings remitted by a household member employed outside. According to customary law, such property does not belong exclusively to the man who acquired it, but is rather the property of the joint estate and should be divided like everything else (Middleton 1919a:130). But, in practice, the employee will often claim it as his own personal possession, while the other household members will insist on their equal rights. Such disputes are likely to be particularly intractable where they concern land. During the period of my fieldwork there was a case of partition in which one of a group of three brothers had worked outside, and had provided the total purchase price of a fertile plot of rice land in which the joint household had invested. When it came to partition he had insisted on its exclusive ownership. In a similar case the brother who was living at home, and who had actually negotiated the purchase, had persuaded the village accountant to enter the land in the revenue records as his own individual property and not as part of the joint estate. Both these cases wound up in court.

In partition disputes, court proceedings are usually a last resort. Partly this is because of the much vaunted ideal that close agnates should always co-operate, an ideal which at least has the effect of generating a certain reluctance to wash their dirty linen in public. But the main reason is that court proceedings are lengthy and expensive, and nobody really imagines that justice will be done. The courts are thought to be corrupt; but leaving that aside they are also considered incompetent to partition the land equitably because they cannot assess, as a villager can, the exact equivalence of two fields. In cases of deadlock, then, other villagers will generally be called in to arbitrate. Certain individuals have established reputations in this field. Generally they are elderly men with a detailed knowledge of local conditions and with a reputation for impartiality and incorruptibility. Significantly, they are almost never the men who occupy leadership positions in the official *panchayats*, or in other formal structures of power.

Partition of the joint household is almost always blamed on quarrels between the women-folk. The relationship between a woman and her husband's mother (*sas*) and sister (*nanan*) is expected to be particularly difficult and tense. But the sister will soon be married – if she is not married already – and will become an increasingly infrequent visitor to the household. Although a woman is expected to wait hand, foot and finger on her husband's married sister when she comes to see them, she can afford to put up with this, because such visits don't usually last very long. Any antipathy here is unlikely to disrupt the unity of the household seriously. Much more likely to endanger it is the relationship between mother-in-law and daughter-in-law, and I knew of several cases where the hostility was open and vicious.

Bidhi Chand's wife, for example, was on bad terms with her *sas*. One day it happened that quite by chance both of them turned up at the same time at the house where I lived. The mother-in-law insisted on sitting in a separate room until her *nunh* (SW) had gone. A short time after this, while the daughter-in-law was staying at her maternal grandmother's house and her husband was away in the military, news reached Chadhiar that her husband's sister's husband had died in hospital in Delhi. The following day all the members of the affinal household were to be purified at the *kapar-dhuai* ceremony. But Bidhi Chand's mother refused to send a message to her daughter-in-law informing her of the death. Bidhi Chand himself retired from the army a month later and, using this as a pretext, immediately demanded partition from his parents and brothers. Popular notions about women sowing the seeds of dissent between male agnates had been vindicated.

As Chadhiar people see it, the relationship which most often disrupts the unity of the joint household is that between wives of brothers. Brothers, they say, are bound together by ties of 'natural' affection, by shared childhood experiences, and by the simple fact of being 'of one blood'. But their wives come as strangers to the household and to each other, and from the outset they are apt to eye each other with suspicion. It is partly in an attempt to contain the potentially disruptive effects of this relationship that a pair of brothers will often be married to a pair of sisters.

Initially the hostility between the wives of brothers is unlikely to be overt, for a newly married bride is expected to submit meekly to the authority of her husband's mother and to her role as maid-of-all-work. Her relationship with her father-in-law (*sohra*), with her husband's elder brother (*jeth*) and with all the men of the lineage who are senior to her husband is expected to be both distant and, on her part, extremely deferential. In the early stages of her marriage the only person with whom she has a fairly relaxed relationship is her husband's younger brother (*der*), though while her mother-in-law rules the roost she may also find a natural ally in her *jethani* (HeBW). But if the mother-in-law is dead, she will be taking orders direct from the *jethani*, and until she has found her feet she will be too timid to disobey her.

During the first few years of her marriage a young bride will probably see more of her parents- and sisters-in-law than of her own husband, for the chances are high that he will be employed outside. When he comes home on leave every member of the household will drop what they are doing and go to meet him and make a fuss of him. Only the young wife will go on with her work as if oblivious to his arrival. To do otherwise would be to invite censure as a brazen hussy with an overdeveloped sexual appetite. Even if the husband lives at home contact between them is much restricted. A young wife is expected never to address her husband directly in the presence of her parents-in-law. At first, then, a woman cannot count on the blind affection of her husband. What she can reckon on is that she will be watched and judged by suspicious in-laws, and she can be fairly certain that if she picks a quarrel, her husband will side with his parents or brothers against her. But after she has borne his children she can be more confident of his loyalty and her position is more secure. It is when the wives of brothers have both had children that the greatest strain is put on their relationship. At this point each is on her guard lest the children of the other should corner more than their fair share of the joint resources. By this time too, the restraining influence of the parents-in-law's authority – if they are still alive – is probably on the wane.

Where one or more brothers from the joint household are employed outside, there may be all sorts of additional tensions between their wives. An employee who returns from the city may bring expensive presents for his wife, but it is rather improbable that he will be equally generous where his brothers' wives are concerned. If one of these brothers lives at home then his wife is especially likely to feel that she is missing out, and she may complain that her husband's brother's earnings belong to the household jointly and should not be squandered on luxuries for his wife. But when the employee is away in the city, the boot is on the other foot, for his wife will be left under the authority of his brother and she may well feel that he is discriminating in favour of his own wife by assigning her all the lightest jobs, while she herself gets all the dreariest and most back-breaking ones.

The difficulties of the *jethani-darani* (HeBW-HyBW) relationship is a theme which receives endless elaboration in folklore and folksongs. In about half the number of cases of witchcraft (*jadu*) I was told about, the accusation had been made by a woman against her husband's brother's wife – though, of course, the theory was that the witch had been named by the diviner (*chela*) she had employed, or by the spirit which had possessed her.

According to the stereotype, the relationship between co-wives (*sokhan*) is even more tense and hostile than that between *jethani* and *darani* or *sas* and *nunh*. Eight of the men of my census currently had two wives. In one case things had become so bad that the husband had to maintain a separate household for each of his wives. But as far as I could tell, popular expectations were not fulfilled in any of the other cases. In all but one of these, the second wife had been taken on after the first wife had failed to produce children, and it was even said that in two or three of these instances it was the barren first wife who had herself insisted on her husband's remarriage, and who had personally selected the bride from her natal village.

The women of the household are almost invariably made the scapegoats when it comes to partition, although my own observations suggest that this is as often an attempt to preserve a façade of solidarity between male agnates as a genuine reflection of reality; and although it is invariably the men who actually take the decision to demand partition. It is thought to be part of the natural order of things that *jethani* and *darani*, or *sas* and *nunh*, should quarrel. But quarrels between brothers flatly contradict the ideal that they should always live in harmony and should pool all their resources. This ambivalence is reflected in the often quoted saying that your brother is either your best friend or your worst enemy. The truth of the matter is not so much that the women of the household don't quarrel. It is rather that their quarrels are frequently not the underlying cause of the partition but simply a good pretext for it, a pretext which allows the brothers to sustain the fiction that even in dividing the household they are not behaving in an unbrotherly way; and which allows them to preserve some room for manoeuvre if they want to co-operate at a later stage, or are ever constrained to re-amalgamate (see below).

Within the the joint household the most common source of tension between brothers is over their respective contributions to the household economy, and the relationship that this bears to the amount that each conjugal family consumes. As I have already noted, any disparity here is likely to be seized on by the wives of brothers; but although the women probably fan the flames, their husbands are rarely impervious to such considerations. Outside employment, and the extension of the cash economy, have introduced an obvious and unambiguous measure of the contribution of each brother. This may have exacerbated the problem but, as I shall argue in the next section, these sorts of conflict are built into the structure of the joint household, even in a purely subsistence economy.

6:7 Partition: the constraints on choice

Partition is a normal phase in the developmental cycle of the household, and typically takes place between brothers after the death of their father. In their analysis of comparable situations in different parts of north India, Madan (1965:167–8) and Gould (1968), taking their cue from Fortes (1949a) have seen partition as the outcome of the conflict between the fraternal bond on the one hand and the conjugal and parental bond on the other. This general line of approach seems to take into account a good deal of the Kangra evidence. A man's marriage creates for him a new focus of interest and responsibility and is the point at which his interests begin to diverge from those of his brothers. This is, perhaps, symbolized by the dowry given at the marriage ceremony, which in theory belongs exclusively to the newly married couple and not to the joint household, and which forms the nucleus of the property of their own individual household (cf. Tambiah 1973a). After his wife has borne him children, a man finds that more and more situations arise in which he is forced to choose between the competing demands of his conjugal family and those of the joint household as a whole. In personal terms, such conflicts often force individual men to face a grave crisis of divided loyalties. People recognize this clearly, and the suicide of a neighbour of mine was widely attributed to a series of rows with his wife and brothers in which each had made insistent but incompatible claims on him. Usually such conflicts are eventually worked out, if not resolved, by partition.

Looked at on a broad time-scale, joint households never survive. Sooner or later collateral joint households are partitioned between brothers or cousins. Lineal joint households either revert to nuclear households after the death of the father and mother or as a result of partition, or expand into collateral joint households in subsequent generations and are eventually partitioned. At this level of objectivity, neither problems of adjustment between individual personalities, nor the constraints which pattern choices about the precise timing of partition, are relevant to understanding why partition occurs. Whatever the constraints on choice in any particular case, and however good or bad the personal relations within any particular joint household, the fact remains that no joint household goes on forever. Seen on a broad canvas, the ultimate reason for this is adequately contained within the orthodox formula that household fission is the inevitable outcome of the opposing pulls of a man's loyalty to his conjugal family on the one hand and to his father and brothers on the other.

But clearly none of this gets us very far if we want to understand how it is that different households split up during different phases of their growth. In other words, it does not explain why partition sometimes occurs between father and son, sometimes between brothers and sometimes between cousins; or why some brothers split up immediately after the death of their father while others go on living in a joint household many years after this event. Although personalities undoubtedly come into it, such decisions are not, I suggest, a purely random outcome of individual whims or of a man's sudden realization that he can no longer face the prospect of living at such close quarters with his brother. The crux of the case I shall argue below is that these individual decisions conform to a pattern which can only be understood in the light of a set of material constraints imposed by the employment and inheritance prospects of men, and by the marriage strategies of fathers *vis-à-vis* their children.

The first and most obvious of the constraints which limit a man's options about the timing of partition is the right of his father to exclude him – temporarily under the old inheritance rules and absolutely under the provisions of the new legislation – from a share in the property. In line with this we find, as I showed earlier, that in nearly all the cases in my census where the division had been between father and son, it had involved people who were either landless, or who had only very small amounts of land.

The division of labour between the sexes also limits the range of possible options about when to set up an independent household. Broadly speaking, women do most of the household chores like cooking, cleaning and fetching water and firewood. The men plough and also do the heaviest of the labouring tasks. There are also all sorts of jobs – like, for example, cutting grass, reaping, and breaking up the sods after first ploughing – which are performed indiscriminately by either sex. At least, that is the position in most castes, though in the past the rules of *purdah* absolutely prohibited aristocratic Rajput and superior Brahman women from doing any sort of work in the fields. (By providing the landlord with a positive inducement to cultivate his own fields, recent tenancy legislation has gone a long way towards undermining this prohibition, although something of the prejudice still remains.) In the lower castes, however, there are no tasks of a technical nature – except ploughing – which are the exclusive preserve of a single sex. But in spite of this relatively flexible division of labour, a household without at least one adult member of each sex is unlikely to be viable, since in practice most men can't cook and most women have no experience of managing the land.

Death, disablement or serious illness may deprive the household of all its able-bodied men or all its women, and the result of this may be that it won't be able to meet its own minimal labour requirements. Under such conditions it will either have to recruit new members, or employ labour on a wage basis, or possibly re-amalgamate with the household from which it had originally split off. If there are no men, a daughter may sometimes be married off to a *ghar-jamwantru*. But it is more likely that labour will be hired to cultivate the fields. A well-to-do household which has been left without women may employ a young girl, or an impoverished Brahman, as a cook. But the less well-off will probably take an adolescent daughter of a close kinsman as a foster-child, or arrange for the marriage of one of the men. In my experience, it is quite common for a man to remarry, or for a father to advance his son's marriage by several years, in order to meet an unexpected demand for more labour.

When I first knew Biswa Nath, for example, his household consisted of his wife, his adolescent daughter, and his three sons aged between sixteen and twenty-two. At that time his daughter was already engaged, but he was in no hurry to find a wife for his eldest son. When his own wife unexpectedly died shortly before his daughter was due to be married, however, the question of his son's marriage became a matter of some urgency and was hastily arranged. Khiali Lohar was faced with a similar problem when his wife had to have her arm amputated in hospital. After the operation she was unable to manage her household duties, so Khiali took her sister as a second wife.

But although many households go through periods when they are temporarily unviable in terms of their minimum labour requirements, and although most of them get by somehow and sooner or later recruit new members to redress the balance, few men would choose to initiate partition under such conditions. An unmarried man, then, is extremely unlikely to press for the division of the joint household. I recorded a number of cases in which a group of three or more brothers had partitioned whilst the youngest was still unmarried. In every one of these cases he had opted to join the household of one of his elder brothers, and had remained in it at least until his own marriage.

I noted earlier that a common cause of dissent between brothers is over their relative contributions to the joint economy, and that this is often acute where one or more of them is employed outside. Bailey observed this in Bisipara and it led him to postulate the breakdown of the joint family under conditions of economic diversification (Bailey 1958). But as a number of other students have recognized (e.g., Cohn 1961; Madan 1965:153; Owens 1971), outside employment may also provide the employee with a powerful incentive to remain in his joint household. Kangra people see this clearly, and sometimes consciously use it as a device to keep the household intact by sending a fractious son or younger brother out to the city to earn his living and cool his head.

Living in a joint household is not only considered to be a moral duty which one owes to one's close agnates, but it is also explicitly recognized that in certain contexts it is also a matter of self-interest. From the point of view of a man who is employed away from home, it has a number of advantages. The army seldom provides married quarters for the lower ranks, so it will not usually be possible for a soldier to take his wife and children along with him. The cost of living in the cities is high, and suitable family accommodation expensive and hard to come by, so the civilian employee may find himself in much the same boat (cf. Owens 1971). But anyway, if he leaves his wife and children in the village, they can live – partly at least – off his own land, and his wife can be productively employed in subsistence agriculture. Most men, however, are reluctant to leave their wives to shoulder all the responsibility for looking after the children and managing the land. It is thought, too, that a woman needs a male guardian to protect her honour. Her brother probably lives too far away to be of much use here, and an unrelated friend could not be trusted with such a delicate matter as a wife's honour – nor gossip to put a charitable interpretation on his interest.

If an employee sets up an independent household he is likely to face a problem about how his land is to be cultivated in his absence. Until recently the obvious solution was to give it out to tenants. But the new tenancy legislation, which increases the difficulty of evicting a tenant and reduces the landlord's share of the crop, has made this a rather unprofitable business, and has added enormously to the attractions of joint living for the man employed outside.

For him, too, the joint household is thought to provide some sort of an insurance against unemployment and for everybody an insurance against sickness and old age, though my later analysis will suggest that it would be unwise to bank too heavily on the readiness of members of other segments of the joint family to subsidize one's own segment indefinitely.

Joint living makes for economies of scale, for if a family is to set up on its own as an independent unit, it will have to make a substantial outlay to duplicate many of those household items it had previously shared. Two water-buffaloes, two pairs of bullocks and two ploughs may be needed where previously there had been one. For some it also makes capital investment in land or in some small-scale enterprise possible (see Chapter 3:2, above). Two of the electrically-powered flour-mills and several of the shops in the vicinity of my home had been started with cash remitted by brothers employed outside.

In addition to these material incentives to maintain a joint household, there are other non-material but no less important considerations to be taken into account. For example, there is the protection of one's political interests and the maintenance of *bartan* exchanges with neighbours, friends and a whole range of kin. In a joint household the brother who remains at home fulfils the *bartan* obligations of the whole household. But after partition each new unit will have to look after its own obligations separately, and this may be rather difficult for a man employed outside. The consequence of failure is social isolation.

While a man is employed outside, then, he has strong incentives to maintain the unity of the joint household, and during this time the opportunities for quarrelling with his brothers are probably rather limited. Consistent with all this is a typical pattern in which employees remain within the same joint household as their brothers just so long as they are working outside, and initiate partition shortly after returning to the village. In Table 18a I have classified the households of each 'type' according to the number of members employed outside. Table 18b is an abstract of this showing the same information for joint households only. Of these last, only 3 out of the total of 133 households do not have at least one member employed outside. Not only do these figures seem to contradict Bailey's argument that outside employment is incompatible with joint living, but they also seem to suggest that precisely the reverse is true, and that many joint households would not be joint were it not for the fact that they have men employed outside.

Looking at it cynically, what does the man who remains at home while his brothers go out to work, get out of all this additional

TABLE 18a *Number of households with 0–5 members employed outside*

Type of household	*Nil*	*1*	*2*	*3*	*4*	*5*	*>5*
1 Nuclear	81	98	7	3			
2 Supplemented nuclear	18	43	10	1			
3 Sub-nuclear	11	22	9	1			
4 Single person	24	1					
5 Supplemented sub-nuclear	5	2					
6 Collateral joint	1	6	1	3	1	1	
7 Supplemented collateral joint	1	11	21	7	2	1	
8 Lineal joint		15	10	4	1		
9 Supplemented lineal joint	1	5					
10 Lineal collateral joint		1	20	4	3	2	1
11 Supplemented lineal collateral joint		1	5	1	2		1
12 Other	2	1					

TABLE 18b

	Nil	*1*	*2*	*3*	*4*	*5*	*>5*
Joint households	3	39	57	19	9	4	2

responsibility? For a start he probably receives fairly substantial cash remittances, and it may well be that he needs these to buy enough grains to feed his own wife and children. Furthermore, while his brothers are employed outside he will be taking the total produce of the undivided land. Although the conjugal families of the employees will probably be drawing on this common stock, the employees themselves will not, and so his own share will be larger than if he lived independently. This advantage may be so great that those left at home may think it worth their while to maintain a joint household even if the employees send back no money at all.

The household represented in Figure 1 is a case in point. It is one of the largest and also one of the richest in my census. Ranjit Singh and Kashmir Singh both live at home while Pratap Singh is a taxi-driver in Delhi. But in spite of earning extremely good money, these days he never contributes a pie to joint household funds, and I happen to know that he has a secret Post Office savings account into which he makes regular payments (a common ploy for a man who wants to hold out on his joint family and hang on to his individual earnings). Pratap Singh's wife and Ranjit Singh's wife fight like cats, and one day after some particularly trying scene between them, Ranjit Singh was complaining

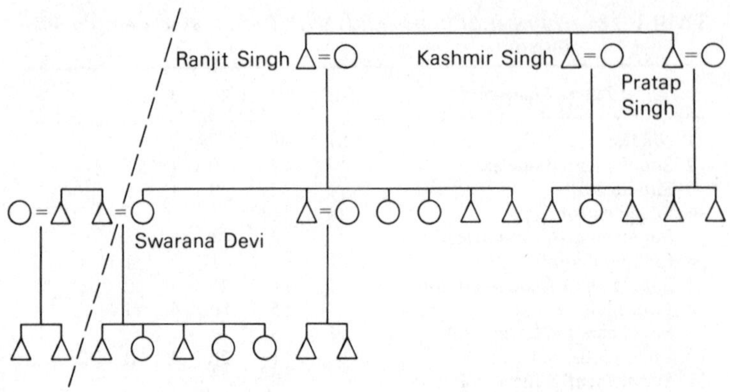

FIGURE 1 *Household of Ranjit Singh*

to me about his difficulties. When I asked him why he didn't demand partition, he explained – after the usual preliminary statement of one's duty to one's brother – that he would lose out badly if he did so. If the three brothers split up, he would be left to feed sixteen people on only a third of the land. But as it is, his segment of the household is, in effect, being subsidized from the land of the other two brothers. The crucial point to note here is that although shares in the land are owned on a *per stirpes* basis, the produce of the land and the other income of the joint household is distributed on the principle of 'to each according to his needs'.

But in this particular instance there were two conditions which made it worth Ranjit Singh's while to keep the joint household intact. First, there was a significant amount of land to partition. Had this not been the case, then it wouldn't have been to his advantage to feed Pratap Singh's wife and children, and to put up with the continual bickering of the women, while Pratap Singh contributed nothing to the common funds. Second and more importantly, it would not have been in his interest to remain in a joint household with Pratap Singh had the size of their conjugal families been more evenly matched.

Where these two conditions do not prevail, and where the employee fails to contribute to the common funds, partition is likely to take place. From Figure 1 it will be seen that Ranjit Singh's married daughter and her children are living as part of his household. The son-in-law is comparatively well-educated and has a post as a clerk in Bombay. Until recently he lived in a joint household with his brother and the latter's wife and two children. But the son-in-law is a drinker and a few years ago he completely stopped contributing to joint household funds. Between them they had little land and the brother soon objected to doing all the work and to subsidizing Swarana Devi and her five children from his own share. He demanded partition and, since her husband hardly ever came home and never sent her any money, Swarana was forced to bring her children to live at her father's house.

Theoretically it would have been within Ranjit Singh's rights to have refused to let his daughter come back to live with them but he could only have done so at the expense of his own good name. But by taking her in he must have known that he was putting the unity of his own joint household at risk, since his brothers were likely to resent this additional drain on their resources. Now it so happens that Pratap Singh stopped sending remittances from Bombay only a few months after Swarana and her children had turned up on her father's doorstep. Though I couldn't say for sure, I strongly suspect that these two facts are not unrelated. On my return to Chadhiar I learnt that at Pratap Singh's instigation the household had been formally partitioned in 1971.

Case material like this raises a general point about Bailey's diversification thesis. As he sees it, outside employment raises fundamentally new questions about the equivalence of the contribution of each brother to the common fund. My own view is that this sort of tension, although perhaps exacerbated by outside employment, exists independently of it, and is inherent in the fact that different segments of the family have different birth rates. In other words, the fact that brothers tend to have unequal numbers of sons is by itself enough to raise the question of the equivalence of their respective contributions. Take Figure 2, for example. If A and B have equal shares in a joint estate, then A and his sons will be contributing a larger amount of

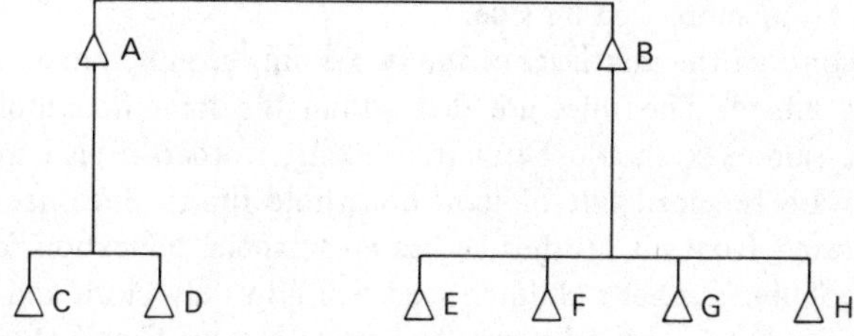

FIGURE 2 *Situations leading to a disparity of contributions*

capital per head than B and his sons. But in a joint household situation B's segment will be consuming the larger share. If land is the scarce resource, and if A is interested in maximizing his economic pay-off, his optimum strategy will be – all other things being equal – to initiate partition. But if labour is scarce and land plentiful, then A's advantage is to be joint and B's advantage is to partition. Of course, in practice all other things are probably not equal; but that does not affect my general point about inequivalence being in the nature of things.

In any particular case this very simple model will have to be complicated to take account of a whole range of different variables which affect the strategy of when to partition. In the Kangra case, for example, even assuming that people ruthlessly pursue their material advantage, the straightforward mechanical functioning of this model will be distorted by outside employment. Still considering Figure 2, A's material interest – given the enormous population pressure on the land in Kangra and the scarcity of grains – lies in partition if all of the men of the household are living at home. But if E, F and G go to work outside, earn good money and contribute regularly to the household expenses, it may then be to A's advantage to remain joint. Not only are he and his sons benefiting from the cash which is coming in in the form of remittances, but they are also consuming a substantial share of the grains which would have gone to feed the three employees had they been at home. In this situation it may even be advantageous for B to initiate partition; and this is especially likely to be the case where the total landholding of the joint household is small. But when E, F and G come back to live in the village permanently, the balance will again be altered decisively, since the income from outside will dry up and since B's segment will then be consuming more than A's. At this stage A's material interests will again be maximized by partition. The general point here is that the balance of advantage shifts over time and depends on the amount of land owned by the household and the number of men in each sibling group employed outside.

If we now consider the marriages of the two sibling groups, a new set of variables is added. The rules are that within the joint household siblings of the same sex should be married in strict order of age, and that marriages are financed out of joint household funds. But once a man has separated from his brother he has no financial obligation for the marriages of the brother's children, and will give only cloth and a comparatively small amount of money as *bartan*. Now if C and D are older than any of B's sons, then A's interests will best be served by sticking with his brother B until they have been married and partitioning before E gets married.

So far I have considered only all-male sibling groups, and have simplified the picture by disregarding the fact that orthodox individuals of high caste are expected to give large dowries when their daughters are married, while low-caste fathers generally demand a bride-price payment. Now if the household shown in Figure 2 are Rajputs or Brahmans, and if C and D have three sisters for whom dowry payments will have to be made, then there will be an even stronger incentive for A to maintain the joint household until after his daughters have married. B's interests, on the other hand, will dictate that he demand partition, since he will have to help finance the dowries made to A's daughters, while – given that a dowry forms the nucleus of the individual property of the newly married couple when the household eventually splits – his segment of the joint family does not stand to reap any lasting benefit from the dowries received by A's sons. But if the household belongs to a caste where bride-price is the rule, then the presence of nubile daughters may tip the scales in the other direction, since the payment received for A's three daughters may be used to subsidize the marriages of B's four sons.

What all this boils down to, then, is that in order to assess optimum strategies we have to take account not only of the size and sexual composition of sibling groups, but also of their relative ages, and whether they belong to a caste which gives dowries or takes bride-price payments.

New manipulations of the model may be necessary to allow for the implications of the different sets of inheritance rules. Suppose, for example, that E is B's son by his first wife, while F, G and H are sons by a second wife. If, on B's death the property is divided according to the traditional *chundabandh* system, then E's interest (*ceteris paribus*) will be in early partition, since he has a right to the exclusive possession of half his father's ancestral property. But if the *pagbandh* rules – or the rules for intestate succession laid down by the Hindu Code Bill – are followed, then none of the siblings will stand to gain more than the others by a division of the household.

Optimal strategies for timing partition may also be affected by a wife's interest in her father's property; and as a result of the Hindu Code Bill this consideration is likely to become increasingly important. Let us assume that H's father-in-law dies and that his wife becomes entitled to, and claims, a share of the estate. H may then find that his most profitable course of action is to initiate partition from his brothers, so that his own conjugal family can enjoy the full produce of the land his wife has inherited without having to share it with the conjugal families of his brothers. But as far as the latter are concerned, of course, H's windfall may tip the balance in favour of maintaining a joint household with him.

The whole of this discussion might seem more appropriate to the analysis of a rather sophisticated parlour game than to any concrete ethnography. Is it really the case that the ideology of joint living is just an irrelevant myth, and that people coldly and cynically weigh up the pros and cons of partition in this way?

In this context I would make two points. The first is that the variables which I have discussed are only parameters which define the limits within which choice is made, and in no sense do I mean to imply that they act as mechanical determinants of choice. The second point goes back to Madan's neat formula, quoted earlier, that as we move along the continuum from the father–son, to the brother–brother, to the cousin relationship, the ideal of joint living becomes gradually weaker, and the demands of personal interest and of the interests of a man's conjugal family, become more insistent. As I see it, the sorts of manipulation of the model that I have been discussing are likely to be most decisive at the cousin end of the continuum and are least likely to influence choice where the father–son relationship is concerned, though even here, as my case histories will show, they are far from irrelevant.

But in spite of these qualifications, the reader may be forgiven for thinking that I have strayed a long way from the conscious motivations of the participants themselves. While the morality of 'prescriptive altruism' should ideally govern relations between close agnatic kin, people recognize that in practice (*pace* Bloch 1973) human frailty makes it unwise to place too much faith in their long-term willingness to sustain one-way flows. I don't want to make it sound as if any of my Kangra acquaintances bear the remotest resemblance to the infamous Ik, but the fact is that they did talk about specific cases of partition in precisely these terms. The Rajput household represented in Figure 3 illustrates this rather neatly, and highlights the interplay of several of the variables I have isolated.

Until 1959 all the people shown here belonged to a single joint household owning a substantial amount of land. By this time Dugal Singh and Joginder were both in their seventies and their sons were all middle-aged. All the named individuals, with the exception of Dugal

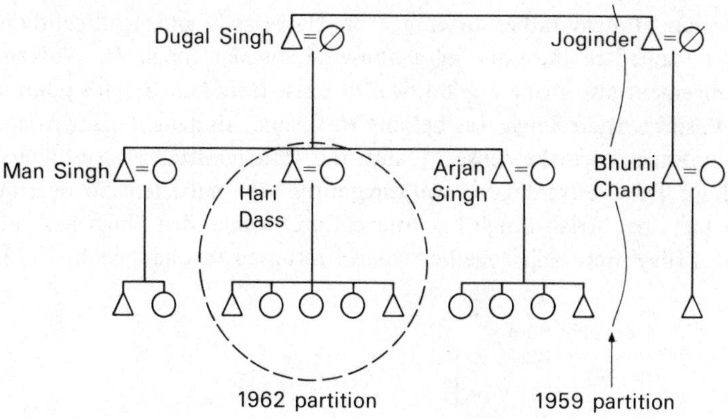

FIGURE 3 *Household of Dugal and Joginder*

Singh, have at one time or another been employed outside, but in 1959 Man Singh and Joginder had both been at home for some years. In that year Hari Dass retired from the military and this left only Arjan Singh and Bhumi Chand employed outside. As soon as Hari Dass was back in the village, Joginder and his son demanded partition. Joginder himself is quite candid about what happened. Bhumi Chand insisted, in spite of his father's reluctance, that they should divide the household; for their cash income had been substantially reduced, and they stood to gain by a partition of the land since they were the smaller unit.

Dugal Singh's segment of the family remained joint only up until 1962. In that year two crucial things happened to tip the scales in favour of partition. First, as a result of the Chinese invasion Hari Dass was recalled by the military; and second, Man Singh got his daughter engaged to a boy of royal clan, a match which clearly demanded a large dowry. Hari Dass immediately initiated partition, and gossip is in no doubt that he did this because he wanted to keep his salary to himself and because he did not want to contribute to the dowry. Dugal Singh was still alive but he acquiesced in the division of the estate. As a military reservist, Hari Dass was assigned for the period of his recall to Cadet Corps training in the neighbouring sub-division to Palampur. This posting gives him the opportunity to pay frequent visits home, and allows him to supervise the cultivation of his land and see that all is well with his wife and children. Arjan Singh, by contrast, is a regular soldier who has never been stationed anywhere near Chadhiar and who can expect to visit home only on his annual leave. This fact makes his optimum strategy rather different from Hari Dass's, and significantly he has remained in the same joint household as Man Singh. In 1962 this arrangement also made a good deal of sense from Man Singh's point of view, since Arjan Singh was helping to finance his daughter's marriage. It continues to make sense because the cash remittances continue to roll in. These advantages have apparently been sufficient to override the fact that Arjan Singh has four children while Man Singh has only two. (They were still together when I returned to Chadhiar in 1974.)

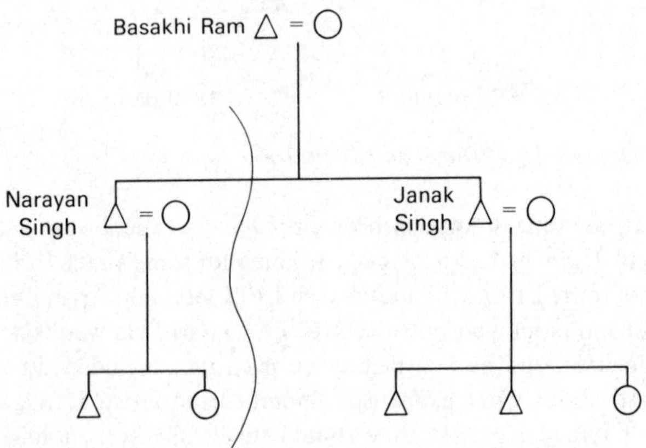

FIGURE 4 *Household of Basakhi Ram*

Fewer variables were involved in the partition of the household represented in Figure 4. Basakhi Ram, the owner of a very modest landholding, is now an old man. At the time I left the field both his sons were employed outside Chadhiar, though Narayan Singh was planning to return home for good within the next six months. Janak Singh was a soldier and Narayan a forest guard, though he too had been a soldier during the Second World War. While he was fighting in the British army he had been captured and interned for some time in a Japanese prisoner-of-war camp. Later he was released after enlisting in the Indian National Army, with whom he had subsequently fought against the British. This fact became relevant again in 1967, when he was eventually awarded a large *ex-gratia* grant and a pension in recognition of his INA services. Right out of the blue, then, a monetary windfall of rather substantial proportions dropped into his lap. To avoid having to pool this with the rest of the joint household Narayan immediately set up on his own. His father and brother were, of course, highly indignant. Basakhi refused to give him a share of the land and made it absolutely plain that he couldn't expect to inherit anything from him when he died. But all the same, there was no doubt that Narayan had done the rational thing in terms of his material self-interest, since the lump sum he was getting from the Government was enough to buy almost twice the amount of land he stood to inherit from his father.

I cannot claim that in every case the timing of partition correlates so precisely with a shift in the strategic balance of advantage between different segments of the joint household. But on the other hand I could multiply case histories like these to the point of tedium. The present anlysis was completed some time before my brief return to Kangra in 1974. As a postscript from that visit I add one final example of a rather different sort, an example which gives me some confidence that I have not misrepresented the sorts of consideration which Kangra people themselves believe to enter into such decisions.

I found one of my closest friends, Krishan, employed as the manager of a small and financially precarious printing works in Palampur on a salary of Rs. 160 per month. His younger brother Onkar is a skilled welder and mechanic who was then earning around Rs. 600 per month. Out of this he regularly gave Krishan Rs. 100 for household expenses but was – on his brother's account – generous to a fault when anything over and above that was needed. Both brothers live at their home some three miles from Palampur. Krishan is married and had two children with a third on the way; Onkar was to be married that summer. The third and youngest brother was away in the military; was drawing pay of roughly Rs. 200 per month while the army provided food, clothing and accommodation, and sent regular remittances of Rs. 100 a month. In addition the family also owns just over three acres of land, which is a very handsome bonus when they are all in work, and which – provided they continued to cultivate it jointly – would support the whole family in straightened circumstances in the unlikely event of their all being unemployed at the same time.

To all appearances Krishan and his brothers were paragons of fraternal solidarity. I was rather surprised, then, when he told me with visible emotion that he was not at all sanguine about their future together. His cause for concern was that there was little prospect that he would ever be in a position to contribute as much as his brothers; yet in the forseeable future it was he and his wife and children who would make the greatest calls on the household's resources. Furthermore, the dubious profitability of the printing works made his employment insecure; and he had already committed the blunder of settling some of the business's debts out of joint household funds and had never been able to recoup the money from his employer. What he sadly but resignedly recognized was that he had become something of a liability to his brothers, and that the chances were that once Onkar was married the unity of their household would not long survive the disparity of their contributions.

I have subsequently remained in close touch with the family and can report that the now unemployed Krishan's gloomy prognostications have already been largely fulfilled. Although there has been no formal decision to partition, Onkar and his wife currently live at his workshop, are increasingly irregular visitors to the family home and no longer contribute directly to joint household funds (though they do provide for an unmarried sister who stays with them). Moreover, Onkar has reportedly invested some of his savings in land (to which he has individual title) in his wife's natal village, while the ancestral property is now shown in the official records as the separate holdings of the siblings – although in practice Krishan has continued to cultivate the whole area as a joint resource.

In most cases what actually seems to happen is that the constituent conjugal families of a joint household are each presented at different points in time with several opportunities when their own immediate material advantage would be maximized if they initiated partition. The ideology of joint living, and the moral stigma which attaches to a man who separates from his father, may prompt some individuals to rule out some of these options. Out of those that remain, one may be taken up when another, just a few years before, had been passed by. The immediate reason why one of these occasions is chosen rather than another is likely to depend on a whole range of purely personal and individual motives; but commonly personal conflict between members of different conjugal families within the joint household provides the immediate motivation for the split. Frequently the real conflict is between brothers, but it is likely to be dressed up for public consumption as conflict between their wives. It is usually problems involving personal relationships, then, that determine which occasion is selected and which actually precipitate the crisis. But personal conflicts tend to remain submerged while it is in everybody's interest to maintain the joint household, and to be brought out into the open only when the balance of advantage shifts decisively in the direction of one segment of the joint family.

6:8 The causes of partition

If my analysis has any merit at all, then I think that it allows us to differentiate between three analytically distinct levels of causation involved in partition. For want of a more precise terminology, I distinguish these three levels as (1) the 'underlying', (2) the 'predisposing' and (3) the 'immediate' causes of partition.

(1) At the highest level of generality partition is a normal phase in the developmental cycle of any household whose membership expands beyond the stage of a linear joint or a nuclear family. A man's conjugal family drives a wedge between him and the rest of the joint household and this fact invariably condemns joint households of the lineal-collateral or collateral types to eventual dismemberment. As I see it, these conflicting loyalties and interests provide the underlying cause of all partitions. By this I mean that in the last resort the ultimate reason why no household survives forever is precisely because it is sooner or later disrupted by the competing demands of individual (or conjugal family) interests versus joint family interests.

(2) But apart from suggesting that married men with children are those who are most likely to initiate the split, this first level of causation tells us very little about why a household is partitioned at one time rather than another. My argument here is that a whole set of material interests constrain the segments of a joint household to remain joint over long periods of time. But these material interests may also make partition an attractive proposition for particular segments of the household at other times. The central point of my analysis is that during certain periods of its history a household may be predisposed to partition by all sorts of fortuitous accidents of a primarily economic kind, accidents which produce situations in which the advantages of joint living are unevenly balanced between the constituent segments of a joint household. These situations of imbalance, then, are the predisposing causes of partition.

(3) Most households will probably pass through several phases during which the material advantages of joint living benefit some members at the expense of others. At no time is partition inevitable, though the likelihood of the split taking place during one of these periods of disequilibrium is much greater than at other times. The immediate cause for a household member deciding to take advantage of one of these occasions rather than another is usually a series of quarrels between individuals of the joint household.

The myth is that it is the women of the household as individual personalities who are always to blame for all the trouble, though in fact quarrels between brothers are much more likely to have a seriously disruptive effect on household unity. While quarrels between the womenfolk are certainly not rare, they are often only a pretext for partition, a pretext which allows the women to be used as convenient scapegoats, and the men to conceal the fact that they themselves do not get on with each other, and that one brother is making use of a favourable opportunity to maximize his profits by opting out of the joint household. The men's need to make scapegoats of the women is related to the enormous value put on the ideal of co-operation and harmony between closely related male agnates.

Whether one chooses to emphasize the first of these levels of causation at the expense of the second and third, will depend a good deal on the distance and time-scale over which the material is viewed. Taken over a substantial period of time, joint households never survive, and at this level of objectivity individual personalities and the constraints on choice in any particular case are irrelevant. But if we examine individual cases of partition over a shorter time-span, or from the participants's point of view, then the direct causes of the split will appear to be the product, either of personal conflict between household members, or of one individual taking a unilateral decision to realize his short-term advantage by cutting loose from the joint household, or – most probably – of both.

7 Rajput hypergamy in an historical perspective

7:1 Preliminary considerations

The next four chapters are all in one way or another concerned with marriage and affinity. For the top three castes of the Chadhiar hierarchy marriage is explicitly conceptualized as a hypergamous relationship in which those of inferior status give wives to their superiors within the caste. The other castes are not stratified internally, and the exchange of women takes place on a symmetrical basis. Throughout the analysis my interest will be focussed primarily on the hypergamous castes.

The practice of hypergamy is a very widespread feature of Rajput social organization, and is general amongst Rajputs of the hill region of Kangra, Mandi, Chamba and Jammu and of the adjacent sub-montane districts of Hoshiarpur and Gurdaspur. Although it is they who have developed the logic of hypergamy in the most extreme manner, there are others throughout this region who also operate a system based on the same general principles. But if the underlying principles are one, their transformations are many. They vary both between castes, and over space and time within a single caste.

In the present chapter the particular variant on which I shall focus is that of the Rajputs of Palampur sub-division between 1846, when the British annexed the area, and 1930, which I have taken – somewhat arbitrarily – to mark the beginning of a period of upheaval during which there was an attempt to undermine the hierarchy from within by a systematic, though short-lived, campaign to deny brides to superiors. Since 1930, then, the system has passed through a phase of reformation and counter-reformation. As a result of the counter-reformation the Rajput clan hierarchy has reverted to something very like its old form, so that the variant which I actually observed in the late 1960s is only a slightly modified version of the model I describe in this chapter. Where appropriate, then, I continue to write in the ethnographic present.

In the next chapter I will attempt to draw out the principal differences between present day practice and my necessarily somewhat idealized model of the situation before the *biradari* reforms. But the main theme of this chapter will concern the causes of the reform movements, and the extent to which they were responsible for the introduction of permanent structural changes. I shall argue that such upheavals are endemic to the system itself, and that the hypergamous hierarchy is like the Phoenix: it contains within itself the seeds of its own destruction and of its own rebirth. In order to reinforce this case I will briefly outline the hypergamous variants of the Brahmans and Temple priests, and call on some rather sketchy data I gathered amongst Rajputs in another part of the district. Chapter 9 focusses on hypergamy in action: the empirical pattern of marriage alliances, and their relationship to the status aspirations of those who contract them. In Chapter 10 I take up Dumont's thesis (1966) that an alliance pattern exists in north India in a 'disguised' form, and that affinity has something of the diachronic dimension associated with south Indian systems with positive marriage rules.

I do not propose to be side-tracked into formulating a technical definition of 'hypergamy'. But at the outset I should perhaps indicate that I use the term in a broader sense than the one Dumont (1964) considers strictly appropriate. In my usage (and thus far I follow Dumont 1970: 117), 'hypergamy' refers to a norm which strongly recommends – but does not necessarily oblige – a man to marry his daughter to a groom of higher status. The minimum requirement of such systems is that a woman should preferably be married to a man of higher rank but may be married to an equal; and as a residual consequence of this, a man must necessarily marry an equal or inferior woman.

It is at first sight tempting to distinguish between a system of 'prescriptive' hypergamy in which it is mandatory to give one's daughters 'up', and a system of 'preferential' hypergamy which merely recommends one to do so. But this distinction is difficult to sustain. Although in the second case a daughter can legitimately be married to an equal, the marriage itself may create an inequality between the wife-givers and the wife-receivers so that after the event *every* marriage is conceptualized as hypergamous.

Dumont (1964:86) favours a narrower definition than the one I have proposed:

> The term can be used loosely, of a marriage (or even a union) in which the man is of higher status than the woman, or it can more strictly designate a kind of rule, as found in Northern India, according to which the said difference of status characterizes all, or may characterize any, of the primary principal marriages. *In this latter case, between recognized limits (those of the endogamous caste group), the inferior status of the wife's natal group does not bring any inferiority to the status of the children* (emphasis added).

There is therefore no distinction of status between the children of an equal and unequal wife, and the male line is indifferent as to whether their wives are from equal or from allowed inferior rank. This then forms the basis for Dumont's contrast between hypergamy and isogamy where 'unequality of status between the parents brings inferiority (of the union and) of the children'. It is also central to a further contrast with the Nayar pattern to which

> in the restricted North Indian sense, the term 'hypergamy' is inapplicable . . . for several reasons. (1) The marriage can be across the caste boundary. (2) The difference of status is meaningful for the status of the children. (3) Moreover the difference of status is reversed if we take into account, not the absolute sexes, but the sexes as lineally relevant or irrelevant to transmission of group membership, etc., for with the Nayar the lineally stressed parent, the mother, is inferior in status to the other parent (1964:86–7).

Only the third of these contrasts seems to me unquestionable. The precise sense in which marriage across the caste boundary distinguishes the two cases is unclear, for it is well known that the strictly hypergamous systems of the north entail frequent breaches of caste endogamy by the men of the lowest ranking groups, and the evidence suggests that such inter-caste unions are commonly accorded the status of valid marriages. As for the second contrast, I will endeavour to show (Chapter 9:4) that in Kangra – as I suspect elsewhere in north India – the status of the mother's natal group is in certain contexts relevant to the status of her children, and that the wife-takers are by no means indifferent to the precise ranking of those who give them brides.[1] For this reason I reject Dumont's use of the criterion of the 'normative neutralization' of the mother's status as the critical feature by which hypergamy should be defined.

North Indian hypergamy is a kind of mirror image of the hypogamy of the Kachins, not simply in the obvious sense that in the one case the woman marries 'up' while in the other case she marries 'down'. In north India the hypergamous marriage *par excellence* is one in which residence is virilocal (that is, *conforms* to the expected pattern); for when a man is constrained to marry uxorilocally, the superiority of the wife-taking affines – and in particular of the son-in-law himself – is somewhat compromised. In the Kachin case by contrast, the status implications of the union are attenuated in the orthodox virilocal case and the hypogamous marriage *par excellence* is one in which residence is uxorilocal, that is *deviates* from the expected pattern (Leach 1954: 84, 168–71; 1961a:87).

Throughout the analysis I treat the prevalence of hypergamy in India, and the general disapproval of hypogamy, as a cultural given, and make no systematic attempt to answer the (perhaps unanswerable) question 'why hypergamy?'

Various hypotheses of a rather speculative nature have been advanced to account for its development. Bouglé (1971:90–1), Risley (1915:179) and Rivers (1921) suggest that its origins lie in the deficit of Aryan women with which the invading Aryan armies had to contend, and in the fact that they were in a position to extract wives from the indigenous population without giving them daughters in return. Others have tried to specify the kinds of conditions under which it is likely to be adopted by contemporary caste groups. Hutton (1969:50–1), for example, associates hypergamy with an intermediary phase in the development of a sub-caste within the wider caste group. On somewhat firmer ground, Ahmad's excellent article (1973) documents the way in which hypergamy and a meticulous adherence to endogamy have been used by different segments of an upwardly mobile Muslim group as two alternative strategies for promoting their status aspirations.

At the synchronic level what can be said is that the hypergamous marriage formula is in tune with the hierarchical spirit which pervades so much of Indian society, and with the values of the great tradition of Hinduism.

> The laws of Manu state unequivocally that *anuloma* unions (with the hair or grain: natural) between a high caste man and a low caste woman are acceptable, but that *pratiloma* unions (against the hair or grain: unnatural) between a high caste woman and a low

> caste man must be punished by excommunication, if not more serious measures. In Ceylon, before British rule, the punishment was drowning (Yalman 1967:179).

Yalman (1963) associates this tolerance of *anuloma* unions and the complete rejection of *pratiloma* with ideas about the purity of women. Men are polluted only 'externally' by sexual intercourse and can be cleansed by a ritual bath. But sex pollutes women 'internally' and the effects of this are much harder to eradicate. From the point of view of the caste as a whole *anuloma* unions are also less menacing in that the bond between genitor and child can be given minimal content or even denied altogether. A man may therefore sow his wild oats without saddling his caste with impure bastards. The bond between mother and child is not so lightly dismissed, however; so that if a woman consorts with an inferior she will bear offspring who introduce impure blood into the caste unless both mother and child are swiftly repudiated. But if her lover is of higher caste the purity of her own caste is in no way jeopardized. The offspring of such a union may be placed in the mother's caste and their rank within it may even be enhanced by the superiority of their genitor. But the progeny of a *pratiloma* union cannot be assimilated to the mother's caste and are not unambiguously entitled to membership of their father's caste either. On the principle of 'compounded degradation' set out in the texts, mother and child are placed right at the bottom of the ladder (Tambiah 1973b). Yalman therefore concludes that:

> In south India and Ceylon at least it makes sense to speak of matrilateral filiation. In the last resort the child belongs to the social group of the mother, unless, of course, the mother herself has been excommunicated because of her contact with low caste men. . . . It is through women (and not men) that the 'purity' of the caste community is ensured and preserved. It is mainly through the women of the group (for the men may be of higher caste) that blood and purity is perpetuated (1963:42–3).

What Yalman clearly shows is that the almost universal disapproval of hypogamy in caste society is closely associated with the degradation of the offspring of such a union; but contrary to his implication it is not clear which is cause and which effect. Moreover when – as in north India or amongst the Catholic Fishermen of Sri Lanka studied by Stirrat (1975) – the children of an *anuloma* union are assigned to the father's caste, it makes little sense to speak of matrilateral filiation, or to argue that the purity of the caste is perpetuated mainly through its women. Such instances must be understood, as Yalman himself indicates, in terms of the emphasis on the patrilineal transmission of status (see below, section 7).

Dumont (1970:117) offers two observations which relate to the question 'why hypergamy?' The first is that 'as the woman is in general considered inferior to the man, the pattern would seem natural to the people concerned'. What he fails to note is that a hypogamous pattern might seem equally natural for precisely the same reason. Furthermore, Kangra people stress that a bride is only 'true' *dan* in the strict sense if she is married before her menarche and that therefore 'the gift of a virgin' is ideally the gift of a pre-pubescent girl. Now, as we have seen (Chapter 5:5), such a girl is symbolically identified as a goddess incarnate. In other words, it might be argued that it is not her inferiority but rather her quasi-divine status which makes her an appropriate gift to a man of higher rank. This ties up with Dumont's second and more insightful observation that the hypergamous pattern harmonizes with the ideology of *dan*. The virgin (*kanya*) is assimilated to the category *dan*, and *dan* – as I noted earlier (Chapter 3:4) – is a meritorious gift made to somebody of superior status, typically a Brahman. In line with this, a Kangra son-in-law, though a non-Brahman by caste, is in certain symbolic contexts treated as if he were a Brahman (see Chapter 10:2).

7:2 The holistic 'biradari' formula

Rajput clans which are in a general way regarded as being of equal status form a single *biradari*. The members of the *biradari* share broadly speaking in a common style of life and a common set of customs which, to some extent, differentiate them from the members of other *biradaris*. But the main consideration here is the symmetrical exchange of women. At least in theory, clans both give and take women in marriage from all other clans of their *biradari*. The relationship between *biradaris* is largely defined by the asymmetrical exchange of women. Wives are taken from the *biradari* immediately inferior to your own, but preferably from your own *biradari*; and daughters are given to your own *biradari*, but preferably to the *biradari* above.

The lower castes say that all the clans of the caste belong to a single *biradari*. At all levels of the hierarchy, then, the *biradari* is equated with the group which exchanges women on a reciprocal basis. This corresponds to the way in which the term is used in Malwa (Mayer 1960: 152). But elsewhere the *biradari* is an exogamous patri-clan or a segment thereof (Cohn 1968:24, 1971:116; Eglar 1960:43, 75; Rowe 1960; Tiemann 1970); while amongst certain Punjabi Muslim groups it is both a patrilineal descent group and the unit within which brides are exchanged in a symmetrical way (Alavi 1972). This variability is reminiscent of the Sinhalese term *variga* which – despite Leach's (1963a) scepticism – may denote an exogamous matrilineal clan (Robinson 1968), an exogamous patrilineal clan (Gamburd n.d.) or an endogamous bilateral kindred (Leach 1961c). What seems to be essential to both concepts is not (*pace* Leach) their endogamy, but their equality of status *vis-à-vis* outsiders, as the term *biradari* ('brotherhood') itself suggests.

But although the Kangra theory is that each *biradari* consists of a series of clans which are of equal status and which engage in the symmetrical exchange of women, there is in practice a tendency towards hypergamy and differentiation of status within the Rajput *biradari*, a tendency which becomes increasingly marked as one moves up the ladder. Only those clans – or more precisely those clan-segments – which are prepared to acknowledge complete equality with each other will exchange women on a reciprocal basis, and this by no means always includes everybody else in the *biradari*. In the early days of the British Raj, there were some people at the very top of the hierarchy for whom it included nobody at all.

In Palampur the Rajput hierarchy is said to consist of four *biradaris*, but within the first and second it is possible to identify various informal and hotly disputed gradations of status. The position is represented schematically in Table 19. In terms of the divisions shown in the table, the most superior royal clans of the first *biradari* takes brides from the other clans of their *biradari*, and from the clans of 2a at the top of the second *biradari*, but will not generally go any lower down the ladder than this. The other royal clans of 1b take from the inferior and non-royal clans of 1c and from the whole of *biradari* 2; 1c also take from 2, though some sub-clans of 2a are not prepared to give them girls. The whole of the second *biradari* take wives from the third, and the third take from the fourth. The system clearly creates a surplus of women at the top of the hierarchy and a shortage at the bottom.

The acid test of the superiority of clan A over clan B is that it takes women from clan B but does not give in return. But this is not to argue

TABLE 19 *The Rajput* Biradari *hierarchy*

Biradari	*Participants' categories*		*Informal sub-divisions (ethnographer's labels)*	*Clans of the* biradari[1]
1	*Jai Karias* or *Mians*	Rajput	(a) Most superior royal clans	*Jamuwal*, *Katoch*, Pathania, Guleria
			(b) Other royal clans	Sepieya, *Dadwal*, Jaswal, Chandel, Mankotia, *et al.*
			(c) Inferior royal and non-royal clans	Bhangalia, Chadhial Rana, *Jaryal*, *Manhas*, Sonkla
2	Some-times referred to as *Thakurs*		(a) Wife-givers to 1a above	*Kanthwal*, *Jaggi*, *Changre*, Khaurwal, Patial, Indauria
			(b) Others	Sanghotra, Bhandari, Guhenay, Dodh Rana, Pathiarch, Chamyal, Samkriya, *et al.*
3		*Rathi*		*Malhotra*, *Kalial*, *Nanwarak*, *Moongla*, *Dagohia*, *Mehta*, Ranot *Phangu*, *Thakur*, *Sohal*, *Dukhe*, *Karihal*, *Sarial*, Bhateriya, *et al.*
4				*Lassai*, *Bhaurwal*, *Makanwal*, *Kathial*, *Bhuriya*, *Dhandola*, *Bhullaniya*, *Rihal*, *Chatwalia*, *Kharbora*, *Saniarch*, *et al.*

[1] This list is by no means exhaustive. The names of those clans which are represented in *mauza* Chadhiar are italicized.

[2] Since the *biradari* classification of certain clans is disputed, and since different sub-clans of the same clan are sometimes assigned to different *biradaris*, it would never be possible to say exactly how many clans belong to each *biradari*.

[3] Unfortunately more detailed figures are not available; and even these figures are of rather doubtful value since the census provided a golden opportunity to lay

<table>
<tr><th rowspan="2">No. of clan names recorded for biradari[2]</th><th colspan="2">Approximate % of population of district[3]</th><th colspan="4">Figures for mauza Chadhiar 1968</th></tr>
<tr><th>1881</th><th>1931</th><th>No. of clans</th><th>No. of households</th><th>% of Rajput population</th><th>% of total population</th></tr>
<tr><td>There are conventionally said to be 22 royal clans but the figures never add up.</td><td>12·7</td><td rowspan="2">15·2</td><td>5</td><td>79</td><td>10·4</td><td>5·3</td></tr>
<tr><td>A list published by the biradari council at the time of the reform movements records 27 clans.</td><td>2.6</td><td>4</td><td>62</td><td>8·1</td><td>4·2</td></tr>
<tr><td>Roughly one-fifth of the total number of clan names recorded by the ethnographer were assigned to this biradari</td><td rowspan="2">15·3</td><td rowspan="2">15·6</td><td>11</td><td>274</td><td>35·9</td><td>18·5</td></tr>
<tr><td>Roughly half the total number of clan names recorded by the ethnographer were assigned to this biradari.</td><td>23</td><td>349</td><td>45·6</td><td>23·6</td></tr>
</table>

claim to membership of a higher *biradari*, and it would be surprising if substantial numbers of get-ahead people in the lower *biradaris* had not taken the chance to register themselves as belonging to a higher status group. The effect of this is obviously to exaggerate the proportion of the population which falls into the top two *biradaris* (cf. Kangra District Gazetteer, 1926:161). The figures for 1881 are from Ibbetson (1883:219); those for 1931 from the Census of India, 1931 (Punjab, Part 2).

that marriage alliances exist in a vacuum independent of other rank variables. They tend rather to express and legitimize a reality of a different order. A man gets rich, he becomes an official in the raja's retinue or an officer in the army, and then tries to translate this newly achieved standing into the more durable sort of status of a prestigious marriage alliance. In other words he starts to give girls to people who had previously not accepted them and to take wives from clans which would not previously have given. Lyall (1889:59) describes the process like this:

> A rich man of a Rathi family . . . marries his daughter to an impoverished Raja, and his whole clan gets a kind of step and becomes Thakur (or second grade) Rajputs. So again the Raja out riding falls in love with a Pathial girl herding cattle, and marries her, thereupon the whole clan begins to give its daughters to Mians.

The general point here is that mobility up and down the ladder is possible because what is immutable is not the fact that the A's rank higher than the B's, but rather the abstract principle that the wife-takers rank higher than the wife-givers, and that those who exchange women on a symmetrical basis are equals. What happens is that the status of the male line is constantly being readjusted to take account of the prestige of its recent alliances. When 'wrong' marriages occur – that is, marriages with affines who are either too high or too low to be compatible with the present status of the group – they do not threaten to undermine the fundamental principles of the hierarchy, for the system can cope by simply reassessing the status of the two parties to the exchange. In other words, it is by contracting marriages which do not conform to the existing pattern that get-ahead people pursue their aspirations; and it is the carrot of eventual success which gives the system its resilience to changes in the distribution of wealth and power between the wife-exchanging units.

But although people tend to conceptualize the hierarchy in terms of broad units of stratification like the *biradari* and clan, my evidence would suggest that the units of mobility which actually move up and down the ladder are, in practice, much smaller groups (cf. Furer-Haimendorf 1966:27). A concerted strategy of social climbing does not seem to be a practical proposition for a group any larger than a sub-clan, and is often pursued by a segment of a sub-clan. But to make such progress a mobile clan-segment needs to be able to jettison its links with less affluent and less respectable collaterals. The sorts of strategies which make this possible will be described at a later stage (Chapter 9:3).

7:3 The attributes and interactions of 'biradaris'

The clans of the most superior *biradari* are those of the royal houses of the petty hill states which used to control the area between the rivers Chenab and Sutlej. It is said that there were 22 of these states, but the number is conventional. Two non-royal clans – the Manhas and Sonkla – are included within the same *biradari*, though in a somewhat subordinate status. Their membership is justified on the grounds that they observe all the rules appropriate to the most aristocratic of Rajputs, and that by any standard their style of life is unimpeachable. Three clans which can legitimately claim royal status are usually assigned to the same rung of the ladder (see Table 19). The relative inferiority of the Jaryal to the other royal clans is attributed to the fact that their raja became a Muslim, and that poverty induced many of them to plough their own land; that of the Bhangalia and the Chadhial Rane to the fact that the kingdoms over which they had ruled were small, remote and politically impotent, and that their numbers are insignificant. This inferiority is reflected in a pattern of marriage alliances in which these clans traditionally give daughters to grooms of other royal clans without receiving wives in return.

Members of the highest *biradari* are classified as Jai Karia Rajputs and are addressed by the honorific Mian, a title of Muslim origin which is said to have been conferred on the hill rajas by their political overlords, the Moghul emperors. The term Jai Karia derives from the greeting *Jai Dewa*, or *Jai Dia*, which is strictly speaking appropriate only to a person of royal clan, and the right to which is jealously guarded.

> in former days . . . unauthorized assumption of the privilege was punished as a misdemeanor by a heavy fine or imprisonment. The Raja, however, could extend the honour to high born Rajputs not strictly belonging to a royal clan, such, for instance, as the Sonklas and the Manhas. Any deviation from the austere rules of caste were sufficient to deprive the offender of the salutation, and the loss was tantamount to excommunication. The Rajputs delight to recount stories illustrating the value of this honour and the vicissitudes endured to prevent its abuse. Raja Dhian Singh, the Sikh Minister, himself a Jamuwal Mian, desired to extort the *jai dia* from Raja

> Bir Singh, the fallen chief of Nurpur. He held in his possession the grant of a *jagir* valued at Rs. 25,000 duly signed and sealed by Ranjit Singh, and delayed presenting the deed until the Nurpur chief should hail with this coveted salutation. But Bir Singh was a Raja by a long line of ancestors, and Dhian Singh was a Raja only by favour of Ranjit Singh. The hereditary chief refused to compromise his honour, and preferred beggary to affluence rather than accord the *jai dia* to one who, by the rules of the brotherhood, was his inferior (Kangra District Gazetteer, 1926:162–3).

Within the Jai Karia *biradari* there are various hotly disputed gradations of rank. Those of lower status should greet their superiors with *Jai Dewa* first, and the greeting is then returned. Between members of a single clan, or clans of equal status, the man who is junior in age or generation should greet his senior first. People of all other castes and *biradaris*, except the Brahmans, also greet the Mians with *Jai Dewa*, and for each there is an appropriate acknowledgment which the Mian might be expected to return. Appropriate to the second *biradari* is the reply *mujara*;[2] to the Rathis and others of clean caste, *Ram Ram*. It is said that formerly low-caste people could consider themselves lucky to get any acknowledgment at all, though if the Mian was feeling particularly benevolent he might deign to respond with *raji raho*, 'stay happy'.

That at least is how the ideal rules are described, though the District Gazetteer (1926:163) observes that 'nowadays the salutation tends more to follow wealth'. At the present time the Mians certainly cannot get away with being quite so uncivil to people of low caste, while Rajputs of other *biradaris* have usurped the greeting *Jai Dia*. These days too – but probably in the past as well – the expected pattern is often modified in encounters between a notable of inferior clan and a nobody of higher ascribed status.

In an earlier part of the analysis we have seen that *nali rasoi*, or food boiled in water, can be taken only if it has been cooked by someone of your own ritual status, or by a superior (Chapter 4:4). People of clans of the first *biradari* could accept *nali rasoi* from each other's houses, but not from people of a lower *biradari*. Some of the most prestigious sub-clans of category 1a were even more exclusive, however, and would not accept boiled food cooked by members of the clans of 1c. Men of the second *biradari* could legitimately eat *nali rasoi* prepared in the house of a third *biradari* clan, but not by members of the fourth *biradari*. The third and fourth engaged in symmetrical transactions in boiled food. What this meant in terms of inter-personal relations between affines was that after his sacred thread ceremony a Mian should not eat from his mother's brother's house, or his wife's parents' house, if they belonged to a lower *biradari*. Although inconsistent with the idea that a woman becomes a member of her husband's clan and *gotra* at the marriage ceremony, no Mian would eat rice cooked by his wife until she had borne him a child, or as Kangra people put it, 'until the blood has mixed' (cf. Stevenson 1954:53). A man of the second *biradari* could eat from his mother's brother's house if his mother's brother cooked the food, but not if his mother's brother's wife was the cook, since the chances were that she belonged to the fourth *biradari*.

It is said that in the past members of the most prestigious royal sub-clans would never sit in the same line of diners (*painth*) to eat *nali rasoi* as members of other sub-clans. Rajputs of the second, third and fourth *biradaris* would sit in a single unbroken line with others of their own *biradari*, but not with people of other *biradaris*. When they attend Nanwarak (third *biradari*) weddings in the neighbouring hamlet of Chhek, the Manhas women of Matial (1c) will even today insist on forming a separate *painth* and on eating off brass utensils rather than off the leaf plates provided to less fastidious guests. (On such an occasion the food will, of course, have been prepared by a Brahman cook.) But when Nanwarak women come to Manhas weddings, they will be allowed to sit in the same line of diners, but will be placed lower down the line than the Manhas.

The formal rules about smoking from a common hookah paralleled the rules about sitting in the same *painth* to eat *nali rasoi*. Clans of the second, third and fourth *biradaris* would smoke with all the clans of their own *biradari* but not with others. People of the first *biradari* would smoke only with members of their own clan. But within category 1a there were divisions within the clan. Those lineages and sub-clans which thought of themselves as being the most superior representatives of their clan would smoke only with other such sub-clans. The Katoch of *mauza* Khera, for example, would smoke only with the Katoch of Durug, Bhullana and Rangher. These four sub-clans all held minor *jagirs* from the raja – a matter of prestige rather than of any great economic significance (Kangra District Gazetteer, 1926:440) – and could trace an equally close collateral kinship with him. Most other Mians were less fussy, however, and would smoke with everybody else in their clan unless they were reputed to be of *sartora* line, that is, the descendants of concubines. Neither *sartoras*, nor their scions, were entitled to the greeting *Jai Dia*, and no Mian of pure descent would give his daughter to a man of bastard lineage, though they would sit in the same *painth* to eat *nali rasoi* on ritual occasions. The *sartoras* of Mians recruited their wives from other lineages with a similar flaw in their pedigree, from the less prestigious clans of the second *biradari*, and from the third *biradari*.

There were four fundamental rules which a Mian had to observe if he was to retain his rank (cf. Kangra District Gazetteer, 1926:163). The first of these was that he should never marry his daughter or sister to a man of lower clan. Local history abounds with heroic tales of the sacrifices which men of honour were prepared to make rather than give a girl to an inferior.

> The Raja of Kangra deserted his hereditary kingdom rather than ally his sister to Dhian Singh, himself a Mian of Jammu stock, but not the equal of the Katoch prince. The Rajputs of Katgarh near Nurpur voluntarily set fire to their houses and immolated their female relatives to avoid the disgrace of Ranjit Singh's alliance (ibid., p. 164).

Second, no Mian should plough. If he did so he would no longer be entitled to the greeting *Jai Dia*, no Mian would give him a daughter in marriage, and he would have to go a step lower in the hierarchy to get wives for his sons. Third, the women of his household should be strictly secluded. From his own experience, Barnes reported a remarkable instance of the dedication with which Mian women observed the rules of *purdah*. A Mian house caught fire in broad daylight, and rather than come out into the open and be seen by strangers, the women allowed themselves to be burnt alive (ibid., p. 164). Finally, a Mian should give dowry at the marriage of his daughter, and under no circumstances accept a bride-price.

This last prohibition ties in closely with the ideology of *kanya dan* ('the gift of a virgin') for it is only when *dan* is freely given without any material recompense that the donor acquires prestige in this world and spiritual merit in the next by the act of giving. Consistent with this notion that a counter-prestation would cancel out the merit acquired by the original gift, the *jajman* should never accept food in his *purohit*'s house, nor the wife-giver in the wife-taker's house. Various forms of exchange marriage like *batta satta* (in which a brother and a sister marry a sister and a brother) and *tarvadla* (in which A marries B's sister,

B marries C's and C marries A's) are also forbidden at the top of the hierarchy, since they are held to contradict this unilateral ideal.[3]

During their monthly course, Mian women should be rigorously secluded. Once widowed they can never remarry, and they are expected to mark their widowhood by renouncing the use of all jewellery, by wearing white clothes, preparing all their own meals, and by strictly avoiding any of the 'hot' foods which produce sexual desire. In pre-British days only the Mians were properly entitled to wear the sacred thread, and the rajas are said to have taken measures of 'barbarous cruelty' to prevent their inferiors from usurping the privilege (Kangra District Gazetteer, 1926:136). Even today, an orthodox *purohit* will not conduct a full sacred thread ceremony for men of the lowest Rajput *biradari*, but only a truncated form at the time of their marriage when they whisper an abridged version of the *gyatri mantra* into the ear of the novitiate. At weddings there are certain rather peripheral rituals which only the Mians perform, and they do not recognize the less prestigious and abbreviated forms of marriage ritual which are acceptable to their inferiors (see section 9 below). While in other *biradaris* it is customary for a young bride to be sent back on a protracted visit to her parents' house almost immediately after her marriage, Mian brides are expected to remain in their husband's house for several months before they return to their natal home for the first time.

Unlike the Mians, the clans of the second *biradari* ploughed, and have never secluded their women. But like the Mians their widows did not remarry; they did not tolerate divorce; they gave dowry and did not accept bride-price. In other essential ways too, their customs seem to be broadly similar to those of the top *biradari*.

The label Rathi is most generally held to apply to both of the lowest two *biradaris*, though there is a tendency for the term to be applied in a hierarchically relative way, by which I mean that people on all but the very lowest rungs of the ladder often talk as though the dividing line between the 'true' Rajputs and the Rathis is located somewhere just below their own particular position. 'A Rathi,' as one stern old aristocrat contemptuously defined the term, 'is somebody whose mother is one but whose fathers are many.' But what really distinguishes the Rathis is said to be the practice of *rakhewa* by which a younger brother is entitled to inherit his deceased elder brother's wife, or to compensation if she goes off with somebody else (though today this is unenforceable). *Rakhewa* is associated with both these *biradaris*, as is an easy tolerance of divorce and extortionate bride-price demands. As a consequence girls are not gifts in the sense that Mian daughters are supposed to be, and there is no restriction on exchange marriages or insistence on preserving the unilaterality of affinal prestations.

I should stress, however, that all this represents a highly idealized account, and that today at any rate the whole hierarchy is a good deal more homogeneous than any of this would imply. Even though most points in my description are directly corroborated by the contemporary literature, there can be little doubt that the situation on the ground was never so tidy or consistent. We have already seen, for example, that ideal rules governing the exchange of greetings have probably always been modified by the extraneous factors of wealth and power, and the chances are that much the same goes for interactions of other kinds.

There are also strong grounds for suspecting that in many empirical situations the contrast between the attributes of two clan-segments belonging to different *biradaris* was not always nearly so sharp as my account would suggest. Some sub-clans undoubtedly fell some way short of the ideal standards of their own *biradari*, while others, anxious to enhance their status, adopted the attributes of their superiors. For example, there is documentary evidence (Tika Assessment Notes of 1915) to support the claim that at the beginning of this century the Kanthwal sub-clan of Chadhiar (with the exception of the Vaid *al*) did not plough, and that they secluded their women like the Mians, though they actually belong to the second *biradari*. By the same token, I learnt of the odd case of *batta satta* (direct exchange) marriage amongst impoverished Jai Karias.

The general point here is that just as the highest sections of an inferior caste may have 'better' attributes than the lowest sections of a higher caste (Chapter 4:4), so some sub-clans of a lower *biradari* may have 'better' attributes than some sub-clans of the *biradari* above. But although the reality is that there is often a good deal of overlap between the attributes of one *biradari* and another, each is nevertheless associated in the popular imagination with a homogeneous style of life and a homogeneous set of customs. What makes this possible is that those with an inferior set of attributes arrogate to themselves the superiority of the more orthodox *biradari* members, who, in order to preserve their own status, must either expel them altogether, or must close ranks and refrain from drawing the attention of outsiders to their shortcomings, since by so doing they would be calling the life-style of the *biradari* as a whole into question. At the same time as the less orthodox sub-clans of the *biradari* include themselves with the more orthodox, the *biradari* as a whole repudiates the pretensions of those inferior sub-clans which have adopted a higher set of attributes, by including them with those who have not.

7:4 The relative wealth of 'biradaris'

Table 20 shows the proportion of land in the district owned by each *biradari* in 1867. What these figures suggest is that even formerly

TABLE 20 *Rajput landholdings in district Kangra in 1867*[1]

Biradari	*% of cultivated area owned (and acres per family) by sub-division*				*Total for district (%)*
	Kangra (including Palampur)	*Nurpur*	*Dehra*	*Hamirpur*	
1	7·1 (10·1)	7·4 (43·7)	5·2 (17·5)	4·5 (22·3)	6
2	12·9 (12·1)	22·3 (46·9)	0·6 (40·0)	19·3 (32·8)	15
3 and 4	15·5 (10·4)	44·7 (18·7)	44·4 (24·3)	41·5 (30·2)	37

[1] Figures based on Lyall 1889.

status within the hierarchy did not faithfully mirror the distribution of landed property. Just in terms of gross area, the Rathis everywhere had more land than anybody else, while in terms of the average size of holding per family, there is only one sub-division in which they were worse off than the Mians. Mian incomes have long been supplemented by military service: first with the rajas, then with the Sikhs, and after with the British. But even so, Mian status does not clearly correlate with affluence and there is considerable economic graduality within the *biradari*. Of the 58 largest landowners in Palampur sub-division, 9 are Rajputs and 6 of these are Mians. At the other end of the scale are those paupers who – as the folk song has it – are proud aristocrats by day but mend their shoes at night. The early British administration papers provide a graphic picture of the sorry financial plight of many Mians as a result of the ban on ploughing:

> It is melancholy to see with what devoted tenacity the Rajputs cling to these deep-rooted prejudices. Their emaciated looks and coarse clothes attest the vicissitudes they have undergone to maintain their fancied purity. . . . They would rather follow any precarious pursuit than submit to the disgrace (of ploughing). Some lounge

away their time on the tops of mountains, spreading nets for the capture of hawks. . . . Others will stay at home and pass their time in sporting either with a hawk, or, if they can afford it, with a gun. . . . At the close of the day, if they have been successful they exchange the game for a little meal, and thus prolong existence over another span (Barnes 1889:38).

Table 21 shows the distribution of land between *biradaris* in the 37 hamlets of *mauza* Chadhiar for the years 1891, 1934 and 1968. The striking thing here is that the proportion of land controlled by each *biradari* is much the same today as it was at the turn of the century, and that no very significant redistribution has taken place. If the two tables are read in conjunction, the broad pattern which emerges is that the status of the Mians is largely independent of their control of the land, but that there seems to be a rough correlation between the average size of holdings, and the rank order between *biradaris* 2, 3 and 4.

My census of eight of the *tikas* of *mauza* Chadhiar included 198 Rajput households. The way in which these households are distributed over the range between the landless and those with 30 acres or more, can be seen by reference back to Table 5 (Chapter 3:1), where they

TABLE 21 *Rajput landholdings in* mauza *Chadhiar in 1891, 1934 and 1968*[1]

Biradari	*% owned in 1891*	*% owned in 1934*	*% owned in 1968*	*Acreage owned in 1968*[2]	*No. of households in 1968*	*Average holding per household in 1968*[3]
1	15·4	14·8	13·4	538	79	6·8
2	16·0	11·9	13·1	529	62	8·5
3	28·3	33·5	31·2	1262	274	4·8
4	27·2	27·6	28·6	1151	349	3·3
Total Rajput	86·9	87·8	86·3	3480	764	4·6
Non-Rajput	13·1	12·2	13·7	554	717	0·8

[1] Figures based on the record of rights for the 37 hamlets of Chadhiar for the years in question.

[2] The area of the *mauza* is much larger than the sum total accounted for in this column since over half the land is *shamlat* vested in the *gram-panchayat*.

[3] These figures include uncultivated grassland as well as cultivated arable. The actual size of cultivated holdings is therefore a good deal smaller.

are classified by *biradari*. Though the samples are small and the general pattern rather inconclusive, it is nevertheless clear that it is the households of the second and third *biradaris* which are comparatively well favoured,[4] and that here the Mians are poorly represented amongst the class of richest landlords.

7:5 The consequences of hypergamy for the Mians

We have seen then that hierarchical notions tend to infect relations between the clans of a single *biradari* and to breed competition between them. In the past, some of the royal clans at the top of the hierarchy took this overweening desire for precedence to such lengths that they absolutely refused to acknowledge the members of any other royal clan as their peers. But clearly any clan which claims absolute pre-eminence in the hierarchy has, by definition, nobody to whom it can give its daughters in marriage.

Theoretically there are several possible solutions to this problem. The most obvious of these would be for the groups at the top of the hierarchy to call a truce in their struggle for precedence and to agree to exchange women on a reciprocal basis. Although the intense rivalry amongst the royal clans militates against the formation of egalitarian marriage circles, this is nevertheless the compromise to which they have eventually been forced to accommodate themselves. But they did so under considerable pressure from the British administration.

A second theoretical possibility is that the daughters of the most superior royal clans should remain unmarried. But this solution too has its drawbacks. The first of these is that the clans at the top of the hierarchy attach enormous importance to female chastity. But chastity does not come easily to most women, since they have nine times as much 'heat' (*garami*) as men, and are consequently sexually predatory by nature. 'Heat' is a sort of energy which manifests itself either in desirable qualities like bravery, or in undesirable lust. (Thus venereal disease is the 'illness of heat' – *garami di bimari.*) But as men tend to see it, 'heat' in a woman is almost invariably converted into sexual desire rather than courage. Hence a widow without a husband to satisfy her carnal appetites is equated with a woman of easy virtue: both are *randis*. As a result of their innate sexual proclivities, a daughter whose marriage is delayed is in grave danger of being overtaken by a fate worse than death, and is a constant source of potential dishonour to her family.

Other societies, of course, cope with problems of this sort by putting the temptations of the flesh out of the way of girls with poor marriage prospects by packing them off to a nunnery. But nunneries would be no solution here since the disgrace of an indiscretion is not the only thing a Rajput father has to worry about. The mere existence of a nubile, but unmarried, daughter is shame enough in itself, for according to the sacred scriptures it is the binding – and supernaturally sanctioned – duty of a father to provide a husband for his daughter before she reaches puberty. This ties in with the classical theory that if she remains unmarried after puberty her guardians will be responsible for the destruction of an embryo every month (Altekar 1938:67), and with the notion, mentioned earlier, that a bride is only 'true' *dan* if she is married before her menarche.

On the face of it, then, the most superior royal clans can't win whatever they do. If they leave their daughters unmarried, they incur both supernatural sanctions and shame in the eyes of the world, while they run the even graver risk of being totally dishonoured by their daughter's unchastity. Yet by giving their daughters in marriage they renounce all claims to absolute supremacy in the hierarchy. Cave-Browne (1857:9) puts the dilemma like this:

> To marry an inferior is, in their eyes, a degradation; but to remain unmarrried is actual dishonour. Not believing in the existence of female virtue, they regard marriage as a woman's only safeguard against shame and infamy. Thus a daughter becomes, from the very first, a source of great anxiety. . . . He cannot allow her to pass even the early years of her childhood unbetrothed, or to attain the first stage of puberty unmarried, without incurring the risk of grievous dishonour.

Before the British took over the area, however, the Rajput aristocrats were at liberty to resolve this dilemma by resorting to female infanticide.

But if female infanticide was the most satisfactory way of safeguarding the Mian's *amour propre*, what sort of a proposition was it for his immortal soul? Did it rate as murder, justifiable homicide, or simply as the disposal of some as yet inanimate object?

The evidence here is difficult to assess. On the one hand, the child is thought to possess a soul and to have life from the moment the mother first feels the foetus quicken in her womb, a notion which would logically seem to imply some equation between infanticide and homicide. Textual justification for this view can be found in the sacred scriptures, where the practice is described as one of the most heinous forms of murder (Cave-Browne 1857:42). But on the other hand, a child of less than 22 months is considered to have no sins. As we have seen (Chapter 5:3), the death of such a child does not involve any of the orthodox mortuary rituals; only the child's mother is polluted by the death, and her pollution is no more severe, either in duration or in intensity, than the pollution she suffers at menstruation. This squares with the contemporary reports that no particular stigma was attached to infanticide (Montgomery 1853), and with the fact that today the Mians do not feel it necessary to repudiate their past conduct, and even view the allegation that the practice is not altogether extinct with a certain amount of complacency. But it needs to be appreciated that at the best of times the Rajput ethic sets little store by the sanctity of human life, and finds it understandable that a man should rate the honour (*ijat*) of his lineage higher than the life of his daughter. Consistent with this the Mians pay lip-service to the ideal that an unmarried daughter who is discovered in a love affair should be killed by those whose duty it was to safeguard her virtue.

Female infanticide was not, of course, confined to Kangra but was widespread throughout large tracts of northern and western India where hypergamy is prevalent, and was in some areas pursued in a spine-chillingly methodical way (see, for example, Cave-Browne 1857: 68, 78 and Panigrahi 1972). In Kangra Rajput daughters were not eliminated with quite such single-minded thoroughness; but even so the proportion of girls born into the top clans who were killed at birth was not inconsiderable.

Statistical records for 1852 show a sex ratio of 585 girls to every 1,000 boys in the top two Rajput *biradaris* of the present-day Kangra and Palampur sub-divisions (Cave-Browne 1857:186). But by averaging the statistics out over such a broad stratum of the Rajput population this figure distorts the true picture. The need to marry one's daughter before she attained puberty lent a certain urgency to the Mian father's search for a groom of appropriate status, while the wide-ranging exogamous prohibitions ruled out many of the available options (see Section 6). His difficulties were further exacerbated by the fact that there were many fathers of inferior *biradari* who were prepared to pay handsomely for the honour of a royal alliance. Unless he was to be hopelessly outbid by his subordinates, a substantial dowry – which made daughters a ruinous financial liability to all but the richest –

had to be offered. The effect of all this was probably to make the phenomena more general within the top *biradari*. But what also needs to be stressed is that people on all but the very highest rungs of the ladder also had a strong incentive to preserve their girls, since it was by giving them away to superiors that they themselves acquired prestige. Infanticide, then, was mainly confined to sub-clans of the very highest status. A more precise idea of its extent in 1852 among three of the most superior royal clans is given in Table 22. But again it should be kept in mind that some sub-clans had considerably more exacting standards than others.

TABLE 22 *Ratio of girls to boys in three of the most superior royal clans in 1852*[1]

Clan	*Girls per 100 boys*	*Total sample*
Katoch	40·31	
Pathania	33·52	33·1
Guleria	21·75	

[1] Figures from Cave-Browne 1857:187.

From the time that they first stumbled on the practice, the British authorities made zealous efforts to stamp it out. But official and missionary propaganda, and even guarantees of financial assistance with the marriages of aristocratic Rajput girls from government-sponsored charities, made very little impact on the problem, and the administration was forced to take a more direct hand in attacking its roots. In many areas the local bureaucracy adopted a systematic strategy of intervening in the hypergamous hierarchy to pressurize the exogamous groups at the top to marry in a circle, and to put a limit on the size of dowry payments. (For the Punjab see Cave-Browne 1857:84–6, 136–40; Montgomery 1853, 1854, Hoshiarpur District Gazetteer, 1906:34; Panigrahi 1972:102–12).

In the early 1850s representatives from the highest-ranking Rajput clans from different parts of the Punjab hills were summoned to a series of meetings convened by British district officers to discuss measures to eliminate infanticide. The largest and most sumptuous of these gatherings was held in Amritsar at Diwali 1853, and was attended by several senior members of the provincial administration, and by delegates from every group known to practise infanticide within a radius of 200 miles, including 11 of the Kangra rajas:

> the arranging of whom according to their rival claims of precedence, was a most difficult task; and only the tact of the officers, who, placing all their chairs together, seated them in the order in which they chanced to enter, saved them, and spared the meeting all the evil consequences of their mutual jealousies and discontent (Cave-Browne 1857:160).

But despite this diplomatic finesse the meeting was not an unqualified success; for although it passed various pious resolutions condemning infanticide and limiting the size of dowries, the hill Rajputs failed to come up with any substantial agreement on the crucial question of forming new marriage circles at the top of the hierarchy (ibid., p. 138ff.; Montgomery 1853:423-32; Panigrahi 1972:108).

Not content to let matters rest at that, the British continued to exert pressure at local level. The district authorities in Kangra, concerned that infanticide appeared to be more firmly entrenched here than elsewhere in the Punjab, and that the destruction of daughters at the top of the hierarchy created something very like a market in women at the bottom, urged the government to give formal recognition to a series of councils which had been organized – with the surreptitious encouragement of the local administration – in an apparently spontaneous attempt to reform the current set of marriage practices (Cave-Browne 1857:172; Montgomery 1854).

Within a very few years of their taking over control of the district, a certain amount of progress towards suppression had been achieved. Shortly after the Amritsar meeting the Collector was able to send his superiors the optimistic report that the Rajputs

> confess the sinfulness of (infanticide) and are now inclined to adopt a more rational policy, which, by enlarging the circle of matrimony will remove all excuse for infanticide (Montgomery 1854).

The results of a survey (Table 23) conducted in 1855 seemed to justify his confidence. But Cave-Browne (1857:199-200) was less sanguine of the chances of sustaining the improvement until the most superior royal clans had actually put the proposal to exchange women on a symmetrical basis into practice. His pessimism proved realistic, and the administration papers for 1864-5 sadly admit that infanticide was still being practised in Kangra, and that further public meetings to hammer out a solution to the problem had been convened (General Report on the Administration of the Punjab, 1864-5).

TABLE 23 *Census of children in villages known to practise infanticide, 1855*[1]

Sub-division	*No. of children aged 4 to 14 years*			*Children of less than 4 years of age*		
	Boys	*Girls*	*No. of girls per 1,000 boys*	*Boys*	*Girls*	*No. of girls per 1,000 boys*
Kangra (including Palampur)	514	245	476	271	212	782
Hamirpur	1,171	515	439	842	682	809
Nurpur	697	203	291	617	286	463
Dehra	760	269	353	531	356	670
Total	3,142	1,232	392	2,261	1,536	679

[1] Figures from Cave-Browne 1857:188.

It is difficult to say exactly when infanticide died out in Kangra, or even whether it is entirely extinct today. The 1911 census reported that it had 'dwindled down to insignificance'. But Bhai Mul Raj (1933:3) thought that certain Rajput families were still killing their daughters in the 1920s, and the Dogra Handbook of 1932 (p. 77) described the practice as 'even now regrettably prevalent'. There seems to be little doubt, however, that the incidence of infanticide declined quite rapidly after the turn of the century,[5] though my own enquiries would suggest that it stubbornly persisted in certain pockets on quite a significant scale up until the time of the *biradari* reform movements in the 1930s. My hunch is that it was the reformation itself which finally put paid to the practice by expanding the field within which the symmetrical exchange of women was permitted at the top of the hierarchy.

But although infanticide is now undoubtedly extremely rare, infant mortality remains higher for girls than for boys (cf. Minturn and Hitchcock 1966:78). It would certainly be an exaggeration to describe this as the result of callous neglect, but it is the case that boys are cherished and pampered and have first call on the household's resources,while the attention devoted to a girl is much more perfunctory. I was always struck, for example, by the contrast between two Rajput twins of the house-cluster in which I lived. The boy was chubby and well dressed; his sister decidedly scraggy and her clothes generally in tatters. When they were babies their mother did not have enough milk to feed both children, and it was the boy who was breast-fed.

With the suppression of infanticide the Mians have been forced to adopt a less uncompromising attitude, and to find other ways of disposing of their daughters. Some are married locally to grooms of other royal sub-clans with similar pretensions to stand on the very highest rung of the ladder; some are married far away to the west, while others are left unmarried. These solutions are not, of course, entirely new, since a proportion of the girls of the most superior royal clans had always been raised. But what was new was the scale on which they were now adopted.

Girls of the most superior royal clans who are married are commonly married a long way from home. Since the mere existence of wife-takers is galling to the self-esteem of a Rajput of royal clan, the desire to be separated from them by as large a distance as possible is perhaps understandable. In other cases, the bride's father may perhaps be motivated by a desire to broaden his range of political contacts by acquiring affines in other areas. But most important of all, the demography of Mian marriages simply reflects the general difficulty of finding wife-takers of a sufficiently elevated status within the immediate vicinity.

The direction in which daughters are given in marriage is by no means random. Girls tend to move westwards. In a certain indirect way status is loosely associated with points of the compass. The most refined and aristocratic Rajputs are thought of as belonging to the west; the most plebeian of Rathis to the east. A sort of chain passes through Kangra, and links district Mandi in the east with Jammu in the west. At the top of the hierarchy brides and dowries are passed along the chain in the same direction; at the bottom of the hierarchy, brides go one way and bride-price the other.

This association of high-status bride-takers with the west, and low-status bride-givers with the east, is a common feature of Rajput social organization in northern India, and is explicitly formulated as an ideal rule of marriage in Rajasthan (Karve 1965:125; cf. Mandelbaum 1962:312). But in Kangra – as in Malwa (Mayer 1960:211) – there is no categorical rule which obliges girls to be given in any particular direction, though empirically they tend to be. In fact, the Kangra Rajputs do not formulate the preference in terms of compass points at all. Instead they tend to associate high or low status with particular localities; and broadly speaking the 'better' the locality, the farther along the chain to the west it is situated. Rajputs from the Dhar area of Palampur sub-division take girls from district Mandi to the east but don't give daughters there because Mandi people are 'uncivilized'. They have 'bad customs', a funny way of talking, and they don't have the same proud traditions of military service. People from the Palam area to the west are in their turn reluctant to give their daughters to men from the Dhar area who are considered to lack refinement and to lead a much more Spartan existence. The inhabitants of Nurpur at the western end of the valley talk in an equally disparaging way about Palam.

This correlation between status and longitude seems to derive not so much from any vague knowledge of a general Rajput tradition of high status being associated with the west, but rather from the hard facts of political and economic power. To the east of Palampur lies increasingly inaccessible and barren hill country; to the west, more fertile and prosperous areas with easier access to the plains. At the most prestigious end of the chain is the state of Jammu. Jammu's royal clan acts as a powerful magnet for the girls of the other highly-rated royal clans, and I would speculate that this is because the state was for a long period the largest and most powerful in the hills, and because its Maharaja retained considerable autonomy throughout the British period. Newell's data (1970) on marriage patterns in the neighbouring district of Chamba suggest a similar westward drift of women at marriage which occurs for precisely comparable reasons.

In Palampur, the clan of the local raja are the Katoch. Katoch girls who were married before the reform movements of the 1930s were generally given to Pathania or Jamuwal men in the west. The higher the Katoch sub-clan rates its own status the farther away to the west it has tended to marry its daughters. Before 1930, most of the sons-in-law of the highly prestigious Katoch sub-clan of *mauza* Khera were Jamuwals from Jammu, some hundred miles away. (The pattern here is to be understood in the light of a long tradition of service in the Jammu army. One member of the sub-clan reached the rank of General in the Maharaja's service, his son is now a General in the Indian army, and others of the *khandan* also became high-ranking officers.) I have records of the marriages of 101 Katoch daughters from three different sub-clans in the sub-division. In 79 cases the girls had been married to a groom from the west, and of these a majority were from outside the sub-division.

The cavalier manner in which the superior royal clans dispose of their daughters has to be seen in the context of a situation in which they are confident of their supply of brides from the clans below them. It is hard to believe that they would squander their assets in quite such a prodigal way if they themselves had to take the full consequences of their own actions and go without wives. But since the spirit of hypergamy fosters ambitions in those lower down the hierarchy to gain prestige by acquiring sons-in-law of the highest possible rank, the men on the very top rungs of the ladder experience a glut rather than a scarcity of potential brides. This situation stimulates competition between the potential wife-givers and leads to an escalation of dowry payments. These substantial dowries, and the often considerable prestations which flow from wife-givers to wife-takers throughout the marriage, encouraged grooms of the highest status to 'sell' several times over the honour they confer by their alliance, and this promoted the polygynous accumulation of women at the top of the ladder. This is, of course, a characteristic feature of these north Indian systems of hypergamy, and seems to have reached its most spectacular proportions amongst the Kulin Brahmans of Bengal who sometimes counted over 50, or even a 100, wives (Kapadia 1955:102). The Kangra Mians certainly did things on a more modest scale, though unfortunately no precise figures for the incidence of polygynous marriages in different castes are available. But judging by the genealogies I collected for three of the Katoch sub-clans of Palampur, it was not unusual for an individual to have 4 or 5 wives, the largest number I have on record being 11.

As far as the abstract structure of the hierarchy is concerned, then, polygyny, infanticide, enforced spinsterhood and marriage far away to the west, all perform an identical function in that they all serve to create an artificial shortage of women in the top *biradari*; and it is this shortage which maintains the whole system by creating a demand for brides all the way down the ladder, and which is passed on to the clans at the very bottom, who have to get by without enough wives to go round.

7:6 The rules of exogamy

The situation which I have described, then, is one in which there is an almost inexhaustible supply of men who would welcome an alliance with the clans at the top. But in practice the range of options which is actually open to an individual bridegroom of the highest status is much more limited than this would imply. The field of choice is narrowed not only by the demands of status, which require that a man should not marry too far beneath himself, but also by the number of clans which are excluded by the rules of exogamy. Marriage is theoretically forbidden with the entire clans shown in Table 24.

TABLE 24 *Clans with which marriage is prohibited*

Excluded clans	*Alternative translation*	*Participants' categories*	
1 Own clan		Own *jat* or *khandan*	
2 Other clans of *gotra* (e.g., in Katoch case five other clans)		Own *gotra* (*sagotra*)	
3 Mother's brother's clan	FWB clan[1]	*Jat* of *succa* (real) *mama*	*Jat* of *mama*
4 Stepmother's brother's clan	FWB clan[1]	*Jat* of *matr-paksh*	*Jat* of *mama*
5 Father's mother's brother's clan	FFWB clan	*Jat* of *succa* (real) *dadkiye*	*Jat* of *dadkiye*[2]
6 Father's stepmother's brother's clan	FFWB clan	*Jat* of father's *matr-paksh*	*Jat* of *dadkiye*[2]
7 Mother's mother's brother's clan	FWFWB clan		*Jat* of *nankiye*[2]
8 Stepmother's mother's brother's clan (?)[3]	FWFWB clan		*Jat* of *nankiye*[2]
9 Father's father's mother's brother's clan if the father is still alive		*Jat* of *pardadkiye*	

[1] A man may not take a wife from any clan into which his own daughters have been married (cf. Middleton 1919a:13). If he did so, then his own daughters would be in breach of the rules of exogamy for they would have been married into their FWB clan.

[2] The term *dadkiye* refers collectively to the members of the household which gave a wife to the father's father; the term *nankiye* to the members of the household which gave a wife to the mother's father. Though linguistically related, the terms are not therefore comparable in meaning to the Punjabi terms *dadke* (FF, i.e. own village) and *nanke* (mother's natal village); cf. Eglar (1960:80).

[3] I have never heard this cited spontaneously as one of the prohibitions, though when pressed informants would agree that it is a logical extension of rules 4 and 6.

The effect of these rules is clearly to prohibit repetition of the marriages of one's immediate lineal ascendants, though as we shall see (Chapter 9:6) it is possible and indeed fairly common to repeat the marriages of collaterals (e.g., of a real or classificatory brother, father's brother or father's father's brother). There is no explicit prohibition, comparable to that of the Sarjupari Brahmans (Dumont 1966), on a reversal in the direction of the gift between local descent groups. But such reversals are somewhat objectionable in that they are considered to run counter to the spirit of *kanya dan* and are empirically uncommon at the higher levels of the hierarchy.

In addition to the whole clans listed in Table 24, marriage is also forbidden with the children of the father's sister and the mother's sister, though there is no restriction on other members of their sub-clan unless they are members of the same household. People of all castes prohibit marriage with the children of ego's wet-nurse[6] or foster-mother (*dharam mata*), while the Brahmans also exclude the whole of their hereditary *kul-purohit* clan and the household of their *guru-purohit*,[7] whose son rates as '*guru*-brother' and whose daughter as a '*guru*-sister' to the children of a household in which their father has initiated a *chela* (disciple).

The rules of exogamy are said to ensure the circulation of blood. If they aren't observed, the blood stagnates and the male line is likely to die out or contract leprosy, 'the illness of untouchability' (*achhut di bimari*).[8] Now this idea that the prohibitions guarantee the revitalization of the blood is clearly inconsistent with the maxim, noted earlier, that blood comes from the father and milk from the mother. The discrepancy here is one which is rooted in local genetic theory itself, for Kangra people switch capriciously between this fomula and a second one which is inconsistent with it (cf. Yalman 1967:140; Mayer 1960: 203–4). According to this second view, blood has two components, which one rather sophisticated informant likened to the positive and negative currents in an electrical charge. The positive is passed through the male line and is common to all the members of the clan. The negative is inherited from the mother and its composition is constantly changing. In your body you have the blood of your own mother and your father's mother, but not of your father's father's mother, a notion which clearly ties in closely with the fact that while there is an absolute ban on marrying into the natal clans of the mother and father's mother, marriage with the natal clan of the father's father's mother is perfectly permissible once the father is dead (and is only excluded during his lifetime 'out of respect').[9] It is sometimes claimed that if the father and grandfather have contracted orthodox marriages with women of appropriate rank, then the impurity which attaches to the descendants of an unorthodox or illicit union fades away in the great-grandson's generation and he can regain the status lost as a result of his forebear's misdemeanour. This is because the blood of the woman who was taken in the illicit union no longer flows in the veins of her son's son's son. The essential point is summed up in a much quoted proverb which says that (non-agnatic) kinship ends in the third generation.[10]

As Orenstein (1970) and Tambiah (1973b) have shown, this possibility of regaining status after several generations by meticulously contracting appropriate marriages is clearly conceptualized in the legal texts. But as far as contemporary Kangra is concerned, the real interest here lies in the ideas themselves rather than in any hard reality to which they correspond, for the chances of being able to repair the damage by consistently marrying spouses of impeccable status are rather slim. As a result the stigma which attaches to the descendants of an illicit union often seems to perpetuate itself well beyond the third generation. Any informed Rajput aristocrat knows which royal sub-clans in the vicinity are reputed to be of *sartora* descent, and any self-respecting Mian will be somewhat reluctant to give his daughters in marriage to such a sub-clan.

Just as there is a logical congruence between the second bilateral theory of blood and the rules of exogamy, so the latter seem to harmonize with the configuration of ancestors to whom *pind* are offered at the *saradh* ceremony which precedes the marriage rites. *Pind* are given in the names of the father and mother, to both their fathers and mothers, and to the father's father's father and mother if the father is alive to make the offering. It is as if those pairs of ascendants whose marriages cannot be repeated must be invoked.

It should be noted, however, that the fit between the rules of exogamy on the one hand, and the alternative theory about blood and the offering of *pind* on the other, is not perfect. The need to revitalize the blood obviously does not demand that the clans of the stepmother and the father's stepmother should be excluded. Again *pind* are not given to the parents of the stepmother – as they are to the parents of the real mother – and will only be given to the stepmother herself if she died without sons to make offerings on her behalf.

The basic pattern of these prohibitions corresponds closely to what is often described in the ethnographic literature on north India as the four-clan (or *gotra*) rule: the four excluded clans being those of ego, his mother, his father's mother, and his mother's mother (Mayer 1960: 202–3; Karve 1965:118–23; Tiemann 1970). But the essential difference between the Kangra pattern, and what is usually reported as the orthodox four-clan formula, is that in the Kangra case the prohibition is on taking wives from the natal clans of all the father's wives and the father's father's wives, and not just from the clans of the mother and the father's mother. In this respect, then, the rules appear to be couched in the idiom of affinity rather than in the idiom of consanguinity. Yet in other respects it is clear that the ultimate justification for this elaborate set of prohibitions is provided by considerations of consanguinity expressed as a need to revitalize the blood. Consistent with this the rules are actually applied in a much less rigorous way to *matr-paksh* (i.e. 'step-') clans; and marriage with the children of the father's sister and mother's sister (who share the same bodily substance as one's parents) is prohibited while other more remote members of their clans are perfectly eligible spouses (cf. Mayer 1960:203). What all this seems to hint at – and here I anticipate a fuller discussion in Chapter 10 – is that the Rajputs themselves have yet to take a firm stand on 'the alliance/descent controversy', and can (and do) present their system in terms of either model.

Apart from the affinal idiom, there is also an important variation between the way in which Kangra people actually apply the prohibitions and the way in which they are applied in some other areas. In Malwa (Mayer 1960:202) and amongst the Jats of Punjab (Karve 1965: 118–19; Tiemann 1970), for instance, marriage is forbidden if any of the four clans which are excluded for the boy are also excluded for the girl.

> A man and a woman cannot marry if any one of their own, their mother's, their father's mother's and their mother's mother's mother's *got* coincide. Or to put it another way, if the *got* names of a prospective bridegroom and bride's father, mother, father's mother and mother's mother are called out, no name must occur twice' (Tiemann 1970:168–9).

The Malwa-Jat rules, then, would prevent a boy of clan X from marrying a girl of clan Y who shares any of the same prohibitions as he does, even though Y itself is not excluded. In Kangra, by contrast, such a marriage would be perfectly acceptable, provided only that clan Y is not itself excluded for the groom (or X for the bride). The former variant requires, as Karve notes (1965:120), an absolute minimum of eight groups in order to function, while the latter would theoretically be possible with only five clans.[11]

Were Kangra people to operate the rules in the more rigorous way in which they are applied in Ramkheri, it would greatly exacerbate the problem of finding eligible spouses for many of the people at the very top of the hierarchy. It can be hard enough as it is for the men of the highest clans to find suitable wives. We have seen that in the past the Mians often married polygynously. Take, then, the case of a Katoch whose father is still alive, and whose father and grandfather have both married three times. In that case there might be a total of 14 clans excluded by the rules of exogamy (5 by the ban on marrying within the *gotra*). In terms of the categories shown in Table 19, Katoch men take girls from the other Jai Karia Rajputs of 1b and 1c, and from the most superior clans of the second *biradari*, but are not supposed to go any lower than this. In other words, there are only about 28 clans from which to select a wife. But in our hypothetical example, half of these are excluded by the rules of exogamy, while others are likely to be ruled out because they are concentrated in areas with which there is no contact. On the face of it, then, the rules look unworkably rigid, and some of the men at the top of the ladder will have to choose between not getting married at all, or marrying a girl of a prohibited clan, or of a clan which is normally regarded as too inferior to merit the honour of being accepted as their wife-givers.

One answer here is that in such a situation the rules have probably always been bent. Describing a similar set of prohibitions for the neighbouring district of Hoshiarpur, the District Gazetteer records that they 'must of necessity be relaxed in the case of tribes who are already strictly limited by status' (Hoshiarpur District Gazetteer, 1906:35). Barnes (1889:7), Griffin (1870:629) and Goswami (n.d.) all cite instances in which a raja had married within his own *gotra*, and I myself came across the odd case in which a Mian had taken a girl from a prohibited clan. Most of the instances I encountered in which a man had broken the ban on marrying into the natal clan of the stepmother involved Katoch aristocrats, which is hardly surprising in view of the fact that it was they who most frequently married polygynously.

But in spite of such lapses it is precisely the clans at the top of the ladder who appear to be most conscientious in their insistence on the full range of prohibitions. Although everybody pays lip-service to the same set of rules, the lower down the ladder one goes the less fussy people tend to be in practice. Apart from the stepmother's clan, my data would suggest that marriage with the mother's mother's clan is more readily tolerated than any of the other prohibited unions, though I also encountered one or two cases where marriage had taken place with the father's mother's clan.[12] But however lax the clans on the bottom of the ladder are with regard to the other rules, the prohibition on marrying into one's own clan, or with a girl of one's real mother's brother's clan, is a kind of uncouth minimum which even the lowest of Rathis cannot ignore with impunity. This is in contrast with the situation in the neighbouring state of Mandi where it is reported that even high-ranking Rajputs sometimes marry with a girl of their mother's brother's clan (Mandi State Gazetteer, 1904:27).

The situation, then, is that the people at the top of the hierarchy attach the highest value to the rules of exogamy while they themselves experience the greatest difficulty in observing them, a difficulty which was especially acute in the days when polygynous marriages were common. In view of this, it is hardly surprising that some Mians of the highest status, encouraged no doubt by the financial incentive of a higher dowry, consented to take brides from lower-ranking clans of the second *biradari*. But the only difference between 2a and 2b (in Table 19) is that the most superior Jai Karias take girls from 2a but not from 2b. My point is that the rules are such that on some occasions Katoch men have precious little option but to marry with the clans of 2b, since there is nobody else; and that this introduces an element of flexibility into the system, since a sub-clan of 2b which starts to give girls to the top Jai Karias becomes part of 2a.

7:7 The consequences of hypergamy for the Rathis

The clans at the bottom of the hierarchy are faced, as we have seen, with a shortage of brides. In the days before the *biradari* reforms their plight was especially acute since at that time a significantly higher proportion of marriages were hypergamous (see Chapter 8:3). One consequence of this shortage was that in some parts of the region substantial numbers of men in the lowest *biradari* were unable to get married at all (cf. Van der Veen 1972:143; Shah 1974:36). The strikingly high proportion of bachelors amongst the Rathis was noted by several writers. Bhai Mul Raj (1933:3), for example, records that:

> in some thirteen families of Thakurs near Dehra town . . . there are no less than twenty unmarried males between the ages of 22 and

> 60, although infant marriage and universal marriage are supposed to be the rule. Similarly the Marhwal families of Tika Mahl have a number of men in search of brides (cf. Middleton 1919b:4).

In other parts of the region their difficulties were so acute that:

> the lower classes appear to be dying out. Their estates are undermanned . . . and badly farmed . . . (while) amongst the higher classes there is a general tendency to increase (Gurdaspur District Gazetteer, 1915:50; cf. Rose 1919:276).

But clearly the wholesale extinction of the groups at the bottom of the ladder is incompatible with the survival of the system itself; and in practice they have adopted a whole series of palliatives which take the edge off the problem. To some extent the deficit is made good, for example, by the fact that the men marry late and the widows remarry, ideally with the deceased husband's younger brother, who even during his elder brother's lifetime enjoys a tolerated licence (if not a formal right) to sexual access to his brother's wife.

The scarcity of brides at the bottom of the ladder also appears to be associated with inflationary bride-price payments, sibling exchange marriages in which a father uses his daughter to secure a wife for his son, and a ready acceptance of divorce. High bride-price payments in turn encourage *rakhewa* unions with the deceased brother's wife, for such marriages represent a considerable economy (cf. Pocock 1972:65).

It would clearly be wrong to argue that hypergamy is the *cause* of such practices, for they are common to the isogamous castes below the Rajputs. But it is equally clear that many of the demeaning attributes which are held to justify the inferiority of those at the bottom of the ladder are entrenched by the system itself. By the same token hypergamy would seem to promote the orthodox Hindu prejudice against widow remarriage at the top of the hierarchy, since the effect of such marriages would be to expand the number of marriageable women available to the royal clans, and so to increase the difficulty of disposing of daughters. Furthermore, it is not easy to imagine who would pay dowry for a widow, or be prepared to accept a widow in marriage without (cf. Bouglé 1971:91–2; Risley 1915:184).

It would appear that as far as the Chadhiar area is concerned, the difficulties which face the clans of the fourth *biradari* are also alleviated by recruiting substantial numbers of brides from district Mandi to the east. Of the 115 men of the lowest *biradari* whose marriages I recorded,

37 (or 32 per cent) had taken wives from Mandi, while in only 5 (8·2 per cent) of the 61 marriages of daughters had the direction of the gift been reversed. But clearly taking brides from the east only helps to ease the problem if they more than replace the number of daughters who are given away to the west. Although my sample is too small to be completely confident, it does seem that this is indeed the case. While 32 per cent of the wives had been born in Mandi, only 10 (16·4 per cent) of the 61 daughters from Chadhiar had been given in Palam to the west, the vast majority being married within the immediate vicinity of Chadhiar.

Assuming that this pattern is general, and that the Rathis of the Dhar area gain on balance more women than they lose, we can begin to understand the distribution of another more drastic remedy to which the clans of the fourth *biradari* have traditionally resorted. Throughout this region the consequences of hypergamy have disposed the men on the bottom rungs of the ladder to transgress the ideal of caste endogamy by contracting unions with women of the cultivating and artisan castes below them (cf. Barnes 1889:36; Lyall 1889: 99). Now such inter-caste unions appear to have been much more common in some places than others, and by this criterion the fourth *biradari* sub-clans of the Chadhiar area seem to score better marks for caste puritanism than their peers from other localities. It is tempting, then, to relate this comparative orthodoxy to a demographic pattern in which more brides come into the area from the east than go out to the west.

In Nurpur sub-division it was largely Jat girls who were recruited by those men who could not find a wife within the *biradari*, while Rose (1919:282) mentions the Water-carriers as an additional source of supply. But in most parts of the valley the majority of these unions were between Rathi men and Girth-cultivator women. In Kangra there is a proverb that in the fifth generation the Girth's daughter becomes a queen.

Although *in certain contexts*, any inferiority in the status of the mother may be held to depreciate the relative status of her offspring within the patrilineal descent group, the individual's rank *vis-à-vis* members of other sub-clans is derived from that of the agnatic group to which he belongs (Chapter 9:4). It is precisely because status is primarily perpetuated in the male line that the Rathis can afford to admit the legitimacy of their children by Girth-cultivator women, and to adopt a rather nonchalant attitude towards breaches of caste endogamy. As Yalman (1967:280) puts it:

> The more emphasis is placed on a unilineal principle of descent, the less there is need for strict endogamy, for the patronymic can be made to carry the status distinction. Alternatively, where marriage is confined to a small endogamous circle, then unilineal principles are rendered redundant for these purposes (cf. Leach 1961c:74; Barth 1960:132).

In other terms, endogamy is not, as Dumont (1964) points out, the ultimate principle, but is rather entailed by the demands of status. Where caste affiliation is purely patrilineal (e.g., Barth 1959, 1960; Stirrat 1975), the endogamous requirement is dispensed with altogether.

Though somewhat less extreme, the Kangra Rajputs are clearly closer to this unilineal pole of the continuum than to the meticulously endogamous bilateral systems of, for example, Kandyan Ceylon. According to local genetic theory there is no fundamental incompatibility between the fact that the men at the bottom of the hierarchy sometimes contract unions with women of inferior caste, and the ideology of caste purity or the notion that each caste has a unique quality of blood. On the formula that all blood comes from the father, the purity of the mother's blood is clearly of no consequence as far as the purity of her children is concerned. According to the second theory, which posits that the blood of both parents flows in the child's veins, that of the mother only dilutes the blood of her offspring to a limited extent, for the 'positive' element derived from the father is the constant one. The woman's contribution is to the volatile 'negative' component, and does no permanent damage to the purity of her descendants, since the inferior element she introduces will be eliminated in subsequent generations. In any case, the royal clans at the top of the hierarchy – those who are considered to be the Rajputs *par excellence* and who sometimes claim to be the only 'true' Rajputs – are completely insulated from the genetic consequences of these inter-caste unions. If a non-Rajput woman marries into the fourth *biradari*, then her daughter (who potentially marries into the third *biradari*), and her daughter's daughter (who potentially marries into the second) are contaminated by the blood of the inferior caste. But her daughter's daughter's daughter is not, and she is the first female descendant of the original inter-caste union who is potentially of appropriate birth status to rate as a gift to a groom of one of the royal clans.

As the second bilateral theory of blood seems to demand, endogamy continues to stand as an ideal for the Kangra Rajputs despite their patrilineal bias; and there is some reason to suppose that as a consequence families of lower caste who gave several daughters in marriage to Rathi grooms could aspire to being eventually reclassified as Rathis themselves. The general point here is that a thoroughgoing regime of hypergamy tends to spread its tentacles ever more widely, for the shortages of women it creates at the bottom of the ladder make the lower fringes of the caste subject to continuous infiltration, and thus promotes a surreptitious but incessant expansion of the endogamous unit. At the same time hypergamy preserves the links between the different grades within the caste and thus maintains its unity (cf. Pocock 1972). As Mandelbaum (1962:317) puts it, hypergamy 'permits the differentiation of groups according to ritual practice, power and rank, yet maintains a certain unity among the parts which are hypergamously differentiated.'

7:8 Rajputs and Rathis

By contracting unions with Girth and Jat women, the men of the fourth *biradari* unambiguously infringe the ideal of caste endogamy. But the precedent they set is not quite so radical as it might at first sight appear, for there are other structural barriers which straddle the hierarchy, which seem to be almost as important as the one which separates the fourth *biradari* from the cultivating castes below them, and which are commonly crossed in marriage.

These days nobody would dispute that the Rathis are as much Rajputs as anybody else, though they are often dismissed as *halke* ('lightweight') Rajputs by their superiors. But they were not generally accorded even this dubious honour in the nineteenth-century administrative reports on the area. Throughout this literature they are usually classified as Shudras, in opposition to the Rajputs who rated, of course, as Kshatriyas. Consistent with this, they were traditionally denied the right to wear the sacred thread or to keep *tulsi* shrines, and they observed a 21-day period of death pollution like the cultivating and artisan castes below them, while those higher up the ladder were held to be polluted for only 13 days (cf. Cunningham 1932:83).

Earlier in this century the Rathis conducted a concerted and eventually successful campaign to have themselves classified as Rajputs in the official records. This campaign was given a certain edge by the pragmatic consideration that clans listed as Rajputs were given preference in recruitment to the army and promotion from the ranks (see below, Chapter 8:7). At the time of the 1921 census the Rathis pressed their case before the census authorities. The Kangra rajas were consulted and used their influence to veto the reform. But when, in the next decade, pressure was brought to bear on the district administration by the increasingly vocal *biradari* councils, and Rathi servicemen started to agitate in the ranks, the authorities capitulated.

The apparent implication might seem to be that during the nineteenth century the Rajputs and Rathis constituted two distinct castes. But on close examination the position turns out to be rather less clear-cut. Ibbetson (1883:251) describes the Rathis as degraded Rajputs who, 'though they are admittedly Rajputs and give their daughters to Rajputs who are styled by that title, do not reach the standard which would entitle them to be called Rajput.' Barnes (1889:39) depicts them as a breed of bastard Rajput, and reports that 'the offspring of a Rajput father by a Shudra mother would be styled a Rathi, and accepted as such by the brotherhood.'

That the Rathis were once reckoned to belong to a completely different caste from the Rajputs seems unlikely in view of the fact that there has never been a complete consensus on the exact point at which the line between the two categories should be drawn. Conventionally the first and second *biradaris* are said to be Rajputs, and the third and fourth to be Rathis; and this is the division which received formal recognition in the British records. But the Mians sometimes explain that the term 'Rajput' derives from *raja putr* – 'the son of a king' – and assert that therefore the only true Rajputs are those of royal clan. Their claim reflects a general tendency for people on all but the lowest rungs of the ladder to classify themselves as Rajputs and those below them as Rathis (cf. Pocock 1972:61). The District Gazetteer (1926: 166) sums all this up when it records that:

> It is not easy to indicate the line which separates the Rajput from the class immediately below him, known in the hills by the appellation Thakur and Rathi. The Mian would restrict the term Rajput to those of royal descent; while the Rathi naturally seeks a broader definition, so as to include his own pretensions. The limit here given on the authority of Mr. Barnes is probably just; and those are legitimately entitled to rank as Rajputs who are themselves the members of a royal clan, or are connected in marriage with them.

By contrast with the proud title of 'Rajput' the label 'Rathi' has distinctly unflattering connotations; and today at any rate the term itself is considered to be so derogatory that it is extremely impolite to refer to somebody as a Rathi in his hearing. Even before their systematic campaign to eliminate the term from the records, members of those Rathi clan-segments which were on the way up went to enormous lengths to persuade the revenue officials to enter them as Rajputs in the land registers (Shuttleworth 1916:13). Success sometimes led to all sorts of bureaucratic anomalies and made complete nonsense of official attempts to maintain a neat and tidy distinction between the two categories. In Chadhiar, for example, the Nanwaraks of *tika* Chhek managed to get themselves entered in the records as Rajputs; while their poorer clansmen from *tika* Nanwar continued to be classified as Rathis.

On the one hand, then, the Rathis used to be classified as Shudras, could not wear the sacred thread, and are said to have observed a period of mourning appropriate to the artisan and cultivating castes below them. But on the other hand they are variously described in the literature as 'bastard Rajputs', or as Rajputs who are too degraded to be allowed that title.

In order to resolve the apparent contradiction here, and to avoid the kind of 'substantialist fallacy' the British authorities committed when they tried to define a precise boundary between the two categories, we need to remember that the people themselves think in segmentary terms, and that neither in language nor in other symbolic aspects of behaviour do they appear to signal an absolute discontinuity between groups at different levels of segmentation. What this points to is that in opposition to the lower *biradaris*, aristocratic Rajputs will define themselves as if they were of an entirely different species. But *vis-à-vis* the artisan and cultivating castes in the middle ranges of the hierarchy, both 'Rajputs' and 'Rathis' will generally be conceptualized as a single unit. Nor is this simply the judgment of outsiders, for in such contexts even the aristocratic Mians have to concede that the Rathis are a kind of Rajput, for the unacceptable alternative is to deny the ideal of caste endogamy.

But what can be said is that between the Rathis and the Rajputs there used to be a 'caste-like' barrier. Similarly relations betwen *biradaris* within the hypergamous hierarchy are governed – as we have seen (section 3 above) – by a set of ideal interactional rules which are strictly comparable to the rules by which castes within the total hierarchy interact. What I am getting at here, then, is that the relationship between Rajputs and Rathis, and between one *biradari* and another is conceptualized as different, not in kind but only in degree, from the relationship between the fourth *biradari* and the cultivating castes. Put in this context, breaches of caste endogamy are not quite such a radical solution to the problem of the shortage of women at the bottom of the hierarchy as they might at first sight appear.

7:9 Legitimacy and the validity of marriage

The union between a Rajput and a Rathi woman, or between a Rathi and a Girth woman, may have the status of a valid marriage the children of which are perfectly legitimate and entitled to inherit. In this respect at least, there is absolutely no discrimination between the sons of an 'equal' and of an 'unequal' wife.

For heuristic purposes we can distinguish between 'marriage' (the offspring of which are legitimate) and 'concubinage' (the offspring of which are illegitimate); and – following Dumont (1961a and b; 1964; 1970:114–16) – between 'primary' and 'secondary' marriage.

> In the case of a woman we shall call the first marriage the *primary* marriage. Once this marriage has been contracted, either it is indissoluble even by the death of the spouse (superior castes) or else the woman may, after her husband's death or even after divorce, contract another union, legitimate, but infinitely less prestigious, involving much less ritual and expense, which we shall call *secondary* marriage. Secondary marriage, being of lower status, is freer, sometimes much freer, than primary marriage (Dumont 1970:114).

These analytical distinctions are closely mirrored by the set of categories with which Kangra people themselves operate, and which serve to discriminate between a *bihoti* (or *bihoyu*), a *rikhorar* and a *sarit*. A *bihoti* is a woman whose current union is her first or 'primary' marriage; a *rikhorar* is a widow or a divorcee who has contracted a secondary union. The third category – *sarit* – are concubines with whom a valid marriage would not be possible on grounds of caste (cf. Middleton 1919a:ii).

Congruent with the distinction between a *bihoti* and a *rikhorar* is the distinction between a *lagan-ved* and a *jhanjarar* marriage. The *lagan-ved* ritual involves an elaborate series of Sanskritic rites which are officiated over by the family *purohits* of the bride and groom, and which require the active participation of a wide range of kin. It is the most lengthy, most expensive and most prestigious type of marriage ceremony, and as far as the clans in the higher echelons of the hierarchy are concerned, it is the only valid form of marriage. For the woman it marks an absolutely crucial turning point in her life, for it transforms her from the status of unmarried girl (*kanya* or *kuari*) into the status of a married woman (*bihoti*). This being so she can only go through such a ceremony once in her lifetime; and even amongst those clans which tolerate remarriage, the *lagan-ved* can never be repeated. Subsequent unions will be solemnized by a *jhanjarar* ceremony if they are solemnized at all.

Looked at from the man's point of view, however, this distinction between *lagan-ved* and *jhanjarar* is of far less critical significance. He may contract any number of *lagan-ved* marriages; and amongst those who tolerate widow remarriage and divorce such rites do not inevitably mark his first marriage which may be with a *rikhorar*. But although a man may pass through more than one *lagan-ved* marriage, in my experience the rites tend to be somewhat telescoped in the case of subsequent unions. A groom who has previously been married is a *duharju* and his bride a *noli*. Amongst Brahmans there is a strong prejudice against giving one's daughter as a *noli* for, quite apart from the difficulties of being a co-wife, this depreciates her value as *dan*. (Indeed, the term itself evokes a girl of suspect pedigree from outside the locality.) As Tambiah (1973a) has pointed out, 'the gift of a virgin' is here associated with the ideal of monogamy. Though the Rajputs do not appear to feel so strongly on the matter, all things being equal they too prefer a previously unmarried groom.

The *jhanjarar* rites are much shorter, less costly and less prestigious. In the crucial part of the ceremony the bride resumes the nose-ring (*balu*) which is the symbol of her married status and which she had put off at the time of the death of her first husband, or after her separation from him. If she is a widow she also discards the white shawl which she had worn as a mark of her widowhood, and resumes a coloured one. The occasion should be presided over by a Brahman and marked by a feast to which close kinsmen are invited. But these days, when those who had traditionally tolerated widow remarriage and divorce are anxious to dissociate themselves from such practices, all public display tends to be avoided and the ceremony is sometimes dispensed with altogether. But whether the couple perform *jhanjarar* or not, a woman who contracts a secondary union with a man of her own caste or of a caste with which she may legitimately marry, rates as a *rikhorar*.

In addition to *lagan-ved* and *jhanjarar* there is a third type of marriage ritual known as *brar-phuki* which represents the minimum ritual possible. According to hearsay, the couple simply set fire to, and walk round a burning *brar* bush. These days at least, *brar-phuki* is extremely rare and almost invariably seems to involve runaway 'love-marriages'.

Though the point is disputed – more I suspect from wishful thinking than actual experience – my information suggests that the *brar-phuki* ceremony can be performed though the bride has never been given in *lagan-ved*. With this rather doubtful exception, we can conclude that as far as a woman is concerned, the *lagan-ved* ceremony is essential before she can enter the status of *bihoti*, and that the prior performance of *lagan-ved* is a necessary qualification for contracting a 'secondary' (*jhanjarar*) union.

The distinction between primary (*lagan-ved*) and secondary (*jhanjarar*) marriage is crucial to understanding the nature of the union of a Rathi man and a Girth or Jat woman. The point here is that such a union cannot be sanctified by *lagan-ved* rites, and can only be solemnized by the less prestigious forms of ritual (cf. Rose 1919:282).

A union with a *sarit* is not generally marked by any sort of ceremony. But it is said that in the old days, people of the élite Rajput families would sometimes give several *sarit* along with the dowry as handmaids for the bride, and as bedmates for the groom; and that these girls would accompany the bridal couple on the seventh round of the sacred fire (*hawan*) at the time of the *vedi* ceremony, at which the bride's father formally makes over his daughter to the groom.

The hypergamous hierarchy divides between those clans which insist that only the children of a *bihoti* who has married according to *lagan-ved* rites are legitimate, and those which recognize the legitimacy of the children of a *rikhorar*. Predictably enough the distinction is congruent with the distinction between those clans which forbid widow remarriage and those which tolerate it. Broadly speaking, then, the dividing line is between the Rajputs of the top two *biradaris*, and the Rathis of the bottom two *biradaris*.

As far as the former are concerned, the children of a *rikhorar*, a *sarit*, or a woman married by *brar-phuki* rites, are *sartoras*, or bastards. By customary law *sartoras* are not entitled to inherit although they can claim a maintenance allowance (*guzara*) from their father's estate. But although it is only the children of a *bihoti* married according to *lagan-ved* rites who are recognized as legitimate, unions with a *rikhorar* or a *sarit* are not categorically forbidden, but merely rated as inferior (cf. Dumont 1961a); they are only likely to lead to excommunication if the woman belongs to one of the outside castes (cf. Kangra District Gazetteer, 1926:141; Middleton 1919a:ii). But even in such a case the miscreant may very well get away with it if he is a man of substance. Chadhiar's most celebrated roué – a Katoch aristocrat who died some years ago – left children by the two Koli mistresses he maintained. It never became essential to boycott him because, it is said, he would never eat with either family.

While the superior Rajputs and the Brahmans distinguish between the legitimate children of a *bihoti* and the illegitimate children of a *rikhorar* and a *sarit*, the Rathis and Girths draw the line in a different place. As far as they are concerned, the children of a *rikhorar* are also legitimate, provided that their mother is of clean caste. Not only do they recognize all three varieties of marriage ceremony as valid – the validity of the *jhanjarar* being upheld by the courts (cf. Kangra District Gazetteer, 1926:142-3) – but in practice they treat cohabitation, unsanctified by any ritual, as enough to establish the legitimacy of the children and their right to inherit (cf. Middleton 1919a:37, 140). Nor do such children suffer any inferiority by virtue of the status of their mother's marriage. This lack of discrimination based on the nature of the marriage itself (i.e. primary or secondary) conforms to the pattern general in north India, 'where the difference is scarcely more than one of ritual and of the prestige of the spouses, and it is not passed on to their descendants' (Dumont 1970:115); but it is in contrast to the southern pattern where the difference between the two sorts of marriage is itself sufficient to establish a rank order between the children (Dumont 1961a).

7:10 Bride-price and dowry

In an earlier part of the analysis we have seen that competition for royal grooms leads to an escalation in the size of dowries, and that the Mians often married several times and collected a large dowry for each wife. Nor do their rewards stop there, for throughout the relationship the husband's family continues to receive gifts from the family of the bride. Every year they get presents of foodstuffs on the occasion of the *Hariali puja*, which is celebrated during the rains. For the first year of her marriage, the bride goes backwards and forwards between the house of her parents and that of her new husband. This period of *ghera-phera* ('coming and going') is brought to an end at the *dobara* (or *maklawa*) ceremony, when the girl, accompanied by a second though far more modest dowry payment, is finally dispatched to live permanently in her husband's home. When the daughter has a baby, her parents send clothes to all the members of her household, and silver ornaments for the child. When *her* daughters get married, her brother or father has to provide various expensive items of apparel for both the bride and her mother, and is expected to help with the cost of entertaining the marriage party. If her husband dies, then all the households of her natal lineage send her condolence gifts of cloth (*randepa*). In addition to these formal prestations, lavish hospitality and many informal gifts are showered on members of the husband's family, and the Mian sons-in-law of well-to-do landlords sometimes receive regular and substantial subventions of grains from the produce of their wife's father's land.

These gift-giving obligations endure through time and the flow of prestations continues to be highly asymmetrical, for the ideology of *kanya dan* inhibits even those who have given wives in previous generations from accepting any but the most token return. Although the natal households of the wife and mother are the major donors, those of the father's mother's brother and mother's mother's brother are also expected to give without receiving (cf. Chapter 10:3). For example, the daughter's daughter of a Bakshi widow of Ther is married to a Manhas of *tika* Matial. Not only did the widow provide a substantial portion of the girl's dowry, but she subsequently gave them a buffalo and takes every opportunity – as I myself witnessed – to send them gifts of a more minor nature. Even though the alliance cannot be directly renewed for three generations, these enduring gift-giving obligations sustain the affinal relationship over this period (cf. Tambiah 1973a:93).

The Mians are able to command the most substantial prestations. In the past, when polygyny was more common, they could do so from a larger number of wife-givers; while at the same time infanticide ensured that there were fewer wife-takers to drain their resources. It is not perhaps immediately apparent, then, why they have not been getting richer and richer, and why they are not the biggest landlords.

The dowry (*daj*) itself generally consists of cooking utensils and furniture for the house; and – by far the most expensive item – gold ornaments and other articles of personal adornment for the bride. This is sometimes, though I believe rarely, supplemented by a surreptitious payment in cash. If the necessity arises, the gold might also be converted into cash; and theoretically, of course, the cash could be invested in land. But it is important to remember that this would not have been possible before the first British Settlement in 1849, since all the land was held in grant from the raja, and the cultivator had no right to sell his holding (Chapter 2:5). But even after Settlement there were few incentives of a purely economic kind to induce the Mians to adopt this strategy. Since the men could not plough, and the women could not work in the fields, they had to give most of their land out on tenancy. But during the British period the demand for tenants often exceeded the supply, and the landlord's share of the profits was not particularly attractive (Chapter 3:2).

The second major reason why the Mians don't accumulate more and more wealth is that their customs and style of life demand a high degree of conspicuous consumption. The whole pattern of affinal prestations can thus be seen as a sort of subsidy which enables them to keep up a highly prestigious, but highly uneconomic, life-style. In economic terms, however, Mian status is a somewhat ambiguous asset, the advantages of which are significantly different for rich and poor members of the *biradari*. Hard physical labour is not greatly admired, and the affinal prestations received by a rich Mian landlord are therefore merely a kind of bonus for the ostentatious indolence he would anyway permit himself. But, despite the hand-outs from his wife-giving affines, a poor Mian's status may be something of an economic liability, since it prevents him from working his own farm with family labour and forces him to live in a manner he can ill afford. It was the plight of such men that led to the lifting of the mandatory ban on ploughing at the time of the *biradari* reforms.

I have no reliable historical data on the size of dowries, but today the value of those given and received by the Chadhiar Rajputs range between a minimum of Rs. 1,000 and a maximum of Rs. 12,000, with an average of Rs. 3,000 to 4,000. A woman's dowry is explicitly conceptualized as the nucleus of the property of the individual conjugal household and as a kind of 'pre-mortem inheritance' (Tambiah 1973a); though it would be more accurate to say that while a son has an enforceable right to inherit a precisely specified share of the ancestral property, a daughter has a moral claim to be provided with a dowry (of unspecified proportions) in lieu of the rights of maintenance she renounces at marriage. As a result, there is some ambivalence about whether the dowry she brings may be used to subsidize that of her husband's sister, though in practice this is often discreetly done.

But 'inheritance' is not the only aspect. One part of the dowry – a gift known as *bagge* consisting of one or more tin trunks containing clothes and some ornaments for the women of the groom's immediate *khandan* and close female kin of other lineages – is purely an affinal prestation which does not become part of the conjugal estate. Nor does the trousseau of the bride herself, to which the groom's side also make a substantial contribution in the form of ornaments, clothes and cosmetics (collectively *barasui*). Before the wedding they will also have sent a smaller gift (*samuht*) of items intended for the beautification of the bride on her wedding day. In addition there are also the gifts (a gold ring, a *dhoti*, a suit of clothes and today perhaps a wrist-watch) presented to the groom himself by the bride's brother and intended for his exclusive use.

One further element which is particularly marked in cases of dramatic hypergamy is that of a groom-price. This is reflected in the fact that the more ambitious a father and the higher in the hierarchy he aspires to marry his daughter, the more he must be prepared to pay as *daj* (cf. Yalman 1967:174; Pocock n.d.; Van der Veen 1972:132; Rivers 1923:17). But the dilemma here is that although a munificent dowry is a matter of pride, it may also draw attention to the wide disparity of status between the two families (cf. Pocock 1972:106; Van der Veen 1972:193). It seems to be primarily in such instances that a hidden cash element, which enables the groom's father to overcome his scruples without unduly publicizing the financial inducement to do so, enters into the transaction.

Having once acquired affines of royal clan, those members of the second *biradari* who could afford to do so had a powerful incentive to continue to subsidize their hard-up sons-in-law with substantial gifts. Not only do these affinal prestations bring prestige in themselves, but they are also held to facilitate the acceptance of the bride by her husband's family and to preserve her from the accusation that she is the daughter of miserly clod-hoppers. Moreover, the consequences of withholding such gifts may well have meant writing off their initial investment represented by the higher dowry they had to pay to acquire a higher-status groom. Since a Mian was liable to be expelled from the *biradari* if financial necessity forced him to take up ploughing, or to make his women work in the fields, and since the father-in-law's own status is critically dependent on the status of his son-in-law, a rich man of the second *biradari* had a direct interest in making it financially possible for his royal son-in-law to maintain his rank. For their part, the Mians obviously had strong material incentives to select the richest in-laws they could find.

The size of the dowry not only reflects the relative status of the two sub-clans, but is also to some extent dependent on the personal attainments of the prospective bride and groom. A well-qualified boy with prospects commands a higher dowry than a dullard without; while an educated girl who can potentially earn her own living may be given less than her illiterate sister (cf. Van der Veen 1972:39–40, 63).

But none of this should be taken to imply that dowry negotiations are open and direct. The very idea that the two fathers should sit down together and strike a bargain as if they were haggling over some business deal is pure anathema to Kangra people. The ideal is rather that the groom's side should accept whatever comes their way without comment or complaint, and that the bride's father should give as much as he can possibly afford. But in practice, the wife-takers seldom remain entirely aloof from such matters; and they are particularly unlikely to do so when the bride's status is appreciably lower than their own. In order to preserve appearances, however, they themselves stolidly maintain the appearance of complete disinterest while a tacit understanding is reached through intermediaries, who subtly communicate the expectations (or even demands) of the groom's side to the bride's father, and who have assessed their ability to fulfil them well before the negotiations have reached a critical stage.

One indication that these expectations are to be met is provided by the scale on which gifts are made at *sagan*, which formally seals the engagement. As a rule of thumb I have heard it said that these prestations, known as *tikka* (a term which may also be used for the occasion itself), are equivalent in value to one-eighth of the bride's father's expenditure on the dowry and the wedding ritual. *Tikka* is brought to the groom's house by the bride's family *purohit* and consists of clothing for the wives and daughters of his lineage, various utensils, some money for the groom himself and a large quantity of sweets. Formerly, however, the engagement was clinched at *cha-pani* ('tea and water') when a party of men from the groom's house (excluding the groom himself) visited the bride's house and were given food, turbans and money. *Cha-pani* is somewhat cheaper than *sagan*, and today it is conventional for the groom's side to suggest that they stick to the custom of their ancestors, but to capitulate graciously to the bride's father's insistence that *sagan* be held.

The literature describes the pre-reformation hierarchy as divided between the top two *biradaris* who pay dowry, and the bottom two *biradaris* who accept bride-price. Reading between the lines, however, it is clear that some upwardly mobile Rathi sub-clans waived payment, while financial necessity drove some impoverished Rajputs to accept it. But although there were always some renegades in the second *biradari*, it is broadly true that most members of the *biradari* gave dowries with their daughters; and while there were some paragons in the third *biradari*, it is broadly true that they took bride-price. This division is clearly closely related to the demand for royal grooms at the top of the ladder and the shortages of brides at the bottom.[13]

It is also clear that the clans of the second *biradari* were victims of the system in that on the one hand they had to pay large dowries, and may even have been expected to support their Mian sons-in-law with grain, while on the other hand they had to pay bride-price to the Rathis. According to O'Brien the current rates of bride-price in 1891 were up to Rs. 400 or more, and this at a time when a soldier in the army was getting Rs. 5 per month.[14] Not surprisingly the effect was that 'where owners are in the habit of giving daughters gratis and buying brides for themselves, they are always poor and in debt and their land is certain to be mortgaged' (O'Brien 1891). The general point here is that the whole pattern of bride-price and dowry transactions made for a good deal of mobility in the middle ranges of the hierarchy, for inevitably some sub-clans could not stand the pace and had to drop out of the competition for Mian husbands. They may even have been forced to take bride-price, in which case they would be expelled into the third *biradari*.

But what inducement is there for the clans at the bottom of the hierarchy to continue to pass women up the ladder? The obvious answers here are that the Rathis get bride-price, and everybody gets a status boost from marrying their daughters and sisters to men of the higher clans. Indeed such marriages were crucial to the Rathis' pretensions to be Rajputs, for it was by virtue of their hypergamous alliances with clans of indubitable Rajput status that they themselves could claim membership of the caste. Moreover, the whole cycle of prestations is closed by the return of land. Since the Mians could not work their own farms, they had to give much of their land out on tenancy, and a large proportion of this area was cultivated by Rathis. Like those whose own daughters and sisters were married to Mians, then, the Rathis too had some sort of stake in the ability of the royal clans to sustain themselves without having to plough.

By contrast with dowry, the bride-price given for the girls of the third and fourth *biradaris* takes the form of a short-term cash transaction which is generally handed over into two instalments; one at the time of the betrothal, and the other at the marriage ceremony itself. During the period of the engagement, a gift known as *chhrolu*, consisting of rice, *chapatis*, dried fruit, and sometimes a small amount of money and known after the large flat-bottomed basket in which it is sent, goes from the groom's house to the house of the bride on the occasion of certain annual festivals. Since the engagement might last ten years or so, *chhrolu* can add up to a considerable expense, and if the engagement is broken off by the bride's people, its value should theoretically be returned along with the down-payment which was made at the betrothal.

While dowries are ostentatiously displayed at the time of the marriage ceremony, bride-price is an under-the-counter transaction, which is thoroughly demeaning to the recipient since its acceptance flatly contradicts the ideology of *dan*. Dowry is a gift which accompanies the gift of a virgin. Bride-price is explicitly a commercial transaction to which the verb *bechna* ('to sell') and the noun *mul* ('price') is applied.

This choice of words is more than a linguistic convention, for there is a good deal of evidence that during the second half of the nineteenth century something very close to a market in nubile girls operated at the bottom of the hypergamous hierarchy. We hear, for example, of debtors repaying their debts by marrying a daughter off to their creditor (Montgomery 1854:241); and that bride-price agreements were sometimes put in writing and signed over a Rs. 5 stamp like deeds of sale (Kangra District Gazetteer, 1926:138). Barnes records that 'a man dying without heirs, and holding a promised bride, or *natha*, as she was called, the *natha* was regularly entered into the inventory of his goods'; and he recounts an instance in which a young girl, whose betrothed husband had died in debt, was put up to auction and sold to the highest bidder (quoted in Montgomery 1854:228; Cave-Browne 1857:171). Other reports observe that the greater the difficulty a man found in getting a wife, the more thoroughly the girl's father was likely to fleece him (O'Brien 1900), and that Mandi State made a regular business out of exporting its women to Kangra (Montgomery 1854: 222).

The fact that the men of the lowest *biradari* were forced to offer considerable bride-prices encouraged frequent breaches of promise, for some fathers exploited the situation by collecting several payments for the same daughter (ibid., p. 288). Even after marriage, a woman did not lose her market value, and a jilted husband would demand exorbitant compensation from her new paramour. The District Commissioner of Kangra summed all this up in 1854 when he informed his superiors that 'a young girl is made the subject of a commercial speculation, and is as liable to enhancement or depreciation in value as any other commodity in the market' (ibid., p. 228).

This situation has to be viewed, I suggest, in the context of a situation in which infanticide and polygyny amongst the most superior royal clans, and the marriage of their daughters far away to the west, combined to create a demand for brides all the way down the ladder, and resulted in an absolute scarcity of wives in the lowest *biradari*. The connection between infanticide at the top of the ladder, and inflationary bride-price rates at the bottom did not escape the attention of the British authorities:

> it appears to me impossible to resist the conclusion that, opposite as are the vices of the upper and lower sections of society in this particular, the latter are, in a very great measure, the result of the former, and that if the Rajpoots . . . who have heretofore regarded their female children with disfavour could be brought universally to cherish and preserve them, the inducements, which at present exist among the lower orders to make traffic of them, would in great measure cease, so that both objects may appropriately form parts of one design – indeed must do so to render our efforts effectual (ibid., p. 223).

At first sight, however, there is one piece of evidence which does not seem to square at all well with this hypothesis. At the time when the British first took control of the area in 1846, bride-price was usually between Rs. 20 and Rs. 40. But by the 1880s the going rate had jumped to between Rs. 200 and Rs. 400 or more (Anderson 1897; O'Brien 1891). If the market in women at the bottom of the hierarchy was really a product of the demand for brides created by the clans at the top, then why this dramatic inflation at the very time when the British had started to make progress towards the suppression of infanticide?

The first point to be made here is that the preservation of Mian daughters did little to slacken their demand for brides from the *biradari* below, since they continued to marry polygynously, and since they either married their own daughters outside the area, or left them unmarried altogether. Now this might explain why the rates did not, as one might expect, go down; but it certainly does not explain why there was such a sharp rise, or why the rise should have been out of all proportion to the rise in the price of other commodities. I suggest that one reason for this was that before annexation land could not be freely mortgaged or sold in order to raise a bride-price, while the opportunities to do so by seeking employment outside the district were much more limited. From contemporary accounts it is absolutely clear that as soon as land became a marketable commodity, vast areas were alienated by men in search of brides (Middleton 1919b; Connolly 1911; O'Brien 1891; Bhai Mul Raj 1933:8). Of the locality round Chadhiar, O'Brien (1891) recorded that:

> Extra Assistant Commissioner Moti Ram and I have gone very closely into the causes of sales and mortgages, and we find that there is hardly a *tika* of the 553 *tikas* in this *taluka* in which land has not been sold or mortgaged, or both, in order to procure wives.

My point, then, is that by providing new employment opportunities, and by allowing land to be bought and sold, the British created the conditions which allowed the market in women to find its 'true' level.

I suggest that one further reason for this enormous increase in bride-price payments was that the Pax Britannica destroyed the sanctions which most effectively curbed the avarice of a calculating father. Formerly a prospective father-in-law who broke faith by marrying his daughter elsewhere ran the risk of violent retribution (cf. Cave-Browne 1857:172). British rule deprived the bridegroom's family of the right of such redress and there was consequently less to inhibit the girl's father from welshing on the agreement. The general effect of the new situation, then, was to allow fathers a far greater freedom to explore the market, and to dispose of their daughters to the highest bidder.

Just as an ambitious member of the second *biradari* who aspires to marry his daughter to a Mian groom must be prepared to pay a higher dowry than he would have to pay for a son-in-law of his own *biradari*, so the Rathis tend to demand smaller bride-price payments from grooms of the *biradari* above than they are prepared to accept from members of their own *biradari* (cf. Middleton 1919b:4). In other words a Rathi father must chose between the status pay-off of marrying his daughter 'up', and the material pay-off of marrying her equally. But if he has a son, the consequence of opting for status over cash is that he will be in deficit when it comes to paying out bride-price for his son's marriage. Clearly a man who has no daughter, or whose daughter is married to a groom of the *biradari* above, is at a pecuniary disadvantage in paying bride-price for his son. Since it takes a number of years to accumulated enough money to make such a payment, the marriages of many fourth *biradari* men are necessarily delayed. Financial necessity, then, forces the men of the fourth *biradari* to postpone their search for brides, and thus helps to disguise the absolute shortage of women at the bottom of the ladder.

8 The 'biradari' reform movement

8:1 Introduction

In the years between 1930 and 1955 the Rajput *biradari* hierarchy passed through a phase of reformation and counter-reformation. During this period the Rathis at the bottom of the ladder attempted to repudiate their inferiority by denying daughters to those who would not give brides in exchange, withdrawing from other asymmetrical exchanges which defined them as inferiors, and appropriating the attributes of their superiors. Although they failed to accomplish their aim of subverting the whole hierarchy and persuading those higher up the ladder to marry with them on a symmetrical basis, they did precipitate a series of convulsions which reverberated through the whole hierarchy, and which temporarily transformed each *biradari* into a unit of endogamy.

In the present chapter I set out to describe this campaign for *biradari* equality; and to analyse the reasons why it took place, and why it eventually failed. I shall argue that such upheavals are a symptom of structural contradictions inherent within the system and are endemic to it. *A priori*, the most likely dissidents would seem to be the men of the fourth *biradari*. Although they are in a position to collect large bride-price payments for their daughters, they themselves experience a perpetual shortage of brides, and are scorned as the most inferior Rajputs of all. Now if they opt out by refusing to give their daughters to the third *biradari*, then the whole hierarchy is in imminent danger of collapse. This is so because the third *biradari*, deprived of brides from below, are likely to react by keeping their girls to themselves, and refusing to pass them up the ladder to the second *biradari*. In other words, if the people at the bottom disrupt the supply of women, then this will set off a chain reaction through the whole system.

Faced with the fourth *biradari*'s refusal to give them girls, there would theoretically of course be other alternatives for the third *biradari*. The shortage of women might, for example, be made good by raising the age at which the men get married, and this would enable them to go on giving girls to the second *biradari*. Such a palliative is not particularly attractive. In terms of customs and style of life there was no difference between the third and fourth *biradaris*, while in terms of economics the difference was comparatively slight (see Table 21, Chapter 7:4). The superiority of the third *biradari*, then, was simply a product of the fact that it was they who were the wife-takers, and the refusal of the fourth *biradari* strikes at the very roots of their superiority. While raising the marriageable age of men may be a solution to the problem of the shortage of women, it is no answer at all to the challenge to their status. If they pass a self-denying ordinance and marry later, they do nothing to repudiate the pretensions of the fourth *biradari*. They simply maintain the superiority of the second, whilst they themselves have to get by without enough wives to go round.

Apart from the fourth *biradari*, the first and second might be predisposed to some modification of the system. The clans at the very top of the ladder continually face the problem of getting married without breaking the rules of exogamy, and this problem becomes acute as soon as they abandon female infanticide. One might expect, then, that these people would be interested in expanding the field of endogamy through some modification of the rules of exogamy. The second *biradari* too are potential reformers since the system of bride-price and dowry puts them under a continual economic strain.

8:2 The Rajput evidence[1]

What actually happened was this. In the years immediately following the First World War there were two apparently unconnected attempts to reform the hierarchy. The impetus for the first came from a clique of influential individuals from fourth *biradari* sub-clans of the Dhar area of Palampur, and was organized on a strictly local basis. The aim was to persuade the *biradari* to refuse to give girls to their traditional wife-takers until such time as the latter would reciprocate. But their campaign proved abortive and soon fizzled out.

The other movement was initiated by a group of retired army officers of the second *biradari* who toured the district preaching the unity of all Rajputs and urging those lower down the ladder to mend their unorthodox ways. Though lip-service was paid to the ideal that all Rajputs should marry on a symmetrical basis, the movement was primarily directed at upgrading the attributes of the backsliders, and the official line maintained by the leadership was that the Rathis could only expect to receive wives from the higher *biradaris* once they had completely divested themselves of their inferior customs. But since it was the regime of hypergamy itself which encouraged the Rathis in their most demeaning practices, it is hardly surprising that their moralizing seems to have fallen on deaf ears. The fact is that those who inspired the movement had no real commitment to abolishing the asymmetrical marriage formula. Their real interest lay in convincing the Rathis of the sinfulness of their exorbitant bride-price demands, for their immediate objective was to remedy the state of affairs by which their *biradari* got caught both ways by the pattern of marriage prestations.

In 1930 the Katoch formed their own clan association. At first they were concerned with hookah relations and with abolishing the distinctions in status between different sub-clans of the same clan. But within three or four years they had expanded their association to include all the clans of the *gotra* and it was decided that these clans should be allowed to intermarry. This decision caused consternation in the ranks of the second *biradari*, who were not slow to realize that this reform would make it increasingly difficult for them to get their own daughters accepted by grooms of the highest rank, and who immediately dispatched a formal deputation to protest. Soon after this several Katoch men of pure descent were formally given permission to marry their daughters to Mians of *sartora* line. By 1937 the association had again been expanded to include all the clans of the first *biradari*, and the most superior royal clans agreed to start exchanging women with all the other clans of their *biradari* on a reciprocal basis.

Meanwhile, the hypergamous hierarchy was being undermined from below. The process started when the Rajputs of district Mandi collectively decided to deny girls to Kangra, and were backed in their action by the local raja. The fourth *biradari* who had recruited the largest numbers of brides from Mandi – and consequently forfeited very substantial sums paid as the first instalment of bride-prices – then cut off their supply of brides to the third *biradari*, refused to greet the Mians with *Jai Dewa*, and tried to push through a series of reforms designed to bring their customs into line with those of the top two *biradaris*.

They asserted that all Rajputs are equal, agitated against their bureaucratic classification as Rathis, and managed to bring enough pressure to bear on the Government to have the term eliminated from the official records. The effects of all this reverberated through the whole hierarchy and those immediately above were forced to take the same measures. By the end of the decade the marriage system had been transformed into one of *biradari* endogamy.

The interests of each *biradari* were articulated by the *biradari sabha*, or council. These councils had not existed in the days immediately before the reform movements and were created – or perhaps revived from an earlier period of upheaval in the 1850s (Cave-Browne 1857: 172; Montgomery 1854) – to cope with the new situation. In every case their active membership seems to have been confined to Palampur sub-division, though the leaders of the fourth *biradari* addressed meetings throughout Kangra and the neighbouring districts, and though representatives from other areas were usually invited to participate in meetings of the Jai Karia *biradari sabha* when important issues were on the agenda, for example, the ban on ploughing or the question of *gotra* exogamy.

The leaders of the *biradari sabha* appear to have exercised a certain discretion about which clans and sub-clans were legitimate members of the *biradari* and which were merely advancing spurious claims. The rather chaotic situation during the early phases of the movement seems to have provided the opportunity for a certain amount of surreptitious reshuffling of the pack. The proceedings of the second *biradari* council, for example, record a protracted dispute about whether the Narial were *bona fide* members, and those who opposed their case alleged that their inclusion was not uninfluenced by the fact that the President's brother's wife was a Narial.

As a consequence of this ambiguity about the precise boundaries of the *biradari*, the Jaryal (1c) found themselves in the temporary predicament of being excluded by both their superiors and their inferiors. The clan is universally admitted to possess a royal pedigree. But their raja was converted to Islam, most of the members of the clan were poor, and many of them ploughed. As a result the more respectable Mians were not traditionally prepared to give them brides. So when they refused to countenance the second *biradari*'s invitation to join their ranks and were consequently denied brides from below, they initially fell between two stools. At the instigation of Mian reformers the Jaryal then formed their own clan council to eliminate their 'deficiencies', and were subsequently formally re-admitted to the Jai Karia *biradari* at a large feast reminiscent of that acknowledging the clean-caste status of the Kolis.

What this points to is that in addition to stage-managing the transformation to *biradari* endogamy, the *biradari* councils also adopted a far-reaching programme for reforming the customs and style of life of their *biradari*. All of them attempted to put a limit on the cost of marriage ceremonies and other life-cycle rituals, and insisted that their members should interact with those above them only on a symmetrical basis. The lower *biradaris* made strenuous efforts to eliminate the inferior practices with which they were associated. Meanwhile the Mians themselves formally abandoned some of the customs which had served to distinguish them from those lower down the ladder. In conformity with more modern and secular notions they forbade the marriage of children below the age of puberty.[2] In 1938 a large meeting of Mians decided to drop the ban on ploughing; and the Raja of Lambagoan and a Katoch General of the Maharaja of Jammu's army sealed the decision by ploughing a token furrow.

8:3 The return to hierarchy

Biradari endogamy had broken down again by the early 1950s as people slid back into giving their daughters to grooms of the *biradari* above. At the height of the movement such renegade wife-givers were zealously boycotted by their *biradari*, but by the turn of the decade there were so many defaulters that the *biradari* councils simply could not enforce their decisions. The last occasion I have been able to trace on which a man was formally boycotted for marrying his daughter 'up' was in 1952.

Today the *biradari* councils are either defunct or wholly ineffective. The Mian council, for example, has not been convened since 1959. The only one which did meet during the period of my fieldwork was the council of the fourth *biradari*, but the occasion merely served to underline its impotence. The meeting was called to consider two cases of betrothal in which the bride's father had accepted the first instalment of a bride-price payment, and had then repudiated the agreement. The *biradari* council threatened that they would be boycotted unless the money was repaid within six weeks. But although they made no effort to comply with the decision, the threat was never implemented.

The significant thing is that the people who reopened the hierarchy by marrying their daughters hypergamously were the men of the more prestigious sub-clans of the second *biradari*, and the richer members of the third and fourth *biradaris*. As I see it, the principal reason for this is that hierarchy in terms of marriage alliance is such a strong value that people are always keen to get one up on their immediate competitors by marrying their daughters to grooms of the highest possible status. For the higher-ranking sub-clans of the *biradari*, endogamy meant a reduction in status since their superiority had consisted in the fact that they gave daughters to the most prestigious wife-takers, and it was not long before they tried to reassert this old distinction.

The rich defectors in the second *baradari*, supported by their Mian affines, naturally tend to gloss their motives rather differently. As they put it, marriage within the *biradari* would have condemned their daughters to a life of labour in the fields. But a Mian son-in-law could be expected to maintain her in the ease to which she, as a rich man's daughter, was accustomed. In many such instances, however, it would be more accurate to say that the father, doubtless to some extent conscious of his own reputation, chose for his daughter a life of sequestered privation over one of public toil.

I would argue that in addition to the disruptive effects of the intense competition for precedence between those who are theoretically peers, strict *biradari* endogamy also proved difficult to sustain because of the importance attached to links with old-established affines in other *biradaris*. Once one or two marriages have been contracted with a given sub-clan more tend to follow, for existing affines act as marriage brokers and exert an informal pressure to reinforce the alliance by the gift of a further daughter (cf. Chapter 9:5). My point, then, is that *biradari* endogamy threatened amicable relations with affines who had already proved their worth; and it would seem reasonable to infer that the conflict of loyalties was particularly acute when the alliance was a cumulative one.

In some cases there is also a political aspect to this relationship in that the pattern of local factional loyalties seems to run in the same groove as the pattern of affinal alliances. Over the last three or four generations, for example, the Nanwaraks of *tika* Chhek (third *biradari*) have given several of their daughters to the Kanthwals of *tika* Ther (second *biradari*). But neither of these clan-segments have any ('direct')[3] affinal relationship with the Manhas of Matial (first *biradari*). This correlates with the fact that within the centrally located *tikas* of *mauza* Chadhiar there is a long-standing and bitter hostility between a block consisting of the Nanwaraks and the Kanthwals and their clients on the one hand, and the Manhas and their clients on the other. Given that I encountered a very similar situation in *mauza* Khera, I would judge that the pattern is fairly typical. The implication, then, is that ties of affinity may form the basis for long-term political alliances, and that the return to hypergamy can be seen in terms of the interest certain sub-clans had in keeping in with their political allies.

In more general terms we can say that if hypergamy maintained the unity of different grades within the caste, *biradari* endogamy threatened to disrupt that unity. As we have seen (Chapter 7:8), the position of the Rathis was a somewhat ambivalent one, and their status as Rajputs was, as it were, vicariously derived from their affinal alliances with those whose authenticity was beyond question. I think that we can now see why they were so concerned to be recorded as Rajputs in the official records at the very time they were repudiating their hypergamous associations. Whatever the disadvantages of such associations, they did at least keep the Rathis within the pale of the dominant caste.

One might speculate that a further reason why *biradari* endogamy broke down again is that it did not pay the immediate dividends hoped for by the people at the bottom of the ladder who had initiated it. By denying daughters to their traditional wife-takers they had aimed to blackmail them into giving them wives on a symmetrical basis. But, as we have seen, what actually happened was that the latter responded by themselves denying brides to their own wife-takers. In short, the aim of the lowest *biradari* was to merge itself with the *biradari* above; but it was repulsed and the hypergamously ranked hierarchy was converted into a set of endogamous *biradaris*. Since each of these was still associated with its old rank position on the hierarchy, their status was not immediately improved. In time, of course, this might have changed; but many members of the *biradari* were undoubtedly looking for a more rapid pay-off, and from their point of view the campaign had been a flop.

With one or two important modifications the system has reverted to its old form. One significant change, however, is that all the clans of the first *biradari* now exchange women on an egalitarian basis. The Manhas, for example, are one of the non-royal clans which belong to the first *biradari*, and they were traditionally assigned to the lowest grade within the *biradari*. I have records of a total of 47 marriages of Manhas men of the Chadhiar sub-clan. Of these 24 were contracted before 1940, and in not a single case had the wife been recruited from a higher grade within

TABLE 25 *Proportion of hypergamous to intra-*biradari *marriages*[1]

A *Showing the total number of Rajput marriages recorded*

	Within biradari	*Hyper-gamous*	*Hypo-gamous*	*Inter-caste*	*Total (100%)*
	No. %	*No. %*	*No. %*	*No. %*	
Total	763 (59·7)	481 (37·7)	24 (1·9)	9 (0·7)	1,277

B *Showing the total number of Rajput marriages for which approximate date established*

Date of Marriage	*Within* biradari	*Hyper-gamous*	*Hypo-gamous*	*Inter-caste*	*Total (100%)*
	No. %	*No. %*	*No. %*	*No. %*	
Before 1940	162 (33·1)	307 (63·0)	14 (2·9)	5 (1·0)	488
1940–50	98 (86·0)	14 (12·3)	–	2 (1·0)	114
Post-1950	185 (64·5)	91 (31·7)	10 (3·5)	1 (0·3)	287
Total	445 (50·0)	412 (46·4)	24 (2·7)	8 (0·9)	889

C *Abstract of B excluding the men of the fourth* biradari *and the daughters of the first* biradari

Date of Marriage	*Within* biradari	*Hyper-gamous*	*Hypo-gamous*	*Inter-caste*	*Total (100%)*
	No. %	*No. %*	*No. %*	*No. %*	
Before 1940	92 (22·5)	307 (75·4)	9 (2·2)	–	408
1940–50	88 (86·1)	14 (13·9)	–	–	102
Post-1950	151 (61·1)	91 (36·8)	5 (2·1)	–	247
Total	331 (43·7)	412 (54·5)	14 (1·8)	–	757

[1] The majority of these marriages are those of Chadhiar Rajputs and their daughters and sisters. But I also recorded details of a number of marriages in *mauza* Khera, and these figures are also included in the table. The details of a significant proportion of the marriages which were contracted before 1940 are taken from genealogies and by no means all the individuals concerned are still alive.

The hypogamous marriages shown in the third column are those in which the birth status of the wife was higher than that of her husband. The inter-caste marriages shown in column four are those between Rathi men and artisan- and cultivator-caste women. Illicit unions contracted by Rajputs of higher status have not been included.

It is difficult to know exactly how much reliance to put on my figures since the problems involved in collecting statistics of this sort are enormous. One diffi-

the *biradari*. But since that time 16 out of the 23 marriages of the men of the sub-clan have been with girls of the most superior royal clans of all.

Another change is that today there are significantly more marriages within the *biradari* than there were before the reformation. The general trend is shown in Table 25. Section A of the table shows the total number of hypergamous and *biradari* endogamous marriages I recorded amongst the Rajputs of Palampur. The marriages for which I was able to establish an approximate date are classified in the second part of the table on the basis of whether they took place before, during or after the reformation. In section C, I have excluded the men of the fourth *biradari* and the girls of the first *biradari* who might be held to distort the figures since they have little alternative but to marry within the *biradari*. The statistics seem to suggest that before the reformation between two-thirds and three-quarters of all marriages were hypergamous while a quarter to a third were within the *biradari*, and that since the reformation these proportions have been reversed.

Both of these changes – the new willingness of the clans of the first *biradari* to exchange women on a symmetrical basis, and the reversal in the proportions of hypergamous to *biradari* endogamous marriages – seem to be directly correlated with the suppression of infanticide. It was this which forced the people at the very top of the ladder to expand their horizons and include new clans in their marriage circle. Together with the legal prohibition of polygyny, the suppression of

---

culty is that people may be tempted to upgrade the status of their affines by giving them the clan name by which they would like to be known, rather than the name by which they are actually known. A second difficulty is that the different sub-clans of the same clan sometimes belong to different *biradaris*, and so by itself the clan name is not always sufficient to establish their rank. It is also necessary to know exactly where they live. The third major difficulty relates to the dates shown in sections B and C, for few people can spontaneously recall the precise year in which they were married.

In collecting these statistics I adopted several very crude devices for cross-checking the information I was given. I found that I was usually able to detect when people were surreptitiously upgrading the status of their affines by comparing the clan name given for a particular set of affines with an independent list of the clans represented in each *mauza*. I also did a double check on a substantial proportion of these marriages by collecting the same information from different individuals. As for the date of marriage, it was usually possible to come up with an approximation sufficient for my purposes by fixing a series of reference points (e.g., the beginning of *biradari* endogamy or the Partition of India) and asking my informant to place the marriage in time in relation to these events. Although I obviously cannot claim that the figures are completely accurate I do consider that they broadly reflect the general pattern.

infanticide has also reduced the capacity of the top *biradari* to absorb girls of the second *biradari*, and has consequently led to a slackening off in the demand for brides of inferior status throughout the whole hierarchy. At the same time the decision to dispense with the theoretical requirement of *gotra* exogamy has widened the field of choice within the *biradari*.

The third really important change is that, in terms of customs and styles of life, the hierarchy has become increasingly homogeneous over the last forty years or so. On the one hand many Mians have taken to ploughing and their women observe *purdah* in a much less rigorous way than formerly, while on the other hand the Rathis have been partly successful in suppressing some of their most conspicuously 'inferior' attributes. These days they affect as great a disapproval of *rakhewa* and *batta satta* marriages as anybody else, though in reality such practices are by no means extinct. While a significant proportion of people of the fourth *biradari* still demand a bride-price payment, they now do so with the utmost discretion and sometimes use part, or even all, of the money they surreptitiously accept to provide their daughter with a dowry for all to see. Current practice with regard to transactions in boiled food between members of different *biradaris*, or the smoking of a common hookah, is a great deal more liberal than the ideal rules which are described for the past. Today it is only the most conservative of Mians who retain their old exclusiveness.

8:4 The Nurpur variant

During the course of a short stay in Indaura, a village close to the border between districts Kangra and Gurdaspur at the extreme western end of the Kangra valley, I encountered a rather different variant of the hypergamous hierarchy I have described for Palampur. Though people in the Indaura area know the four-*biradari* model current in other parts of the district, it bears little relation to the reality they actually experience, and they are unable to decide how to assign the clans of their local area to the four categories. Rather they divide the hierarchy into two broad divisions: the Jai Karias and the Salaamiyas. The Jai Karias are the royal clans who are entitled to the greeting *Jai Dewa*; the Salaamiyas are all the rest to whom the greeting *salaam* is appropriate. But within these two broad divisions there are a very large number of hypergamously defined gradations of status.

Until recently there were some people for whom hypergamy was compulsory. That is, they did not exchange women on a symmetrical basis with anybody at all, but gave all their daughters to acknowledged superiors and recruited all their wives from acknowledged inferiors. The situation seems to have been precisely comparable to that described for the neighbouring district of Gurdaspur where clans with an exclusively unilateral pattern of marriage alliances are distinguished as *kahri*, while those which marry with other clans on a symmetrical basis rate as *dohri* (Gurdaspur District Gazetteer, 1915:50–1; cf. Rose 1919:276; Kashmir Census Report, 1912). The former seem to have been concentrated in the middle ranges of the hierarchy and constituted a Salaamiya elite competing amongst themselves for Mian grooms. Amongst the Jai Karias at the top there were two or three loosely defined groups of clans which married in a circle, while at the bottom of the ladder the lower-ranking Salaamiyas engaged in the direct exchange of women. The position can be represented thus: (1) Jai Karias – optional hypergamy and marriage in a circle; (2) Salaamiyas (a) *kahri* clans – mandatory hypergamy; (b) *dohri* clans – optional hypergamy and direct exchange.

The Nurpur variant has displayed all the symptoms of the same instability which shook the Palampur hierarchy during the 1930s and 1940s – symptoms which in this case manifested themselves in the years immediately following the First World War. Some of my evidence suggests that these upheavals were precipitated by the middle-ranking *kahri* clans, who endeavoured to abrogate compulsive hypergamy by agreements to exchange women on a symmetrical basis. But other accounts indicate that this was a consequence of the fact that the clans on the lowest rungs of the ladder had already banded together and agreed to deny brides to their superiors. But whoever touched the initial spark, the result was that the *kahris* negotiated an agreement to marry on a symmetrical basis with other clans of approximately equal standing. The Indauria, for example, formed a new marriage circle with the Dadhwal, Manhas, Harchand and Jaryal, clans with whom they had no previous affinal connection. In Nurpur the attempt to deny brides to those of superior status seems to have been much less effective than in Palampur, and at no stage did each marriage circle become a hermetically sealed unit of endogamy. But on the other hand the system never simply reverted to its original state, for the upper-crust Salaamiyas have continued to participate in a marriage circle with their new affines, and did not return to the regime of obligatory hypergamy.

8:5 The Brahmans and Temple priests

Though in Kangra it is the Rajputs who push the logic of hypergamy to its furthest extreme, they are not the only caste which is internally stratified on the basis of the asymmetrical marriage formula. The Brahmans also operate a system which closely resembles that of the Rajputs, and they too conceptualize their clan hierarchy in terms of a model of four hypergamously ranked *biradaris*. In order of precedence these *biradaris* are known as Nagerkotias, Pucca Bhateru, Kacha Bhateru and Halbah, divisions which appear to be confined to *tehsils* Palampur and Kangra and which are said to have been created by the sixteenth-century Katoch raja, Dharam Chand.

At least today, however, it is impossible to establish any clear distinction between Kacha Bhateru and Halbah either on the level of marriage alliances or on the level of the attributes with which they are identified. Indeed the same people may be described by both labels, the term Halbah (from *hal*, a plough) being reserved for those one wishes to denigrate. In practice, then, the hierarchy has the appearance of consisting of three hypergamously related categories.

But in addition to these there is a further *biradari*, the Dogras, who are identified with an exclusively endogamous pattern. The Dogras are considered to be 'good' Brahmans with a pure and respectable style of life. Their enforced endogamy is said to stem from an occasion, now in the distant past, when one of their number committed suicide at the gates of the royal palace in order to bring disaster on the house of the Katoch raja who renegued a debt.

In terms of the attributes associated with each *biradari* the hypergamous hierarchy divides broadly between the Nagerkotias and Pucca Bhateru on the one hand, and the Kacha Bhateru/Halbah on the other. The clans of the top two *biradaris* do not plough and set themselves the strictest standards of conformity to the ideology of *kanya dan*. That is, they give dowries, abhor bride-price payments and *batta satta* marriages, and rigidly refuse to accept the hospitality of those to whom they have given daughters lest it be taken as a return for the original gift. In all these respects the attributes associated with the clans at the bottom of the ladder are diametrically opposed.

As regards interactions between *biradaris*, the ideal expectations are broadly similar to those described for the Rajputs. A Nagerkotia, for example, should not smoke a common hookah with a man of lower *biradari* or accept *nali rasoi* which has been prepared in his kitchen.

The Nagerkotias are the *kul-purohits* of the Mian Rajputs, and in theory they will perform their *purohitchari* duties only for *jajman* of the highest castes – that is, for other Brahmans and for Rajputs. In practice, however, the only Nagerkotias in *mauza* Chadhiar are prepared to officiate at the household rituals of all the clean castes, and even of the Kolis.

Each Brahman clan itself acts as *jajman* to a linked clan of *kul-purohits*. This relationship is always asymmetrical and in no case is there a direct exchange of priestly services (which would contradict the ideology of *dan*). At least in the context of the relationship, the hereditary priest is superior to his *jajman*, and though there is the odd exception the *kul-purohit* clan does not generally belong to a lower *biradari*. But given that the relationship has hierarchical connotations, what happens amongst those who claim to be the most superior Brahmans of all? A system involving the generalized exchange of services at the top would theoretically be possible, though this would further limit the already constricted field of potential wife-takers since clans associated in this way are not potential affines. In fact the problem is ingeniously solved by the dogma that one of the thirteen Nagerkotia clans, Bipp, is extinct; and that Bipp are the 'true' *kul-purohits* of those who claim to be the highest Brahmans of all. Since they no longer exist, the latter are constrained to call on individual wife-taking affines to officiate at their domestic rituals.

The problems which hypergamy creates at the top of the ladder are familiar from the Mian case. The Nagerkotias accept brides from the Pucca Bhateru and are obliged to marry their own daughters within the *biradari*, with the result that women are supernumerary, competition for grooms intense, and dowry payments large. But while the desire for unrivalled superiority drove the members of some Mian sub-clans to kill their daughters rather than give them in marriage, the most superior Nagerkotia sub-clans have traditionally participated in a single marriage circle, and have never indulged in infanticide.

The Brahman hierarchy has passed through a series of upheavals strictly comparable to those I have described for the Rajputs, and this has happened twice within living memory. The first time was at the beginning of the century. The hierarchy, then, reasserted itself in preparation for a further period of revolt in the late 1930s. When I returned to Palampur in 1974 there were some indications that Brahman hypergamy was again on the brink of a further convulsion. A series of hand-bills were circulating which called on members of the caste to reject the old divisions, to place a mandatory limit on the size of dowries, and to curb all unnecessary expenditure on the rituals of marriage.

The third of the Chadhiar castes which is directly associated with the asymmetrical formula are the Temple priests. As their local representatives describe it, the caste is divided into two hypergamously ranked *biradaris*. The highest *biradari* consists of those who are priests at the big Kangra temples, who have grown extremely rich from the offerings of large numbers of pilgrims, and who do not plough the land themselves. The lower *biradari*, to which the Chadhiar Temple Priests belong, is made up of those sub-clans which live mainly by agriculture, and which plough. In the early 1950s the sub-clans of this lower *biradari* organized a revolt against the higher, and began to deny them brides. During the period of my fieldwork the ban was still in force, and the caste had the appearance of being divided into two endogamous sub-castes. But there is no reason to suppose that this is a stable state, for again there is some historical evidence (Rose 1919:108) to suggest that before now hypergamy between Bhojki marriage circles has broken down into an endogamy which proved ultimately unviable.

8:6 Comparative evidence

From other areas of northern and western India there is comparable evidence that such upheavals are endemic to hierarchies ranked by the asymmetrical marriage formula. For the Punjab alone the examples are numerous. The Sialkot District Gazetteer (1921:45), for example, records that in 1915 some of the Rajputs on the bottom rungs of the ladder of hypergamy began a campaign to deny brides to clans which were not prepared to marry with them on a symmetrical basis. In 1852, Montgomery (1853:1:478) reported that the lower divisions of Sureen Khatris had started to deny brides to Sureen aristocrats, and that the latter 'are preparing to yield to pressure from without'. The Hoshiarpur District Gazetteer of 1906 (p. 34) records that 'for the past thirty years certain classes of Khatris (have) . . . been agitating to extend the principle of isogamy and free themselves from the necessity of contracting hypergamous alliances for their daughters.' Rose (1919:514) mentions such movements in Patiala, Jollundur and Gujarat districts, and notes (p. 126) that documentary evidence tells of a similar revolt amongst certain Brahman groups at the beginning of the nineteenth century.

More familiar perhaps is the evidence for the Patidar and Anavil Brahmans of Gujarat (Kapadia 1955:108; Van der Veen 1972:173-6). In the Patidar case at least it is clear that such movements have been recurrent throughout the past century (Risley 1915:166; Morris 1968: 98, 194; Pocock n.d.; 1972).

Pocock's (1972) analysis would suggest that these *ekada* movements are bound up with the importance attached to repeated intermarriage. The Patidar dilemma is that while a father aspires to marry his daughter to a groom of the highest possible standing, instances of dramatic hypergamy are not easily reduplicated. The notion that 'good' marriages are contracted with the same families generation after generation thus produces recurrent attempts to require that all marriages be within the circle of equals (the *ekada*), attempts which stem not so much from a dislike of hypergamy *per se* as from a dislike of individual affinal ties.

It is the families of highest standing within the circle of nominal equals who come closest to the ideal of repeated intermarriage, and it was they who initiated the move to make such marriages mandatory. But while it is still possible to acquire prestige from the superiority of one's wife-takers, it is paradoxically these same people who are most susceptible to the temptation to defy the ban on marrying their daughters 'up'. Only the ideal of the repeated alliance marriage holds this disruptive tendency in check.

A second contradiction which is built into the *ekada* movement is that while its objective is to enhance the standing of its members by limiting the range of affinity, the rigorous enforcement of *ekada* regulations pushes in the direction of exchange marriage. But exchange marriages – whether direct or indirect – are discountenanced by Patidars of high standing since they undermine the ideal asymmetry of affines and run counter to the ethic of *kanya dan*.

The Kangra material parallels the Patidar pattern in that it was the leading sections of each *biradari* which initiated the move towards mandatory endogamy; and that it was they who subsequently undermined the regulation by succumbing to the temptation to acquire prestige by marrying their daughters 'up'. But there is little evidence to suggest that *biradari* endogamy was in the long term self-destructive because it increasingly approximated to exchange marriage; or that it was precipitated by a dislike of individual affinal ties. While on a statistical level there is a discernible tendency to repeat alliances (Chapter 9:5), the extent to which this happens is scarcely recognized by the people themselves. Nor is there any explicitly articulated ideal that a 'good' marriage is contracted with existing affines, even though the latter's willingness to renew the alliance may certainly be cited as testimony to one's respectability. Furthermore, my data suggest that repeated alliances are no more common within the *biradari* than between sub-clans of adjacent *biradaris*. In other words, the Kangra reform movements do not seem to be a logical development of an ideological stress on repeated alliance, for even if such an emphasis existed, it would as likely inhibit as promote the move to endogamy.

I am not altogether convinced that the distaste for individual alliances is anything like the whole story in the Patidar case either. In an earlier discussion, Pocock (n.d.) observes that the *ekada* (like the Kangra *biradari*) is primarily concerned to deny brides to superiors, but 'does not object to the taking of daughters and dowries from inferior groups'. What seems to be at issue here is not so much the desire to ensure that all marriages are with established affines, as the desire to repudiate the superiority of those who are exclusively wife-takers.

8:7 The predisposing causes

At the beginning of this chapter I suggested that the *biradari* movements are to be seen as a symptom of structural contradictions inherent within the regime of hypergamy. But it might be argued that they are more plausibly seen as a response to some stimulus of a political or economic kind outside the marriage system: to a redistribution of land in favour of the lower *biradaris*, for example, or to an opening up of new opportunities for the Rathis to achieve high standing independent of their clan status.

In Table 21 (Chapter 7:4) I have shown the proportion of land owned by each of the Rajput *biradaris* in the 37 hamlets of *mauza* Chadhiar in 1891, 1935 and 1968. Over this period no significant shift in the pattern is apparent, and I have no reason to suppose that the figures would be any different for other parts of the district.

There is a good deal of evidence that in the pre-British period the Kangra rajas exerted considerable influence and control over caste matters. From this one might conclude that the *biradari* hierarchy was propped up by the authority of the raja, and that as soon as his power was removed the whole system collapsed. But the real powers of the rajas were annihilated by the Sikhs in the early nineteenth century, and during the British period they were reduced to the position of petty *jagirdars*. If the reform movements had been a direct result of a decline in their authority, then it was strange that they did not happen a hundred years before. The removal of the raja's influence may have been a necessary condition for, but could hardly be described as the immediate cause of the reformation. Although the Raja of Kangra continued to legitimate reforms in the caste hierarchy right up until the beginning of this century, the evidence would suggest that he had long since ceased to be capable of imposing his will (see Chapter 4:6).

Before the First World War, British army recruiting policy was to enlist only Rajputs. In recruitment, and more especially in promotion, there was a marked preference for men of superior *biradari*, and a certain number of recruits from influential Mian families were taken directly as Indian Officers (cf. Cunningham 1932:101; Mason 1974: 350ff). The general effect of this was to keep army rank broadly congruent with clan status. But during the course of the War the rules were liberalized, and by the late 1930s a substantial proportion of those who became Indian Officers in the Dogra regiments must have been Rathis. Could it be, then, that this change of policy led to such an incongruence between achievement and ascription that a reordering of the whole hierarchy became inevitable? This is certainly plausible since there were an estimated 40,000 servicemen from the district in 1921 (Kangra District Gazetteer, 1926:125), and by the late 1930s there must have been several hundred retired and serving Rathi officers from Palampur. What is more most of the leaders of the *biradari sabhas* were themselves retired army officers. At most, however, British army promotion policy can only be part of the answer, since the Brahman hierarchy passed through a precisely equivalent series of upheavals at the beginning of the century – that is, at a time when the military authorities refused to enlist Brahmans.

But there is perhaps something to be salvaged here, for my argument that periods of upheaval are always a latent potentiality within the system in no way excludes the possible influence of external stimuli, stimuli which may have the effect of activating the contradictions inherent within the structure itself. By analogy with the case I have argued about the causes for the partition of the joint family, I suggest that it is possible to discern more than one level of causation behind the *biradari* reform movements. As I see it, structural contradictions within the system are the underlying cause of the convulsions I have described, while all sorts of political and economic factors (e.g., the decline of the raja's authority, or the promotion of non-Mians in the army) may exacerbate this inherent proclivity, and provide the catalyst which actually precipitates the crisis.

That these 'external' precipitating causes were not the only causes seems clear from the fact that the hierarchy soon reasserted itself. But if the reforms were merely the result of external stimuli one would expect to find a permanent change in the system. If, for example, the moves towards *biradari* endogamy were a straightforward response to the fact that a great number of Rathis became army officers, then the effects of the reformation would have been permanent, since the factors which led to it are still part of the environment. In other words, the changes would be one-way changes.

At least in the Rajput case, however, there was one factor outside the system which did influence the course of the reformation, and significantly this did lead to a one-way change. As British control over the area became more complete the clans at the top of the ladder were forced to stop killing their daughters. The Brahman case clearly illustrates that infanticide was not an absolute prerequisite of the system, and the reform movements cannot therefore be seen as a simple consequence of its suppression. But the suppression of infanticide did mean that the Mians had to modify the rules if they were to marry off their daughters, and the obvious way of doing this was to expand the field of endogamy and create a marriage circle of equal clans. In line with this, reforms were introduced by which marriage within the *gotra* was allowed, and the gradations of status within the top *biradari* are no longer validated by the rigorously asymmetrical exchange of women and are consequently much attenuated.

If, as I have argued, the *biradari* reforms are a symptom of contradictions inherent within the system itself, then one might expect that movements of this sort would be a recurring phenomenon. There is some evidence that this is, in fact, the case. There are hints in the contemporary literature of a similar attempt to reorganize the hierarchy in the 1850s (Cave-Browne 1857:172; Montgomery 1854), and in Palampur the fourth *biradari* initiated an abortive attempt to deny girls to their superiors just after the First World War, some twenty years before the main movement got under way. In Nurpur sub-division, 60 miles to the west of Palampur, a similar movement took place in the early 1920s. The Brahman and Bhojki hierarchies have proved prone to the same weakness, and evidence from other parts of north India would suggest that upheavals of this sort have not been confined to Kangra, but are a characteristic feature of hypergamous structures throughout the region.

8:8 Instability or oscillating equilibrium?

In the light of the data I have already presented, I turn in the last part of this chapter to a more abstract consideration of Lévi-Strauss's thesis (1969) that systems of generalized exchange are intrinsically unstable.

For Lévi-Strauss the paradigmatic case of 'generalized exchange' is a system of 'circulating connubium'. The simplest model of such a system is one in which group A gives its girls to group B, group B to C, and C to A. If marriage circles of this sort are to function harmoniously, he argues, each of the wife-exchanging groups must be of roughly equal status. In other words, the system presupposes that the 'C' woman who is offered in marriage to the 'A' man is fair exchange for the 'A' girl who is given in marriage to a 'B' man. It further requires that group A should be prepared to extend credit to group B in the expectation that group C will fulfil their obligations to give them wives (pp. 265–8).

By resisting the temptation to keep their girls to themselves (i.e. to marry them endogamously), or the temptation to offer them only to people who will give wives in return (i.e. to give them only in reciprocal or 'restricted exchange'), the group extends the range of its alliances. But although a system of circulating connubium has the advantage of linking the group with a wider set of affines (and is consequently seen as a more efficient way of integrating the society), it also involves risks; and, as Lévi-Strauss sees it, the more links in the chain, and the more indirect the reciprocity, the greater these risks are likely to be (1969:238). Individual groups try to insure themselves against the contingency that their wife-givers will default, by multiplying the cycles of exchange in which they participate, and by cornering as large a proportion of the girls of their wife-giving groups as they can.

The result is that there is competition for women, and since the rich and the powerful will be in a position to net the largest haul, there is a tendency for women to accumulate at one point in the cycle at the expense of everybody else. So on the one hand systems of circulating connubium presuppose the equality of the wife-exchanging groups, while on the other hand

> the speculative character of the system, the widening of the cycle, the establishment of secondary cycles between certain enterprising lineages for their own advantage, and, finally, the inevitable preference for certain alliances, resulting in the accumulation of women at some stage in the cycle, are all factors of inequality, which may at any point force a rupture. Thus one comes to the conclusion that generalized exchange leads almost unavoidably to anisogamy, i.e. to marriage between spouses of different status; that this must appear all the more clearly when the cycles of exchange are multiplied or widened; but that at the same time it is at variance with the system, and must therefore lead to its downfall (p. 266).

The argument, then, is that systems of generalized exchange of the 'circulating connubium' variety break down into hypergamy or hypogamy. But hypergamous regimes are themselves unstable, for they prevent the cycle of prestations from being closed by the return of women; and they pose problems about how the girls of the highest status are to marry.

> The cycle is interrupted, the infinite chain of prestations seizes up. The partners mark time, and, placed in a position where it is impossible for them to fulfil their prestations, keep their daughters by marrying them to their sons. . . . Needless to say, such a process is contagious. It must gradually reach every member of the body social, and change hypergamy to endogamy. Only India has systematically and durably adopted this solution (Lévi-Strauss 1969:475).

Elsewhere two other possibilities have been developed. The first is that the system breaks down into one of restricted exchange or patrilateral cross-cousin marriage as individuals seek to insure themselves by demanding a direct reciprocation from those who take their daughters. The second possibility, which foreshadows the European system, is that anisogamy is forced to introduce a complex element. India conceives of this possibility in the form of the legendary *swyamvara* marriage which closes the cycle by allowing the king's daughter to marry a man of any status who has performed some extraordinary feat, or who is chosen by the princess herself. As Lévi-Strauss observes, the resolution is mythological; 'yet the transfiguration into mythological form conceals a real problem, and probably positive institutions as well' (p. 475). We have already seen (Chapter 7:5) what these 'positive institutions' are.

Lévi-Strauss's argument is not always entirely consistent. Sometimes, for example, it would appear that bride-price payments allow the contradictions to develop by permitting 'the accumulation of alliances . . . for groups which are economically and socially the most powerful' (p. 397). But elsewhere they are seen as providing 'a solution to certain difficulties inherent in generalized exchange' (p. 466). In the Kangra case the first proposition is clearly fallacious. It is the high status of the Mians and not their (comparatively modest) financial standing which allows them to accumulate an excess of wives. Rather than pay bride-price, they themselves are in a position to command substantial dowries for the honour they confer by their alliance. The second argument is more plausible, for the exorbitant bride-price demands of the Rathis may serve as a temporary check on their willingness to subvert the system.

In a subsequent paper (Lévi-Strauss 1963:311), the evolutionary sequence postulated in *Elementary Structures* is reversed (cf. Barnes 1971:164–5). Anisogamy now succumbs to its contradictions and – 'temporarily and locally' – breaks down into circulating connubium. I prefer this later formulation, for the Kangra facts suggest that it is short-lived (and possibly recurring) periods of *biradari* endogamy which appear to be the 'pathological' development, and that it is hypergamy which is the norm. The whole ideology stresses the asymmetrical status of affines; the doctrine of *kanya dan* emphasizes that the virgin is an appropriate gift to a superior, while *tarvadla* – the paradigmatic case of circulating connubium – is frowned on by people with any pretensions to orthodoxy.

What this perhaps suggests is that not all systems of circulating connubium are necessarily unstable. (Evidence from other parts of the world does not unequivocally permit any such inference.) It is rather that such systems are in the long-term unviable when (as in north India and amongst the Kachin) they are located in milieus thoroughly permeated by the values of hierarchy; and where the egalitarian marriage circle has been formed in response to the problems of anisogamy, the ethic of which continually subverts it.

Lévi-Strauss's thesis has been severely criticized by Leach (1961a, 1969) who argues that although the cycle may not be closed by the return of women in a ranked system, the wife-givers are nevertheless compensated by counter-prestations of a different nature. It is because Lévi-Strauss fails to appreciate that women are only one item in this total set of prestations that 'he is led to attribute to the Kachin system an instability which it does not in fact possess' (Leach 1961a:90). Lévi-Strauss's response (1969:239–40) is that Leach himself (1954) has clearly demonstrated that the system is not in equilibrium. But while for Lévi-Strauss the contradictions are inherent in the formal properties of the marriage system itself, for Leach the 'instability' of 'aristocratic' *gumsa* political organization derives essentially from a contradiction between the principles of rank and the principles of kinship (1954:203). A second contrast is that for Lévi-Strauss the system is 'unstable' in the sense that it leads to genuine one-way structural changes and does not return to its original starting point: (A → B → C). But Leach's model of 'oscillating equilibrium' posits just such a return (A ⇄ B). The system is in perpetual motion between two poles and radical structural change does not occur (cf. Leach 1969).

The situation I have described seems to be one of oscillating equilibrium rather than the kind of instability which Lévi-Strauss envisaged. But – against Leach – I would agree with Lévi-Strauss that the contradictions which have generated such movements are a structural property of the marriage system itself, and ultimately derive from the surplus of unmarriageable girls at the top of the ladder and the deficit of brides at the bottom. Although these north-Indian systems exist in a totally different politico-economic context, they have proved prone to recurrent rejections of the hierarchy reminiscent of Kachin 'democratic' *gumlao* rebellions. Given these parallels it is surely insufficient to posit a purely local explanation in terms of such features as the assimilation of Shan ideas about class (Leach 1954), the productive capacity of the Kachin economy (Friedman 1971, 1975), or the promotion of Rathi soldiers from the ranks. These may be predisposing causes but are not the underlying ones.

Friedman (1975) has cogently argued that 'the dynamic of the Kachin system might be envisaged as an evolution towards an increasing hierarchy and state formation which comes into contradiction with its own material constraints of reproduction but which, by means of *gumlao* revolts, succeeds in re-establishing the conditions for a renewed evolution'. Where the economy has a greater productive capacity – as amongst those Kachin who have moved down into the fertile plains of Assam – we find an uninterrupted development towards state formation. The analysis makes a laudable attempt to go beyond both Leach and Lévi-Strauss by specifying the precise material and demographic conditions under which the contradictions inherent in the system will manifest themselves. But despite the illusory air of precision lent by the algebra, the argument remains highly speculative, since much of the demographic data on which it critically depends is not presented. More importantly, the material pre-conditions Friedman considers essential to the development of a stable hierarchical system seem to be present in the north-Indian case; yet this does not appear to inhibit the kind of oscillation he attributes to the insufficient surpluses generated by the Kachin economy.

One final comment concerns the reasons why both *gumlao* rebellions and *biradari* endogamy seem ultimately to fail. Leach (1954:210–11) sees the weakness of the former in terms of a contradiction between 'the asymmetry of the *mayu-dama* [wife-giver/wife-receiver] relationship . . . [and] the dogma of status equality between the lineages which dominates *gumlao* theory'. I would add that to the extent that *gumlao* organization realizes its own ideal of local group endogamy, it demands some other mechanism to integrate these local groups into the wider society. But in fact the atomistic tendencies of endogamy do not appear to be counteracted by other integrative mechanisms, and consequently *gumlao* polities seem to exist in a state of chronic hostility with their neighbours. In the same way *biradari* endogamy severed the links between *biradaris*, and thus between established affines and political allies; while it prohibited the Rathis from contracting alliances with those whose connection would prove them 'true' Rajputs. My supplementary hypothesis, then, is that under such conditions endogamy poses its own structural problems which push the system back in the direction of anisogamy.

9 Marriage strategies

9:1 Status and standing

Readers familiar with the background literature will have noted that I use the terms 'status' and 'standing' in an apparently promiscuous way; and do not follow Pocock (1972) in drawing a sharp distinction between 'standing' within the caste and 'status' between castes. For Pocock status is of a religious nature and derives from Hindu purity values; standing is much more flexible and is largely a product of wealth judiciously invested in prestigious marriage alliances. If we speak of differences of status within the caste we imply that the relationship between different levels within the caste is homologous with the relationship between different castes, a position which he dismisses as 'absurd' (p. 65).

As it is formulated I find this distinction, uncomfortably reminiscent of Leach's (1960) emphatic opposition between 'castes' and 'caste-grades', rather misleading. The evidence presented in Chapter 7 (sections 3 and 8) clearly suggests that at least *in certain contexts* the Kangra Rajputs perceive relations between one *biradari* and another as analogous to relations between one caste and another, and that they mark the boundary between them in much the same way as they mark the boundary between one caste and another: that is, in terms of a complex set of interactions involving the asymmetrical exchange of food, hookahs, greetings and so on. It also suggests that between Rajputs and Rathis there was, during the nineteenth century, a 'caste-like' barrier signalled in terms of the length of mourning prescribed, and the right to keep *tulsi* shrines or to wear the sacred thread. In defence of this 'absurd' position, Dumont's authoritative and convincing demonstration that 'there is no absolute distinction between what happens inside and outside a caste group' (1957) and that 'the caste boundary is only one more marked cleavage than others' (1964) may be cited.

I emphasize the caveat 'in certain contexts', for whether it appears more appropriate to speak of 'status' or 'standing' within the caste will often depend on whose point of view is adopted. Seen from above, what distinguishes us from inferiors is likely to be conceptualized as a quality of status based on differential purity. As the inferior tends to present it, however, the difference is merely one of standing based on the crude pretensions of wealth. But this may be true not only of relations within the caste but also of relations between castes, for in my experience people of lower caste often talk as if the superiority of others is a consequence of their affluence and quite devoid of religious significance.

I would argue, then, that there is no neat congruence between the status/standing distinction and the distinction between inter-caste and intra-caste relations; and that grades within the caste are sometimes represented as grades of relative purity. But this is not to deny that there is an analytically distinct dimension of achieved rank (military rank, educational attainment, personal and family reputation and so on) which might appropriately be called 'standing'. While status is conceptualized as the permanent and immutable attribute of groups, the other dimension is impermanent and mutable. But impermanent standing is continually being surreptitiously converted into status through the mechanism of hypergamous marriage alliances. The present chapter describes the strategies by which this transmutation is accomplished.

9:2 The spouse's credentials

All things being equal, an ambitious father would like to marry his daughter as high in the hierarchy as possible. But he would also like a lieutenant or a clerk for a son-in-law, and may be forced to recognize that this is not compatible with the first aspiration. Though others will undoubtedly criticize him if he allows himself to be dazzled by the achievements of prospective affines of dubious pedigree, the prestige of this occupational elite is sufficient to induce some fathers to overcome their misgivings.

This concern with standing is highly elaborated, and especially so within the ranks of the occupational elite itself. Those with commissions in the army command the greatest respect.[1] Teaching is definitely a second best, and Rajput graduates who fail to get a direct commission in the army often become schoolmasters. But schoolmasters enjoy a higher regard than most clerks or the para-medical staff of the Primary Health Centres. Educational attainments are another important dimension of personal rank,[2] and these tend to be minutely catalogued when introductions are made. Related to this concern with academic qualifications is the prestige attached to fluency in English, candidly summarized by the acquaintance who observed that: 'If somebody comes to my office and he speaks high-flown English I attend to his work in a flash. If he speaks Pahari I just go on signing papers. There must be some respect for the chair.'

The most sought-after groom, then, is a lad with the prospect of a commission in the army. But it would seem that the standing of white-collar civilian employment has recently been gaining ground against other army ranks. As Mata Ji put it: 'Ten years ago it was *fauji* (a soldier), now it is *babu Ji* (a clerk) that everybody wants'. The boy's educational attainments are also weighed. A schoolmaster friend explained he was working hard to improve on the third-class MA he already possessed in order to make himself a more eligible groom. At all levels of the occupational ladder, Government service (which offers considerable security) is preferred over employment in the private sector.

In many cases, of course, the groom himself will be too young to be far advanced in his career. But the personal attainments of the members of his immediate *khandan* will also be taken into account. How many soldiers are there, and what are their ranks? Is the captaincy of his 'brother' a substantive or merely a field rank? Might his 'uncle' who is a peon in the DEO's office be in a position to find him employment?

Even more pertinent is the quality of the marriage alliances contracted by the family; and these are themselves in part a product of their occupational standing. High standing makes for 'good' marriages; and one 'good' marriage follows another. Conversely a shady reputation may force even a Mian to arrange an exchange marriage which will be held against the family in subsequent negotiations. A combination of unorthodox ways, irascible temper, lack of either kin or land in Chadhiar, and the inability to provide an adequate dowry, forced Hari Singh – a Mian of somewhat questionable credentials – to give his daughter in *batta satta* in order to secure a second wife for his son.

(The first was dying of tuberculosis.) This shoddy behaviour made it difficult to find a bride for his younger son (employed as a watchman in Delhi) who eventually absconded with a Rajasthani girl of dubious caste; which in turn has proved a matrimonial handicap to Hari Singh's daughter's daughters.

In terms of physical attributes the ideal bride and groom are both fair-skinned, sharp-featured, and more plump than skinny. The boy should be older and taller than the girl, and their horoscopes should match (which they are normally found to do when the alliance has much to recommend it). The girl should be obedient and modest, especially in sexual matters. Unless she is 'without shame' she is a virgin at marriage; after intercourse she is 'spoilt' and 'without value'. There is some ambivalence about whether she should be well-educated. Provided that she does not over-step the mark by being better qualified than her husband, an educated wife is a matter of pride. But on the other hand, such girls are held to be less ready to submit to the authority of their mother-in-law and less conscientious about the domestic chores.

More mercenary considerations are also important. I refer here not only to the matter of bride-price and dowry, but also to the inheritance prospects of both bride and groom. In the past no marriages were contracted between the Manhas and Kanthwal sub-clans of Chadhiar. But recently a Kanthwal of the Vaid *al* married one of his two daughters to a Manhas captain. The father-in-law has no sons and it is understood that each of his two daughters will inherit half of his fairly substantial landholding. As a result of this new alliance, the relationship between the two sub-clans is now said to be 'open', and more marriages are expected to follow. But when the idea was floated that a Kanthwal girl of the Bakshi *al* might marry one of the captain's five brothers, it was swiftly rejected on the grounds that with so many brothers his potential inheritance was too small. (Long-standing factional rivalry was probably also at stake here.)

In the rather extreme circumstances of one family I knew well, such pragmatic concerns make it difficult for the youngest daughter to get married at all. Kamla Devi is a widow and the mother of three daughters, two of whom are already respectably married. The eldest sent her first-born son for the mother to foster on the understanding that he would eventually look after her in her old age. But the boy runs wild, never goes to school, and Kamla feels she cannot count on his support in the future. Since her husband left too little land to attract an uxorilocally resident son-in-law, her problem is that if she gives her youngest daughter in marriage she will spend the rest of her days in lonely penury. Despite the fact that the girl is of an age, Kamla has resisted pressure from several affines who want to arrange a match, and has devoted a considerable part of her meagre resources to keeping the girl in school in the (rather forlorn) hope that she will eventually get a job and support them both.

All things being equal people prefer not to marry too close to home. One reason for this is that they do not like to feel that their in-laws are keeping close tabs on them, or to risk their continual interference. The other major consideration is one of status. For the wife-givers such proximity entails a continual and mortifying subservience; while the wife-takers regard it as undesirable since such marriages are said to tar the groom with the same brush as a *ghar-jamwantru*. On the principle that familiarity breeds contempt, the boy's side also feel that they will not receive the respect which is their due.

The marriage negotiations themselves are an extremely delicate matter, for a refusal may be interpreted as an affront to the family's honour (*ijat*) and a slur on the character of a prospective bride or groom. It is elementary discretion, then, to leave the matter in the hands of intermediaries whose tact may be relied on to temper the humiliation of a rejection, or whose ineptness may be blamed for bungling the match.

9:3 The manipulation of 'als'

One of the implications of a system like this, in which status is expressed in terms of marriage, would seem to be a tendency to the repeated fragmentation of the status group, since it is unlikely that any two localized segments of the clan will make a set of alliances of exactly equivalent prestige. Although people talk in terms of an ideal model in which the hierarchy consists of *biradaris* and *biradaris* consist of dispersed clans, the facts on the ground are that in many contexts it is more often the localized sub-clan which *seems* to be the real unit of stratification. Different sub-clans of the same clan are sometimes assigned to different *biradaris*, just as they sometimes call on different clans of Brahmans as their *purohits*, worship different clan deities, and claim allegiance to different *gotras*. In the larger sub-clans this tendency towards the fragmentation of the status group may go even further, and lineages of slightly different status may be distinguished.

The term *al* refers to a title or a nickname which is applied to a whole clan, a clan-segment of any generation depth, or even to the unrelated members of a local neighbourhood group. These titles are relevant to the present discussion because they frequently serve to discriminate segments of different status within the clan, and because they are often manipulated to advantage by ambitious sub-clans or lineages anxious to enhance their status. In this context, it is useful to distinguish between two varieties of *al*: those which derive from an ancestor and those which derive from a locality.

The majority of those *als* which derive from an ancestor refer to the title of an office he occupied, the title being used by all his descendants to remind everybody else of their illustrious history. But sometimes *als* of this sort refer to a rather more mundane characteristic of a forebear (like, for instance, his prodigious strength) or even occasionally to some shameful incident in the lineage's past (for example, the sobriquet Nihang which is applied to the descendants of a man who is reputed to have behaved shamelessly with his debtors).

These ancestor-derived *als* typically serve to distinguish lineages of different status within the *sub-clan*. It may, for example, be recalled that the Kanthwal sub-clan of Chadhiar is divided into four *als*: the Bakshis, Wazirs, Roos and Vaids (cf. Chapter 5:4). The Bakshis and Wazirs are reckoned to be of rather higher status than the others, and their marriage alliances reflect this superiority. The Vaids are considered definitely inferior, for they are reputed to be a bastard line. What is more, they have always ploughed and they beat drums at local fairs – things that until recently no other self-respecting Kanthwal would have done.

The second sort of *al*, derived from a place name, is usually attached to the whole of a localized clan-segment; and typically serves to distinguish sub-clans of different status within the *clan*. But in some cases the name of the clan itself has an obvious association with a place name. Among the lower ranking Rajput clans of Chadhiar, for example, are the Moonglas who concentrated in *tika* Moongal, the Nanwaraks in Nanwar, the Bhullaniyas in Bhullana, and the Dhandolas in Dhandol. Popular theory accounts for this correspondence between clan and local name in terms of a process of clan fission in which a sub-clan splits off from its parent stock to found an independent clan named after the locality in which it lives. Thus the royal clan of Guler is said to have originally been a branch of the Katoch, but is now rated as a separate clan and is known as Guleria.

Now all this may seem to be highly ambiguous. But it is precisely this ambiguity which I want to underline, since time and again it is exploited by low-status clans with aspirations to a higher rank. The fact that both clans and sub-clans have names associated with a locality lends a certain plausibility to an assertion by the members of upwardly mobile clan that in reality they are – or were originally – just a sub-clan of such and such a high-status clan. What the parvenus claim is that their clan name is really just an *al* derived from their place of residence, and the fact that they are usually identified by their *al* has tended to obscure their 'true' clan affiliation.

A concrete example may help to clarify the main points here. The Nanwaraks are associated with *tika* Nanwar, and it is in the hamlets around Nanwar that the bulk of their population is concentrated. Although for all practical purposes they are counted as a clan of the third *biradari*, they claim that by rights they ought to be more highly ranked. Their story is that Nanwarak is not their real clan name, but simply an *al* deriving from the name of the place in which their founding ancestor had settled. The latter, they say, was a Chadhial Rana of the first *biradari* who fled his ancestral home as the result of a feud. This 'true' origin had been 'forgotten', and was only recently 'rediscovered', a 'rediscovery' which is clearly of more than antiquarian interest. It is of particular concern to one of the Chhek house-clusters whose high standing has enabled them to contract a series of rather spectacular alliances (see Figure 11, section 5, below). In addition to the four daughters they have given to Mians, two Nanwarak men shown on the genealogy have married a girl of a higher *biradari*. The case of the Forest Ranger is of particular interest here in that it is said that the wife-givers (who belong to a different part of the district) acted under the illusion that the Nanwaraks are *bona fide* Mians.

In the days of the British administration it was possible to put such claims on official record by convincing the gullible authorities that the name under which their clan had been classified in the records was really just an *al* of a higher ranking clan. The Dogra Handbook, for example, records that:

> In Mandi State there is a caste of Rajputs known as Saroch. This has been classed as first grade in Mandi, and as a better grade of Rathi in other parts, whereas it is one of the *als* of royal Guler. Had the members of this *al* remained in their original village of Saroya, near Guler, they would never have given up their clan designation for that of their *al*. . . . The investigation of these *als* cleans up the

origin of some castes, which have been improperly classified (Cunningham 1932:52).

Occasionally the name of a place may be used as a nickname for all of its inhabitants. This creates a further area of ambiguity which is this time used to advantage by upstart segments of the sub-clan to enable them to dissociate themselves from the inconvenient encumbrance of poor relations with discreditable customs by claiming that although they share a common *al*, derived from a common place of residence, they are not really of the same clan at all. The Indauria Rajputs, for example, say that Indauria is just an *al* derived from the name of their village which is Indaura. Indaura got its name from their founding ancestor, Indu Chand, who was the younger brother of the Katoch raja; and from this they conclude that they are really Mians of the highest *biradari* – a claim repudiated by the 'true' Katoch. But the Indauria are divided into the Headmen (Chowdhury) and Clerk (Babu) *als*, who are extremely rich, and all the rest who are rather poor. The Headmen and the Clerks say that it is they, and only they, who are the real Katoch, and all the rest are something else and nothing to do with them. Although they certainly share a common *al* – derived from the name of their village – they most emphatically are not members of the same clan.

All this seems to raise several puzzles. One problem here is that in a situation where status is derived from marriage, there seems to be no logical limit to the process of the fragmentation of the status group. On the face of it, there is no obvious reason why more and more minute gradations of status should not be discerned on this basis, so that in the last resort even the nuclear families of real brothers might be ranked. In practice tacit comparisons of this sort are going on all the time, though they are seldom made explicitly. The puzzle, then, is just how lineages of the depth – or sub-clans of the size – of those we encounter in Kangra survive these fissiparous tendencies.

As I see it, the centrifugal forces generated by hypergamy are, in part at least, counterbalanced by the large proportion of marriages which are repetitions or renewals of affinal relationships previously established by sub-clan members other than the father and the father's father. My point is that a proclivity to repeat alliances contracted by (collateral) lineage kin means that two lineage segments are frequently affinally related to some of the same clans of wife-givers and wife-takers, and this clearly has the effect of inhibiting the development of a status distinction between them, since at least a proportion of their affinal relationships are of precisely equivalent prestige.

On a broader canvas, I would suggest that in Kangra this tendency to an extreme parcellization of status might usefully be viewed in the context of a species of *raiyatwari* tenure where land is held on a highly individualistic basis, and the wider descent group has not traditionally been a coparcenary (cf. Chapter 2:5). At the other extreme of north-Indian tenurial patterns are the 'true' *bhaiachara* systems associated with large coparcenary bodies within which the principles of sharing are highly egalitarian ones. Here – in theory at least – shares are allotted on a *per capita* basis, or in proportion to family size; and this principle of equality is often developed in the most exhaustive manner such that the equivalence of each holding is minutely calculated, and the holdings themselves are subject to systematic rotation (Baden-Powell 1892). The egalitarian principles on which such systems are founded seem to delimit a substantive group on the ground within which hierarchical values have little or no place. It is as if the boundary which delimits the share-holding brotherhood constitutes a severe obstacle, if not an impermeable barrier, to the further intrusion of the hierarchical principle (cf. Parry 1974). Somewhere between these two poles is the other major species of joint tenure, the *pattidari* system, where shares are calculated on a *per stirpes* basis from the founder of the estate. While such a principle does not prevent the parcellization of status within the descent group, secession from it is likely to be inhibited by the fact that land rights are based directly on a genealogical charter.

A second difficulty is that if even two lineages of the same sub-clan may have different status positions deriving from different sets of marriage alliances, then to what reality does the *biradari* – conceived of as a group of clans of roughly equal status – correspond? The answer to this, I suggest, is to be found in an analogy with a function Srinivas (1962) attributes to the *varna* categories: that is, the holistic *biradari* model provides a broad framework which enables people to translate status outside the purely local context. Like the *varna*, the *biradari* is homogeneous in status only when it is viewed from the outside. Seen from the inside there are infinite gradations and refinements of rank.

The British certainly found that the *biradari* model provided a useful way of conceptualizing the system, which allowed them to compare the status of clans concentrated in different parts of the region. Nowhere was such a rough and ready guide of greater importance than in the implementation of British army recruiting and promotion policy which, as we have seen (Chapter 8:7), systematically favoured those of superior clan. In order to accomplish this the British needed a general framework of the hierarchy, so they took over the *biradari* categories and drew up the first formal lists of the clans of each *biradari*. Since the Rajputs accord high army rank an enormous prestige, it would be reasonable to assume that the effect was to enhance the importance which local people themselves attached to these categories.

Related to both these problems is a third difficulty, that of identifying the precise nature of the groups which are ranked on the hierarchy, and between which women are exchanged. Writing of broadly similar sorts of situation, both Leach (1961a) and Dumont (1964, 1966) have confronted this problem (though from slightly different angles), and both have come up with much the same conclusion. For Dumont it is the local descent line which tends to be the real unit of ranking; while Leach emphasizes that it is local lineages which are the corporate groups for the purposes of the exchange of women.

One obvious difficulty here is that of specifying exactly what a 'local group' would be in this area of highly dispersed settlement where social ties based on common residence receive little or no explicit recognition. A second difficulty is that – as we shall see (Chapter 10:3) – the role of the bride's mother's brother in the marriage ceremony suggests that he has a major hand in donating the girl to the groom's family. In other words, Kangra people seem to be saying that the wife-giving group is neither a local group, nor even a descent group, for it includes the wife-givers to the wife-givers.

But my major concern here is to suggest that in Kangra there are no real corporate groups which exchange women in marriage, and no real status-bearing units which can be precisely identified as empirical groups on the ground. As I see it, the whole system operates not in terms of firmly delineated groups which exist as substantial entities, but rather in terms of a whole series of shifting categories which are capable of almost infinite segmentation. In different contexts people talk as if different sorts of group – *biradaris*, clans, sub-clans or even segments of the sub-clan – are the units which are ranked on the hierarchy and which are engaged in the exchange of women. But none of

ons. Each is simply a slightly
ons. Ech is simply a slightly
, and in different contexts
.

Page 279, line 36 onwards should read:—

But none of these groups can be singled out as being in some sense the 'real' units in terms of which the system actually functions.

People tend to visualize their local hierarchy, for example, as consisting of a series of localized clan-segments. But just as the *biradari* is only homogeneous in status when it is viewed from the outside, so the equality of the members of the sub-clan is only a manner of speaking which is adopted in specific contexts. *Vis-à-vis* like units, the members of a single sub-clan share in a corporate status, and the prestige of the marriages of each of the segments reflects on the status of the group as a whole. Seen from this point of view, the members of the local agnatic group rate as equals, and there is no difference in status between a man whose sister marries 'up' and one whose sister marries 'equally'. *Vis-à-vis* other segments of their own sub-clan, however, people are able to make increasingly minute discriminations in status, though they are only likely to bring these out into the open when they themselves come off best by the comparison.

The whole situation allows a good deal of scope for different interpretations to be put on the same facts by the selection of a different frame of reference. The members of a sub-clan which is on the way up, and which has made a series of highly prestigious marriages, will probably choose to talk about the hierarchy as if it were made up of sub-clans. But the members of the less prestigious sub-clans will talk as if it were whole clans or even whole *biradaris* which are ranged on the ladder, for this allows them to derive vicarious prestige from the marriages of their more successful associates.

My argument, then, is that although people talk as if marriage were a transaction between groups, the members of which participate in a corporate status, there are, on the ground, no real corporate groups engaged in the exchange of women. There are simply a large number of harassed fathers being bombarded with gratuitous advice from all sides, and making decisions with a view to maximizing their personal prestige in the eyes of their neighbours and immediate competitors in the status game – that is, those who belong to other segments of their own clan, but more importantly those who belong to other sub-clans of their own *biradari* within the local area.

Seen from the father's standpoint, then, 'we' who are giving away a girl, or recruiting a bride, tend to be conceptualized as an extremely small group whose status can be meticulously defined and differentiated. But, by contrast, 'they' – the potential affines – are viewed against the background of a wider set of categories rather more vaguely possessed of high or low status. Without these background categories to impose an order on the system and to define the field of choice, it would be difficult to see how matrimonial decisions compatible with an ordered hierarchy could ever be reached, for status would become an attribute of small-scale lineages or even households, and the merits of potential affines could never be objectively assessed, but would always be a matter of widely differing interpretations. In short, it would be impossible to derive a consistent ladder of prestige based on hypergamous principles.

In passing, I would suggest that my argument here may have implications for a wide variety of other material. It seems to me, for example, that Leach's attribution of some ultimate reality to the local descent group, and his contention that while the *mayu-dama* relationship does not operate consistently at the clan level it does at the level of the local lineage, is not altogether consistent with his own data. For a start, the pattern of marriage prestations he describes (1961a:117; 1963b) seems somewhat discordant with his thesis that it is the local lineage which is the wife-exchanging unit. As Leach himself recognizes elsewhere (1961b), the division of the bride-price (in the Lakher case into nearly equal shares) between representatives of the bride's natal lineage and the lineage of her mother's brother, suggests a configuration in which the wife-givers and *their* wife-givers act as a single unit in relation to the wife-takers.[3]

One example of the sort of confusion which I believe Leach (1963b) introduces by reifying the alliance categories is provided by his contrast between the Kachin term *dama* (a wife-receiving *lineage*) and the Lakher term *ngazua* (a wife-receiving *household*); and the further contrast he draws for the Lakher between the recipient *ngazua* household and the wife-giving *lineage* (*patong*). I suggest that absolute distinctions of this sort exist mainly in the mind of the anthropologist, and probably have very little to do with the native categories whose application is purely contextual.

This argument might also have some bearing on the question which Wilder (1971) has recently posed, and which Needham (1971:lxxxi) has endorsed as 'the kind of inquiry that in my opinion most needs to be conducted': the question: 'How many alliance groups do the Purum have?' Both these authors seem to imagine that we can discover alliance groups which exist as substantial entities and which we can count; and the suggestion is that these entities will tend to be the *local* descent groups. But as I see it, Wilder's search for the 'real' alliance units is a 'substantialist fallacy' and his question is somewhat analogous to asking how many castes there are in India, or how many lineages in Nuerland.

In reality, the range of people on the ground to whom the affinal categories are applied varies with context, so that marriages which are 'wrong' from one point of view, are perfectly orthodox from another. Depending on which frame of reference you select, Needham's statement (1958:87) that among the Purum 'there might well be no irregular marriages at all' is either hopelessly inaccurate, or completely accurate – though the tautology it has become in the hands of Wilder when he, in effect, discovers that the 'real' alliance units are those for which no direct exchange is reported. Once we admit that there might be no empirically-bounded alliance units, Needham's conjecture (1958:85) that once upon a time the system operated in terms of clans, and that now 'the place of the clan as the wife-exchanging group has been taken by the lineage', becomes redundant.

9:4 The status of the wife-givers

In a brief discussion of hypergamy in northern India, Dumont (1964: 86–90) formulates two closely related general propositions about the nature of such systems. The first is that – provided the marriage takes place within the permissible limits – the status of the children is not affected by the status of the mother's natal group; the second, that it is therefore a matter of indifference to the wife-taking line whether their brides are recruited from equal or inferior groups, and that 'it is (only) for the family of the bride that there is a difference between marrying "up" or "equal" ' (p. 89). The Kangra evidence suggests that Dumont is guilty of some over-simplification here.[4]

The matter is complicated, however, and some of the evidence certainly supports Dumont's position. Everything, for example, points to the conclusion that the *biradari* reform movements were directed only against the giving of daughters to superiors and not against the taking of brides from inferiors. But if the status of the wife-takers is compromised by any inferiority in their wife-giving affines, one might have expected the *biradari* to object to the recruitment of brides from lower groups, and to the re-establishment of hypergamous relations with them. Furthermore, those fathers who defied the *biradari* by marrying their daughters 'up' did so in the full knowledge that they would be boycotted, and would therefore have to find a bride for their son in an inferior *biradari*. It is clear that such men were making the judgment that the increment in prestige to be derived from superior wife-takers is not forfeited as a consequence of accepting wives from inferiors.

On an ideological level, the notion of *dan* puts all the stress on the merit and prestige to be derived from giving to superiors. Just as the *purohit* may not accept *dan* from the lowest castes, so the wife-takers may not accept brides from people who are substantially inferior to themselves. But provided that the recipient stays within the prescribed limits the acceptance of *dan* does not appear to be considered demeaning.

But despite all this, the fact is that most Rajput fathers of my acquaintance did not strike me as being in the least bit indifferent to the status of the wife-givers, and aspired to marry both sons and daughters as high in the hierarchy as possible. Some went out of their way to mislead me about the status of those who had given them brides, and apparently did so because they felt that their own prestige was at stake.

Moreover there is a tendency for larger dowries to be paid in marriages in which wife-givers rank lower than the wife-takers; and the greater the difference in status, the higher the dowry. I interpret this as reflecting a reluctance to marry wives of an inferior group. It might, of course, be argued that it simply reflects the fact that inferiors are prepared to pay more for the privilege of acquiring superior sons-in-law than equals are prepared to pay for the same grooms. But a father has to marry his daughter somewhere, and must accept a son-in-law of his own *biradari* if he cannot find one in the *biradari* above. As a result he could not afford to offer a lower dowry than his inferiors unless the wife-takers showed some preference for a girl of their own *biradari*.

In the previous section I have tried to show that there is a tendency to the repeated fragmentation of the status group, since no two segments of the same clan are likely to make a set of alliances of exactly equivalent prestige. But in the case of the most superior royal clans it is difficult to believe that these distinctions are generated solely by reference to the relative rank of those to whom they have given daughters. In the past infanticide deprived many such lineages of wife-taking affines; while the fact that today their daughters are for the most part married within a narrow circle of equals has precisely the same effect in that it provides little scope for distinctions within the clan to be based on the relative status of the wife-takers. In so far as marriage forms the basis for the ranking of segments within the most superior royal clans, then, it must be the taking of wives and not the giving of daughters which counts.

Kangra people put it explicitly. The Pathanias are the clan of the

Raja of Nurpur. Those of *mauza* Re rate as one of the most prestigious Pathania sub-clans, and regard themselves as being of somewhat higher status than the nearby sub-clans of Ladori and Suliali. But all three local groups are said to have practised infanticide on a fairly large scale in the past, and most of the daughters from all three groups have been given to grooms from precisely the same range of clans, and even in some cases to the same sub-clans. People variously attribute the superiority of the Re Pathanias to their (allegedly) closer collateral relationship to the Raja, to a more exacting observance of all the rules of the Mian *biradari*, and to the larger number of high-ranking military officers who belong to the sub-clan. But above all their pre-eminence is conclusively validated by the fact that they refuse to take brides from some of the clans whom their less aristocratic collaterals are content to accept as wife-givers.

What, then, are we to make of this apparently contradictory evidence? Some resolution seems possible if we bear in mind that Kangra people treat it as axiomatic that wife-takers rank higher than wife-givers; and that they picture the hierarchy as consisting of a series of *biradaris*, each of which is thought of *as if* it were homogeneous in status. What this implies is that a man who accepts a wife from the *biradari* below and gives a daughter to the *biradari* above, is simply reasserting the *status quo*. He is giving to recognized superiors and taking from recognized inferiors. But by taking a wife from his own *biradari* he is converting an assumed equal into an inferior; and by giving his daughter in marriage to a groom of the *biradari* he is putting himself in a position of inferiority.

Once it is formulated like this I think we can see why people apparently care more about marrying a daughter 'up' than about marrying a son 'equally'. Since exchange marriages (which imply equality between the wife-exchanging units) are strongly disapproved of by people with any pretensions to high status, there is little option but to give one's girls to grooms of an obviously higher status if one is to avoid the galling admission that people one had claimed as peers are in fact superiors. But from this point of view it is of no consequence whether one marries one's son with a girl from an equal or an inferior clan since – provided the wife-givers fall within the allowed limits – there is nothing *lost* by so doing. One is simply supplying redundant information about one's status *vis-à-vis* acknowledged inferiors. My argument, then, is that just in order to be able to mark time in the same place without being forced to concede precedence to anybody one considers an equal, one has to give one's daughter up, but can afford to go down for a bride.

But those who aim to get ahead in the hierarchy need to acquire the most prestigious wife-giving and wife-taking affines possible. By consistently giving daughters higher in the hierarchy than their competitors they demonstrate their superiority. By taking brides from their own *biradari* they simultaneously dispose of potential rivals by converting them into inferiors, and implicitly claim that they are too superior to marry with the *biradari* below.

In order to make a radical break with the past, an upwardly mobile clan-segment has to restructure its pattern of alliances to bring them into line with the alliances of the *biradari* above. They must get some girls accepted by the men of the *biradari* above the one they are trying to enter; and must refuse either to give daughters to the men of the *biradari* they are trying to leave, or to accept wives from the *biradari* below that. But by itself none of this is enough. It is only when the people of the higher *biradari* start to marry with them on a reciprocal basis that they can finally be said to have arrived. The really major obstacle which the parvenus have to overcome, then, lies in recruiting wives from people who had previously counted them as inferiors. In such circumstances, it is impossible to believe that the male line is in the least bit indifferent to the status of the wife-givers.

But what of the proposition that the status of the offspring is not affected by the precise circumstances of their mother's birth? Faced with a series of hypothetical situations, informants would generally assert the equality of half-siblings with mothers of different status. By the same token a man does not rank lower than a close lineage 'brother' on account of having taken a wife from an inferior group. But nor does he rank higher by virtue of the superiority of his sister's husband, for as 'brothers' they must be equals. If one extends these comparisons outwards to include more and more distant collaterals, people usually continue to assert their equality, justifying their view on the principle that they are 'brothers', or members of a single *khandan*, and are therefore to be ranked only on the basis of age or generation.

These formalized responses are only part of the story, however, for when such questions arise in less academic contexts, people sometimes make invidious comparisons between their own status and that of their collaterals. Such comparisons may either be couched in terms of the comparative superiority of one's wife-takers, or of the inferior maternal origins of those one is concerned to denigrate.

When people refuse to rank classificatory brothers, the implication seems to be that A's status is affected by the marriages contracted by members of B's lineage segment, and vice versa. If A makes a particularly good match for his sister, the prestige of the alliance also has the effect of boosting that of the group as a whole. But what is the nature of these groups? I have argued that they are not empirically fixed entities, but rather a set of flexible conceptual categories whose boundaries shift and change according to context. Seen in relation to other sub-clans, all sub-clan members are equals; and a segment whose daughters have married 'up' and whose wives and mothers are of equal birth status does not rank higher than one with less desirable connections. But viewed from the inside the disparity is unlikely to pass without comment.

9:5 The repetition of marriage

If the Kangra data does not entirely support Dumont's conclusion that in these hypergamous regimes the status of the wife-givers is 'neutralized', it does, I think, corroborate his more fundamental thesis (1966) that even in the absence of a positive marriage rule elements of the south-Indian alliance pattern exist in north India in a 'disguised' form, and that here too affinity has a diachronic dimension. I suspect, however, that the common features Dumont discovers may be more revealing about the relationship between 'elementary' and 'complex' kinship systems in general than about the relationship between Indian kinship systems in particular. I return to this point in the next chapter, which deals with the actors' models of affinity and non-agnatic kinship. In the last part of this chapter I aim to show that empirically a pattern of repeated intermarriage between sub-clans does occur.

But how, given the second bilateral theory of blood, discussed in Chapter 7:6, the rules of exogamy listed in Table 24, and the absence of a positive marriage rule, can it possibly be meaningful to talk in terms of marriage alliance in Kangra?

Now admittedly the Kangra rules of exogamy are cast in a mould which is at variance with the classic alliance pattern in that they are ego-focussed, and only full and paternal half-siblings share precisely the same range of prohibitions. But in spite of this they appear to be couched in the idiom of affinity rather than in the idiom of consanguinity. The prohibition is on taking wives from the natal clans of the father's wives and the father's father's wives, and not just from the clans of the mother and the father's mother.

On the face of it this prohibition would seem to militate against the repetition of marriage, and consequently inhibit the development of an enduring alliance type relationship. But the crucial point here is that it is only the direct repetition of the marriages of one's immediate lineal ascendants which is excluded, and there is a good deal of scope for renewing the alliance in other indirect ways (which are illustrated in Figure 5).

Without infringing the rules, for example, marriage is repeated *within the same generation* when real or classificatory brothers marry real or classificatory sisters. Such marriages are frequent and approved, especially when they are between real brothers and sisters, for this is seen as a way of maintaining harmony within the joint family, and of containing the disruptive effects of what is conceived to be a naturally antagonistic relationship between the wives of brothers. (In one rather extreme case, five real sisters from *tika* Nanwar are married to five real brothers in Katheru. The latter's three FBDs are married to three real brothers in Khooh). Alternatively, reversals of the *batta satta* kind may occur when a brother and a sister marry a sister and a brother. Though such marriages are not uncommon at the bottom of the hierarchy, they are strongly disapproved of by the more orthodox when they involve real siblings, first or even second cousins. In the case of more distant classificatory siblings, however, reversals of this sort are tolerated, though it is felt that they are not quite nice.

Marriage may also be repeated in an 'indirect' way in *successive generations*. Though the *household* of the real father's sister's husband is excluded, a girl may be given to a groom of other households of the same sub-clan, or to a groom of the sub-clan of a classificatory FZH. Though the natal clan of the father's wife, and the father's father's wife is excluded, a boy may take a bride from the same sub-clan which gave a wife to his father's brother, or his father's father's brother. In other words, the rules of exogamy exclude repetition only in the direct line of descent, and there is nothing to prevent one from marrying with the same people as one's collateral lineage kin.

In the third generation the alliance can be renewed directly. That is, a man is free to repeat the marriage of his father's father's father.

Empirically, a very substantial proportion of all marriages are repetitions of one kind or another. Of the 375 married Rajput men living in the eight hamlets of my census, 247 had recruited a wife from the same sub-clan as one or more of the living agnates of their own hamlet.

1 Same generation

(a.)

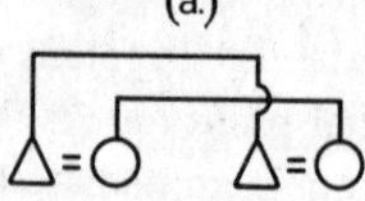

(b.)

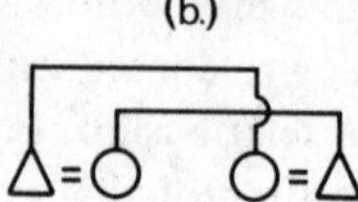

2 Successive generations

(a.)

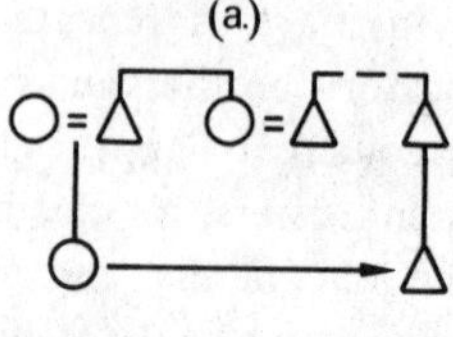

(b.)

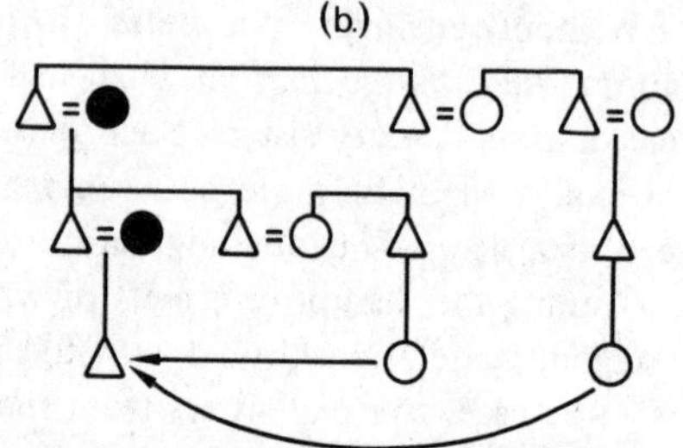

3 Direct repetition in third generation

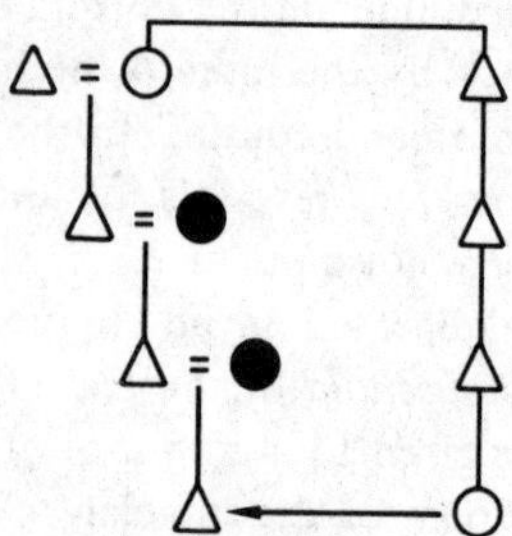

← Potential marriage

● Natal clan excluded

FIGURE 5 *Potential repetitions not excluded by rules of exogamy*

If anything this figure grossly *underestimates* the extent of the repetition, since it take no account of the marriages of deceased agnates or of the daughters of the group. In other words, some marriages have been counted as unique though in fact they duplicate the marriage of a daughter, or of a deceased agnate. Of the 28 marriages of Manhas girls from *tika* Matial whose marriages I recorded, 24 are married to Katoch grooms, and 11 of these to the Katoch sub-clan of Molag.

But far more revealing than any set of raw statistics are the genealogies shown in Figures 6, 7, 8, 9, 10 and 11. The last of these – admittedly one of the more extreme cases I recorded – is particularly

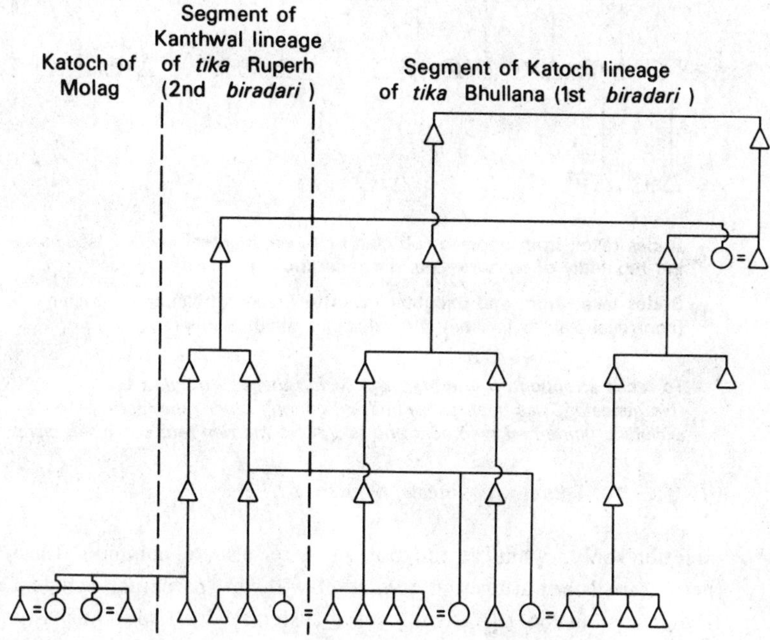

FIGURE 6 *Segment of Kanthwal lineage of* tika *Ruperh*

instructive. There are 36 Bakshi men shown in the genealogy; 33 of them in generations 3 to 6, that is, subsequent to the first Nanwarak marriage. Of these, 15 could not have renewed the alliance without infringing the rules of exogamy; 9 did not though they might legitimately have done so; and the remaining 9 did marry a Nanwarak bride. In short, the alliance was perpetuated by half of the men for whom such a marriage was permissible.

The sum effect of such marriages is that a small-scale lineage may stand in an affinal relationship to two or three of the same sub-clans over a period of several generations. At the top of the ladder such relationships tend to be asymmetrical, with women moving in one

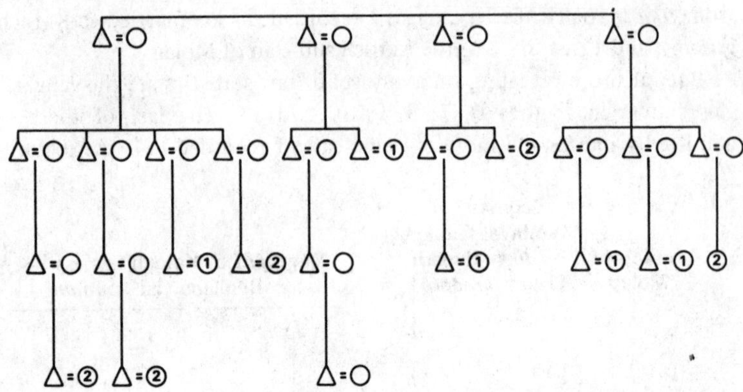

① Brides taken from Sepieye sub-clan of Alampur (royal clan of 1st *biradari*, but reputedly of *sartora* line; distance about 10 miles)

② Brides taken from and daughter given to Sonkla of Nanaun sub-clan (non-royal clan of 1st *biradari*; distance about 8 miles)

To focus attention on intermarriage within these two sub-clans, this genealogy has been simplified by ignoring other repetitions, and by excluding unmarried members and daughters married into other sub-clans.

FIGURE 7 *A Bhangalia lineage of* mauza *Khera*

direction only; while at the bottom reversals are common. Clearly the pattern is not altogether consistent with the 'perpetual turbulence' Lévi-Strauss (1966:19) envisages for systems with Crow-Omaha-type rules of exogamy, and which he contrasts with 'that regularity of functioning and periodicity of returns which conform with the ideal model of an asymmetric system'.

Now all this poses a rather difficult problem. On the one hand the rules of exogamy would appear to discourage the repetition of marriage, the statistical pattern is largely unconscious, and continually repeated alliances are certainly not represented as the norm to which all respectable lineages must approximate. On the contrary, people sometimes make reference to the explicit ideal that the bride and groom should come as total strangers to each other, and that they – and even their close agnates – should never have set eyes on each other before the wedding day. But on the other hand the empirical situation is that repeated intermarriage is not at all uncommon. It is almost as if people were cheating on the spirit of the rules by doing in an indirect

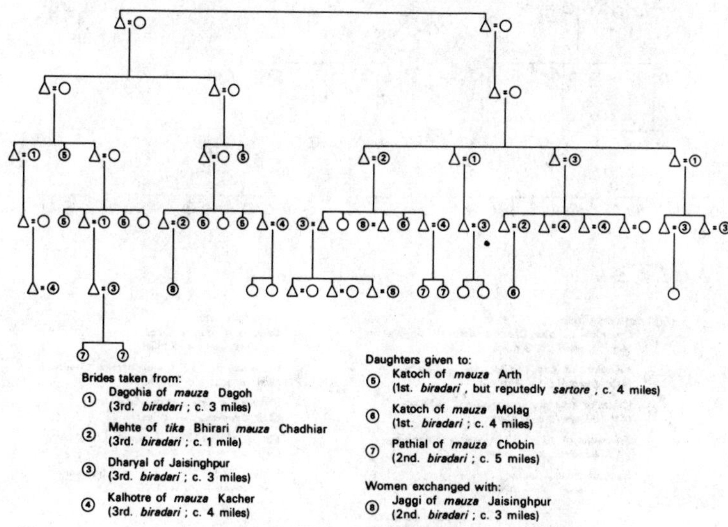

FIGURE 8 *The Vaid* al *of the Kanthwal sub-clan of* mauza *Chadhiar*

way what they forbid in a direct way. The whole pattern is the more remarkable in its contrast to the wife-scatter of marriages reported by Mayer (1960:208), Lewis (1965:161) and Rowe (1960) for other areas of north India; and this contrast requires us to ask why Kangra Rajputs continually renew their ties with old-established affines. The question is one which Dumont fails to pose, although he perceives that 'north India is not universally averse to the repetition of marriage' (1966:106).

One way of approaching the problem would be to argue that the rules of exogamy, combined with the demands of status, exclude such a wide range of clans that people have to repeat the alliances contracted by other members of their sub-clan simply because there are no other viable alternatives. In other words, the range of prohibitions and the requirements of prestige amount to a sort of positive marriage rule defined negatively, and the density of repetition is a residual consequence of what is forbidden (cf. Lévi-Strauss 1966). But it is necessary to proceed with caution here, for at most points in the hierarchy there are still a number of clans of appropriate status left over after those prohibited by the rules of exogamy have been excluded. Even in the case of the most superior royal clans for whom the problem is most

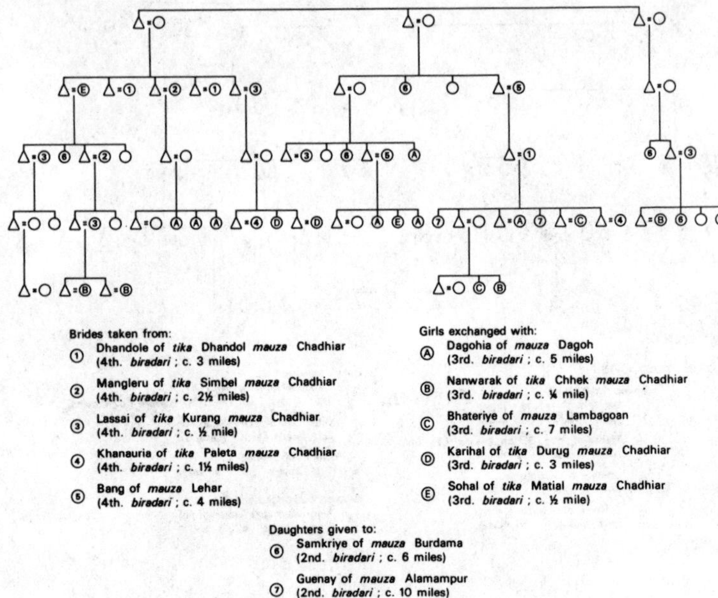

FIGURE 9 *A Moongla lineage of* tika *Khooh*

acute (see Chapter 7:6), the extent of the negative prohibitions does not fully account for the pattern, for the fact is that people go on marrying into the same set of *sub-clans.* Although the rules may severely curtail the number of clans which are possible options, they cannot have the effect of prescribing the particular localized segments of those clans with which marriage should take place.

The most obvious reason why new marriages should duplicate old ones is that most betrothals are arranged by existing affines. All things being equal, people prefer not to marry too close to home, and given that their non-agnatic kinsmen are their principle source of contact with other areas, it is perhaps natural that most matches should be arranged through relatives already connected by marriage. It is also natural that parents should be keen to give their daughter to a sub-clan where one of the daughters of the lineage is already married, since the lot of a young bride is a hard and lonely one, and they don't like the idea of her being completely isolated and friendless in her new home. From the point of view of the wife-receivers, one of the advantages of taking a bride from a group which has already given wives is that it is

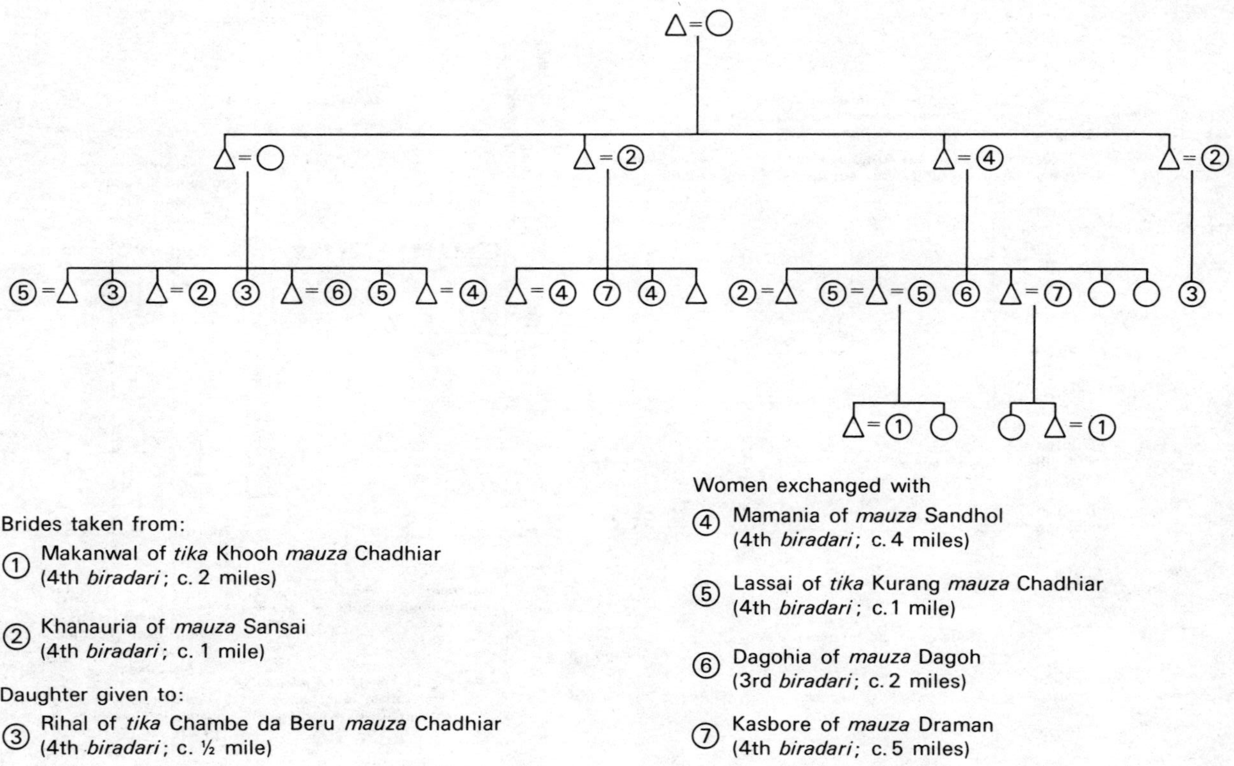

FIGURE 10 *A Bhullaniya lineage of* tika *Bhullana*

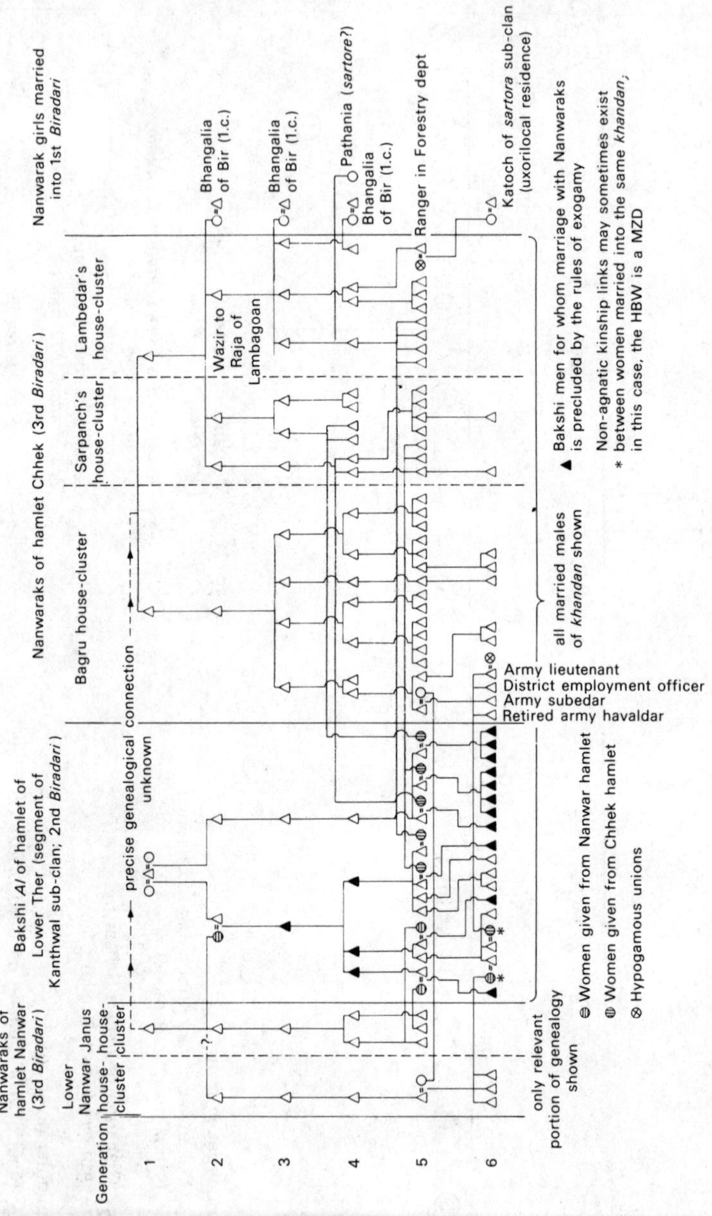

FIGURE 11 *Repetition of marriage between members of the Bakshi* al *of Lower Ther and the Nanwaraks*

thought that if the wives of agnates are sisters, they are less likely to quarrel and to sow dissension between the men of the lineage.

Moreover, one's old-established affines are a known quantity who have demonstrated their respectability and their willingness to meet their obligations in the past. As we have seen, they may also be one's major political allies within the local community. We have also seen that a refused proposal calls one's honour into question. As a result, a pressing offer from an affine may be more difficult to resist than one from a mere stranger. What is more, the marriage negotiations are likely to be smoother with those to whom one is already related. One consideration here is that the wife-takers may be expected to demonstrate the trust they place in the bride's family, and the value they attach to the alliance, by foreswearing the temptation to exert pressure in the matter of dowry. The chances are that subsequent relations will also be less tense. Within the space of a week or two I accompanied the marriage parties of two Manhas grooms, one of whom was marrying the real sister of his brother's wife, and the other into a sub-clan with whom no previous alliances existed. The contrast between the comparatively relaxed atmosphere of the first wedding and the stiff formality of the second was striking.

As I see it, repeated alliances also represent a kind of minimum risk strategy in terms of the values of hypergamy. Because the empirical situation on the ground is that there is a marked graduality of status within the *biradari*, the clan and even the sub-clan, people experience a certain difficulty in assessing the relative merits of the options which are open to them; and if no unambiguously more attractive alternative presents itself, the temptation is to play safe by repeating an alliance which has already proved its worth. Since other members of the sub-clan have made the same choice, the individual is at least immune to the accusation that he has brought his agnates into disrepute by the quality of his affinal relations, and to invidious comparisons between their status and his own.

Now all this is somewhat at odds with Tambiah's claim that:

> The consequence of the North Indian notion of affinity is seemingly to drive marriage outwards towards the formation of newer and newer affinal links. This meshes in beautifully with the ideals of hypergamy, which demands a constant search for more and more prestigious wife-takers on the one hand, and richer and richer wife-givers to exploit on the other. Correspondingly, since repeated

> marriage would fix and solidify status inequalities between takers and givers, it is antithetical to the spirit of the hypergamous system which constantly seeks an elevation of status, or less ambitiously at least a validation and maintenance of status (Tambiah 1973a: 93; cf. 1973b:222 and Morris 1968:98).

But it would surely be equally plausible to argue that by giving to the same set of wife-takers the bride's father is merely re-stating an inferiority which is already established, and thus avoids placing himself and the members of his sub-clan in a new relationship of subordination (which is likely to be unacceptable when the wife-takers are not of self-evidently superior rank). I do not want to suggest that Tambiah is wrong, but that he puts all the emphasis on one of two opposing pulls, and confuses the strategies of those who seek an elevation of status with those who must be content with its validation. On the one hand hypergamy does encourage an upwardly mobile clan segment to search for more and more prestigious affines. But, paradoxically, the intensely competitive nature of the system also constrains the less ambitious to avoid at all costs the risk of a misalliance, and thus to renew existing affinal relationships.

10 Affines and consanguines

10:1 The kinship terminology

I claim to have demonstrated, then, that there is a pattern of cumulative alliances between sub-clans. But clearly no discussion of the empirical *facts* of repetition is sufficient to establish the existence of an *ideology* of alliance recognized by the people themselves. Nor, at first sight, does the kinship terminology provide any obvious clues of an alliance pattern.

All affines and non-agnatic kin fall into the general category of *ristedar.* Included within this broad category are members of both wife-taking and wife-giving lineages, and there is no simple distinction between a class of wife-givers and a class of wife-takers along the lines of the *mayu-dama* categories of the Kachin. While for the most part the terms of reference (Table 26) distinguish wife-givers like the mother's brother (*mama*) and WB (*sala*), from wife-takers like the FZH (*buai*) and the ZH (*jija*), they also discriminate between those who have given brides, or taken daughters, in successive generations. The same goes for the terms applied collectively to the members of various affinal households (Table 27). In short, there is nothing here which would hint at the persistence of affinity across generations. The inclusion of the MBC, MZC, and FZC within the category 'sibling' would rather suggest that affinal ties disappear into consanguinity in subsequent generations.

Table 26 is modelled on Vatuk's (1969) tabulation of the terminology used in western Uttar Pradesh. In specifying a genealogical referent for each term I follow Kangra people themselves, who readily assert that their *succa* ('real') *mama* is their mother's true brother, their *succa dadu* is their actual father's father, and so on. To my mind, the

TABLE 26 *Kinship terms of reference*

Term	Genealogical referent	Other referents include
1 *dādū* (*bābā*)	FF	FFB, FFZH, FMB, FZHFB
dādī (*bari ammā*)	FM	W of any *dādū*
nānū	MF	MFZH, MMB, MMZH, MBWF, FBWF
nānī	MM	W of any *nānū*
dadorā	HFF/WFF	any *dādū* of H/W
dadhes	HFM/WFM	W of any *dadorā*
nanohrā	HMF/WMF	any *nānū* of H/W
nanehs	HMM/WMM	W of any *nanohrā*
2 *chāchū (chāchā)/tāū*	FyB/FeB	FFBS, FFZS, FMBS, FMZS
chāchī/tāī	FyBW/FeBW	W of any *chāchū/tāū*
māmā	MB	MFBS, MFZS, MMZS, MMBS, FBWB
māmī	MBW	W of any *māmā*
bū	FZ	FFZD, FFBD, FMBD, FMZD
buāī	FZH	H of any *bū*
māsī	MZ	MFBD, MMBD, MFZD, MMZD
māsar	MZH	H of any *māsi*
ammā (*mātā jī*)	M	
mātren	FW	
pitā (*bāpū jī*)	F	
sohrā[1]	WF/HF	
sas	WM/HM	
patrorā	HFyB/WFyB	any *chāchū* of H/W
patres	HFyBW/WFyBW	any *chāchī* of H/W
tatorā (*tohrā*)	HFeB/WFeB	any *tāū* of H/W
tatres (*tahes*)	HFeBW/WFeBW	any *tāi* of H/W
marūlā	HMB/WMB	any *māmā* of H/W
malehs	HMBW/WMBW	any *māmī* of H/W
busohrā	HFZH/WFZH	any *buāī* of H/W
bues	HFZ/WFZ	any *bū* of H/W
masohrā	HMZH/WMZH	any *māsar* of H/W
masehs	HMZ/WMZ	any *māsī* of H/W
3 *bhāū* (*bhāī*)	B	FBS, FZS, MBS, MZS[3]
bhābhī	eBW (yBW classified with SW)	W of any eB
bobo (*bahen*)	Z	FBD, FZD, MBD, MZD[3]
jījā (*bhanoa*)[1]	ZH	
sālā	WB	WFBS, WMBS, WFZS, WMZS
sarāl	WBW (more commonly rated *nunh*)	W of any *sālā*
sālī/jethāl[2]	WyZ/WeZ	any *bobo* of W
sādhu	WZH	
der/jeth	HyB/HeB	HFBS, HMBS, HFZS, HMZS
darānī/jethānī	HyBW/HeBW	W of any *der/jeth*
nanān	HZ	HMBD, HFBD, HFZD, HMZD
narnoi	HZH	H of any *nanān*

Term	Genealogical referent	Other referents include
(cont.)		
kurum	SWF/DHF	F of *jāwāī/nūnh*
kurumni	SWM/DHM	W of any *kurum*
4 *betā (munnū)*	S	
betī (munnī)	D	
bhatījā (bhatrīyā)	BS	S of *bhāū, sālā*
bhatījī (bhatrī)	BD	D of *bhāū, sālā*
jathūtr/darūtr	HeBS/HyBS	S of any *jeth/der*
jathūtri/darūtri	HeBD/HyBD	D of any *jeth/der*
bhānjā	ZS	S of *bobo, sālī, nanān*
bhānjī	ZD	D of *bobo, sālī, nanān*
jawāī (juāī)	DH	H of *betī, bhatījī, bhānjī, potrī, dhyotrī*
nūnh	SW	yBW, WBW (see also *saral*), W of any *bhatījā, bhānjā, potrū, dyhotrū, darūtr, jathūtr*[4]
5 *potrū*	SS	S of *bhatījā, bhānjā*
potrī	SD	D of *bhatījā, bhānjā*
dhyotrū	DS	S of *bhatījī, bhānjī*
dhyotrī	DD	D of *bhatījī, bhānjī*

[1] There is no term for the ZHF or BWF (though one touches the feet of the former). Nor is there any term for the ZHZ which is here characterized by avoidance rather than the joking reported for Uttar Pradesh.

[2] Vatuk (1969) does not record any distinction between the WyZ and WeZ. In Kangra this distinction has an important behavioural content in that a man jokes with the former, but is avoided by the latter, who is said to be like his WM.

[3] If a more precise description is required, these terms may be qualified by the adjectives *chacherā, maler, buyer, maser* for the FyBC, MBC, FZC and MZC respectively.

[4] The term *nūnh* may be qualified thus: *bhatij nūnh, bhānj nūnh, potr nūnh, dhyotr nūnh, darūtr nūnh* and *jathūtr nūnh*.

TABLE 27 *Terms applied to affinal households*

Generation		
+2	*dadkiye* (FMB household)	*nankiye* (MMB household)
+1	*maruliye* (HMB/WMB household)	
0	*sohriye* (HF/WF household)	*piochiyon* (married woman's natal household)

most striking variation between the Kangra terminology and the one which Vatuk has recorded is that the tendency of the latter towards an almost infinite extension to include the affines of one's affines and their affines, is much attenuated in the Kangra case.

The affines of one's agnates and the agnates of one's affines are, however, subsumed by the kinship categories. Thus the Nanwaraks of *tika* Chhek collectively refer to the Bakshis of Ther as their 'sisters' sons'; while the Bakshis refer to the Nanwaraks as 'mother's brothers'. Nor is this merely a matter of a courteous extension of the kinship terminology. It also has a behavioural aspect in the deference owed by wife-givers to their wife-taking affines.

10:2 Inter-personal relations between 'ristedar'

Whether they belong to different *biradaris* or not, the hypergamous marriage formula defines wife-givers as inferior to wife-takers, and this inequality is acted out in the most explicit manner. When two affines of the same generation meet, the man of the wife-giving group touches the feet of the man of the wife-receiving group. People of superior status are never addressed by their personal name but always by some honorific or by a kinship term. Wife-takers of the same generation are addressed by a kinship term but wife-givers by their personal name.

A man can expect to be treated in an unceremonious, even rather contemptuous, way by his wife-taking affines. The most superior royal sub-clans have a reputation for behaving in a particularly cavàlier fashion; and it is said that in the past a Mian bride's father or brother would never gain entry to the main part of the house when he came on a visit lest he disturb the *purdah* of the other women of the household, and that his presence would scarcely be acknowledged by anybody but the bride herself. It is almost as if these aristocrats would be glad to repudiate all connection with their wife-giving affines, and especially with those of lower *biradari*. One elderly Mian informant told me that, although he had taught for ten years in a school just two miles away, he had visited his mother's brother's house only three times in his life; and it was clear that he regarded this as a matter of pride rather than regret.

Of significance here is the fact that the word *sala* (WB) is itself a term of abuse. The term *mama* (MB) is also tinged with connotations of familiarity and disrespect, and he too is a rather inferior sort of person. I have heard Mians scornfully refer to their mother's brother as *bapu da sala,* 'father's *sala*' – and in Kangra that is just about the most disparaging way you could talk about your uncle. The mother's father comes in for ridicule at every *rite de passage*, when the women of the lineage dance with a rag doll by which he is represented while they relate in song how he has come to attend the ritual, and is shamelessly dancing naked instead of conducting himself in the restrained and self-effacing way expected of him in his married daughter's house.

By contrast with all this, wife-takers, and especially the ZH, DH and DDH, are *parone*, 'honoured guests' for whom one rolls out the proverbial red carpet. In many symbolic contexts they are treated as if they were Brahmans or even deities. On the fourth anniversary of a death, for example, a number of Brahmans, and a ZS, DS, or DH, are invited to receive a gift known as *nimantran*. Brahman and wife-taker are once more equated at the symbolic marriage of the goddess Lachmi when the Rajput *jajman* acts as wife-giver to his *purohit* (cf. p. 64). When a bride returns to her father's home for the first time after marriage she is worshipped as a deity by her brother's wives; and the latter will often address the *dhiyans* (married sisters) of the lineage as *Dewi Ji* as though they were incarnate goddesses. When the husband of a *dhiyan* of any generation dies, then every household of the lineage will send her a gift of money and cloth (known as *randepa*). A man shaves his head in mourning five days after the death of his FZH and ZH, and seven days after the death of a married sister or FZ, but is not obliged to shave for any relative of a wife-giving group. Again, the most superior Brahman clans consider a wife-taking affine as the most appropriate person to act as their *purohit*; while on ritual occasions the Barber to the Barber, and the Sanyasi to the Sanyasi (Funeral priest), is also a wife-taker.

Two strikingly obvious points seem to emerge from the data here. The first is that the inequality established by the original marriage does not fade away when it comes to relations between non-agnatic kin of different generations; and the second is that in many symbolic contexts there is an explicit identification between wife-takers of successive generations, and by the same token between wife-givers of successive generations. What all this seems to amount to, then, is that *in these contexts* relatives like the ZS or the MB are viewed as affines, for the alternative would be to reckon the daughter's husband or wife's brother as consanguines. In the case of the mother's brother, the Mians formulate the point explicitly by contemptuously referring to him as the 'father's brother-in-law'.

But if, in certain contexts, the mother's brother is an affine, people also undoubtedly think of him as a uterine kinsman. While the formula that all blood comes from the father seems to be consistent with the affinity of the mother's natal group, the second bilateral theory of blood (Chapter 7:6) clearly suggests that the child is linked with his mother's natal kin, not just through the marriage of his father, but also through filiation with his mother. Consistent with this is the fact that although the rules of exogamy forbid marriage with the natal clans of all the father's wives, the prohibition is enforced in a markedly more rigorous way in the case of the clan of the real mother. Furthermore, the hierarchical distinction between *sala* (WB) and *jija* (ZH) disappears from the terminology in the next generation when their sons rate as 'brothers'. In theory the pattern of deference between 'brothers' is purely a matter of relative age; though in practice the FZS is unlikely to be entirely oblivious to his superiority as a wife-taker. A child's affection for his mother's brother was sometimes spontaneously explained to me in the field in terms of a pure Radcliffe-Brownian 'extension of sentiments' theory. Though he may be despised as the brother-in-law of the father, he is also loved as the brother of the mother.

As I see it, then, both 'alliance' and 'complementary filiation' are actors' models of the system. The one is premised on a bio-genetic theory which asserts the uniqueness of the male line, and affirms an ideology of asymmetric exchange between affines. The other is premised on a theory of common substance, and stresses an ideology of equality between consanguines. Which of these two models the participants will choose to stress at any one time is largely a matter of context; but not unnaturally it is the wife-takers – and especially those of Mian status – who tend to emphasize the affinal aspect of the relationship, and the wife-givers who whenever possible present it in terms of consanguinity. What we have here, then, is yet another play on the twin principles of exclusion and inclusion.

Something of this double view of the relationship appears to be encapsulated in the requirement that man should have his head tonsured on the death of various wife-taking relatives but not on the death of a wife-giver. Now according to Shastric theory a man is polluted by the demise of those who share the same body particles. By this logic, then, the stricter purification of the wife-givers proclaims a closer genetic link with the wife-takers than the latter are obliged to concede (cf. Chapter 5:3).

What also needs to be said is that there is some variation between the top and the bottom of the hypergamous hierarchy in the extent to which affinity is symbolized as a relationship of pure asymmetry and hierarchy. This variation parallels, at the level of the 'mechanical' model, the statistical tendency towards exclusively unilateral exchanges of women in the superior *biradaris* and towards symmetrical exchanges amongst their inferiors. It is most clearly illustrated by the relationship between co-parents-in-law of the same sex (those of opposite sex avoid each other). The SWF touches the feet of his DHF, and at the highest levels of the caste this relationship is characterized by a dignified reserve and a self-deprecating modesty on the part of the wife-giving *kurum.* The kind of broad jokes which are traded reciprocally between *kurum* of the lower *biradaris* would, I think, be regarded as sheer impudence in aristocratic circles. At any rate joking is a strikingly pronounced feature of the *kurum* relationship in the lowest *biradari*, but is progressively attenuated as one moves up the ladder until it all but disappears under the weight of deference.[1]

10.3 The 'ristedar' of the 'ristedar'

Joking begins at the engagement and may involve not only the two men whose children are to be married but also other members of the two *khandans* of appropriate sex and generation. Sometimes this joking relationship is extended to include the *kurum* of the *kurum.* For example, the daughters of two retired army subedars of fourth *biradari* sub-clans of Chadhiar are married to two real brothers (Figure 12a).

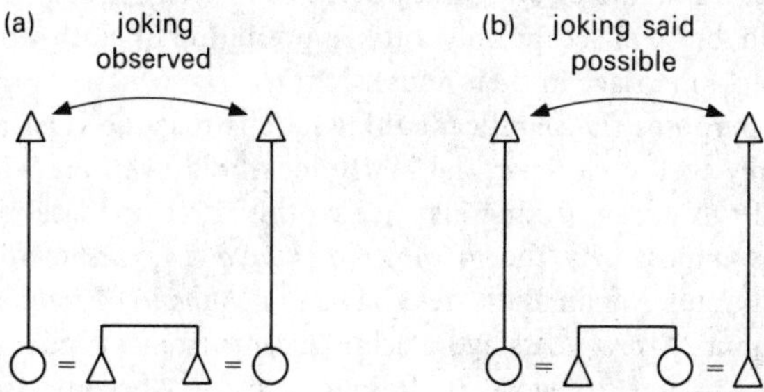

FIGURE 12 *Joking between classificatory* kurum

The subedars refer to each other as *kurum*, and joke. I do not think it significant that in this case the two men are both wife-givers to the same set of wife-takers, for I have also heard the wife-taking *kurum*'s wife-taking *kurum* (Figure 12b) described as a *kurum* with whom one might in theory joke.

The logic here, then, seems to be that the affine of my affine is my affine. Consistent with the symmetrical joking which is a pronounced feature of the relationship between co-parents-in-law at lower levels of the hierarchy, no distinction is made between my *kurum*'s wife-giving and wife-taking *kurum*. But when we consider the *ristedar* of other kinds of *ristedar*, an asymmetry is introduced. This is particularly clear at the top of the hierarchy where – in certain contexts – the affine of my affine is explicitly conceptualized, not just as an affine but as a wife-giver or wife-taker.

I noted earlier that the ideology of *kanya dan* requires that those who give a girl should not accept any form of return for their gift. The logic of this is held to require that a man should not eat in the house of his married daughter or younger sister, and ideally the prohibition should be extended to include the households of married daughters and sisters of collateral lineage kin. But those who are really fastidious about these matters take the interdiction even further and claim that those members of the mother's brother's household, the father's mother's brother's household (*dadkiye*), *and* the mother's mother's brother's household (*nankiye*) who are senior in age or generation to ego should not accept food in his house. Precisely the same pattern is repeated by the prestations made on the occasion of marriage in affinal households. All these wife-giving households make a substantial *bartan* prestation of cloth and money when they attend a marriage in the wife-taking household, but will accept only a token prestation of cloth when the latter come to a marriage in their house.

For present purposes the significant thing here is that the rules are also held to apply to the *nankiye*, the MMB household, who are wife-givers to the wife-givers. A striking instance of this lateral extension of the prohibitions imposed by the ideology of *kanya dan* is shown in Figure 13. Tillok and Narain Datt are Vedwe (1st *biradari*) Brahmans from *mauza* Rajpur. A few years ago a schoolmaster from Langu, also a Vedwe by clan, came to work in Rajpur, and soon become firm friends with the two brothers. Some time later Tillok engaged his daughter to the schoolmaster's WFBS. From that day on the two brothers refused to eat at their friend's house because, they said, his wife was a daughter of their wife-takers, and it would be accepting a return for the girl they had given. In other words, they extended the prohibition to include the wife-takers to their wife-takers, and thereby

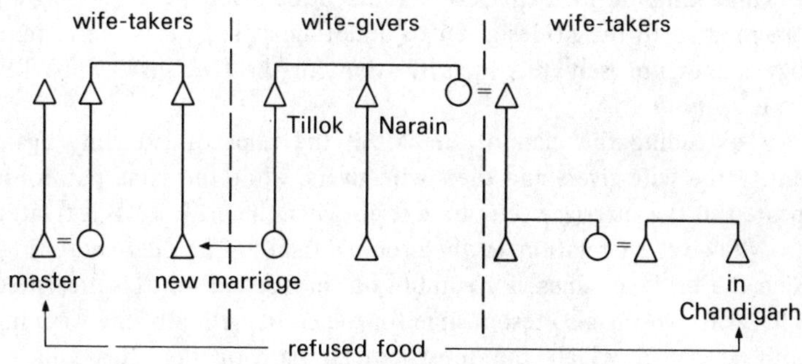

FIGURE 13 *Example of the lateral extension of the prohibitions imposed by the ideology of* kanya dan

converted a putative agnate into an affine. (There is also a tenuous sense in which they converted a kind of wife-giver into a wife-taker, for Narain Datt's wife also came from Langu and considered herself a 'village sister' of the master.)

Towards the end of my fieldwork Narain Datt became seriously ill and his son took him for treatment to Chandigarh, where they paid a courtesy call on his ZDHB who was employed in the city. But both declined to take tea at the latter's lodgings – again on the grounds that he was a wife-taker.

Narain died shortly after their return, and when his corpse was laid out in the courtyard before being taken to the cremation ground, it was circumambulated and offered obeisance by his SW and WBW, but not by his sister or daughters (Figure 14). What we seem to have here is

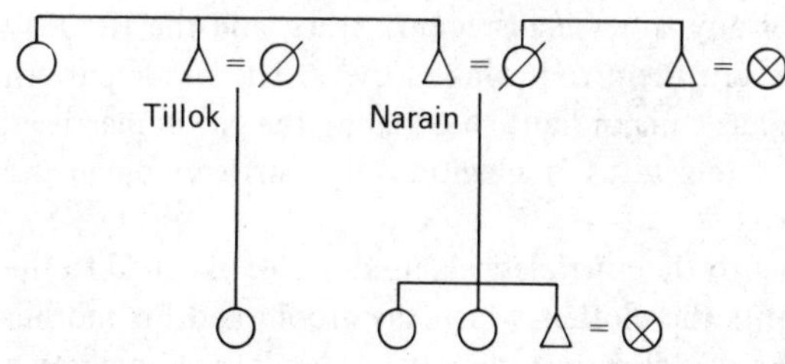

FIGURE 14 *Circumambulating the corpse*

the same kind of logic in reverse: the bride given to the wife-giver is assimilated to the brides given to junior agnates. In fact the terminology makes precisely this identification for the SW, yBW and WBW all rate as *nunh.*

By excluding the clan of the MMB the rules of exogamy again identify the wife-givers and their wife-givers, while the same pattern is repeated in the marriage ceremony itself when the bride's MB is treated as a wife-giver in relation to the groom's family, The *balu* (nose-ring) which the bride assumes as a symbol of her married status is presented by her MB, who is also responsible for the construction of the wedding booth (*ved*) in which the most crucial part of the rites will be performed, and in which his presence is essential at the time when the bride is made over to the groom (cf. Pocock 1972:112, who reports that a Patidar bride is received from the hand of her MB). In preparation for this role, he and the bride's mother and father have fasted throughout the day. One of the most solemn parts of the ritual is when the bride and groom circumambulate the sacred fire. In Palampur the bride is helped on each round by one of her sisters. But at a wedding I attended across the border in district Mandi she was carried bodily around the fire by, in turn, her two brothers and her MB. At a later stage in the rites, the MB presents the couple with an evergreen plant (*sanspan*) with many roots, which is a symbol of fertility and by which he confers the blessing of many children on the newly married couple. When the marriage party sets off on the return journey to the groom's house, it is her mother's brother who carries the bride to the palanquin and instals her in it. He also has a crucial part to play in the final rite of the wedding, known as *marula* ('the spouse's MB'), when he makes gifts to the bridal couple. Before *marula* is celebrated the couple may not attend a funeral or any other inauspicious ritual, and the rite may therefore be said to return them to profane society. The whole pattern suggests, then, that he has a major hand in donating the girl in marriage; and in conferring on her the status of a legitimately married woman and the blessing of fertility.

All this is in contrast to the much less elaborated role assigned to the groom's MB. He presents the clothes which the groom and his mother wear at the time of the wedding, including the groom's wedding crown (*sehra*). In addition he may also pay for one of the main meals served to the guests at the groom's house. But while the bride's MB makes an 'external' prestation of the bride to the groom and is thus symbolized as a wife-giver in relation to the groom, the gifts of the groom's MB are exclusively 'internal' prestations directed at his own wife-takers and nothing suggests that he is a wife-taker in relation to the bride's family. Indeed his presence on the marriage party is not considered absolutely essential.

On the face of it one difficulty with this interpretation concerns the distribution to the groom's kinswomen of that part of the dowry known as *bagge*. The way in which this distribution was made in the case of the marriage of one of Narain Datt's daughters is shown in Figure 15, where the second largest gift went to the groom's MBW. Here, then, we

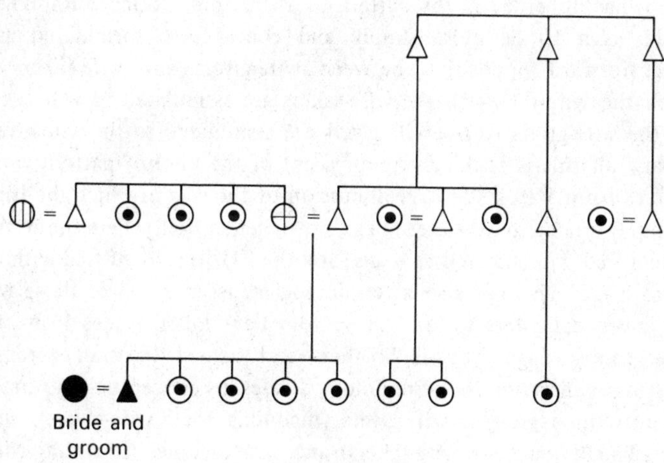

FIGURE 15 *The distribution of* bagge

appear to have a context in which the wife-givers to the wife-takers become appropriate recipients of an 'external' prestation from the bride's side, and are apparently treated as wife-takers. But the significant point is that this prestation is 'mediated' by the groom's parents, who decide on the recipients, submit a list of those for whom gifts must be provided to the bride's parents, and effect the distribution. What starts as an 'external' prestation from the bride's family is thus converted into an 'internal' prestation received from the groom's parents. Nor does the fact that it is received by a wife-giver place in question the ideal unilaterality of the gift, for the *bagge* given to the MBW merely constitutes a token return for the much more substantial gifts her household provides to the groom and his mother on the occasion of the marriage. By the same token, *potari*, a gift of clothing made to the bride and groom by his married sister or FZ, is returned with increment by the prestations they will later receive.

The general point I have been driving at here, then, is that the opposition between wife-givers and agnates plus wife-takers which Dumont (1966) has discerned in the pattern of affinal prestations in Ramkheri, would seem to be more simply and consistently formulated as a straightforward opposition between wife-givers and wife-takers, in which the wife-takers to the wife-takers are assimilated to wife-takers and the wife-givers to the wife-givers are assimilated to the wife-givers.

Now all this is strikingly reminiscent of the kind of pattern which emerges from Vatuk's (1969) discussion of the way in which the Hindi kinship terminology operates in ego's own generation, where the WBWB is identified with the WB as a *sala*, and the ZHZH is identified with the ZH as a *jija*. There is also a terminological assimilation of those who have given daughters to, and those who have taken brides from, the same groups as ego with his 'brothers' and 'sisters'. In other words, in ego's own generation the terminology divides his conceptual universe of kin into three groups: wife-givers (including their wife-givers), wife-takers (including their wife-takers) and consanguines (including those who have taken wives from the same wife-givers and given to the same wife-takers).

Were Kangra people to make these identifications in as systematic a form as Vatuk describes it would perhaps be appropriate to echo Needham's Purum analysis (1962:96) in concluding that the terminology – or at least certain aspects of it – reveals a triadic system while the symbolism of affinal prestations displays its component dyadic relation. In fact, something of this terminological configuration does exist, though in a somewhat equivocal form.

Consistent with the Uttar Pradesh schema, 'quasi-consanguines' like the WZH (*sadhu*) and the WZHB are addressed as 'brothers' and are said to be 'like brothers'; while a woman's HBW and a man's ZHBW are called 'sister' and are 'like sisters'.[2] (Of course, given the pattern of repetition described in Chapter 9:5, such individuals may in fact be biological siblings.) What fits less well, however, is that in abstract contexts informants invariably refused to classify their ZHZH as a *jija* (ZH), their WBWB as a *sala* (WB); or – in the first ascending generation – their MBWB as a *mama* (MB), or their FZHZH as a *buai* (FZH). Faced with my intransigent insistence in taking her through some of the more mind-bending extensions Vatuk lists for Uttar Pradesh, Mata Ji's exasperated last word on the subject was to invoke the proverb '*nanan da narnoi tamak toi*', 'the HZH of the HZ is just a drumstick (without a drum)'. Since nobody can hear him there is no need to bother about him.

But in other contexts the kind of lateral extensions reported for Uttar Pradesh are in fact made when there is some particular tactical advantage to be gained. The principle that the MBWB is a kind of MB was invoked, for example, by Lambedar Fakir Chand's factional opponents to cast doubt on the propriety of his son's marriage to the former's daughter (Figure 16). The match was criticized on the grounds that Kehar Chand is his 'brother', and Nirmala is Kehar Chand's 'sister', and that therefore his son had married his 'sister', the daughter of his classificatory *mama*. When there are no political axes to grind, however, considerations of this kind are totally ignored and such matches pass without comment.

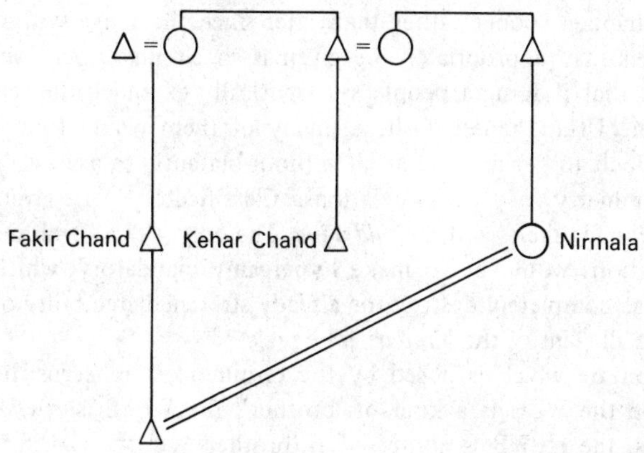

FIGURE 16 *Example of the assimilation of MBWB to MB*

Now we have seen that in the context of joking between *kurum* and in the context of affinal prestations, the affine of my affine is my affine. It is therefore rather puzzling that in theory (if not always in practice) my informants adamantly repudiated many of the terminological corollaries of such a principle; and that – by contrast with the almost infinite lateral spread of the Uttar Pradesh categories – the proverb of the drumstick disclaims all connection between those linked by more than two marriages. I would tentatively associate this comparative impoverishment of the classificatory potential of the terminology with two other features of the system.

My first, rather piecemeal, observation is that as a term of reference *jija* – unlike *sala* – applies only to a specific individual (though it is used more widely in address). The implicit emphasis here seems to be on the fact that the *jija* is not just a wife-taker, but *the* wife-taker *par excellence*. It is therefore inappropriate to confound him with others.

The second and more general point concerns the fact that the whole ideology of hypergamy requires that wives should not be taken from people one classifies as wife-givers; and the logic of the widely ramifying extensions Vatuk records is therefore that 'not only bride-takers but also bride-takers of bride-takers – and so on, as far as memory serves – are equally disapproved as a source of brides for one's own males' (1969:110). But in Kangra a substantial proportion of marriages are within the *biradari*, where for the majority the circuit is inevitably closed by the return of women. At the very top of the ladder this closure must happen sooner rather than later since the range within which daughters may appropriately be given is so circumscribed. My point, then, is that if Kangra people systematically extended the terminology in the Uttar Pradesh fashion, many of them would find it extremely difficult to get married at all without blatantly transgressing the ideal asymmetry of affinal relations. Classificatory wife-givers would become wife-takers, and the *sala* a *jija*. The only way of avoiding such contradictions would be to make hypergamy mandatory, which would of course completely destroy the already stretched credibility of the notion that all clans of the *biradari* are equals.

A further puzzle which is posed by the terminology concerns the fact that while the WZH is a kind of 'brother', the WFZS is a *sala*. Parallel to this, the HBWB is addressed as 'brother', yet the HMBS is either a *der* (HyB), or a *jeth* (HeB) in front of whom a woman should respectfully veil her face. In other words, the WZH and HBWB are conceptualized in terms of the logic of hypergamous alliance according to which the wife-taker to the wife-giver and the wife-giver to the wife-taker is an equal and a 'brother'. But this logic is negated in the other two instances. As we have seen, the sons of ZH, WB and WZH are classified as consanguines; and the distinction between wife-givers and wife-takers disappears from the terminology. At this level of the system, then, the marked asymmetry of affinal relations of the previous generation is superseded by a kind of symmetry between consanguines of ego's own generation who collectively rate as wife-givers or wife-receivers in relation to the marriages they contract. Thus the WFZS is a wife-giver and the HMBS is a wife-taker. As a result marriage notionally assumes the character of an exchange between two bilaterally recruited groups, and this is at variance with the triadic schema implicit in other aspects of the system.

I would claim that this contradiction belongs, not just to my analysis, but to the system itself. By one principle the WFZS is a 'brother' of the bride and therefore a *sala* of the groom; yet by another way of reckoning he is a conceptual equal who, given the pattern of repeated intermarriage, may in fact be a real or classificatory FBS. This ambivalence was clearly reflected by my informants' ambivalence about the pattern of deference appropriate between such individuals. Everybody was agreed that the WMBS should touch the feet of his FZDH regardless of their relative ages. But while some people said that since he is a *sala* the same rule applies to the WFZS, some claimed that, as between brothers, this would only be appropriate if the latter were his senior in age. In practice, however, this conflict is unlikely to cause much anxiety since the occasions on which these individuals will meet are limited – unless, of course, they belong to the same sub-clan in which the rules of precedence appropriate between agnates will apply.

Further, the symmetric element to which the terminology directs us does not appear to be reflected in the pattern of affinal prestations, where a distinction is re-established between those who have given brides to and taken daughters from the household of one's affines. We have seen, for example, that a man should properly refuse to accept food in the house of the wife-taker to his wife-taker. But – and my evidence here is purely negative – I have never heard it suggested that he should not eat in the house of the wife-taker to his wife-giver (e.g., at the house of his WBDH, a terminological *jawai* or DH) though this would be implied by the notion that he is a kind of wife-giver in relation to the latter. One further illustration of the point I am concerned to make here is provided by my earlier contrast between the roles of the two mother's brothers at the wedding ceremony. While the bride's MB is represented as a wife-giver in relation to the groom, the groom's MB does not become a wife-taker in relation to the bride.

Symmetry is thus – as it were – suppressed in favour of an asymmetry in which the wife-givers to the wife-givers are wife-givers and the wife-takers to the wife-takers are wife-takers, but the wife-givers to the wife-takers and the wife-takers to the wife-givers are placed in an ambiguous limbo in which they are not overtly recognized as either.

10:4 Comparative implications

I have tried to show that, both on the level of the statistical facts and on the level of the mechanical model, Dumont's thesis that an alliance pattern exists in north India and that here too affinity has a diachronic dimension, is broadly applicable to my Kangra data. But quite how much this tells us about the relationship between north- and south-Indian kinship systems is perhaps open to question. It seems likely that a very similar pattern of repeated alliances with a unilateral flow of women between groups is to be found in other systems with Crow-Omaha-type rules of exogamy. The Tallensi, as Hershman (n.d.) has recently suggested, are very probably a case in point (see also Héritier 1974). Moreover, at the level of the mechanical model, Dumont (1961a) has cogently argued that an alliance aspect is present in the MB/ZS relationship in West Africa. Given that in both these respects there may well turn out to be a certain comparability between the north-Indian and West African patterns, are we then to conclude that the latter are also basically south Indians in disguise? The question is not entirely flippant, for I suspect that Dumont's acute insights into the north-Indian system may be more revealing about the dangers of drawing an over-rigid dichotomy between complex and elementary systems in general, than about the relationship between north- and south-Indian kinship systems in particular.

At any rate, the situation I have described does not altogether square with the view that descent theory is best suited to the analysis of Crow-Omaha systems, 'while alliance theory is irrelevant outside the field of simple kinship systems' (Kuper 1970:785). Despite a complex set of exogamic prohibitions, a rule of mandatory hypergamy (or any other rule which prohibits a reversal in the direction of marriage) is structurally similar to the classic systems of asymmetric alliance in that it demands an absolute distinction between wife-giving and wife-receiving groups. In neither case is the category of potential spouses defined by genealogical criteria. The difference is rather that in the first case the MBD and other members of her descent group are excluded from, while in the second case they are included in, the category of possible wives. But – as the Kangra case illustrates – this exclusion of the matrilateral cross-cousin in Crow-Omaha systems does not necessarily preclude the development of a pattern of repeated alliances between descent groups.

11 Conclusion: The limits of hierarchy

The theme which I have tried to emphasize throughout this study is that almost every social relationship in Kangra is pervaded by the spirit of hierarchy, and that in this respect there is no fundamental distinction between inter-caste and intra-caste relations. The relationship between junior agnates and their seniors, between wife-givers and wife-takers and between members of different *biradaris* of the same caste has something of the same quality as the relationship between one caste and another.

By way of conclusion, however, it is perhaps worth stressing that this hierarchical view of the world is not entirely unqualified. We have seen, for example, how at one stage the Leather-workers threatened to repudiate their position in the system by mass conversion to Islam (Chapter 4:6). We have also seen how a rigorous application of hypergamous principles has pragmatic consequences which result in recurrent attempts to undermine the hypergamous hierarchy and to make marriages between equals mandatory (Chapter 8). Again the explicit denial of any relationship between those linked by more than two marriages sets a limit on the extent to which any given marriage sets up relations of superordination and subordination, and thus helps to preserve the notional equality of the *biradari* (Chapter 10:3).

The clans of a single *biradari* constitute a 'brotherhood' and their putative equality points to a certain ambivalence in relations between those who rate as 'brothers'. On the one hand brothers are ranked according to relative age; and this ranking makes it inappropriate for an elder brother to handle the saliva-polluted remnants of the meal consumed by his younger brother, in the same way as he must avoid contact with the *jutha* of a person of lower caste. Yet at the same time full brothers have rights to equal shares of the ancestral property, and there is a marked reluctance to acknowledge that close classificatory 'brothers' may be ranked on the basis of the relative prestige of their marriage alliances. In certain respects, then, 'brotherhood' appears to provide a paradigm for relations of equality, and this is at variance with the dominant ideology of hierarchy.

Aside from his observation that hierarchy inevitably implies equality within the hierarchically ranked units, Dumont (1970) finds no significant place for egalitarian values in his model of traditional Indian society. Relations of equality *within* the ranked units are overshadowed by relations of hierarchy *between* them. Furthermore, the system is a segmentary one and the ranked units are not a set of fixed groups. As a consequence, the equality which exists at one level of segmentation breaks down at another (lower) level. It is a purely relative matter; a logically necessary but ideologically subordinated corollary of the similarly relative principle of hierarchy.

Yet in certain parts of 'traditional' India the concept of a brotherhood of equals is a highly elaborated one and seems to reveal equality as a stressed principle in its own right rather than as a mere adjunct of hierarchy. One example of what I have in mind here is provided by the emphatically egalitarian theory which underlies certain systems of land tenure described by Baden-Powell (1892).

Baden-Powell classifies Indian villages into two broad types: 'severalty' (*raiyatwari*) and joint. There are various kinds of joint tenure but it is the 'true' *bhaiachara* systems which are of interest here. By contrast with *pattidari* tenures where shares in the estate are calculated on the basis of genealogical reckoning from its founder, in a *bhaiachara* system they are typically assigned on egalitarian principle. The difference can be illustrated by the simple example shown in Figure 17. In both systems B and C stand to inherit one half of the estate each from its original founder, their father A. In the next generation the *pattidari* system allocates shares on a *per stirpes* basis such that D and E will each receive one quarter of the total estate; while C's four sons will divide the other half (i.e. one-eighth each); and the

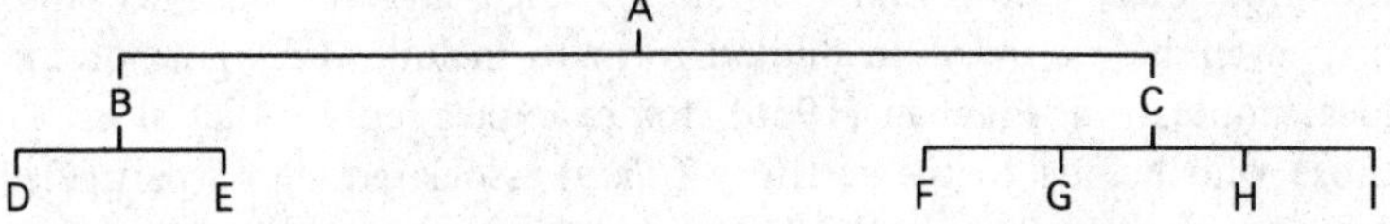

FIGURE 17 *Principles of sharing in* pattidari *and* bhaiachara *systems*

same principle applies in subsequent generations. But in a 'true' *bhaiachara* system all the grandsons inherit an equal share on a *per capita* basis (one-sixth each) or are allotted land in proportion to the size of their families 'so that the father of a family would . . . have an area suitable to his wants, while a single man, or a childless pair would have a smaller area' (ibid., vol. 2:639).

The principle of equality within the proprietary body (which after several generations may include a substantial number of households) is often developed in the most exhaustive manner. Not only are shares assigned on an egalitarian basis, but each unit of land which makes up the holding is equivalent, not in terms of area but in terms of yield, and consists of all the different kinds of soil. Lands adjacent to a river are commonly divided into long narrow strips which run at right angles to its course, so that the risk of erosion, and the benefit from the proximity of the river are equal for each plot.

In such a system rights are not to any particular set of fields but to a share in the total estate. This is, of course, necessarily the case if the egalitarian ideal is to be realized in practice, for some redistribution of the actual plots must be possible in order to counter inequities arising from the demographic expansion of some families and the contraction of others. But the reallocation of holdings sometimes went much further than a simple readjustment of this sort, and the principle of equality was carried through in such a meticulous fashion that the holdings themselves were subject to a systematic rotation by which all the proprietors took turns at each part of the estate. Where this included lands in several different villages a periodic shift of residence was sometimes involved.

Equality, then, would seem to be a central feature of such land tenure arrangements, not just as a matter of empirical fact unsanctioned by the ideology, but above all as a matter of values. Nor is it simply a question of economic equity amongst the shareholders, but also of an equality of status and of political rights. By contrast with the considerable powers of the headman in a *raiyatwari* village, here village government is in the hands of a 'democratic' council of household heads of the proprietary body. Some of the evidence suggests that this ethic may even be extended in diluted form to include the whole of the local population. Pradhan (1966), for example, reports that since all those who belong to the territory (*khap*) associated with a particular Jat clan constitute a single 'brotherhood', sexual relations between members of different castes of the same *khap* rate as 'incest' (p. 86), and representatives of all castes have – in theory at least – the right to participate in the *khap* council *as equals* (p. 36). In such situations, then, equality as a value would seem to demand some more explicit recognition than it receives when it is considered only as the reverse and ideologically unembellished side of the hierarchical coin.

It is also worth pointing out that it is difficult to regard these *bhaiachara* systems as totally atypical aberrations perpetually confined to isolated corners of the country. Cohn (1969) and Fox (1971) have both discerned a developmental cycle of tenurial patterns in the historical material on north India. At certain stages in the cycle other forms of tenure break down into a *bhaiachara* system, which may in turn evolve into a new form. My point here, then, is that if the *bhaiachara* type is part of a developmental cycle which also includes other forms, then the egalitarian principles it elaborates are a constant *potentiality* within apparently quite diverse systems.

More generally it would seem that even in the sphere of inter-caste relations the principle of hierarchy is in certain instances qualified by an extension of the egalitarian ideal of brotherhood (e.g., in the case described by Pradhan). But elsewhere it would seem more appropriate to speak of the equality of brothers being disrupted by the intrusion of the hierarchical principle (e.g., in Kangra). Yet even in this second case the idea that 'brothers' are equals is nonetheless present, although in a somewhat compromised form. Seen as a totality, then, the ideology does not appear to constitute a perfectly articulated and wholly consistent system. It contains a contradiction which allows it to be elaborated in different ways, and which gives it a potential for change and development.

Glossary

achhut	untouchable
al	title or nickname
andarke	'inside' or 'clean' (of castes)
babu	a clerk or white-collar worker
bagge	a prestation of clothes and ornaments given as part of the dowry for distribution amongst the groom's female relatives
baharke	'outside' or 'untouchable' (of castes)
bajhiya	landlord
balu	nose-ring symbolic of a woman's married status
bartan	relationship involving material prestations and mutual support between households at important life-cycle rituals; the prestations themselves
batta satta	marriage involving a direct exchange of brides between households
bhat	a meal of boiled rice and a garnish
bihoti	a woman whose current union is her first or 'primary' marriage
biradari	a group of clans of the same caste which are reckoned to be of roughly equal status and which exchange women on a symmetrical basis
bitsha	alms; prestation made to the Basket-maker, Jogi-ascetic and Musician after the performance of certain caste duties
boti	a Brahman cook employed at life-cycle rituals
chauka	an area of purity surrounding a cooking hearth or an object of worship

chillum	a small stemless clay pipe
chulah	a cooking hearth
chundabandh	principle of inheritance by which shares are calculated on a (uterine) *per stirpes* basis
dadkiye	father's mother's brother's household
daj	dowry
dan	a religiously meritorious gift to a superior for which no material recompense may properly be accepted
devi	a goddess
dham	an elaborate meal given at the bride's house before the departure of the marriage party and at the groom's house after their return
dhi	an unmarried girl of the lineage
dhyan	a married daughter of the lineage
gala-batai	share-cropping arrangement
ghar-jamwantru	an uxorilocally resident son-in-law
ghee	clarified butter
gotra	grouping of clans between which marriage is prohibited
gram panchayat	'village' council
gret	patrikin
guru-purohit	spiritual preceptor
gyatri mantra	an extremely potent incantation which is whispered into the ear of the initiate at the sacred thread ceremony and which can subsequently be used to ward off spiritual and even physical danger
hali	ploughman
ijat	honour
jaddi	ancestral property
jagir	an assignment of land from a ruler to his 'feudal' subordinate in return for military or other services
jagirdar	one who holds a *jagir*
jajman	patron of a Brahman or a Barber
jar kharid	self-acquired property
jat/jati	breed; type; species
jhanjarar	rites which solemnize a woman's 'secondary' marriage
jutha	anything contaminated by saliva from the mouth
kama	a general farm servant
kamin	craftsman

kanya dan	'the gift of a virgin'
kapar-dhuai	a ritual purifying the mourners after a death
khandan	clan or lineage
kulaj	clan deity
kul-purohit	hereditary domestic priest
kutumb	lineage of shallow depth
lagan-ved	rites which accompany a woman's 'primary' marriage
lambedar	'village' headman
mauza	a revenue circle or 'parish' consisting of several hamlets
nali rasoi	food boiled in water
nankiye	mother's mother's brother's household
narar	house-cluster
nari	removable stem of hookah
nasran	grains collected by Brahman on first day of Hindu month
nimantran	a prestation made on the fourth anniversary of a death
pagbandh	principle of inheritance by which the shares of sons are calculated on a *per capita* basis
pahu	a house-tenant
painth	unbroken line of diners
panchayat	council
Panchayat Samiti	elected council representing all the village councils of a Community Development Block
panjap	a ritual which purifies a newly born child and its mother and integrates them into profane society
patak	death pollution
patwari	village accountant
pind	flour-balls offered to ancestors
piochiyon	married woman's natal household
pitr kop	ancestral curse
prasad	sanctified food
pret	the disembodied and malevolently disposed soul of a deceased person before it is converted into an ancestor
puja	act of worship; ritualized veneration
raiyatwari	system of land tenure in which individual proprietors hold direct from the state and the local group does not constitute a co-parcenary body

rakhewa	custom by which a younger brother inherits his deceased elder brother's wife
randepa	a gift of money and cloth sent to a recently widowed woman by the households of her natal lineage
rikhorar	a widow or divorcee who has contracted a 'secondary' union
ristedar	non-agnatic kin and affines
roti	unleavened bread
rurhu	fixed grain rent
sajhi	tenant; partner
sapinda	the bilateral grouping of kin discussed in the Sanskrit texts as those who share common body particles
sapindi	a ritual at which the wandering soul of the deceased is incorporated into the society of the ancestors
saradh	ceremony at which offerings are made to the ancestral dead
sartora	an illegitimate child or one descended from an illegitimate son
seri	festival which marks the end of the rainy season; the crop harvested at this time
shamlat	common land
sohriye	spouse's parents' household
suji rasoi	food prepared with clarified butter
sutak	birth pollution
tapas	the 'heat' of asceticism
tarvadla	marriages involving the indirect exchange of women (e.g., A gives to B, B to C, and C to A)
tehsil	administrative sub-division of a district
thakur	household deity
tika	hamlet
tulsi	basil plant (sacred to the goddess Lachmi)
vaid	an Ayurvedic doctor
varna	classical division of Hindu society
ved	a wedding booth
zaildar	appointed official who oversaw a group of *lambedars*
zamindar	a landholder
Zila Parishad	Government-constituted district council

Notes

2 The setting

1 These figures exclude Tensil Una (population 175,927 in 1961), which did not become part of Kangra until 1966.

2 In that part of Nurpur *tehsil* which borders on the plains, and where the pattern of settlement is a nucleated one, the village is treated as a unit of local exogamy.

3 The economy

1 The standard acre is not a fixed measurement of area, but a measurement of that area which will produce a certain yield. It varies with the quality of the soil, and in the hills it is almost always considerably larger than an ordinary (4,840-square yard) acre.

2 This figure is based on a list prepared by the sub-division revenue authorities for the Land Reform Committee set up to review the proposed Himachal Pradesh (Transferred Territory) Tenants (Protection of Rights) Bill of 1968.

3 The Punjab Security of Land Tenures Act, 1953.

4 Information supplied by the District Commissioner of Kangra for a question in the State Assembly on June 26, 1968.

5 This figure is not comparable to the official census statistic for these hamlets since the latter excludes all those employed outside.

6 Figures quoted by the President of the District Soldiers', Sailors' and Airmen's Board, in a speech given to the Kangra Zamindar Sabha in March 1968.

7 Figures for the number of government employees in each *tika* in 1915 are given in the hand-written 'Tika Assessment Notes' which are kept in the D.C.'s office in Dharamsala (Palampur Tehsil, Rajgiri circle, vol. 5).

8 This includes the ranks of Subedar-Major, Subedar and Naib-Subedar (Jamedar). Known in British days as Viceroy's Commissioned

Officers (VCOs) or simply as Indian Officers (IOs) these ranks are intermediate between full commissioned officers and the NCOs and approximate very roughly to Warrant Officers in the British army.

9 The number of shops has been increasing steadily. Forty years ago there were only 4 shops within easy walking distance of the house in which I lived. Now there are over 20, and 6 new ones opened during my period in the field while two of the old ones went bust.

Most shopkeepers charge no interest on goods supplied on credit, though some of them are widely alleged to make up for this by fiddling the books. The alternative sources of credit are the private money-lenders (*shahukars*), most of whom are Rajputs in Chadhiar, and the government-sponsored co-operative societies. The latter offer short-term loans of modest proportions at annual interest rates of 8 per cent, but most of these go to the high-caste peasant proprietors who control their operations. Unless he can find an influential sponsor to act as a front man, the landless labourer has little prospect of obtaining credit from this source, and probably no great desire to do so since such loans involve a great deal of tiresome red-tape and a commitment to repay the principal within a set period. Although the *shahukars* charge much higher rates of interest (between 18 and 24 per cent p.a.) it was not my impression that people generally entertain the common European stereotype of the money-lender as an avaricious and grasping Shylock. On the contrary, some of them seem to be regarded as social benefactors, and the reluctance I encountered to acknowledge such transactions stemmed rather from the shame of being in debt and an outraged sense of propriety occasioned by my brazen enquiries on such a delicate topic.

10 But the problem here is that the appropriate academic qualifications are no longer an automatic passport to white-collar status. Increasingly one also needs what is locally known as 'approach', a relationship with an influential local politician who is prepared to drop a word in the right official ear at the right time. On my last visit to Kangra I was repeatedly told that even the most menial jobs in a government department are now being filled on the recommendation of a Minister and – from the many concrete instances I was offered – I am inclined to believe that this is not much of an exaggeration.

11 The district figures are taken from the 1931 census, which was the last at which caste populations were systematically enumerated (Census of India 1931a).

12 I exclude *tehsil* Una, which was not part of the district at that time. The figures are based on Boughey (1914) for Palampur; Middleton (1919b) for Nurpur and Kangra; and Shuttleworth (1916) for Dehra and Hamirpur.

13 There are also four co-opted representatives of the Scheduled Castes and two co-opted women.

14 These figures are based on an analysis of the Record of Rights of

each of the 37 hamlets for these years.

15 Of these, the tailor, watchman, forest guard and *vaid* traditionally received seasonal grain payments by way of remuneration.

16 Inferior Rajputs and the artisan castes are not regarded as sufficiently pure to merit the honour of keeping such a shrine.

17 The conventional formula which people present as past practice, is that *sapindi* is celebrated on the day after *karam-kriya* which Brahmans perform on the eleventh, Rajputs on the thirteenth and the lower castes on the twenty-second day after the death. But in current practice, *sapindi* and *kriya* are commonly telescoped into one ceremony which the low castes now celebrate on the thirteenth day in imitation of the Rajputs.

18 Today the *boti*'s remuneration is largely in cash. From a Rajput wedding he would expect to make a minimum of around Rs. 25, the exact amount depending on the amount of rice he cooks.

19 In fact only one of the 15 Dumna households in *mauza* Chadhiar derives a significant proportion of its income from basket-work.

20 In addition to the gifts of grain and cloth which the Barber receives at marriage, he can expect to make at least Rs. 45 in cash, and at a run-of-the-mill Rajput wedding would expect his cash receipts to be nearer Rs. 100. Though none of the 4 Barber households in my census owns more than one acre of land (see Table 5) they are amongst the most affluent members of the specialist castes. One of these households had no need to make any significant purchases from the shops during my fieldwork since all its needs, including minor luxuries like tobacco, were provided by its patrons. It is said that in the previous generation this household was regularly (though secretly) approached by certain of its Rajput patrons for a loan of grains to tide them over a temporary embarrassment.

21 Only a person of indisputably higher status may touch the head. When an inferior greets his superior he will stoop to touch his feet, and as he rises the latter will lightly lay his hands on his head in blessing.

22 Each set of three *aggars* is held to represent one of the four stages of life (*asramas*) of orthodox Sanskritic theory. The first set, which makes up the Barber's *janeo*, associate him with the second stage (*ghriyast asrama*) – that of the householder. The next three *aggars* added to the *janeo* of the Rajputs and Brahmans are identified with *vanaprastha asrama* (a stage of partial withdrawal from the mundane world for a life of contemplation). The third set worn by the Bhojkis represent the final stage of ascetic renunciation (*sanyas asrama*) and appear to correlate with their role as officiants (*pujaris*) at temples dedicated to Lord Siva, the great ascetic. While the pure Brahmans will not eat offerings made at Siva temples, the Bhojkis will.

23 For the Kangra Leather-workers the term is particularly apposite, not only because the Brahman and the Chamar stand in a relationship of complementary opposition in the sense that one confers

purity while the other removes pollution, but also because both are intermediaries with the supernatural world and possess the most potent of curses. An individual of any caste who feels that he has been wronged by another, can make an invocation (*dochch*) to Chano Sidh, the patron deity of the Leather-workers. Chano Sidh may then take retribution (*khot*) on the offender's household by causing illness or death in the family. There is only one possible way of placating the deity, and that is through the intercession of a Leather-worker.

4 The hierarchical aspects of caste

1 A secondary school headmaster explained that 'the Germans and Rajputs are both light-skinned Aryans. They have the same *gotras* and castes, and worship of the swastika just like we do.' In token of his admiration, a retired army subedar of my acquaintance had named his son German Chand. More extreme was the abrasive insistence of another schoolteacher that the Nuremberg Trials had destroyed the flower of Germany; that the Jews had deserved to die for they were all traitors 'like the Muslims', and that Hitler – a vegetarian and life-long celibate – had been the victim of a malicious campaign of slander and character assassination. Less controversial is the widely held notion that German Sanskrit scholars discovered the secret of the atom bomb from the Vedas.

2 A notion that I several times encountered is that there are two castes in England: the *Sahib log* who provide officers for the army, and the *gore* (a colloquial term for European soldiers; literally 'the fair-skinned') who are recruited as Other Ranks and who include the illegitimate children of the Sahibs.

3 The appearance of a child is determined by the first thing its mother sees after intercourse – ideally the father, though terrible mistakes have been known to occur. The notion that the sex of the offspring is determined by the relative proportions of male and female seed occurs in The Laws of Manu (III:49).

4 In general, high-caste widows are expected to observe more stringent rules for the avoidance of pollution, or for its elimination, than married women. But no menstrual taboos are held to apply to unmarried girls. It is as if the purity of a widow has been so enfeebled by her widowhood that extraordinary precautions against pollution are called for. Conversely, the super-normal state of purity of an unmarried virgin is sufficient to immunize her from sources of pollution which would defile lesser mortals. Quite independently, two particularly astute informants suggested a more pragmatic view, however. They pointed out that the sacred scriptures require that a young girl be married before puberty; but that these days very few of them are. If they were to observe menstrual pollution, then, they would be subtly shaming their fathers by drawing attention to this departure from the ideal.

5 Various popular etymologies are suggested for this greeting. The District Gazetteer (1926:49) suggests that it derives from the Sanskrit *Jayatu Devak* – 'May the king be victorious'. An alternative theory claims it as a corruption of *Jai Dewi* – 'Long live the goddess' (Durga). Durga is clearly associated with the Rajputs, and in particular with the royal clan of Kangra state whose progenitor was born from the sweat on the brow of the goddess.

6 Current practice, however, is rather less exclusive than the ideal suggests. Even in the past this may well have been the case; but there is some reason to suppose that recent upheavals in the hypergamous hierarchies of both the Rajputs and Brahmans have been accompanied by a marked decline in the exclusiveness of the top *biradaris*. I elaborate on these points in Chapters 7 and 8.

7 Mata Ji normally cooked all the food for our household, and I ate with the family in the kitchen (though outside the *chauka* when *bhat* was served). But whenever any of the more orthodox Brahman men came to visit us, my 'uncle' would prepare the *bhat* with all due formality, the women were expected to stay out of the *chauka*, and I to absent myself from the kitchen.

8 While the standing of the Rajput patron is loosely associated with that of the Brahmans who serve him, the latter's own standing is to some extent bound up with that of their patrons. The rather catholic nature of my 'uncle's' clientele as a *vaid* and a *boti*, for example, was the subject of many invidious comparisons with his own father, whose astrological expertise and priestly ministrations were reportedly only at the disposal of other Brahmans and of Rajputs of the top two *biradaris.*

9 The two concluding sections of this chapter reproduce some of the material included in my article 'The Koli Dilemma', published in *Contributions to Indian Sociology*, 1970 (N.S.) IV, pp. 84–104. I am grateful to the Editor for permission to incorporate this material.

10 Pocock's analytical distinction between 'status' and 'standing' is discussed in Chapter 9:1.

11 In the following paragraphs, dealing with the Backward Classes and Scheduled castes in general, I draw heavily on Béteille (1969) and Dushkin (1961). Other sources are cited in the text.

12 The Blacksmiths and Carpenters are ambivalent. Sometimes they identify themselves as Rajputs while at other times they claim to be Dhiman Brahmans. The Jogis also lay a half-hearted claim to Brahman origins, but the model they emulate is really that of the casteless world-renouncer. Like the *Sanyasi* they bury rather than burn their dead, and when they go begging they carry the *jhola* (bag) of the renouncer.

13 Mayer (1960:62) reports that several castes in Ramkheri tell an identical story.

5 Clans and their segments

1 The term *bans* belongs to the same lexical set as the Sanskrit *vamsa*, which designates a patriline in other parts of north India; and as *vamsavali*, a genealogy.

2 An alternative theory, which posits that blood is derived from both parents, is discussed in Chapter 7.

3 The motif of sweat as semen is common in Hindu mythology. The 'heat' which is generated by the austerities of the ascetic produces both. Siva – the ascetic *par excellence* – 'wanders naked, doing *tapas*, and when he sheds a drop of sweat from his forehead the Earth nourishes it and raises the child born from it, just as she receives Siva's seed to bear Skanda' (O'Flaherty 1973:372).

4 There is no commonly known word for incest in the Kangra dialect, and people make no category distinction between marriage and/or sexual relations within the *gotra*, within the clan and within the lineage, though there is a marked difference in the degree of disapproval in each case.

5 Various exceptions should be noted. A boy whose tonsure ceremony (*jagra*) has yet to be performed is not shaved, and nor are those who have recently married. The chief mourner does not have his head shaved at *kapar-dhuai*. He is shaved before the cremation and again at *kriya* on the eleventh or thirteenth day (depending on caste).

6 Madan (1965:203) and Chauhan (1967:36) both report that in their respective field areas the *kutumb* consists exclusively, as in Kangra, of agnates and their wives.

7 This, of course, recalls the requirement that a Nayar woman and her child observe death pollution for her *tali*-tier, while the latter remains unaffected by their death or that of any of their matrikin.

8 Karve (1965:188) records that in Central India individual offerings are made to precisely this range of ancestors. By contrast, Madan (1965:90–1, 205) notes that in Kashmir the Brahmans make offerings to six male and female lineal ascendants. In addition to these ancestors in the direct line of descent, Kangra people also offer *pind* to the mother's father and mother on all occasions when *saradh* is performed for the ancestors collectively. At *sola* ('sixteen') *saradh* during the rains, a wider range of deceased agnates – for instance a childless brother and his wife – are likely to be included.

9 There are certain five-day periods called *panchak* when a corpse must not be cremated lest the deceased's spirit drag other members of the *khandan* after him. If the corpse were cremated on the first day of *panchak*, four other members of the lineage would die; if on the second day three others, and so on. In fact, however, the cremation will go ahead in the normal way and the *pret* spirit is fooled by burning the appropriate number of small effigies along with the corpse.

10 In Chapter 9 I try to show that, by ranking sub-clan segments on the basis of the relative prestige of their marriage alliances, hypergamy fosters fissiparous tendencies within the descent group and its repeated fragmentation. Here I draw attention to the formal possibility that this process would be greatly exacerbated by consistently ranking lines of descent according to the relative age of their founders. In other words, ever more rapid fission and secession would be promoted by the ability of senior lines to attract consistently the more prestigious affines.

6 Households and their partition

1 Epstein (1973:201) has subsequently noted that 'my recent observations . . . bear out much of my earlier hypothesis', but does not substantiate this claim by any serious attempt to dispose of the criticisms noted above.

2 *Nimantran* generally consists of a red scarf, a metal beaker, a *dhoti*, some rice and a small amount of money. In standard Hindi the term translates as 'invitation', but in the local dialect it is used only for the gifts given at *chabarakh*.

3 I was told that in the past one could always tell whether a man's father was alive by the colour of his head-gear. Only those whose fathers were deceased would wear a white *topi.*

4 Given the two-year post-parturition period of abstinence from sexual intercourse which is considered desirable for the health of the child, this asymmetry should be reinforced by an age gap (cf. Minturn and Hitchcock 1966:98). Siblings born within three years of each other are *daduru*, and are likely to be sickly. After the second birth the milk of the mother is said to be poisonous to the elder child.

5 Amongst those who tolerate widow remarriage, the ideal is that it should take the form of *rakhewa*: that is, remarriage with the deceased's husband's younger brother (*der*). The latter has the theoretical though today unenforceable right (*huk*) to inherit his *bhabhi* (eBW), and a legitimate claim to compensation if she chooses to marry somebody else. By contrast, the marriage of a widow to her deceased husband's elder brother is held to be quite impossible since terminologically she is assimilated to the son's wife, and should be treated in the same sort of way. But as high-caste people with pretensions to respectability see it, there is little to choose between the sinfulness of a union with either variety of sister-in-law. Just as your younger brother's wife is a kind of daughter-in-law, so your elder brother's wife is 'just like a mother'.

6 The Kangra data do not entirely lend themselves to the contrast which Tambiah draws between the emphasis which India characteristically places on the lineal before the collateral heir, and the West African stress on the rules of male survivorship, reversion

to male collaterals and the exclusion of women (Tambiah 1973a: 78–9).

7 Some of my informants drew a distinction between a *ghar-jamwantru* in the strict sense, who himself inherits from his father-in-law; and an uxorilocally resident son-in-law whose wife inherits. More opprobrium attaches to the first case, in which it is felt the element of calculated self-interest is stronger.

8 This contrasts with the situation Madan (1962b) reports for the Pandits of rural Kashmir, where brothers continue to perform *saradh* jointly even after partition.

7 Rajput hypergamy in an historical perspective

1 Compare Harper (1968b:60) who appears to arrive at precisely the opposite conclusion to Dumont. He implies that, by contrast with the Nayar, the status of the Patidar lineage is diminished by any inferiority in their wife-givers. If – as I shall argue – Dumont's conclusion is misleading for the north, Harper's characterization of the Nayar situation is even more over-simplified. We obviously need to distinguish between the *tali*-tying 'husband' (*manavalan*) and the *sambandham* partner. It seems clear that the status of the former was impaired by tying *talis* for inferior girls. This at any rate was certainly true for the Nambudiris who performed the rite for Nayar royals (Mencher and Goldberg 1967).

2 The term *mujara* is popularly supposed to be derived from the Hindi *manzur hogaya*, 'accepted'. It is rather more likely, however, that it is related to the Persian *mijra'i*, 'one who pays respects', and *mujir*, 'a protector from oppression'.

3 *Batta satta* (literally 'the exchange of like for like') is also known as *lad batai* ('the swopping of shawls'). Since the reciprocity is direct, and is consequently a more obvious contradiction of the ideology of *kanya dan*, *batta satta* meets with even greater disapproval than *tarvadla*. But that is not the only reason people give for disliking such marriages. They say that, on a purely practical level, experience shows that if there are quarrels between one couple, the conflict will tend to spread to the other couple, since each of the spouses will side with their own sibling. They also say that the wives will tend to demand strict equivalence of treatment. If one wife is given a new piece of jewellery, for example, the husband of the other will not get a moment's peace from his wife until he too gets her a new ornament. People sometimes explain their dislike of *batta satta* marriages in other, equally familiar, terms. It is often explained, for example, that since deference is due to a wife-taker, and since wife-takers are also wife-givers in a *batta satta* marriage, the exchange leads to a confusion of relationships. One informant told me that the reason why he would never consider giving his sister to his wife's brother was that he would then be depriving himself of an additional set of *ristedar* (affines).

Tripartite *tarvadla* exchanges are sometimes more complicated than the simple example I have given above. I recorded instances, for example, in which the cycle was completed when a male ego married his ZHZHFBD, ZHZD, DHZHZ, FBDHFBD and ZHFBSD.

4 As it happened, most of the richest members of the third *biradari* in the *mauza* were concentrated in the area of my census, so that the proportion of owners of large holdings which belong to this *biradari* would probably be rather less marked in a larger sample.

5 Largely because the area never came under the direct control of the British administration, infanticide continued to be practised in a fairly major way in the neighbouring Province of Jammu for some time after it had been almost eradicated in Kangra. The 1931 census report for the Province congratulates the Maharaja on a marked improvement in the situation when the sex ratio recorded for the Rajputs as a whole was only 754 girls per 1,000 boys. The improvement is attributed to the foundation of the Dhandevi Memorial Fund set up by the Maharaja to finance the marriages of Rajput girls, and to his announcement that he would grant an acre of land to the father of every girl born in a Rajput clan of the highest status (Census of India, 1931b, XXIV, Jammu and Kashmir State, pt. 1, p. 136).

6 Colostrum is considered to be poisonous, and until the mother's milk supply is established the baby may be suckled by a neighbour who has milk.

7 In my experience the Brahmans stick to these rules quite conscientiously, for I know of several cases where an otherwise desirable match proposed by a third party was rejected out of hand on these grounds.

8 On account of their predilection for close-kin marriage, leprosy is supposed to be particularly common amongst Muslims. Lepers are liable to be turned out by their own families, and in the neighbouring state of Mandi they used to be drowned or burnt alive (Griffin 1870:648–9).

9 Bakshi Bhag Singh's father (2nd *biradari*) married a Nanwarak girl (3rd *biradari*) from the house-cluster of Janus. Two of Bhag Singh's eight grandsons renewed this alliance by repeating the marriage of their FFF. Bhag Singh himself was still alive when the first of these marriages was celebrated, but would not accompany the marriage party to Janus 'because they were his *mame* ("mother's brothers")'; cf. Figure 11 (Chapter 9:5).

10 *Par piya tan sakh giya.* This might be more literally rendered as: 'When "great" is put (in front) then the relationship has gone.' *Par* is a prefix which is attached to kinship terms, and which performs much the same function as the English prefix 'great' as in great-grandfather. Thus the father's father is *dadu* and *his* father *pardada*; the son's son is *potru* and his son *par-potru*; the mother's father *nanu* and the father's mother's father *parnanu*. When the proverb says, then, that the prefix *par* signifies the end of the

relationship, it does not specify whether the reference is to agnatic or to non-agnatic kinship, or to both. But in most contexts in which people invoke this principle, the reference is unambiguously to relationships initiated by marriage, for in theory at least, agnatic ties never lapse. It thus embodies much the same idea as the Kashmiri proverb 'I began as a daughter, became a sister, a father's sister, a father's father's sister and then – a nobody' (Madan 1963). But I have nevertheless also heard people appeal to this maxim in the context of agnatic kinship to explain why pollution-cum-mourning obligations fall heaviest on those agnates who are descended from a single *pardada*, and to justify the view that ancestral property should not automatically pass to a collateral descended from an ancestor more remote than the father's father's father of the deceased.

11 One further contrast is that the Malwa-Jat rules serve automatically to exclude, among others, *all* those individuals who trace links of filiation to any of ego's great-grandparents, while the Kangra variant excludes only some of these individuals. For example, the MMZDD is excluded in the first case (as she shares the same MM clan as ego) but not in the second.

Most writers have treated the four-*gotra* rules and the bilaterally conceived *sapinda* regulations of the medieval commentaries as being quite heterogeneous, and Karve's (1965) implication to the contrary has been severely castigated by Dumont and Pocock (1957). Quite apart from registering surprise at finding these authors apparently arguing that there is no common denominator between the textual ideas and the modern practice (despite a somersault when they concede that it is 'not impossible after all that there is a relation'), I find their criticism of Karve too harsh and some of their own generalizations open to question. Thus they are simply wrong when they assert that 'even in the most extreme cases, the children of the mother's and father's *female* cousins do not appear to be barred', for the Malwa-Jat rules do precisely that. They are obviously right to insist that there is a fundamental difference between the exogamy of lineal *groups*, and a set of prohibitions which bear on cognatically related *individuals*, a consideration of which Karve (p. 123) was not unaware. It is not that there is any question of an identity between the two sets of rules; but rather that in effect the Malwa-Jat variant of the four-*gotra* rule is an extremely economical way of requiring the exclusion of, amongst others, 'near kin of the same type as given in the ancient rules' (ibid., p. 123).

12 These days *gotra* exogamy is more honoured in the breach, but I am confident that this was not so in the past. At the time of the *biradari* reforms the Katoch council did a good deal of agonizing over whether to dispense with this requirement, and although there was a general agreement to do so, it was not until a Katoch General of the Jammu and Kashmir army married one of his sons (a

Colonel) to a girl from the Raja of Guler's family that others followed suit. Three of the third *biradari* sub-clans of Chadhiar – the Nanwaraks, Moonglas and Dagohias – claim to share a common *gotra*, though marriage between them is now common. But prior to the *biradari* reforms there does not appear to have been a single such marriage, and I am convinced that this is not merely an illusion created by doctoring the genealogies.

13 The argument that it might also be understood in terms of dowry being a compensation for the burden of shouldering an additional unproductive household member, and bride-price a compensation for the loss of a productive daughter (Van der Veen 1972:29; Epstein 1973:199) does not apply. Today dowry payments are increasingly common in the lower ranges of the hierarchy, but women are no less important than formerly in agricultural production. Moreover girls of the second *biradari* receive a dowry, yet only the most affluent second *biradari* sub-clans exempt their women from labour in the fields.

14 Today bride-price rates range between about Rs. 700 and Rs. 3,000.

8 The 'biradari' reform movement

1 This account is based partly on the recollections of a wide range of informants, including nearly all those who had been really influential in initiating the *biradari* reforms in the Palampur area, and who were still alive at the time of my fieldwork. But I was also able to consult the records of the first, second and fourth *biradari* councils. These include minutes of meetings, lists of office-bearers, a voluminous correspondence about boycotted individuals, and in some cases lists of people who attended meetings.

2 Today most Rajput girls are married between the ages of 15 and 19.

3 In one case – noted in the previous chapter – the Manhas are wife-takers to the wife-takers of the Kanthwals of Ther.

9 Marriage strategies

1 Here one enters a world whose own symbols of standing are totally alien to the village. Thus the Katoch son-in-law of a Chadhiar peasant farmer told me of the insecurity he experienced during his preliminary training for a commission when his non-existent skill at 'real officer games like tennis and cricket' was exposed.

2 I often observed that relations between superordinate and subordinate in the same administrative department are markedly uneasy when the latter's formal qualifications are higher.

3 Cf. Parry's report (1932:379–80) that the fertility of a Lakher bride is conferred by her brother *and* mother's brother.

4 Nor, on my reading, is he entirely supported by either the Patidar

or the Anavil Brahman data (see, for example, Pocock 1972:136; Van der Veen 1972:108, 150).

10 Affines and consanguines

1 In the past, a Rathi would take a goat to be slaughtered at his deceased *kurum*'s house at the end of the period of mourning and would cut coarse jokes at the dead man's expense. Today this custom is generally regarded as somewhat uncouth and is no longer practised by Chadhiar Rajputs of any *biradari*.

2 Although the wives of brothers will generally address each other reciprocally as 'sister', it is open to the eBW to call her HyBW '*lari*' – 'bride' – if she wants to maintain her distance.

Bibliography

ABBI, B. L. (1969), 'Urban Family in India', *Contributions to Indian Sociology*, New Series, vol. 3, pp. 116–27.

AHMAD, I. (1973), 'Endogamy and Status among the Siddique Sheikhs of Allahabad, Uttar Pradesh' in I. Ahmad (ed.), *Caste and Social Stratification*, pp. 157–94, Manohar Books, Delhi.

AIYAPPAN, A. (1965), *Social Revolution in a Kerala Village*, Asia Publishing House, Bombay.

ALAVI, H. A. (1972), 'Kinship in West Punjab Villages', *Contributions to Indian Sociology*, New Series, vol. 4, pp. 1–27.

ALTEKAR, A. S. (1938), *The Position of Women in Hindu Civilization from Pre-Historic Times to the Present Day*, Probsthain, London.

ANDERSON, A. (1897), *Final Report of the Revised Settlement of Kangra Proper*, Civil and Military Gazette Press, Lahore.

BADEN-POWELL, B. H. (1892), *The Land Systems of British India*, 3 vols, Clarendon Press, Oxford.

BADEN-POWELL, B. H. (1899), *The Origin and Growth of Village Communities in India*, Swan Sonnenschein, London.

BAILEY, F. G. (1958), *Caste and the Economic Frontier: A Village in Highland Orissa*, Manchester University Press.

BAILEY, F. G. (1959), 'For a Sociology of India?', *Contributions to Indian Sociology*, Old Series, vol. 3, pp. 88–101.

BARNES, G. C. (1889), *Report of the Land Revenue Settlement of the Kangra District, Punjab*, Civil and Military Gazette Press, Lahore.

BARNES, J. A. (1971), *Three Styles in the Study of Kinship*, Tavistock Publications, London.

BARTH, F. (1959), *Political Leadership among the Swat Pathans*, Athlone Press, London.

BARTH, F. (1960), 'The System of Social Stratification in Swat, North Pakistan', in E. R. Leach (ed.), *Aspects of Caste in South India, Ceylon and North-west Pakistan*, pp. 113–46, Cambridge Papers in Social Anthropology No. 2, Cambridge University Press.

BARTH, F. (1966), *Models of Social Organisation*, Royal Anthropological Institute Occasional Paper No. 23, London.

BECK, E. F. (1972), *Peasant Society in Konku: A Study of Right and Left Subcastes in South India*, University of British Columbia Press, Vancouver.

BEIDELMAN, T. O. (1959), *A Comparative Analysis of the 'Jajmani' System*, Monographs for the Association for Asian Studies VIII, New York.

BERREMAN, G. D. (1962), 'Caste and Economy in the Himalayas', *Economic Development and Cultural Change*, X, pp. 386–94.

BERREMAN, G. D. (1963), *Hindus of the Himalayas*, University of California Press, Berkeley and Los Angeles.

BÉTEILLE, A. (1964), 'A Note on the Referents of Caste', *European Journal of Sociology*, V, pp. 130–4.

BÉTEILLE, A. (1965), *Caste, Class and Power*, University of California Press, Berkeley and Los Angeles.

BÉTEILLE, A. (1969), 'The Future of the Backward Classes: The Competing Demands of Status and Power', in A. Béteille, *Castes: Old and New*, Asia Publishing House, Bombay.

BHAI MUL RAJ (1933), *Economic Survey of the Haripur and Mangarh Taluqas of the Kangra District of the Punjab*, The Board of Economic Enquiry, Punjab, Publication No. 9, Lahore.

BLOCH, M. (1973), 'The Long Term and the Short Term: The Economic and Political Significance of the Morality of Kinship' in J. Goody (ed.), *The Character of Kinship*, pp. 75–87, Cambridge University Press.

BLUNT, E. A. H. (1969), *The Caste System of Northern India*, S. Chand, India.

BOUGHEY, G. M. (1914), *Preliminary Assessment of the Palampur Tehsil of the District Kangra*, Government Printing, Lahore.

BOUGLÉ, C. (1971), *Essays on the Caste System*, translated by D. F. Pocock, Cambridge University Press.

BREMAN JAN (1974), *Patronage and Exploitation: Changing Agrarian Relations in South Gujarat, India*, University of California Press, Berkeley and Los Angeles.

BRISTOW, Brigadier R. C. B. (1974), *Memories of the British Raj: A Soldier in India*, Johnson, London.

CARSTAIRS, G. MORRIS (1957), *The Twice Born: A Study of a Community of High-Caste Hindus*, Hogarth Press, London.

CAVE-BROWNE, J. (1857), *Indian Infanticide: Its Origin, Progress and Suppression*, W. H. Allen, London.

CENSUS OF INDIA (1921), vol. XV, pt 1, Punjab and Delhi. Report by L. Middleton and S. M. Jacob, 1923, Civil and Military Gazette Press, Lahore.

CENSUS OF INDIA (1931a), vol. XVII, Punjab, pts 1 and 2, Report and Tables by Khan Ahmad Hasan Khan, 1933, Civil and Military Gazette Press, Lahore.

CENSUS OF INDIA (1931b), vol. XXIV, pt 1, *Jammu and Kashmir State*, Report by Rai Bahadur, Pt Anant Ram and Pt Hira Nand Raina, The Ranbir Government Press, Jammu.

CHAUHAN, B. R. (1967), *A Rajasthan Village*, Vir Publishing House, New Delhi.

COHN, B. S. (1955), 'The Changing Status of a Depressed Caste', in M. Marriott (ed.), *Village India*, pp. 53–77, University of Chicago Press.

COHN, B. S. (1959), 'The Changing Traditions of a Low Caste', in M. Singer (ed.), *Traditional India: Structure and Change*, American Folklore Society, Philadelphia.

COHN, B. S. (1961), 'Chamar Family in a North Indian Village: A Structural Contingent', *Economic Weekly*, July 1961, vol. XIII, Special Number, pp. 1051–5.

COHN, B. S. (1968), 'Notes on the Study of Indian Society and Culture', in M. Singer and B. S. Cohn (eds), *Structure and Change in Indian Society*, pp. 3–28, Aldine, Chicago.

COHN, B. S. (1969), 'Structural Change in Indian Rural Society', in R. E. Frykenberg (ed.), *Land Control and Social Structure in Indian History*, pp. 53–121, University of Wisconsin Press, Madison.

COHN, B. S. (1971), *India: The Social Anthropology of a Civilization*, Prentice-Hall, Englewood Cliffs, New Jersey.

CONNOLLY, V. (1911), *Preliminary Assessment Report of the Dehra and Hamirpur Tahsils of the Kangra District*, Punjab Government Press, Lahore.

CUNNINGHAM, Lt. Col. W. B. (1932), *Dogra Handbook: Handbooks for the Indian Army, Dogras*, revised edn, Government of India Press, New Delhi.

DUMÉZIL, G. (1940), *Mitra-Varuna*, Paris.

DUMONT, L. (1957), *Hierarchy and Marriage Alliance in South Indian Kinship*, Royal Anthropological Institute Occasional Paper No. 22, London.

DUMONT, L. (1961a), 'Marriage in India, The Present State of the Question, I. Alliance in S.E. India and Ceylon', *Contributions to Indian Sociology*, Old Series, vol. 5, pp. 75–90.

DUMONT, L. (1961b), 'Les mariages Nayars comme faits indiens', *L'homme*, vol. 1, no. 1, pp. 11–36.

DUMONT, L. (1962), 'The Conception of Kingship in Ancient India', *Contributions to Indian Sociology*, Old Series, vol. 6, pp. 48–77.

DUMONT, L. (1964), 'Marriage in India: The Present State of the Question. Postscript to Part I, II. Marriage and Status, Nayar and Newar, *Contributions to Indian Sociology*, Old Series, vol. 7, pp. 77–98.

DUMONT, L. (1966), 'Marriage in India: The Present State of the Question, III. North India in Relation to South India', *Contributions to Indian Sociology*, Old Series, vol. 9, pp. 90–114.

DUMONT, L. (1967), 'Caste: A Phenomenon of Social Structure or an Aspect of Indian Culture?' in A. de Reuck and J. Knight (eds), *CIBA Foundation Symposium on Caste and Race: Comparative Approaches*, J. & A. Churchill, London.

DUMONT, L. (1970), *Homo Hierarchicus: The Caste System and its Implications*, Translated by M. Sainsbury, Weidenfeld & Nicolson, London.

DUMONT, L. and POCOCK, D. F. (1957), 'Kinship', *Contributions to Indian Sociology*, Old Series, vol. 1, pp. 43–64.

DUMONT, L. and POCOCK, D. F. (1959), 'Pure and Impure', *Contributions to Indian Sociology*, Old Series, vol. 3, pp. 9–39.

DUSHKIN, L. (1961), 'The Backward Classes', *Economic Weekly*, 29 October, 4 and 18 November 1961, pp. 1665–8, 1695–705, 1729–38, Bombay.

EGLAR, Z. (1960), *A Punjab Village in Pakistan*, Columbia University Press, New York and London.

EPSTEIN, T. S. (1962), *Economic Development and Social Change in South India*, Manchester University Press.

EPSTEIN, T. S. (1967), 'Productive Efficiency and Customary Systems of Rewards in Rural South India', in R. Firth (ed.), *Themes in Economic Anthropology*, (A.S.A.6), Tavistock Publications, London.

EPSTEIN, T. S. (1973), *South India: Yesterday, Today and Tomorrow*, Macmillan, London.

FORTES, M. (1949a), 'Time and Social Structure: An Ashanti Case Study', in M. Fortes (ed.), *Social Structure: Essays Presented to A. R. Radcliffe-Brown*, Oxford University Press, London.

FORTES, M. (1949b), *The Web of Kinship among the Tallensi*, Oxford University Press, London.

FORTES, M. (1969), *Kinship and the Social Order: The Legacy of Lewis Henry Morgan*, Routledge & Kegan Paul, London.

FOX, R. G. (1971), *Kin, Clan, Raja and Rule: State-Hinterland Relations in Pre-Industrial India*, University of California Press, Berkeley and Los Angeles.

FRIEDMAN, J. (1971), 'Marxism, Structuralism and Vulgar Materialism' in *Man*, New Series, vol. 9.

FRIEDMAN, J. (1975), 'Tribes, States and Transformations', in M. Bloch (ed.), *Marxist Analyses and Social Anthropology*, pp. 161–202, Malaby Press, London.

FURER-HAIMENDORF, C. von (1966), 'Unity and Diversity in the Chetri Caste of Nepal' in C. von Furer-Haimendorf (ed.), *Caste and Kin in Nepal, India and Ceylon*, pp. 11–67, Asia Publishing House, Bombay.

GALANTER, M. (1966), 'The Religious Aspects of Caste: A Legal View' in D. E. Smith (ed.), *South Asian Politics and Religion*, pp. 277–310, Princeton University Press.

GALANTER, M. (1968), 'Changing Legal Conceptions of Caste', in M. Singer and B. S. Cohn (eds), *Structure and Change in Indian Society*, pp. 299–338, Aldine, Chicago.

GAMBURD, G. (n.d.), 'Disharmonic Regimes in South-West Ceylon', mimeographed.

GEERTZ, H. and GEERTZ, C. (1975), *Kinship in Bali*, University of Chicago Press.

GOSWAMI, B. N. (n.d.), 'The Social Background of the Kangra Valley Paintings', Unpublished PhD Thesis, Punjab University, Chandigarh.

GOULD, H. A. (1967), 'Priest and Contra-Priest: A Study of "Jajmani" Relationships in the Hindu Plains and the Nilgiri Hills', *Contributions to Indian Sociology*, New Series, vol. 1, pp. 26–55.

GOULD, H. A. (1968), 'Time-Dimension and Structural Change in an Indian Kinship System: A Problem of Conceptual Refinement', in M. Singer and B. S. Cohn (eds), *Structure and Change in Indian Society*, pp. 413–22, Aldine, Chicago.

GRIERSON, Sir G. A. (1916), Linguistic Survey of India, vol. IX, pt. 4, Calcutta.

GRIFFIN, L. H. (1870), *The Rajas of the Punjab: Being the History of the Principal States in the Punjab and their Political Relations with the British Government*, Punjab Printing, Lahore.

GUPTA, G. R. (1974), *Marriage, Religion and Society: Pattern of Change in an Indian Village*, Curzon Press, London and Dublin.

HARDGRAVE, R. (1969), *The Nadars of Tamilnad: The Political Culture of a Community in Change*, University of California Press, Berkeley and Los Angeles.

HARPER, E. B. (1959), 'Two Systems of Economic Exchange in Village India', *American Anthropologist*, vol. LXI, pp. 760–78.

HARPER, E. B. (1968a), 'Social Consequence of an "Unsuccessful" Low Caste Movement', in J. Silverberg (ed.), *Social Mobility in the Caste System in India*, pp. 33–65, Mouton, The Hague.

HARPER, E. B. (1968b), 'A Comparative Analysis of Caste: The United States and India' in M. Singer and B. S. Cohn (eds), *Structure and Change in Indian Society*, pp. 51–77, Aldine, Chicago.

HÉRITIER, F. (1974), 'Systèmes omaha de parenté et d'alliance: étude en ordinateur du fonctionnement matrimonial réel d'une société africaine (Samo, Haute-Volta)' in P. Ballanoff (ed.), *Genealogical Mathematics*, pp. 197–213, Mouton, Paris–The Hague.

HERSHMAN, P. (n.d.), 'A Comparison between the Punjabi and Tallensi Marriage Systems', Unpublished MS.

HERTZ, R. (1960), *Death and the Right Hand*, translated by R. and C. Needham, Free Press, Chicago.

HIEBERT, P. G. (1969), 'Caste and Personal Rank in an Indian Village: An Extension in Techniques', *American Anthropologist*, LXXI, pp. 434–53.

HILL, P. (1963), *The Migrant Cocoa Farmers of Southern Ghana*, Cambridge University Press.

HOGART, A. M. (1968), *Caste: A Comparative Study*, Russell & Russell, New York.

HOWELL, G. C. (1917), 'Some Notes on Ancient Kulu Politics', *Journal of the Punjab Historical Society*, vol. VI, no. 2, pp. 69–81.

HUTCHINSON, J. and VOGEL, J. Ph. (1933), *History of the Punjab Hill States*, Government Printing, Lahore.

HUTTON, J. H. (1969), *Caste in India: Its Nature, Function and Origins*, Oxford University Press, London.

IBBETSON, D. (1883), *Report on the Census of the Punjab Taken on 17th February, 1881*, vol. 1, Government Printing, Calcutta.

INDEN, R. and NICHOLAS, R. W. (n.d.), 'The Defining Features of Kinship in Bengali Culture', mimeographed.

ISAACS, H. R. (1965), *India's Ex-Untouchables*, Asia Publishing House, Bombay.

ISHWARAN, K. (1966), *Tradition and Economy in Village India*, Routledge & Kegan Paul, London.

KAPADIA, K. M. (1955), *Marriage and Family in India*, Oxford University Press, London.

KARVE, I. (1965), *Kinship Organization in India*, Asia Publishing House, Bombay.

KAYASTHA, S. L. (1964), *The Himalayan Beas Basin: A Study in Habitat, Economy and Society*, Benares Hindu University Press.

KOLENDA, P. M. (1968) 'Region, Caste and Family Structure: A Comparative Study of the Indian "Joint" Family' in M. Singer and B. S. Cohn (eds), *Structure and Change in Indian Society*, pp. 339–96, Aldine, Chicago.

KOLENDA, P. M. (1970), 'Family Structure in Village Lonikand, India: 1819, 1958 and 1967', *Contributions to Indian Sociology*, New Series, no. 4, pp. 50–72.

KUPER, A. (1970), 'Lévi-Strauss Comes to Africa, Speaking English', *African Social Research*, 10, pp. 769–88.

LEACH, E. R. (1954) *Political Systems of Highland Burma: A Study of Kachin Social Structure*, Athlone Press, London.

LEACH, E. R. (1960), 'Introduction: What should we mean by Caste', in E. R. Leach (ed.), *Aspects of Caste in South India, Ceylon and North-West Pakistan*, Cambridge Papers in Social Anthropology No. 2, Cambridge University Press.

LEACH, E. R. (1961a), *Rethinking Anthropology*, Athlone Press, London.

LEACH, E. R. (1961b), 'Asymmetric Marriage Rules, Status Difference, and Direct Reciprocity: Comments on Alleged Fallacy', *Southwestern Journal of Anthropology*, vol. 17, pp. 49–55.

LEACH, E. R. (1961c), *Pul Eliya, A Village in Ceylon: A Study of Land Tenure and Kinship*, Cambridge University Press.

LEACH, E. R. (1963a), 'Did The Wild Veddas have Matrilineal Clans', in I. Schapera (ed.), *Studies in Kinship and Marriage*, Royal Anthropological Institute, Occasional Paper No. 16, pp. 68–78.

LEACH, E. R. (1963b), 'Alliance and Descent among the Lakher: A Reconsideration', *Ethnos*, Nos 2–4, pp. 237–49.

LEACH, E. R. (1969), ' "Kachin" and "Haka Chin": A rejoinder to Lévi-Strauss', *Man*, New Series, vol. 4, pp. 277–85.

LÉVI-STRAUSS, C. (1963), 'Social Structure', in C. Lévi-Strauss, *Structural Anthropology* (translated by C. Jacobson and B. G. Schoepf), Allen Lane, The Penguin Press, London.

LÉVI-STRAUSS, C. (1966), 'The Future of Kinship Studies: The Huxley Memorial Lecture 1965', *Proceedings of the Royal Anthropological Institute*, pp. 13–22.

LÉVI-STRAUSS, C. (1969), *The Elementary Structures of Kinship*, translated by J. Bell, J. von Sturmer and R. Needham, Eyre & Spottiswoode, London (first French edition, 1949).

LEWIS, O. (1965), *Village Life in Northern India: Studies in a Delhi Village*, Random House, New York.

LINTON, R. (1952), 'Cultural and Personality Factors Affecting Economic Growth', in B. F. Hoselitz (ed.), *The Progress of Underdeveloped Areas*, University of Chicago Press.

LYALL, J. B. (1889), *Report of the Land Revenue Settlement of the Kangra District*, Civil and Military Gazette Press, Lahore.

LYNCH, O. M. (1968), 'The Politics of Untouchability: A Case from Agra, India', in M. Singer and B. S. Cohn (eds), *Structure and Change in Indian Society*, pp. 209–42, Aldine, Chicago.

MacMILLAN, M. C. (1968), 'The Indian Army 1947–65', Unpublished BPhil Thesis, University of Oxford.

MADAN, T. N. (1962a), 'Is the Brahmanic *Gotra* a Grouping of Kin?', *Southwestern Journal of Anthropology*, vol. 18, pp. 59–77.

MADAN, T. N. (1962b), 'The Joint Family: A Terminological Clarification', *International Journal of Comparative Sociology*, vol. III, pp. 1–16.

MADAN, T. N. (1963), 'Proverbs: The Single-Meaning Category', *Man*, June 1963, Art. 114, p. 9.

MADAN, T. N. (1965), *Family and Kinship: A Study of the Pandits of Rural Kashmir*, Asia Publishing House, London.

MAHAR, J. M. (1972), 'Agents of Dharma in a North Indian Village', in J. M. Mahar (ed.), *The Untouchables in Contemporary India*, pp. 17–36, University of Arizona Press, Tucson.

MANDELBAUM, D. G. (1949), 'The Family in India', in R. Anshen (ed.), *The Family, its Function and Destiny*, pp. 93–110, Harper & Row, New York.

MANDELBAUM, D. G. (1962), 'Role Variation in Caste Relations', in T. Madan and A. Sarana (eds), *Indian Anthropology: Essays in Memory of D. N. Majumdar*, pp. 310–24, Asia, London.

MANDELBAUM, D. G. (1970), *Society in India*, 2 vols, University of California Press, Berkeley, Los Angeles, London.

MARRIOTT, M. (1959), 'Interactional and Attributional Theories of Caste Ranking', *Man in India*, XXXIX, pp. 92–107.

MARRIOTT, M. (1968a), 'Multiple Reference in Indian Caste Systems', in J. Silverberg (ed.), *Social Mobility in the Caste System in India*, pp. 103–4, Mouton, The Hague.

MARRIOTT, M. (1968b), 'Caste Ranking and Food Transactions: A Matrix Analysis', in M. Singer and B. S. Cohn (eds), *Structure and Change in Indian Society*, pp. 133–72, Aldine, Chicago.

MASON, P. (1974), *A Matter of Honour: An Account of the Indian Army, Its Officers and Men*, Jonathan Cape, London.

MAYER, A. C. (1960), 'Caste and Kinship in Central India', Routledge & Kegan Paul, London.

MAYNARD, H. J. (1917), 'Influence of the Indian King Upon the Growth of Caste', *Journal of the Punjab Historical Society*, vol. XI, pp. 88–100.

MENCHER, J. P. (1972), 'Continuity and Change in an Ex-Untouchable Community of South India', in J. M. Mahar (ed.), *The Untouchables in Contemporary India*, pp. 37–56, University of Arizona Press, Tucson.

MENCHER, J. P. and GOLDBERG, H. (1967), 'Kinship and Marriage Regulations Amongst the Namboodiri Brahmans of Kerala', *Man*, New Series, vol. 2, pp. 87–106.

MIDDLETON, L. (1915), *Preliminary Assessment Report of the Kangra Tehsil of the District Kangra*, Civil and Military Gazette Press, Lahore.

MIDDLETON, L. (1919a), *Customary Law of the Kangra District (Excluding Kulu)*, Government Printing, Lahore.

MIDDLETON, L. (1919b), *Final Report of the Third Revised Settlement of the Palampur, Kangra and Nurpur Tehsils of the Kangra District*, Civil and Military Gazette Press, Lahore.

MINTURN, L. and HITCHCOCK, J. T. (1966), *The Rajputs of Khalapur, India*, Six Cultures Series, Volume III, John Wiley, New York, London, Sydney.

MONTGOMERY, R. (1853), 'Minute on Infanticide in the Punjab', *Selections from the Public Correspondence of the Administration for the Affairs of the Punjab*, vol. I, No. 6.

MONTGOMERY, R. (1854), 'Supplementary Papers on Infanticide', *Selections from the Records of the Government of India: The Punjab*, vol. 2, nos 7–12.

MOORCROFT, W. and TREBECK, G. (1841), *Travels in the Himalayan Provinces of Hindustan and the Punjab; in Ladakh and Kashmir; in Peshawar, Kabul, Kunduz and Bokhara*, vol. I, John Murray, London.

MORRIS, H. S. (1968), *The Indians in Uganda*, Weidenfeld & Nicolson, London.

NAYAR, B. R. (1966), *Minority Politics in the Punjab*, Princeton University Press.

NAYAR, B. R. (1968), 'Punjab', in M. Weiner (ed.), *State Politics in India*, pp. 435–502, Princeton University Press.

NEALE, W. C. (1957), 'Reciprocity and Redistribution in the Indian Village: Sequel to Some Notable Discussions', in K. Polanyi, C. M. Arensberg and H. W. Pearson (eds), *Trade and Market in the Early Empires*, Free Press, Chicago.

NEEDHAM, R. (1958), 'A Structural Analysis of Purum Society', *American Anthropologist*, vol. 60, pp. 75–101.

NEEDHAM, R. (1962), *Structure and Sentiment: A Test Case in Social Anthropology*, University of Chicago Press.

NEEDHAM, R. (1971), 'Introduction', in R. Needham (ed.), *Rethinking Kinship and Marriage* (A.S.A. 11), Tavistock, London.

NEWELL, W. H. (1970), 'An Upper Ravi Village: The Process of Social Change in Himachal Pradesh', in K. Ishwaran (ed.), *Change and Continuity in India's Villages*, pp. 21–36, Columbia University Press, New York and London.

O'BRIEN, E. (1891), *Assessment Report of Taluka Rajgiri in the Palampur Tehsil of the Kangra District*, Civil and Military Gazette Press, Lahore.

O'BRIEN, E. (1900), 'The Kangra Girths', *Punjab Ethnography*, no. III, Punjab Government Press, Lahore.

O'FLAHERTY, W. D. (1973), *Asceticism and Eroticism in the Mythology of Siva*, Oxford University Press, London.

ORENSTEIN, H. (1962), 'Exploitation and Function in the Interpretation of "Jajmani"', *Southwestern Journal of Anthropology*, XVIII, no. 4, pp. 302–15.

ORENSTEIN, H. (1970), 'Death and Kinship in Hinduism: Structural and Functional Interpretations', *American Anthropologist*, vol. 72, pp. 1357–77.

OWENS, R. (1971), 'Industrialization and the Joint Family', *Ethnology*, vol. X, no. 2, pp. 223–50.

PANIGRAHI, L. (1972), *British Social Policy and Female Infanticide in India*, Munshiram Manoharlal, New Delhi.

PARRY, J. P. (1970), 'The Koli Dilemma', *Contributions to Indian Sociology*, New Series, no. 4, pp. 84–104.

PARRY, J. P. (1974), 'Egalitarian Values in a Hierarchical Society', *South Asian Review*, vol. 7, no. 2, pp. 95–121.

PARRY, N. E. (1932), *The Lakhers*, Macmillan, London.

PARSONS, T. (1949), 'The Social Structure of the Family', in R. Anshen (ed.), *The Family, its Function and Destiny*, Harper & Row, New York.

PETTIGREW, J. (1975), *Robber Noblemen: A Study of the Political System of the Sikh Jats*, Routledge & Kegan Paul, London.

POCOCK, D. F. (n.d.), 'The Hypergamy of the Patidars', in K. M. Kapadia (ed.), *Ghurye Felicitation Volume*, pp. 195–204, New York.

POCOCK, D. F. (1957), 'Inclusion and Exclusion: A Process in the Caste System of Gujerat', *Southwestern Journal of Anthropology*, vol. XXIII, pp. 19–31.

POCOCK, D. F. (1962), 'Notes on Jajmani Relationships', *Contributions to Indian Sociology*, Old Series, vol. 4, pp. 78–95.

POCOCK, D. F. (1972), *Kanbi and Patidar: A Study of the Patidar Community of Gujarat*, Clarendon Press, Oxford.

POCOCK, D. F. (1973), *Mind, Body and Wealth: A Study of Belief and Practice in an Indian Village*, Blackwell, Oxford.

PRADHAN, M. C. (1966), *The Political System of the Jats of Northern India*, Oxford University Press, London.

PUNJAB DISTRICT GAZETTEER (1906), *Hoshiarpur District*, Punjab Government Press, Lahore.

PUNJAB DISTRICT GAZETTEER (1915), *Gurdaspur District*, Government Printing, Lahore.

PUNJAB DISTRICT GAZETTEER (1921), *Sialkot District*, Government Printing, Lahore.

PUNJAB DISTRICT GAZETTEER (1926), vol. VII, part A, *Kangra District*, Government Printing, Lahore.

PUNJAB DISTRICT GAZETTEER (1934), vol. VII, *Kangra District* (Statistical Tables), part B, Government Printing, Lahore.

PUNJAB STATES GAZETTEERS (1904), vol. XII A, *Mandi and Suket States*, Civil and Military Gazette Press, Lahore.

RADCLIFFE-BROWN, A. R. (1950), 'Introduction' in A. R. Radcliffe-Brown and Daryll Forde (eds), *African Systems of Kinship and Marriage*, Oxford University Press, London.

RAO, M. S. A. (1968), 'Occupational Diversification and Joint Household Organization', *Contributions to Indian Sociology*, New Series, vol. 2, pp. 98–111.

REDDY, N. S. (1955), 'Functional Relations of Lohars in a North Indian Village', *Eastern Anthropologist*, vol. 8, pp. 129–40.

RISLEY, Sir Hubert Hope (1915), *The People of India*, Thacker, London.

RIVERS, W. H. R. (1921), 'The Origin of Hypergamy', *Journal of the Bihar and Orissa Research Society*, Patna, vol. VIII, pp. 9–24.

ROBINSON, M. S. (1968), 'Some Observations on the Kandyan Sinhalese Kinship System', *Man*, New Series, vol. 3, no. 3, pp. 402–23.

ROSE, H. A. (1919), *A Glossary of the Castes and Tribes of the Punjab and North-West Frontier Province*, vol. I, Lahore.

ROSS, A. D. (1962), *The Hindu Family in its Urban Setting*, University of Toronto Press.

ROSSER, C. (1966), 'Social Mobility in the Newar Caste System', in C. von Furer-Haimendorf (ed.), *Caste and Kin in Nepal, India and Ceylon*, pp. 68–139, Asia Publishing House, Bombay.

ROWE, W. L. (1960), 'A Marriage Network in a North Indian Community', *Southwestern Journal of Anthropology*, vol. 16, No. 3, pp. 299–311.

ROWE, W. L. (1968), 'The New Chauhans: A Caste Mobility Movement in North India', in J. Silverberg (ed.), *Social Mobility in the Caste System in India*, pp. 66–77, Mouton, The Hague.

ROWE, W. L. (1973), 'Caste, Kinship and Association in Urban India', in A. Southall (ed.), *Cross-Cultural Studies of Urbanisation*, Oxford University Press, London.

RUDOLPH, L. I. and RUDOLPH, S. H. (1967), *The Modernity of Tradition*, University of Chicago Press.

SARMA, J. (1964), 'The Nuclearization of Joint Family Households in West Bengal', *Man in India*, vol. XLIV, pp. 193-206.

SCHAPERA, I. (1950), 'Kinship and Marriage among the Tswana', in A. R. Radcliffe-Brown and Daryll Forde (eds), *African Systems of Kinship and Marriage*, pp. 140–65, Oxford University Press, London.

SCHAPERA, I. (1957), 'Marriage of Near Kin among the Tswana', *Africa*, vol. 27, pp. 139–59.

SHAH, A. M. (1964), 'Basic Terms and Concepts in the Study of the Family in India', *Indian Economic and Social History Review*, vol. 1, no. 3, pp. 1-36.

SHAH, A. M. (1974), *The Household Dimension of the Family in India*, University of California Press, Berkeley and Los Angeles.

SHARMA, SATYA P. (1973), 'Marriage, Family and Kinship among the Jats and the Thakurs of North India: Some Comparisons', *Contributions to Indian Sociology*, New Series 7, pp. 81-103.

SHARMA, U. M. (1969), 'Hinduism in a Kangra Village', unpublished PhD Thesis, University of London.

SHARMA, U. M. (1970), 'The Problem of Village Hinduism: "Fragmentation" and "Integration" ', *Contributions to Indian Sociology*, New Series, vol. 4, pp. 1-21.

SHUTTLEWORTH, H. L. (1916), *Final Report of the Land Revenue Settlement of the Dehra and Hamirpur Tahsils of the Kangra District*, pp. 1910-15, Government Printing, Lahore.

SRINIVAS, M. N. (1959), 'The Dominant Caste in Rampura', *American Anthropologist*, LXI, pp. 1-16.

SRINIVAS, M. N. (1962), *Caste in Modern India and Other Essays*, Asia Publishing House, Bombay.

SRINIVAS, M. N. (1966), *Social Change in Modern India*, University of California Press, Berkeley and Los Angeles.

SRINIVAS, M. N. (1968), 'Mobility in the Caste System' in M. Singer and B. S. Cohn (eds), *Structure and Change in Modern India*, pp. 189–200, Aldine, Chicago.

STEVENSON, H. N. C. (1954), 'Status Evaluation in the Hindu Caste System', *Journal of the Royal Anthropological Institute*, vol. LXXXIV, no. 1-2, pp. 45–65.

STEVENSON, MRS SINCLAIR (1920), *The Rites of the Twice Born*, Oxford University Press, London.

STIRRAT, R. L. (1975), 'Compadrazgo in Catholic Sri Lanka', *Man*, New Series, vol. 10, no. 4, pp. 589–606.

TAMBIAH, S. J. (1973a), 'Dowry and Bridewealth and the Property Rights of Women in South Asia', in J. Goody and S. J. Tambiah,

Bridewealth and Dowry, Cambridge Papers in Social Anthropology No.7, Cambridge University Press.

TAMBIAH, S. J. (1973b), 'From Varna to Caste through Mixed Unions', in J. Goody (ed.), *The Character of Kinship*, pp. 191–229, Cambridge University Press.

TANDON, P. (1972), *Punjabi Century*, Hind Pocket Books.

TIEMANN, G. (1970), 'The Four-*Gotra* Rule among the Jat of Haryana in Northern India', *Anthropos*, vol. 65, pp. 166–77.

VAN DER VEEN, K. W. (1972), *I Give Thee My Daughter: A Study of Marriage and Hierarchy among the Anavil Brahmans of South Gujarat*, Van Gorcum, Assen, Holland.

VAN DER VEEN, K. W. (1973), 'Marriage and Hierarchy among the Anavil Brahmans of South Gujarat', *Contributions to Indian Sociology*, New Series, No. 7, pp. 36–52.

VATUK, S. (1969), 'A Structural Analysis of the Hindi Kinship Terminology', *Contributions to Indian Sociology*, New Series, no. 3, pp. 94–115.

VATUK, S. (1972), *Kinship and Urbanisation: White Collar Migrants in North India*, University of California Press, London.

WATSON, W. (1958), *Tribal Cohesion in a Money Economy*, Manchester University Press.

WILDER, W. (1971), 'Purum Descent Groups: Some Vagaries of Method', in R. Needham (ed.), *Rethinking Kinship and Marriage* (A.S.A. 11), Tavistock Publications, London.

WISER, W. H. (1936), *The Hindu Jajmani System*, Lucknow Publishing House, India.

YALMAN, N. (1963), 'On the Purity of Women in the Castes of Ceylon and Malabar', *Journal of the Royal Anthropological Institute*, vol. 93 (part 1), pp. 25–58.

YALMAN, N. (1967), *Under the Bo Tree: Studies in Caste, Kinship and Marriage in the Interior of Ceylon*, University of California Press, Berkeley and Los Angeles.

ZELLIOT, E. (1966), 'Buddhism and Politics in Maharashtra', in D. E. Smith (ed.) *South Asian Politics and Religion*, pp. 191–212, Princeton University Press.

MISCELLANEOUS

'General Report of the Administration of the Punjab and its Dependencies for 1864–5', *Administration Reports of the Government of India*, vol. XV.

'Tika Assessment Notes', 1915. Handwritten MS, in the Office of the District Commissioner, Dharamsala, Rajgiri, vol. V.

Index

Routledge Social Science Series

Routledge & Kegan Paul London, Henley and Boston

39 Store Street, London WC1E 7DD
Broadway House, Newtown Road, Henley-on-Thames, Oxon RG9 1EN
9 Park Street, Boston, Mass. 02108

Contents

Authors wishing to submit manuscripts for any series in this catalogue should send them to the Social Science Editor, Routledge & Kegan Paul Ltd, 39 Store Street, London WC1E 7DD

● *Books so marked are available in paperback*
All books are in Metric Demy 8vo format (216×138mm approx.)

International Library of Sociology

General Editor John Rex

GENERAL SOCIOLOGY

Barnsley, J. H. The Social Reality of Ethics. *464 pp.*

Belshaw, Cyril. The Conditions of Social Performance. *An Exploratory Theory. 144 pp.*

Brown, Robert. Explanation in Social Science. *208 pp.*

● Rules and Laws in Sociology. *192 pp.*

Bruford, W. H. Chekhov and His Russia. *A Sociological Study. 244 pp.*

Cain, Maureen E. Society and the Policeman's Role. *326 pp.*

●**Fletcher, Colin.** Beneath the Surface. *An Account of Three Styles of Sociological Research. 221 pp.*

Gibson, Quentin. The Logic of Social Enquiry. *240 pp.*

Glucksmann, M. Structuralist Analysis in Contemporary Social Thought. *212 pp.*

Gurvitch, Georges. Sociology of Law. *Preface by Roscoe Pound. 264 pp.*

Hodge, H. A. Wilhelm Dilthey. *An Introduction. 184 pp.*

Homans, George C. Sentiments and Activities. *336 pp.*

Johnson, Harry M. Sociology: *a Systematic Introduction. Foreword by Robert K. Merton. 710 pp.*

●**Keat, Russell,** and **Urry, John.** Social Theory as Science. *278 pp.*

Mannheim, Karl. Essays on Sociology and Social Psychology. *Edited by Paul Keckskemeti. With Editorial Note by Adolph Lowe. 344 pp.*

Systematic Sociology: *An Introduction to the Study of Society. Edited by J. S. Erös and Professor W. A. C. Stewart. 220 pp.*

Martindale, Don. The Nature and Types of Sociological Theory. *292 pp.*

●**Maus, Heinz.** A Short History of Sociology. *234 pp.*

Mey, Harald. Field-Theory. *A Study of its Application in the Social Sciences. 352 pp.*

Myrdal, Gunnar. Value in Social Theory: *A Collection of Essays on Methodology. Edited by Paul Streeten. 332 pp.*

Ogburn, William F., and **Nimkoff, Meyer F.** A Handbook of Sociology. *Preface by Karl Mannheim. 656 pp. 46 figures. 35 tables.*

Parsons, Talcott, and **Smelser, Neil J.** Economy and Society: *A Study in the Integration of Economic and Social Theory. 362 pp.*

Podgórecki, Adam. Practical Social Sciences. *About 200 pp.*

●**Rex, John.** Key Problems of Sociological Theory. *220 pp.*

Sociology and the Demystification of the Modern World. *282 pp.*

●**Rex, John** (Ed.) Approaches to Sociology. *Contributions by Peter Abell, Frank Bechhofer, Basil Bernstein, Ronald Fletcher, David Frisby, Miriam Glucksmann, Peter Lassman, Herminio Martins, John Rex, Roland Robertson, John Westergaard and Jock Young. 302 pp.*

Rigby, A. Alternative Realities. *352 pp.*

Roche, M. Phenomenology, Language and the Social Sciences. *374 pp.*

Sahay, A. Sociological Analysis. *220 pp.*

Simirenko, Alex (Ed.) Soviet Sociology. *Historical Antecedents and Current Appraisals. Introduction by Alex Simirenko. 376 pp.*

Strasser, Hermann. The Normative Structure of Sociology. *Conservative and Emancipatory Themes in Social Thought. About 340 pp.*

Urry, John. Reference Groups and the Theory of Revolution. *244 pp.*

Weinberg, E. Development of Sociology in the Soviet Union. *173 pp.*

FOREIGN CLASSICS OF SOCIOLOGY

●**Durkheim, Emile.** Suicide. *A Study in Sociology. Edited and with an Introduction by George Simpson. 404 pp.*

●**Gerth, H. H.,** and **Mills, C. Wright.** From Max Weber: *Essays in Sociology. 502 pp.*

●**Tönnies, Ferdinand.** Community and Association. (*Gemeinschaft und Gesellschaft.) Translated and Supplemented by Charles P. Loomis. Foreword by Pitirim A. Sorokin. 334 pp.*

SOCIAL STRUCTURE

Andreski, Stanislav. Military Organization and Society. *Foreword by Professor A. R. Radcliffe-Brown. 226 pp. 1 folder.*

Carlton, Eric. Ideology and Social Order. *Preface by Professor Philip Abrahams. About 320 pp.*

Coontz, Sydney H. Population Theories and the Economic Interpretation. *202 pp.*

Coser, Lewis. The Functions of Social Conflict. *204 pp.*

Dickie-Clark, H. F. Marginal Situation: *A Sociological Study of a Coloured Group. 240 pp. 11 tables.*

Glaser, Barney, and **Strauss, Anselm L.** Status Passage. *A Formal Theory. 208 pp.*

Glass, D. V. (Ed.) Social Mobility in Britain. *Contributions by J. Berent, T. Bottomore, R. C. Chambers, J. Floud, D. V. Glass, J. R. Hall, H. T. Himmelweit, R. K. Kelsall, F. M. Martin, C. A. Moser, R. Mukherjee, and W. Ziegel. 420 pp.*

Johnstone, Frederick A. Class, Race and Gold. *A Study of Class Relations and Racial Discrimination in South Africa. 312 pp.*

Jones, Garth N. Planned Organizational Change: *An Exploratory Study Using an Empirical Approach. 268 pp.*

Kelsall, R. K. Higher Civil Servants in Britain: *From 1870 to the Present Day. 268 pp. 31 tables.*

König, René. The Community. *232 pp. Illustrated.*

●**Lawton, Denis.** Social Class, Language and Education. *192 pp.*

McLeish, John. The Theory of Social Change: *Four Views Considered. 128 pp.*

Marsh, David C. The Changing Social Structure of England and Wales, 1871-1961. *288 pp.*

Menzies, Ken. Talcott Parsons and the Social Image of Man. *About 208 pp.*

●**Mouzelis, Nicos.** Organization and Bureaucracy. *An Analysis of Modern Theories. 240 pp.*

Mulkay, M. J. Functionalism, Exchange and Theoretical Strategy. *272 pp.*

Ossowski, Stanislaw. Class Structure in the Social Consciousness. *210 pp.*

●**Podgórecki, Adam.** Law and Society. *302 pp.*

Renner, Karl. Institutions of Private Law and Their Social Functions. *Edited, with an Introduction and Notes, by O. Kahn-Freud. Translated by Agnes Schwarzschild. 316 pp.*

SOCIOLOGY AND POLITICS

Acton, T. A. Gypsy Politics and Social Change. *316 pp.*

Clegg, Stuart. Power, Rule and Domination. *A Critical and Empirical Understanding of Power in Sociological Theory and Organisational Life. About 300 pp.*

Hechter, Michael. Internal Colonialism. *The Celtic Fringe in British National Development, 1536–1966. 361 pp.*

Hertz, Frederick. Nationality in History and Politics: *A Psychology and Sociology of National Sentiment and Nationalism. 432 pp.*

Kornhauser, William. The Politics of Mass Society. *272 pp. 20 tables.*

●**Kroes, R.** Soldiers and Students. *A Study of Right- and Left-wing Students. 174 pp.*

Laidler, Harry W. History of Socialism. *Social-Economic Movements: An Historical and Comparative Survey of Socialism, Communism, Co-operation, Utopianism; and other Systems of Reform and Reconstruction. 992 pp.*

Lasswell, H. D. Analysis of Political Behaviour. *324 pp.*

Martin, David A. Pacifism: *an Historical and Sociological Study. 262 pp.*

Martin, Roderick. Sociology of Power. *About 272 pp.*

Myrdal, Gunnar. The Political Element in the Development of Economic Theory. *Translated from the German by Paul Streeten. 282 pp.*

Wilson, H. T. The American Ideology. *Science, Technology and Organization of Modes of Rationality. About 280 pp.*

Wootton, Graham. Workers, Unions and the State. *188 pp.*

CRIMINOLOGY

Ancel, Marc. Social Defence: *A Modern Approach to Criminal Problems. Foreword by Leon Radzinowicz. 240 pp.*

Cain, Maureen E. Society and the Policeman's Role. *326 pp.*

Cloward, Richard A., and **Ohlin, Lloyd E.** Delinquency and Opportunity: *A Theory of Delinquent Gangs. 248 pp.*

Downes, David M. The Delinquent Solution. *A Study in Subcultural Theory. 296 pp.*

Dunlop, A. B., and **McCabe, S.** Young Men in Detention Centres. *192 pp.*

Friedlander, Kate. The Psycho-Analytical Approach to Juvenile Delinquency: *Theory, Case Studies, Treatment. 320 pp.*

Glueck, Sheldon, and **Eleanor.** Family Environment and Delinquency. *With the statistical assistance of Rose W. Kneznek. 340 pp.*

Lopez-Rey, Manuel. Crime. *An Analytical Appraisal. 288 pp.*

Mannheim, Hermann. Comparative Criminology: *a Text Book. Two volumes. 442 pp. and 380 pp.*

Morris, Terence. The Criminal Area: *A Study in Social Ecology. Foreword by Hermann Mannheim. 232 pp. 25 tables. 4 maps.*

Rock, Paul. Making People Pay. *338 pp.*

●**Taylor, Ian, Walton, Paul,** and **Young, Jock.** The New Criminology. *For a Social Theory of Deviance. 325 pp.*

●**Taylor, Ian, Walton, Paul,** and **Young, Jock** (Eds). Critical Criminology. *268 pp.*

SOCIAL PSYCHOLOGY

Bagley, Christopher. The Social Psychology of the Epileptic Child. *320 pp.*

Barbu, Zevedei. Problems of Historical Psychology. *248 pp.*

Blackburn, Julian. Psychology and the Social Pattern. *184 pp.*

●**Brittan, Arthur.** Meanings and Situations. *224 pp.*

Carroll, J. Break-Out from the Crystal Palace. *200 pp.*

●**Fleming, C. M.** Adolescence: Its Social Psychology. *With an Introduction to recent findings from the fields of Anthropology, Physiology, Medicine, Psychometrics and Sociometry. 288 pp.*

● The Social Psychology of Education: *An Introduction and Guide to Its Study. 136 pp.*

●**Homans, George C.** The Human Group. *Foreword by Bernard DeVoto. Introduction by Robert K. Merton. 526 pp.*

● Social Behaviour: *its Elementary Forms. 416 pp.*

●**Klein, Josephine.** The Study of Groups. *226 pp. 31 figures. 5 tables.*

Linton, Ralph. The Cultural Background of Personality. *132 pp.*

●**Mayo, Elton.** The Social Problems of an Industrial Civilization. *With an appendix on the Political Problem. 180 pp.*

Ottaway, A. K. C. Learning Through Group Experience. *176 pp.*

Plummer, Ken. Sexual Stigma. *An Interactionist Account. 254 pp.*

●**Rose, Arnold M.** (Ed.) Human Behaviour and Social Processes: *an Interactionist Approach. Contributions by Arnold M. Rose, Ralph H. Turner, Anselm Strauss, Everett C. Hughes, E. Franklin Frazier, Howard S. Becker, et al. 696 pp.*

Smelser, Neil J. Theory of Collective Behaviour. *448 pp.*

Stephenson, Geoffrey M. The Development of Conscience. *128 pp.*

Young, Kimball. Handbook of Social Psychology. *658 pp. 16 figures. 10 tables.*

SOCIOLOGY OF THE FAMILY

Banks, J. A. Prosperity and Parenthood: *A Study of Family Planning among The Victorian Middle Classes. 262 pp.*

Bell, Colin R. Middle Class Families: *Social and Geographical Mobility. 224 pp.*

Burton, Lindy. Vulnerable Children. *272 pp.*

Gavron, Hannah. The Captive Wife: *Conflicts of Household Mothers. 190 pp.*

George, Victor, and **Wilding, Paul.** Motherless Families. *248 pp.*

Klein, Josephine. Samples from English Cultures.

1. Three Preliminary Studies and Aspects of Adult Life in England. *447 pp.*
2. Child-Rearing Practices and Index. *247 pp.*

Klein, Viola. The Feminine Character. *History of an Ideology. 244 pp.*

McWhinnie, Alexina M. Adopted Children. *How They Grow Up. 304 pp.*

● **Morgan, D. H. J.** Social Theory and the Family. *About 320 pp.*

● **Myrdal, Alva,** and **Klein, Viola.** Women's Two Roles: *Home and Work. 238 pp. 27 tables.*

Parsons, Talcott, and **Bales, Robert F.** Family: Socialization and Interaction Process. *In collaboration with James Olds, Morris Zelditch and Philip E. Slater. 456 pp. 50 figures and tables.*

SOCIAL SERVICES

Bastide, Roger. The Sociology of Mental Disorder. *Translated from the French by Jean McNeil. 260 pp.*

Carlebach, Julius. Caring For Children in Trouble. *266 pp.*

George, Victor. Foster Care. *Theory and Practice. 234 pp.*

Social Security: *Beveridge and After. 258 pp.*

George, V., and **Wilding, P.** Motherless Families. *248 pp.*

● **Goetschius, George W.** Working with Community Groups. *256 pp.*

Goetschius, George W., and **Tash, Joan.** Working with Unattached Youth. *416 pp.*

Hall, M. P., and **Howes, I. V.** The Church in Social Work. *A Study of Moral Welfare Work undertaken by the Church of England. 320 pp.*

Heywood, Jean S. Children in Care: *the Development of the Service for the Deprived Child. 264 pp.*

Hoenig, J., and **Hamilton, Marian W.** The De-Segregation of the Mentally Ill. *284 pp.*

Jones, Kathleen. Mental Health and Social Policy, 1845-1959. *264 pp.*

King, Roy D., Raynes, Norma V., and **Tizard, Jack.** Patterns of Residential Care. *356 pp.*

Leigh, John. Young People and Leisure. *256 pp.*

● **Mays, John.** (Ed.) Penelope Hall's Social Services of England and Wales. *About 324 pp.*

Morris, Mary. Voluntary Work and the Welfare State. *300 pp.*

Nokes, P. L. The Professional Task in Welfare Practice. *152 pp.*

Timms, Noel. Psychiatric Social Work in Great Britain (1939-1962). *280 pp.*

● Social Casework: *Principles and Practice. 256 pp.*

Young, A. F. Social Services in British Industry. *272 pp.*

SOCIOLOGY OF EDUCATION

Banks, Olive. Parity and Prestige in English Secondary Education: a Study in Educational Sociology. *272 pp.*

Bentwich, Joseph. Education in Israel. *224 pp. 8 pp. plates.*

● **Blyth, W. A. L.** English Primary Education. *A Sociological Description.*
1. Schools. *232 pp.*
2. Background. *168 pp.*

Collier, K. G. The Social Purposes of Education: *Personal and Social Values in Education. 268 pp.*

Dale, R. R., and **Griffith, S.** Down Stream: *Failure in the Grammar School. 108 pp.*

Evans, K. M. Sociometry and Education. *158 pp.*

● **Ford, Julienne.** Social Class and the Comprehensive School. *192 pp.*

Foster, P. J. Education and Social Change in Ghana. *336 pp. 3 maps.*

Fraser, W. R. Education and Society in Modern France. *150 pp.*

Grace, Gerald R. Role Conflict and the Teacher. *150 pp.*

Hans, Nicholas. New Trends in Education in the Eighteenth Century. *278 pp. 19 tables.*

● Comparative Education: *A Study of Educational Factors and Traditions. 360 pp.*

● **Hargreaves, David.** Interpersonal Relations and Education. *432 pp.*

● Social Relations in a Secondary School. *240 pp.*

Holmes, Brian. Problems in Education. *A Comparative Approach. 336 pp.*

King, Ronald. Values and Involvement in a Grammar School. *164 pp.*

School Organization and Pupil Involvement. *A Study of Secondary Schools.*

● **Mannheim, Karl,** and **Stewart, W. A. C.** An Introduction to the Sociology of Education. *206 pp.*

Morris, Raymond N. The Sixth Form and College Entrance. *231 pp.*

● **Musgrove, F.** Youth and the Social Order. *176 pp.*

● **Ottaway, A. K. C.** Education and Society: An Introduction to the Sociology of Education. *With an Introduction by W. O. Lester Smith. 212 pp.*

Peers, Robert. Adult Education: *A Comparative Study. 398 pp.*

Pritchard, D. G. Education and the Handicapped: *1760 to 1960. 258 pp.*

Stratta, Erica. The Education of Borstal Boys. *A Study of their Educational Experiences prior to, and during, Borstal Training. 256 pp.*

Taylor, P. H., Reid, W. A., and **Holley, B. J.** The English Sixth Form. *A Case Study in Curriculum Research. 200 pp.*

SOCIOLOGY OF CULTURE

Eppel, E. M., and **M.** Adolescents and Morality: *A Study of some Moral Values and Dilemmas of Working Adolescents in the Context of a changing Climate of Opinion. Foreword by W. J. H. Sprott. 268 pp. 39 tables.*

● **Fromm, Erich.** The Fear of Freedom. *286 pp.*

● The Sane Society. *400 pp.*

Mannheim, Karl. Essays on the Sociology of Culture. *Edited by Ernst Mannheim in co-operation with Paul Kecskemeti. Editorial Note by Adolph Lowe. 280 pp.*

Weber, Alfred. Farewell to European History: *or The Conquest of Nihilism. Translated from the German by R. F. C. Hull. 224 pp.*

SOCIOLOGY OF RELIGION

Argyle, Michael and **Beit-Hallahmi, Benjamin.** The Social Psychology of Religion. *About 256 pp.*

Glasner, Peter E. The Sociology of Secularisation. *A Critique of a Concept. About 180 pp.*

Nelson, G. K. Spiritualism and Society. *313 pp.*

Stark, Werner. The Sociology of Religion. *A Study of Christendom.*

Volume I. *Established Religion. 248 pp.*

Volume II. *Sectarian Religion. 368 pp.*

Volume III. *The Universal Church. 464 pp.*

Volume IV. *Types of Religious Man. 352 pp.*

Volume V. *Types of Religious Culture. 464 pp.*

Turner, B. S. Weber and Islam. *216 pp.*

Watt, W. Montgomery. Islam and the Integration of Society. *320 pp.*

SOCIOLOGY OF ART AND LITERATURE

Jarvie, Ian C. Towards a Sociology of the Cinema. *A Comparative Essay on the Structure and Functioning of a Major Entertainment Industry. 405 pp.*

Rust, Frances S. Dance in Society. *An Analysis of the Relationships between the Social Dance and Society in England from the Middle Ages to the Present Day. 256 pp. 8 pp. of plates.*

Schücking, L. L. The Sociology of Literary Taste. *112 pp.*

Wolff, Janet. Hermeneutic Philosophy and the Sociology of Art. *150 pp.*

SOCIOLOGY OF KNOWLEDGE

Diesing, P. Patterns of Discovery in the Social Sciences. *262 pp.*

● **Douglas, J. D.** (Ed.) Understanding Everyday Life. *370 pp.*

● **Hamilton, P.** Knowledge and Social Structure. *174 pp.*

Jarvie, I. C. Concepts and Society. *232 pp.*

Mannheim, Karl. Essays on the Sociology of Knowledge. *Edited by Paul Kecskemeti. Editorial Note by Adolph Lowe. 353 pp.*

Remmling, Gunter W. The Sociology of Karl Mannheim. *With a Bibliographical Guide to the Sociology of Knowledge, Ideological Analysis, and Social Planning. 255 pp.*

Remmling, Gunter W. (Ed.) Towards the Sociology of Knowledge. *Origin and Development of a Sociological Thought Style. 463 pp.*

Stark, Werner. The Sociology of Knowledge: *An Essay in Aid of a Deeper Understanding of the History of Ideas. 384 pp.*

URBAN SOCIOLOGY

Ashworth, William. The Genesis of Modern British Town Planning: *A Study in Economic and Social History of the Nineteenth and Twentieth Centuries. 288 pp.*

Cullingworth, J. B. Housing Needs and Planning Policy: *A Restatement of the Problems of Housing Need and 'Overspill' in England and Wales. 232 pp. 44 tables. 8 maps.*

Dickinson, Robert E. City and Region: *A Geographical Interpretation 608 pp. 125 figures.*

The West European City: *A Geographical Interpretation. 600 pp. 129 maps. 29 plates.*

● The City Region in Western Europe. *320 pp. Maps.*

Humphreys, Alexander J. New Dubliners: *Urbanization and the Irish Family. Foreword by George C. Homans. 304 pp.*

Jackson, Brian. Working Class Community: *Some General Notions raised by a Series of Studies in Northern England. 192 pp.*

Jennings, Hilda. Societies in the Making: *a Study of Development and Redevelopment within a County Borough. Foreword by D. A. Clark. 286 pp.*

●**Mann, P. H.** An Approach to Urban Sociology. *240 pp.*

Morris, R. N., and **Mogey, J.** The Sociology of Housing. *Studies at Berinsfield. 232 pp. 4 pp. plates.*

Rosser, C., and **Harris, C.** The Family and Social Change. *A Study of Family and Kinship in a South Wales Town. 352 pp. 8 maps.*

●**Stacey, Margaret, Batsone, Eric, Bell, Colin,** and **Thurcott, Anne.** Power, Persistence and Change. *A Second Study of Banbury. 196 pp.*

RURAL SOCIOLOGY

Haswell, M. R. The Economics of Development in Village India. *120 pp.*

Littlejohn, James. Westrigg: *the Sociology of a Cheviot Parish. 172 pp. 5 figures.*

Mayer, Adrian C. Peasants in the Pacific. *A Study of Fiji Indian Rural Society. 248 pp. 20 plates.*

Williams, W. M. The Sociology of an English Village: *Gosforth. 272 pp. 12 figures. 13 tables.*

SOCIOLOGY OF INDUSTRY AND DISTRIBUTION

Anderson, Nels. Work and Leisure. *280 pp.*

●**Blau, Peter M.**, and **Scott, W. Richard.** Formal Organizations: *a Comparative approach. Introduction and Additional Bibliography by J. H. Smith. 326 pp.*

Dunkerley, David. The Foreman. *Aspects of Task and Structure. 192 pp.*

Eldridge, J. E. T. Industrial Disputes. *Essays in the Sociology of Industrial Relations. 288 pp.*

Hetzler, Stanley. Applied Measures for Promoting Technological Growth. *352 pp.*

Technological Growth and Social Change. *Achieving Modernization. 269 pp.*

Hollowell, Peter G. The Lorry Driver. *272 pp.*

●**Oxaal, I., Barnett, T.,** and **Booth, D.** (Eds). Beyond the Sociology of Development. *Economy and Society in Latin America and Africa. 295 pp.*

Smelser, Neil J. Social Change in the Industrial Revolution: *An Application of Theory to the Lancashire Cotton Industry, 1770–1840. 468 pp. 12 figures. 14 tables.*

ANTHROPOLOGY

Ammar, Hamed. Growing up in an Egyptian Village: *Silwa, Province of Aswan. 336 pp.*

Brandel-Syrier, Mia. Reeftown Elite. *A Study of Social Mobility in a Modern African Community on the Reef. 376 pp.*

Dickie-Clark, H. F. The Marginal Situation. *A Sociological Study of a Coloured Group. 236 pp.*

Dube, S. C. Indian Village. *Foreword by Morris Edward Opler. 276 pp. 4 plates.*

India's Changing Villages: *Human Factors in Community Development. 260 pp. 8 plates. 1 map.*

Firth, Raymond. Malay Fishermen. *Their Peasant Economy. 420 pp. 17 pp. plates.*

Gulliver, P. H. Social Control in an African Society: a Study of the Arusha, Agricultural Masai of Northern Tanganyika. *320 pp. 8 plates. 10 figures.*

Family Herds. *288 pp.*

Ishwaran, K. Tradition and Economy in Village India: *An Interactionist Approach.*
Foreword by Conrad Arensburg. 176 pp.

Jarvie, Ian C. The Revolution in Anthropology. *268 pp.*

Little, Kenneth L. Mende of Sierra Leone. *308 pp. and folder.*

Negroes in Britain. *With a New Introduction and Contemporary Study by Leonard Bloom. 320 pp.*

Lowie, Robert H. Social Organization. *494 pp.*

Mayer, A. C. Peasants in the Pacific. *A Study of Fiji Indian Rural Society. 248 pp.*

Meer, Fatima. Race and Suicide in South Africa. *325 pp.*

Smith, Raymond T. The Negro Family in British Guiana: *Family Structure and Social Status in the Villages. With a Foreword by Meyer Fortes. 314 pp. 8 plates. 1 figure. 4 maps.*

Smooha, Sammy. Israel: Pluralism and Conflict. *About 320 pp.*

SOCIOLOGY AND PHILOSOPHY

Barnsley, John H. The Social Reality of Ethics. *A Comparative Analysis of Moral Codes. 448 pp.*

Diesing, Paul. Patterns of Discovery in the Social Sciences. *362 pp.*

●**Douglas, Jack D.** (Ed.) Understanding Everyday Life. *Toward the Reconstruction of Sociological Knowledge. Contributions by Alan F. Blum. Aaron W. Cicourel, Norman K. Denzin, Jack D. Douglas, John Heeren, Peter McHugh, Peter K. Manning, Melvin Power, Matthew Speier, Roy Turner, D. Lawrence Wieder, Thomas P. Wilson and Don H. Zimmerman. 370 pp.*

Gorman, Robert A. The Dual Vision. *Alfred Schutz and the Myth of Phenomenological Social Science. About 300 pp.*

Jarvie, Ian C. Concepts and Society. *216 pp.*

●**Pelz, Werner.** The Scope of Understanding in Sociology. *Towards a more radical reorientation in the social humanistic sciences. 283 pp.*

Roche, Maurice. Phenomenology, Language and the Social Sciences. *371 pp.*

Sahay, Arun. Sociological Analysis. *212 pp.*

Sklair, Leslie. The Sociology of Progress. *320 pp.*

Slater, P. Origin and Significance of the Frankfurt School. *A Marxist Perspective. About 192 pp.*

Smart, Barry. Sociology, Phenomenology and Marxian Analysis. *A Critical Discussion of the Theory and Practice of a Science of Society. 220 pp.*

International Library of Anthropology

General Editor Adam Kuper

Ahmed, A. S. Millenium and Charisma Among Pathans. *A Critical Essay in Social Anthropology. 192 pp.*

Brown, Paula. The Chimbu. *A Study of Change in the New Guinea Highlands. 151 pp.*

Gudeman, Stephen. Relationships, Residence and the Individual. *A Rural Panamanian Community. 288 pp. 11 Plates, 5 Figures, 2 Maps, 10 Tables.*

Hamnett, Ian. Chieftainship and Legitimacy. *An Anthropological Study of Executive Law in Lesotho. 163 pp.*

Hanson, F. Allan. Meaning in Culture. *127 pp.*

Lloyd, P. C. Power and Independence. *Urban Africans' Perception of Social Inequality. 264 pp.*

Pettigrew, Joyce. Robber Noblemen. *A Study of the Political System of the Sikh Jats. 284 pp.*

Street, Brian V. The Savage in Literature. *Representations of 'Primitive' Society in English Fiction, 1858–1920. 207 pp.*

Van Den Berghe, Pierre L. Power and Privilege at an African University. *278 pp.*

International Library of Social Policy

General Editor Kathleen Jones

Bayley, M. Mental Handicap and Community Care. *426 pp.*

Bottoms, A. E., and **McClean, J. D.** Defendants in the Criminal Process. *284 pp.*

Butler, J. R. Family Doctors and Public Policy. *208 pp.*

Davies, Martin. Prisoners of Society. *Attitudes and Aftercare. 204 pp.*

Gittus, Elizabeth. Flats, Families and the Under-Fives. *285 pp.*

Holman, Robert. Trading in Children. *A Study of Private Fostering. 355 pp.*

Jones, Howard, and **Cornes, Paul.** Open Prisons. *About 248 pp.*

Jones, Kathleen. History of the Mental Health Service. *428 pp.*

Jones, Kathleen, with **Brown, John, Cunningham, W. J., Roberts, Julian,** and **Williams, Peter.** Opening the Door. *A Study of New Policies for the Mentally Handicapped. 278 pp.*

Karn, Valerie. Retiring to the Seaside. *About 280 pp. 2 maps. Numerous tables.*

Thomas, J. E. The English Prison Officer since 1850: *A Study in Conflict. 258 pp.*

Walton, R. G. Women in Social Work. *303 pp.*

Woodward, J. To Do the Sick No Harm. *A Study of the British Voluntary Hospital System to 1875. 221 pp.*

International Library of Welfare and Philosophy

General Editors Noel Timms and David Watson

● **Plant, Raymond.** Community and Ideology. *104 pp.*

● **McDermott, F. E.** (Ed.) Self-Determination in Social Work. *A Collection of Essays on Self-determination and Related Concepts by Philosophers and Social Work Theorists. Contributors: F. P. Biestek, S. Bernstein, A. Keith-Lucas, D. Sayer, H. H. Perelman, C. Whittington, R. F. Stalley, F. E. McDermott, I. Berlin, H. J. McCloskey, H. L. A. Hart, J. Wilson, A. I. Melden, S. I. Benn. 254 pp.*

Ragg, Nicholas M. People Not Cases. *A Philosophical Approach to Social Work. About 250 pp.*

● **Timms, Noel,** and **Watson, David** (Eds). Talking About Welfare. *Readings in Philosophy and Social Policy. Contributors: T. H. Marshall, R. B. Brandt, G. H. von Wright, K. Nielsen, M. Cranston, R. M. Titmuss, R. S. Downie, E. Telfer, D. Donnison, J. Benson, P. Leonard, A. Keith-Lucas, D. Walsh, I. T. Ramsey. 320 pp.*

Primary Socialization, Language and Education

General Editor Basil Bernstein

Adlam, Diana S., *with the assistance of Geoffrey Turner and Lesley Lineker.* Code in Context. *About 272 pp.*

Bernstein, Basil. Class, Codes and Control. *3 volumes.*

1. *Theoretical Studies Towards a Sociology of Language. 254 pp.*
2. *Applied Studies Towards a Sociology of Language. 377 pp.*
3. ● *Towards a Theory of Educatiomal Transmission. 167 pp.*

Brandis, W., and **Bernstein, B.** Selection and Control. *176 pp.*

Brandis, Walter, and **Henderson, Dorothy.** Social Class, Language and Communication. *288 pp.*

Cook-Gumperz, Jenny. Social Control and Socialization. *A Study of Class Differences in the Language of Maternal Control. 290 pp.*

● **Gahagan, D. M.,** and **G. A.** Talk Reform. *Exploration in Language for Infant School Children. 160 pp.*

Hawkins, P. R. Social Class, the Nominal Group and Verbal Strategies. *About 220 pp.*

Robinson, W. P., and **Rackstraw, Susan D. A.** A Question of Answers. *2 volumes. 192 pp. and 180 pp.*

Turner, Geoffrey J., and **Mohan, Bernard A.** A Linguistic Description and Computer Programme for Children's Speech. *208 pp.*

Reports of the Institute of Community Studies

● **Cartwright, Ann.** Parents and Family Planning Services. *306 pp.*

Patients and their Doctors. *A Study of General Practice. 304 pp.*

Dench, Geoff. Maltese in London. *A Case-study in the Erosion of Ethnic Consciousness. 302 pp.*

● **Jackson, Brian.** Streaming: *an Education System in Miniature. 168 pp.*

Jackson, Brian, and **Marsden, Dennis.** Education and the Working Class: *Some General Themes raised by a Study of 88 Working-class Children in a Northern Industrial City. 268 pp. 2 folders.*

Marris, Peter. The Experience of Higher Education. *232 pp. 27 tables.*

Loss and Change. *192 pp.*

Marris, Peter, and **Rein, Martin.** Dilemmas of Social Reform. *Poverty and Community Action in the United States. 256 pp.*

Marris, Peter, and **Somerset, Anthony.** African Businessmen. *A Study of Entrepreneurship and Development in Kenya. 256 pp.*

Mills, Richard. Young Outsiders: *a Study in Alternative Communities. 216 pp.*

Runciman, W. G. Relative Deprivation and Social Justice. *A Study of Attitudes to Social Inequality in Twentieth-Century England. 352 pp.*

Willmott, Peter. Adolescent Boys in East London. *230 pp.*

Willmott, Peter, and **Young, Michael.** Family and Class in a London Suburb. *202 pp. 47 tables.*

Young, Michael. Innovation and Research in Education. *192 pp.*

● **Young, Michael,** and **McGeeney, Patrick.** Learning Begins at Home. *A Study of a Junior School and its Parents. 128 pp.*

Young, Michael, and **Willmott, Peter.** Family and Kinship in East London. *Foreword by Richard M. Titmuss. 252 pp. 39 tables.*

The Symmetrical Family. *410 pp.*

Reports of the Institute for Social Studies in Medical Care

Cartwright, Ann, Hockey, Lisbeth, and **Anderson, John L.** Life Before Death. *310 pp.*

Dunnell, Karen, and **Cartwright, Ann.** Medicine Takers, Prescribers and Hoarders. *190 pp.*

Medicine, Illness and Society

General Editor W. M. Williams

Robinson, David. The Process of Becoming Ill. *142 pp.*

Stacey, Margaret, *et al.* Hospitals, Children and Their Families. *The Report of a Pilot Study. 202 pp.*

Stimson, G. V., and **Webb, B.** Going to See the Doctor. *The Consultation Process in General Practice. 155 pp.*

Monographs in Social Theory

General Editor Arthur Brittan

● **Barnes, B.** Scientific Knowledge and Sociological Theory. *192 pp.*

Bauman, Zygmunt. Culture as Praxis. *204 pp.*

● **Dixon, Keith.** Sociological Theory. *Pretence and Possibility. 142 pp.*

Meltzer, B. N., Petras, J. W., and **Reynolds, L. T.** Symbolic Interactionism. *Genesis, Varieties and Criticisms. 144 pp.*

● **Smith, Anthony D.** The Concept of Social Change. *A Critique of the Functionalist Theory of Social Change. 208 pp.*

Routledge Social Science Journals

The British Journal of Sociology. *Editor – Angus Stewart; Associate Editor – Leslie Sklair. Vol. 1, No. 1 – March 1950 and Quarterly. Roy. 8vo. All back issues available. An international journal publishing original papers in the field of sociology and related areas.*

Community Work. *Edited by David Jones and Marjorie Mayo. 1973. Published annually.*

Economy and Society. *Vol. 1, No. 1. February 1972 and Quarterly. Metric Roy. 8vo. A journal for all social scientists covering sociology, philosophy, anthropology, economics and history. All back numbers available.*

Religion. Journal of Religion and Religions. *Chairman of Editorial Board, Ninian Smart. Vol. 1, No. 1, Spring 1971. A journal with an inter-disciplinary approach to the study of the phenomena of religion. All back numbers available.*

Year Book of Social Policy in Britain, The. *Edited by Kathleen Jones. 1971. Published annually.*

Social and Psychological Aspects of Medical Practice

Editor Trevor Silverstone

Lader, Malcolm. Psychophysiology of Mental Illness. *280 pp.*

● **Silverstone, Trevor,** and **Turner, Paul.** Drug Treatment in Psychiatry. *232 pp.*

Printed in Great Britain by
Lowe & Brydone Printers Limited, Thetford, Norfolk